KT-117-936

Selections from
CLARENDON

EDWARD HYDE
FIRST EARL OF CLARENDON

Born: Dinton, Wiltshire, 18 February 1608/9
Died: Rouen, 9 December 1674

CLARENDON

SELECTIONS FROM

The History of the Rebellion

AND

The Life by Himself

EDITED BY G. HUEHNS

WITH A NEW INTRODUCTION BY
HUGH TREVOR-ROPER

1978

OXFORD UNIVERSITY PRESS

OXFORD   NEW YORK   MELBOURNE

Oxford University Press, Walton Street, Oxford OX2 6DP

OXFORD LONDON GLASGOW
NEW YORK TORONTO MELBOURNE WELLINGTON
IBADAN NAIROBI DAR ES SALAAM CAPE TOWN
KUALA LUMPUR SINGAPORE JAKARTA HONG KONG TOKYO
DELHI BOMBAY CALCUTTA MADRAS KARACHI

The True Historical Narrative of the Rebellion and the Civil Wars in England was
first published in three volumes in 1702, 1703, and 1704. *The Life of Clarendon
by himself* was first published in 1759. This selection, which follows the text
of the 1843 editions of both the *History* and the *Life*, was first published in a
World's Classics edition in 1955. The present edition was first published as
a hardback and as an Oxford University Press paperback in 1978

Introduction copyright © Hugh Trevor-Roper 1978
All other material copyright © Oxford University Press

*All rights reserved. No part of this publication may be reproduced,
stored in a retrieval system, or transmitted, in any form or by any means,
electronic, mechanical, photocopying, recording, or otherwise, without
the prior permission of Oxford University Press*

*This book is sold subject to the condition that it shall not by way of
trade or otherwise, be lent, re-sold, hired out, or otherwise circulated
without the publisher's prior consent in any form of binding or cover
other than that in which it is published and without a similar condition
including this condition being imposed on the subsequent purchaser*

British Library Cataloguing in Publication Data
Clarendon, Edward Hyde, *Earl of*
Selections from "The History of the Rebellion"; and "The life by
himself"
  1. Great Britain – History – Civil War, 1642–1649 – Early works to 1800
  2. Clarendon, Edward Hyde, *Earl of*
  3. Statesman – England – Biography
  I. Title II. Clarendon, Edward Hyde, Earl of
  The history of the Rebellion. Selections
  III. Clarendon, Edward Hyde, Earl of. The life of
  Edward Earl of Clarendon.
  Selections IV. Huehns, Gertrude
  942.06'2 DA415 78-40717

ISBN 0-19-215852-x ISBN 0-19-285079-2 Pbk

Printed in Great Britain by
Fletcher & Son, Ltd, Norwich

INTRODUCTION

EDWARD HYDE, first Earl of Clarendon, was the greatest
English statesman on the royalist side in the period of the
English Puritan Revolution. Born in 1608, educated at
Oxford University (to which he remained always devoted), trained as a lawyer, but always interested in literature and historical studies, he entered politics in November 1640, as a member of the Long Parliament, whose
opposition to Charles I gradually turned into civil war.
For the first year of that Parliament, Hyde supported the
party of reform; but in the summer of 1641, believing
that the essential reforms had been achieved and that
further opposition to the Crown and the Church would
irreparably damage the fabric of government, he moved
over to the royal side and sought to persuade Charles I to
accept and maintain the constitutional reforms already
achieved, at least on paper, by the concessions of the last
year. Charles I did not do so. Early in 1642, after his
abortive attempt to seize the leaders of Parliament, he
withdrew from London to York and prepared for civil
war. Hyde, who was now a royal minister, joined him
there in May, and put his pen at his disposal. He drafted
manifestos in which the King asserted his moderation,
his belief in 'mixed monarchy', and his acceptance of reform. In this way he made an important contribution to
the royal cause: he helped to create what had previously
been lacking, a royalist party.

Hyde undoubtedly believed his own propaganda. Unfortunately the King did not: he merely used it. Throughout the first civil war (1642-6) Hyde had to compete, in
the royal council, with the 'Cavaliers', the men of war,
who encouraged the King to believe in a war not for
'settlement' but for 'conquest'. The competition was unequal, for the Cavaliers had the support of Charles I's
French queen, Henrietta Maria, who in the end always
prevailed. After the Battle of Naseby, which heralded the
final defeat of the King, Hyde was removed from the
royal capital at Oxford and sent with the Prince of Wales,

afterwards Charles II, to the West country. Later he
accompanied the Prince to the Isles of Scilly and to
Jersey. When the Queen sought to remove the Prince to
France, Hyde resisted. He believed that although the
King had lost the war, he could still, if properly advised,
win the peace. But he insisted that settlement must be on
a purely English basis: the Crown must not seek to re-
conquer England from a foreign base. Here too, in the
end, the Queen prevailed. The Prince was removed to
France. Hyde stayed on in Jersey till the second civil war
and the revolution which followed forced him too to
withdraw to France.

Charles I had lost the first civil war by refusing to accept Hyde's political advice; but he still, as in 1642, saw
Hyde as a useful propagandist. Early in 1646 the Parliament decided to sponsor an official history of the struggle,
representing, of course, the parliamentary view. The his-
torian appointed was Tom May, a minor poet who had
formerly been a friend of Hyde but had defected to the
parliamentary side. As if in response to this venture,
Charles I encouraged Hyde once again to use his pen in the
royalist cause. This was the origin of *The History of the Rebellion*, which Hyde began in Scilly and continued in Jersey.
However, if he undertook it as a work of propaganda,
he soon showed that he intended it to be very different
from Tom May's *History of the Parliament*. He intended
it to be not public propaganda for the King, but private
political advice to the King. He also intended it to be a
great work of literature.

This dual role of Hyde's *History*, as political advice and
as historical literature, is made clear in his correspondence while he was writing it. In letters to his friends he
admitted that he was writing an explosive document
which, if published, would 'make mad work among
friends and foes'. But it was not to be published. It was
'unfit in this age for communication'. It was a state paper
for the eyes of the King only. This was not at all what the
King had intended. On the other hand Hyde made it
clear that he hoped for ultimate publication, when 'the
passion, rage, and fury of this time shall be forgotten'.

In other words, he proposed to write an English classic. For this purpose he read, as models, the great historians, ancient and modern. He reflected on historical causation. He wrote great set pieces. And in his studies of character he aimed at impartiality: he was resolved to do justice, he said, to all who fell in the struggle, on whichever side. Besides being a secret political treatise advising Charles I how to restore and make permanent the royal authority, the *History* was addressed to posterity as a philosophical vindication of the threatened English political system in Church and State.

In May 1648, when a series of royalist revolts in England, the prelude to the second civil war, precipitated him back into political activity, Hyde had written seven books of his *History*. The events of the next year, culminating in the execution of the King and the establishment of the English Republic, not only pre-empted his time: they also deprived him of part at least of his animating purpose. What was the point of writing advice to Charles I, how to repair Church and State, when not only Charles I but the English monarchy and the English Church had been completely destroyed? In the next twelve years Hyde lived uncomfortably as an exile in France or the Netherlands. In spite of the defection of many of his friends, he never lost his faith either in the English monarchy or in the English Church—or in himself and his formula for their restoration. He continued to resist the powerful machinations of the exiled 'Cavaliers' and of Queen Henrietta Maria, who sought to restore the Stuart monarchy with foreign help. But he never returned to his unfinished *History*. Friends urged him to do so, but he could never be persuaded. Apart from the mere problem of survival in exile, the political conjuncture had changed out of recognition. Hyde was fully occupied in maintaining unity at the exiled court, preventing the Queen from converting her sons to Catholicism, organizing, encouraging, and restraining the royalists and the Anglicans in England. Meanwhile, his unpublished *History*, so far as it was written, remained in manuscript in his hands.

In 1658 Cromwell died, and eighteen months later all Hyde's hopes, which had once seemed so quixotic, were realized. The English monarchy and Church were restored, without foreign aid, by Englishmen alone, on his terms. For seven years Hyde, as Earl of Clarendon and Lord Chancellor, ruled England. The basis of his rule was not the absolutism, the royal conquest, vainly demanded by the Cavaliers, but the 'settlement' achieved on paper—but only on paper—in 1641. In his years of power, Hyde had reason to congratulate himself. He had seen his programme realized at last. He was the undisputed maker of the Restoration, the hero of the resuscitated national Church. His daughter was married— against his will, he protested—to the heir presumptive to the throne. His granddaughters would be Queens Regnant of England.

In those years Clarendon lived magnificently: at Clarendon House in London, with its great gallery of portraits, formed by him—the pictorial equivalent of the great 'characters' of his *History*; at Cornbury Park in Oxfordshire, with its Virgilian inscription. But such prosperity bred envy. Old enemies (and some old friends) resented it. The King disliked the heavy shadow of his old mentor. The King's mistresses sensed his disapproval. The Cavaliers suggested that the 'settlement' of 1660 unreasonably restricted the royal power. There was a new generation of politicians, unmoved by the events of the civil war. Above all, there was an unsuccessful foreign war, the Second Dutch War (which Clarendon himself had opposed). In 1667 the Dutch victories animated all other English grievances, and in a sudden 'gust of envy' Clarendon was hurled from power. The King raised no finger to save him: 'Bid the Chancellor begone' was his only message; and the Chancellor fled abroad, pursued by unjust charges, to spend the remaining seven years of his life in a second exile, hardly more comfortable than the first. Old and homeless, subjected to petty persecution, sometimes in danger of his life, he was harried from place to place—Avignon, Moulins, Montpellier, Rouen —and finally died in Rouen in 1674.

However painful to him, we should be grateful for Clarendon's second exile, for it gave him, at last, the opportunity to complete his *History*. As in his first exile, so now, he refused to accept defeat or to be soured by misfortune. Instead, now as then, he congratulated himself on possessing those internal resources which enable the scholar, unlike the courtier, not only not to resent, but positively to enjoy, the loss of power. It was while he was in France, cut off from his library, his documents, his friends (for Parliament had declared it treason to communicate with him), that Clarendon at last resumed his pen and sought to complete the record of his own times. At first he wrote, from memory alone, a new work: a long autobiography, or *apologia pro vita sua*. This is a majestic work, quite untouched by the bitterness of exile. Later, his son was allowed to visit him, and to bring him, among other papers, the long discarded manuscript of his *History*. Thereupon Clarendon changed his mind. He decided not, after all, to spend time on his own vindication—posterity, he thought, would take care of that. Instead he resolved now to complete his *History*: to fill it out, to bring it up to date, to convert it from an *aide-mémoire* for Charles I, into a classic history of his own time.

So he started work again. He carved great chunks out of the autobiography, stitched them into and on to the old *History*, and produced that single great work which we know as *The History of the Rebellion*. However, even now, he did not think of publishing it. He still saw it as an indiscreet work which might do him harm by prejudicing Charles II against him. For he always hoped to be recalled from banishment and to end his life in the houses which he had built and the England which he loved. So, while he published occasional works—polemical works against those who had despaired of the English monarchy or the English Church—he left this great work, on which he relied for immortality, in manuscript. In his last will, signed on his deathbed in Rouen, he charged his two sons to dispose of it, 'either by suppressing or publishing', as they should be advised by the Archbishop of Canterbury and the Bishop of Winchester. Archbishop Sheldon and

Bishop Morley had been his closest friends since the 1630s, his allies in the days of despondency in the 1640s and 1650s, the restorers, with him, in the 1660s, of the Anglican Church.

It was in the reign of Queen Anne, Clarendon's grand-daughter, that the *History* was at last published, by the authority of his sons, the leaders of the now dominant tory party. It at once became a best-seller, and its profits, which had been given to Oxford University, enabled the University to build a new home—the Clarendon Building—to house its learned press, long known as the Clarendon Press. Indeed, the work was so successful, both as tory propaganda and commercially, that positive steps were taken both by the whigs, to counter its influence, and by the University, to perpetuate its profits. The whigs sourly maintained that the work had no real authority, not being by Clarendon at all but the work of its modern editors, the high tory clergy of Oxford. The University, faced by a parliamentary bill which would have put a term to its copyright, lobbied the House of Lords and sought to preserve, in this particular work, a perpetual copyright. In both matters, the tories prevailed. Clarendon's authorship was successfully vindicated, and the *History of the Rebellion* is still the perpetual copyright of the Clarendon Press. In the 19th century the profits were still sufficient to finance the building of the Clarendon Laboratory. Clarendon's other works, in so far as they had not already been published, were published by that Press in the course of the 18th century. Among them were the relics of his autobiography, after the excision, by him, of the passages which he transferred to the *History*. These were published in 1759, as *The Life of Edward, Earl of Clarendon, by Himself.*

Thus Clarendon's History is not a unitary work. It is a composite work put together from distinct material—the *History* and the *Life*—written at different times, twenty years apart, in very different circumstances, and for different purposes. As a record of fact, its accuracy inevitably varies, and the critical reader will always bear in mind the circumstances in which any passage was written:

whether the author was in touch with events, equipped with documents, and dealing with matters still fresh in recollection, or whether he was at a distance in space and time, relying on hearsay or faded memory. Such unity as the work has is provided by the writer: by the philosophy which inspired him throughout the vicissitudes, personal and political, of the revolutionary period.

In fact that philosophy was remarkably consistent. From the beginning, Clarendon had a firm belief in the essential validity of the English constitution, both of State and of Church, in the 'mixed monarchy' of Elizabethan times, and in the Anglican Church as defined and defended by Richard Hooker. He did not approve of the 'personal government' of Charles I—he disliked Strafford's 'tyranny' and he thought Laud (whom he respected personally) injudicious and narrow-minded. But he believed that the mistakes of the 1630s could easily have been corrected. He did not believe that there was any crisis in society, or that revolution was in any sense inevitable. This was not because he was blind to economic forces or social tensions. Far from it. No contemporary writer was more acute in his perception of such factors in the rebellion. But he did not believe that they were the essential motor of revolution. The revolution, in his view, was essentially political. It developed out of small mistakes which in turn were compounded by human weakness and error. This being so, human intelligence and human courage could, at almost any time, have repaired the damage. Unfortunately, that intelligence and that courage were lacking where they were most needed, and so, through weakness and folly the country drifted into an odious and unnecessary civil war. However, as the constitution of Church and State was inherently sound, Clarendon never despaired of restoring it. To him the English constitution was the product of a long, continuous history, and that history gave it a surer validity than could be derived from any theoretically more perfect structure, such as the 'classical' Church system of the Calvinists or the 'mathematical' political system of his old friend Thomas Hobbes.

Moreover, since the history which validated the English constitution was a purely English history, Clarendon repudiated any attempt to regulate it by appeal to foreign arms or foreign models. Such attempts were not only, in his eyes, unpatriotic: they were also, of necessity, counter-productive. Even if successful, they were bound to aggravate the problems of politics by the betrayal of English interests. So he would never forgive the parliamentary leaders for buying Scottish support at the price of surrender to a Presbyterian church system, and he would oppose the attempts of Charles I, and afterwards of Henrietta Maria, to restore the fortunes of the Crown by compliance with parties in Scotland or France. The problems of English history, he believed, must be solved by Englishmen alone; and if they had been left to Englishmen, they could have been solved without civil war or revolution.

This interpretation of the Puritan Revolution was of course a challenge to the 'whig' writers of the time. It runs counter to some modern historical theories. It is not capable of demonstration. However, it equally cannot be disproved, and it has always found powerful historians to defend it. It also proved powerful as a conviction, a philosophy of action. It inspired Clarendon throughout his career. It enabled him to hope when almost all his allies despaired and to achieve a restoration which had seemed impossible. And it enabled him to write the greatest contemporary history of the 17th century Revolution in England.

HUGH TREVOR-ROPER

Chiefswood, Melrose
JUNE 1978

PREFACE

THE selections following are taken from the historical writings of Edward Hyde, first Earl of Clarendon. As he is best known by his title, this has been used throughout except in the more strictly historical portions of the Introduction. To give the reader some idea of the whole work it has been thought advisable not to disrupt Clarendon's narrative too much. The arrangement therefore follows roughly the chronological order of events. Within the separate sections, however, I have aimed at continuity of thought and expression. Only in the character sketches have Clarendon's repetitions been sometimes retained, since complete elimination might have given a misleading impression of his method.

I take this opportunity to express my sincere thanks to Mr. E. S. de Beer, F.S.A., F.R.Hist.S., for his help and advice, and to the Oxford University Press for their patience and co-operation.

G. HUEHNS

New Zealand and London
1953

CONTENTS

BIBLIOGRAPHY

G. Davies, *The Early Stuarts*, 2nd ed., 1959

G. N. Clark, *The Later Stuarts*, 2nd ed., 1956

C. V. Wedgwood, *The Great Rebellion*:
  vol. i, *The King's Peace*, 1955
  vol. ii, *The King's War*, 1958

Sir Charles Firth, *Cromwell and the rule of Puritans in England*, latest ed., 1953

K. Feiling, *History of the Tory Party, 1649–1714*, 1924

D. Bush, *English Literature in the Earlier Seventeenth Century*, 1945

T. H. Lister, *Life and administration of Edward, First Earl of Clarendon*, 3 vols., 1837–8

B. H. G. Wormald, *Clarendon: Politics, History, and Religion, 1640–1660*, 1951

Sir Charles Firth, 'Edward Hyde, Earl of Clarendon', in *Essays, historical and literary*, 1938

Hugh Trevor-Roper, *Edward Hyde, Earl of Clarendon*, 1975

Hyde were of that opinion'; and they always very ingenuously confessed, that he was not: but his having no relation
of service, and so no pretence to be seen often at court, and
the great jealousy that was entertained towards him, made
it necessary to him to repair only in the dark to the king
upon emergent occasions, and leave the rest to be imparted
by the other two: and the differences in their natures and
opinions never produced any disunion between them in
those councils which concerned the conduct of the king's
service; but they proceeded with great unanimity, and
very manifestly much advanced the king's business from
the very low state it was in when they were first trusted;
the other two having always much deference to the lord
Falkland, who allayed their passions; to which they were
both enough inclined.

[After the Restoration] the king brought with him from
beyond the seas that council which had always attended
him, and whose advice he had always received in his transactions of greatest importance; and his small family, that
consisted of gentlemen who had for the most part been put
about him by his father, and constantly waited upon his
person in all his distresses, with as much submission and
patience undergoing their part in it, as could reasonably
be expected from such a people; and therefore had the
keener appetites, and the stronger presumption to push on
their fortunes (as they called it) in the infancy of their
master's restoration, that other men might not be preferred before them, who had not 'borne the heat of the
day', as they had done.

Of the council were the chancellor, the marquis of Ormond, the lord Colepepper, and secretary Nicholas, who
lived in great unity and concurrence in the communication of the most secret counsels. There had been more of
his council abroad with him, who, according to the motions
he made, and the places he had resided in, were sometimes
with him, but other remained in France, or in some parts of
Holland and Flanders, for their convenience, ready to
repair to his majesty when they should be called. The four
nominated above were they who constantly attended, were
privy to all counsels, and waited upon him in his return.

The chancellor was the highest in place, and thought to be so in trust, because he was most in private with the king, had managed most of the secret correspondence in England, and all despatches of importance had passed through his hands; which had hitherto been with the less envy, because the indefatigable pains he took were very visible, and it was as visible that he gained nothing by it. His wants and necessities were as great as any man's, nor was the allowance assigned to him by the king in the least degree more, or better paid, than every one of the council received. Besides, the friendship was so entire between the marquis of Ormond and him, that no arts that were used could dissolve it; and it was enough known, that as he had an entire and full confidence from the king, and a greater esteem than any man, so that the chancellor so entirely communicated all particulars with him, that there was not the least resolution taken without his privity and approbation. The chancellor had been employed by the last king in all the affairs of the greatest trust and secrecy; had been made privy counsellor and chancellor of the exchequer in the very beginning of the troubles; and had been sent by that king into the west with his son, when he thought their interest would be best preserved and provided for by separating their persons. A greater testimony and recommendation, a servant could not receive from his master, than the king gave of him to the prince, who from that time treated him with as much affection and confidence as any man, and which (notwithstanding very powerful opposition) he continued and improved to this time of his restoration; and even then rejected some intimations rather than propositions, which were secretly made to him at the Hague, that the chancellor was a man very much in the prejudice of the presbyterian party, as in truth he was, and therefore that his majesty would do best to leave him behind, till he should be himself settled in England: which the king received with that indignation and disdain, and answered the person, who privately presumed to give the advice, in such a manner, that he was troubled no more with the importunity, nor did any man ever own the advice. Yet the chancellor had besought the king, upon some rumours which had been spread, that if any exception or prejudice to his person should be so insisted on, as might delay his return one hour, he would decline giving him any protection, till he should find it more in his power, after his arrival in England: which desire of his, though it found no reception with the king, proceeded from so much sincerity, that it is well known the chancellor did positively resolve, that if any such thing had been urged by any authority, he would render the king's indulgence and grace of no inconvenience to his majesty, by his secret and voluntary withdrawing himself, without his privity, and without the reach of his discovery for some time: so far he was from being biassed by his own particular benefit and advantage.

That the king might be the more vacant to those thoughts and divertisements which pleased him best, he appointed the chancellor and some others to have frequent consultations with such members of the parliament who were most able and willing to serve him; and to concert all the ways and means by which the transactions in the houses might be carried with the more expedition, and attended with the best success. These daily conferences proved very beneficial to his majesty's service; the members of both houses being very willing to receive advice and direction, and to pursue what they were directed; and all things were done there in good order, and succeeded well. All the courts of justice in Westminster hall were presently filled with grave and learned judges, who had either deserted their practice and profession during all the rebellious times, or had given full evidence of their affection to the king and the established laws, in many weighty instances: and they were then quickly sent in their several circuits, to administer justice to the people according to the old forms of law, which was universally received and submitted to with all possible joy and satisfaction. All commissions of the peace were renewed, and the names of those persons inserted therein, who had been most eminent sufferers for the king, and were known to have entire affections for his majesty and the laws; though it was not possible, but some would get and continue in, who were of more doubtful inclinations, by their not being known to him, whose province it was to depute them. Denied it cannot be, that there appeared, sooner than was thought possible, a general settlement in the civil justice of the kingdom; that no man complained without remedy, and 'every man dwelt again under the shadow of his own vine', without any complaint of injustice and oppression.

The king exposed himself with more condescension than was necessary to persons of all conditions, heard all that they had a mind to say to him, and gave them such answers as for the present seemed full of grace. He was too well pleased to hear both the men and the women of all factions and fancies in religion discourse in their own method, and enlarged himself in debate with them; which made every one believe that they were more favoured by him than they had cause: which kind of liberty, though at first it was accompanied with acclamations, and acknowledgment of his being a prince of rare parts and affability, yet it was attended afterwards with ill consequences, and gave many men opportunity to declare and publish, that the king had said many things to them which he had never said; and made many concessions and promises to them which he had never uttered or thought upon.

The chancellor was generally thought to have most credit with his master, and most power in the counsels, because the king referred all matters of what kind soever to him. And whosoever repaired to him for his direction in any business was sent to the chancellor, not only because he had a great confidence in his integrity, having been with him so many years, and of whose indefatigable industry he and all men had great experience; but because he saw those men, whom he was as willing to trust, and who had at least an equal share in his affections, more inclined to ease and pleasure, and willing that the weight of the work should lie on the chancellor's shoulders, with whom they had an entire friendship, and knew well that they should with more ease be consulted by him in all matters of importance. Nor was it possible for him, at the first coming, to avoid the being engaged in all the counsels, of how

distinct a nature soever, because he had been best acquainted with all transactions whilst the king was abroad;
and therefore communication with him in all things was
thought necessary by those, who were to have any part in
them. Besides that, he continued still chancellor of the
exchequer, by virtue of the grant formerly made to him by
the last king, during whose time he executed that office,
but resolved to surrender it into the king's hand as soon as
his majesty should resolve on whom to confer it; he proposing nothing to himself, but to be left at liberty to intend
only the discharge of his own office, which he thought himself unequal to, and hoped only to improve his talent that
way by a most diligent application, well knowing the
great abilities of those, who had formerly sat in that office,
and that they found it required their full time and all their
faculties. And therefore he did most heartily desire to
meddle with nothing but that province, which though in
itself and the constant perquisites of it is not sufficient to
support the dignity of it, yet was then, upon the king's
return; and, after it had been so many years without a lawful officer, would unquestionably bring in money enough
to be a foundation to a future fortune, competent to his
ambition, and enough to provoke the envy of many, who
believed they deserved better than he. And that this
was the temper and resolution he brought with him into
England, and how unwillingly he departed from it, will
evidently appear by two or three instances, which shall be
given in their proper place. However, he could not expect
that freedom till the council should be settled, (into which
the king admitted all who had been counsellors to his
father, and had not eminently forfeited that promotion
by their revolt, and many of those who had been and still
were recommended by the general, amongst whom there
were some who would not have been received upon any
other title,) and until those officers could be settled, who
might take particular care of their several provinces.

3. *John Earle*

Born 1601; author of 'Micro-cosmographie'; Bishop of Worcester 1662; Bishop of Salisbury 1663; died 1665. Chaplain and Tutor to the Prince of Wales 1641

DOCTOR EARLES was at that time chaplain in the house to the earl of Pembroke, lord chamberlain of his majesty's household, and had a lodging in the court under that relation. He was a person very notable for his elegance in the Greek and Latin tongues; and being Fellow of Merton college in Oxford, and having been proctor of the university, and some very witty and sharp discourses being published in print without his consent, though known to be his, he grew suddenly into a very general esteem with all men; being a man of great piety and devotion; a most eloquent and powerful preacher; and of a conversation so pleasant and delightful, so very innocent, and so very facetious, that no man's company was more desired and more loved. No man was more negligent in his dress, and habit, and mien; no man more wary and cultivated in his behaviour and discourse; insomuch as he had the greater advantage when he was known, by promising so little before he was known. He was an excellent poet, both in Latin, Greek, and English, as appears by many pieces yet abroad; though he suppressed many more himself, especially of English, incomparably good, out of an austerity to those sallies of his youth. He was very dear to the lord Falkland, with whom he spent as much time as he could make his own; and as that lord would impute the speedy progress he made in the Greek tongue, to the information and assistance he had from Mr. Earles, so Mr. Earles would frequently profess, that he had got more useful learning by his conversation at Tew, (the lord Falkland's house,) than he had at Oxford. In the first settling of the prince's family, he was made one of his chaplains; and attended on him when he was forced to leave the kingdom, and therefore we shall often have occasion to mention him hereafter. He was amongst the few excellent men who never had, nor ever could have an enemy, but such a one who was an enemy to all learning and virtue, and therefore would never make himself known.

4. *John Hales*

Born 1584; Fellow of Merton College 1605; Regius Professor of Greek 1615; at the Synod of Dort November 1618–February 1619; Fellow of Eton 1619; Canon of Windsor 1635; died 1656

MR. JOHN HALES had been Greek professor in the university of Oxford; and had borne all the labour of that excellent edition and impression of St. Chrysostom's Works, set out by sir Harry Savile; who was then warden of Merton college, when the other was fellow of that house. He was chaplain in the house with sir Dudley Carleton, ambassador at the Hague in Holland, at the time when the synod of Dort was held, and so had liberty to be present at the consultations in that assembly; and hath left the best memorial behind him, of the ignorance, and passion, and animosity, and injustice of that convention; of which he often made very pleasant relations; though at that time it received too much countenance from England. Being a person of the greatest eminency for learning, and other abilities, from which he might have promised himself any preferment in the church, he withdrew himself from all pursuits of that kind into a private fellowship in the college of Eton, where his friend sir Harry Savile was provost; where he lived among his books, and the most separated from the world of any man then living: though he was not in the least degree inclined to melancholy, but, on the contrary, of a very open and pleasant conversation; and therefore was very well pleased with the resort of his friends to him, who were such as he had chosen, and in whose company he delighted, and for whose sake he would sometimes, once in a year, resort to London, only to enjoy their cheerful conversation.

He would never take any cure of souls; and was so great a contemner of money, that he was wont to say, that his fellowship, and the bursar's place, (which, for the good of the college, he held many years,) was worth him fifty pounds a year more than he could spend; and yet, besides his being very charitable to all poor people, even to liberality, he had made a greater and better collection of books, than were to be found in any other private library that I have seen; as he had sure read more, and carried more about him in his excellent memory, than any man I ever knew, my lord Falkland only excepted, who I think sided him. He had, whether from his natural temper and constitution, or from his long retirement from all crowds, or from his profound judgment and discerning spirit, contracted some opinions which were not received, nor by him published, except in private discourses; and then rather upon occasion of dispute, than of positive opinion: and he would often say, his opinions he was sure did him no harm, but he was far from being confident that they might not do others harm who entertained them, and might entertain other results from them than he did; and therefore he was very reserved in communicating what he thought himself in those points, in which he differed from what was received.

Nothing troubled him more than the brawls which were grown from religion; and he therefore exceedingly detested the tyranny of the church of Rome; more for their imposing uncharitably upon the consciences of other men, than for the errors in their own opinions: and would often say that he would renounce the religion of the church of England to-morrow, if it obliged him to believe that any other Christians should be damned; and that nobody would conclude another man to be damned, who did not wish him so. No man more strict and severe to himself; to other men so charitable as to their opinions, that he thought that other men were more in fault for their carriage towards them, than the men themselves were who erred; and he thought that pride, and passion, more than conscience, were the cause of all separation from each other's communion; and he frequently said, that that only kept the world from agreeing upon such a liturgy, as might bring them into one communion; all doctrinal points,

upon which men differed in their opinions, being to have
no place in any liturgy. Upon an occasional discourse with
a friend, of the frequent and uncharitable reproaches of
heretic and schismatic, too lightly thrown at each other,
amongst men who differ in their judgment, he writ a little
discourse of schism, contained in less than two sheets of
paper; which being transmitted from friend to friend in
writing, was at last, without any malice, brought to the
view of the archbishop of Canterbury, Dr. Laud, who was
a very rigid surveyor of all things which never so little
bordered upon schism; and thought the church could not
be too vigilant against, and jealous of, such incursions.

He sent for Mr. Hales, whom, when they had both lived
in the university of Oxford, he had known well; and told
him, that he had in truth believed him to be long since
dead; and chid him very kindly for having never come to
him, having been of his old acquaintance: then asked him,
whether he had lately written a short discourse of schism,
and whether he was of that opinion which the discourse
implied. He told him, that he had, for the satisfaction of
a private friend, (who was not of his mind,) a year or two
before, writ such a small tract, without any imagination
that it would be communicated; and that he believed it
did not contain any thing that was not agreeable to the
judgment of the primitive fathers: upon which the archbishop debated with him upon some expressions of
Irenaeus, and the most ancient fathers; and concluded
with saying, that the time was very apt to set new doctrines
on foot, of which the wits of the age were too susceptible;
and that there could not be too much care taken to preserve the peace and unity of the church; and from thence
asked him of his condition, and whether he wanted anything: and the other answering, that he had enough, and
wanted or desired no addition, so dismissed him with great
courtesy; and shortly after sent for him again, when there
was a prebendary of Windsor fallen, and told him, the king
had given him the preferment, because it lay so convenient
to his fellowship of Eton; which (though indeed the most
convenient preferment that could be thought of for him)
the archbishop could not without great difficulty persuade

him to accept, and he did accept it rather to please him than himself; because he really believed he had enough before. He was one of the least men in the kingdom; and one of the greatest scholars in Europe.

5. *William Chillingworth*

*Born 1602; author of 'The Religion of Protestants';
died 1644*

MR. CHILLINGWORTH was of a stature little superior to Mr. Hales, (and it was an age in which there were many great and wonderful men of that size,) and a man of so great a subtilty of understanding, and so rare a temper in debate, that, as it was impossible to provoke him into any passion, so it was very difficult to keep a man's self from being a little discomposed by his sharpness and quickness of argument, and instances, in which he had a rare facility, and a great advantage over all the men I ever knew. He had spent all his younger time in disputation, and had arrived to so great a mastery, as he was inferior to no man in those skirmishes: but he had, with his notable perfection, in this exercise, contracted such an irresolution and habit of doubting, that by degrees he grew confident of nothing, and a sceptic, at least, in the greatest mysteries of faith.

This made him, from first wavering in religion, and indulging to scruples, to reconcile himself too soon and too easily to the church of Rome; and carrying still his own inquisitiveness about him, without any resignation to their authority, (which is the only temper can make that church sure of its proselytes,) having made a journey to St. Omer's, purely to perfect his conversion by the conversation of those who had the greatest name, he found as little satisfaction there; and returned with as much haste from them; with a belief, that an entire exemption from error was neither inherent in, nor necessary to any church: which occasioned that war, which was carried on by the Jesuits with so great asperity and reproaches against him, and in which he defended himself by such an admirable eloquence of language, and clear and incomparable power of reason, that he not only made them appear unequal adversaries, but carried the war into their own quarters; and made the pope's infallibility to be as much shaken, and declined by their own doctors, (and as great an acrimony amongst themselves upon that subject,) and to be at least as much doubted, as in the schools of the reformed, or protestant; and forced them since to defend and maintain those unhappy controversies in religion, with arms and weapons of another nature than were used or known in the church of Rome when Bellarmine died; and which probably will in time undermine the very foundation that supports it.

Such a levity, and propensity to change, is commonly attended with great infirmities in, and no less reproach and prejudice to the person; but the sincerity of his heart was so conspicuous, and without the least temptation or any corrupt end; and the innocence and candour of his nature so evident, and without any perverseness; that all who knew him clearly discerned, that all those restless motions and fluctuations proceeded only from the warmth and jealousy of his own thoughts, in a too nice inquisition for truth. Neither the books of the adversary, nor any of their persons, though he was acquainted with the best of both, had ever made great impression upon him; all his doubts grew out of himself, when he assisted his scruples with all the strength of his own reason, and was then too hard for himself; but finding as little quiet and repose in those victories, he quickly recovered, by a new appeal to his own judgment; so that he was, in truth, upon the matter, in all his sallies and retreats, his own convert; though he was not so totally divested of all thoughts of this world, but that when he was ready for it, he admitted some great and considerable churchmen, to be sharers with him in his public conversion.

Whilst he was in perplexity, or rather some passionate disinclination to the religion he had been educated in, he had the misfortune to have much acquaintance with one Mr. Lugar, a minister of that church; a man of a competency of learning in those points most controverted with the Romanists, but of no acute parts of wit, or judgment;

and wrought so far upon him, by weakening and enervating those arguments, by which he found he was governed, (as he had all the logic, and all the rhetoric, that was necessary to persuade very powerfully men of the greatest talents,) that the poor man, not able to live long in doubt, too hastily deserted his own church, and betook himself to the Roman: nor could all the arguments and reasons of Mr. Chillingworth make him pause in the expedition he was using, or reduce him from that church after he had given himself to it; but he had always a great animosity against him, for having (as he said) unkindly betrayed him, and carried him into another religion, and there left him. So unfit are some constitutions to be troubled with doubts, after they are once fixed.

He did really believe all war to be unlawful; and did not think that the parliament (whose proceedings he perfectly abhorred) did in truth intend to involve the nation in a civil war, till after the battle of Edge-hill; and then he thought any expedient or stratagem that was like to put a speedy end to it, to be the most commendable: and so having too mathematically conceived an engine, that should move so lightly as to be a breastwork in all encounters and assaults in the field, he carried it, to make the experiment, into that part of his majesty's army, which was only in that winter season in the field, under the command of lord Hopton, in Hampshire, upon the borders of Sussex; where he was shut up in the castle of Arundel; which was forced, after a short, sharp siege, to yield for want of victual; and poor Mr. Chillingworth with it, falling into the rebels' hands; and being most barbarously treated by them, especially by that clergy which followed them; and being broken with sickness, contracted by the ill accommodation, and want of meat, and fire during the siege, which was in a terrible season of frost and snow, he died shortly after in prison. He was a man of excellent parts, and of a cheerful disposition; void of all kind of vice, and endued with many notable virtues; of a very public heart, and an indefatigable desire to do good; his only unhappiness proceeded from his sleeping too little, and thinking too much; which sometimes threw him into violent fevers.

6. *Ben Jonson and John Selden*

Jonson 1573–1637
Selden 1584–1654; M.P. 1623 and 1626; imprisoned 1629–31;
M.P. of Long Parliament, though less active, 1645–9

BEN JOHNSON's name can never be forgotten, having by his very good learning, and the severity of his nature and manners, very much reformed the stage; and indeed the English poetry itself. His natural advantages were, judgment to order and govern fancy, rather than excess of fancy, his productions being slow and upon deliberation, yet then abounding with great wit and fancy, and will live accordingly; and surely as he did exceedingly exalt the English language in eloquence, propriety, and masculine expressions, so he was the best judge of, and fittest to prescribe rules to poetry and poets of any man, who had lived with, or before him, or since: if Mr. Cowley had not made a flight beyond all men, with that modesty yet, to ascribe much of this to the example and learning of Ben Johnson. His conversation was very good, and with the men of most note; and he had for many years an extraordinary kindness for Mr. Hyde, till he found he betook himself to business, which he believed ought never to be preferred before his company. He lived to be very old, and till the palsy made a deep impression upon his body and his mind.

Mr. Selden was a person whom no character can flatter, or transmit in any expressions equal to his merit and virtue. He was of so stupendous learning in all kinds and in all languages, (as may appear in his excellent and transcendent writings,) that a man would have thought he had been entirely conversant amongst books, and had never spent an hour but in reading and writing; yet his humanity, courtesy, and affability was such, that he would have been thought to have been bred in the best courts, but that his good nature, charity, and delight in doing good, and in communicating all he knew, exceeded that breeding. His style in all his writings seems harsh and sometimes obscure; which is not wholly to be imputed to the abstruse subjects of which he commonly treated, out of the paths

trod by other men; but to a little undervaluing the beauty
of a style, and too much propensity to the language of
antiquity: but in his conversation he was the most clear
discourser, and had the best faculty of making hard things
easy, and presenting them to the understanding, of any
man that hath been known. Mr. Hyde was wont to say,
that he valued himself upon nothing more than upon
having had Mr. Selden's acquaintance from the time he
was very young: and held it with great delight as long as
they were suffered to continue together in London; and he
was very much troubled always when he heard him blamed,
censured, and reproached, for staying in London, and in
the parliament, after they were in rebellion, and in the
worst times, which his age obliged him to do; and how
wicked soever the actions were which were every day done,
he was confident he had not given his consent to them; but
would have hindered them if he could with his own safety,
to which he was always enough indulgent. If he had some
infirmities with other men, they were weighed down with
wonderful and prodigious abilities and excellencies in the
other scale.

7. Dr. Gilbert Sheldon

*Born 1598; various preferments; Bishop of London
1660; P.C. and Master of Savoy chapel 1660; Archbishop of Canterbury 1663; Chancellor of Oxford University after Clarendon's fall 1667; died 1677*

OF Doctor Sheldon there needs no more be said in this
place, there being frequent occasions to mention him hereafter in the prosecution of this discourse, than that his
learning, and gravity, and prudence, had in that time
raised him to such a reputation, when he was chaplain in
the house to the lord keeper Coventry, (who exceedingly
esteemed him, and used his service not only in all matters
relating to the church, but in many other businesses of
importance, and in which that great and good lord was
nearly concerned,) and when he was afterwards warden of
All Souls' college in Oxford, that he then was looked upon
as very equal to any preferment the church could, or hath

since yielded unto him; and sir Francis Wenman would often say, when the doctor resorted to the conversation at the lord Falkland's house, as he frequently did, that 'Dr. Sheldon was born and bred to be archbishop of Canterbury'.

8. *Sidney Godolphin and Edmund Waller*

Godolphin, born 1610; M.P. 1628–43; fell at Chagford 1643
Waller, born 1606; M.P. 1621; died 1687

SIDNEY GODOLPHIN was a younger brother of Godolphin, but by the provision left by his father, and by the death of a younger brother, liberally supplied for a very good education, and for a cheerful subsistence, in any course of life he proposed to himself. There was never so great a mind and spirit contained in so little room; so large an understanding and so unrestrained a fancy in so very small a body; so that the lord Falkland used to say merrily, that he thought it was a great ingredient into his friendship for Mr. Godolphin, that he was pleased to be found in his company, where he was the properer man; and it may be, the very remarkableness of his little person made the sharpness of his wit, and the composed quickness of his judgment and understanding, the more notorious and notable. He had spent some years in France, and in the Low Countries; and accompanied the earl of Leicester in his ambassage into Denmark, before he resolved to be quiet, and attend some promotion in the court; where his excellent disposition and manners, and extraordinary qualifications, made him very acceptable. Though every body loved his company very well, yet he loved very much to be alone, being in his constitution inclined somewhat to melancholy, and to retirement amongst his books; and was so far from being active, that he was contented to be reproached by his friends with laziness; and was of so nice and tender a composition, that a little rain or wind would disorder him, and divert him from any short journey he had most willingly proposed to himself; insomuch as, when he rid abroad with those in whose company he most delighted, if the wind chanced to be in his face, he would (after a little pleasant murmuring) suddenly turn his horse, and go home. Yet the civil war no sooner began, (the first approaches towards which he discovered as soon as any man, by the proceedings in parliament, where he was a member, and opposed with great indignation,) than he put himself into the first troops which were raised in the west for the king; and bore the uneasiness and fatigue of winter marches, with an exemplar courage and alacrity; until by too brave a pursuit of the enemy into an obscure village in Devonshire, he was shot with a musket; with which (without saying any word more, than, Oh God! I am hurt) he fell dead from his horse; to the excessive grief of his friends, who were all that knew him; and the irreparable damage of the public.

Edmund Waller was born to a very fair estate, by the parsimony or frugality of a wise father and mother; and he thought it so commendable an advantage, that he resolved to improve it with his utmost care, upon which in his nature he was too much intent; and in order to that, he was so much reserved and retired, that he was scarce ever heard of, till by his address and dexterity he had gotten a very rich wife in the city, against all the recommendation, and countenance, and authority of the court, which was thoroughly engaged on the behalf of Mr. Crofts; and which used to be successful, in that age, against any opposition. He had the good fortune to have an alliance and friendship with Dr. Morley, who had assisted and instructed him in the reading many good books, to which his natural parts and promptitude inclined him; especially the poets: and at the age when other men used to give over writing verses, (for he was near thirty years of age when he first engaged himself in that exercise, at least that he was known to do so,) he surprised the town with two or three pieces of that kind; as if a tenth muse had been newly born, to cherish drooping poetry. The doctor at that time brought him into that company which was most celebrated for good conversation; where he was received, and esteemed, with great applause and respect. He was a very pleasant discourser, in earnest and in jest, and there-

fore very grateful to all kind of company, where he was not
the less esteemed for being very rich.

He had been even nursed in parliaments, where he sat
in his infancy; and so when they were resumed again,
(after a long intermission and interdiction,) he appeared in
those assemblies with great advantage, having a graceful
way of speaking; and by thinking much upon several arguments, (which his temper and complexion, that had much
of melancholic, inclined him to,) he seemed often to speak
upon the sudden, when the occasion had only administered
the opportunity of saying what he had thoroughly considered, which gave a great lustre to all he said; which
yet was rather of delight than weight. There needs no
more be said to extol the excellence and power of his wit,
and pleasantness of his conversation, than that it was of
magnitude enough to cover a world of very great faults;
that is, so to cover them, that they were not taken notice of
to his reproach; viz. a narrowness in his nature to the
lowest degree; an abjectness, and want of courage to support him in any virtuous undertaking; and insinuation
and servile flattery to the height the vainest and most
imperious nature could be contented with; that it preserved and won his life from those who were most resolved
to take it, and in an occasion in which he ought to have
been ambitious to have lost it; and then preserved him
again, from the reproach and contempt that was due to him
for so preserving it, and for vindicating it at such a price;
that it had power to reconcile him to those whom he had
most offended and provoked; and continued to his age
with that rare felicity, that his company was acceptable,
where his spirit was odious; and he was at least pitied,
where he was most detested.

9. *Lord Falkland*

*Lucius Cary, born 1610; Viscount Falkland 1633;
Secretary of State 1641; died at battle of Newbury
20 September 1643*

BUT I must here take leave a little longer to discontinue
this narration: and if the celebrating the memory of emi-

nent and extraordinary persons, and transmitting their great virtues, for the imitation of posterity, be one of the principal ends and duties of history, it will not be thought impertinent, in this place, to remember a loss which no time will suffer to be forgotten, and no success or good fortune could repair. In this unhappy battle was slain the lord viscount Falkland; a person of such prodigious parts of learning and knowledge, of that inimitable sweetness and delight in conversation, of so flowing and obliging a humanity and goodness to mankind, and of that primitive simplicity and integrity of life, that if there were no other brand upon this odious and accursed civil war, than that single loss, it must be most infamous, and execrable to all posterity.

Turpe mori, post te, solo non posse dolore.

Before this parliament, his condition of life was so happy that it was hardly capable of improvement. Before he came to twenty years of age, he was master of a noble fortune, which descended to him by the gift of a grandfather, without passing through his father or mother, who were then both alive, and not well enough contented to find themselves passed by in the descent. His education for some years had been in Ireland, where his father was lord deputy; so that, when he returned into England, to the possession of his fortune, he was unentangled with any acquaintance or friends, which usually grow up by the custom of conversation; and therefore was to make a pure election of his company; which he chose by other rules than were prescribed to the young nobility of that time. And it cannot be denied, though he admitted some few to his friendship for the agreeableness of their natures, and their undoubted affection to him, that his familiarity and friendship, for the most part, was with men of the most eminent and sublime parts, and of untouched reputation in point of integrity; and such men had a title to his bosom.

He was a great cherisher of wit, and fancy, and good parts in any man; and, if he found them clouded with poverty or want, a most liberal and bountiful patron towards them, even above his fortune; of which, in those administrations, he was such a dispenser, as, if he had been trusted with it to such uses, and if there had been the least of vice in his expense, he might have been thought too prodigal. He was constant and pertinacious in whatsoever he resolved to do, and not to be wearied by any pains that were necessary to that end. And therefore having once resolved not to see London, which he loved above all places, till he had perfectly learned the Greek tongue, he went to his own house in the country, and pursued it with that indefatigable industry, that it will not be believed in how short a time he was master of it, and accurately read all the Greek historians.

In this time, his house being within ten miles of Oxford, he contracted familiarity and friendship with the most polite and accurate men of that university; who found such an immenseness of wit, and such a solidity of judgment in him, so infinite a fancy, bound in by a most logical ratiocination, such a vast knowledge, that he was not ignorant in any thing, yet such an excessive humility, as if he had known nothing, that they frequently resorted, and dwelt with him, as in a college situated in a purer air; so that his house was a university in a less volume; whither they came not so much for repose as study; and to examine and refine those grosser propositions, which laziness and consent made current in vulgar conversation.

Many attempts were made upon him by the instigation of his mother (who was a lady of another persuasion in religion, and of a most masculine understanding, allayed with the passion and infirmities of her own sex) to pervert him in his piety to the church of England, and to reconcile him to that of Rome; which they prosecuted with the more confidence, because he declined no opportunity or occasion of confidence with those of that religion, whether priests or laics; having diligently studied the controversies, and exactly read all, or the choicest of the Greek and Latin fathers, and having a memory so stupendous, that he remembered, on all occasions, whatsoever he read. And he was so great an enemy to that passion and uncharitableness, which he saw produced, by difference of opinion, in matters of religion, that in all those disputations with priests, and others of the Roman church, he affected to manifest all possible civility to their persons, and estimation of their parts; which made them retain still some hope of his reduction, even when they had given over offering farther reasons to him to that purpose. But this charity towards them was much lessened, and any correspondence with them quite declined, when, by sinister arts, they had corrupted his two younger brothers, being both children, and stolen them from his house, and transported them beyond seas, and perverted his sisters: upon which occasion he writ two large discourses against the principal positions of that religion, with that sharpness of style, and full weight of reason, that the church is deprived of great jewels in the concealment of them, and that they are not published to the world.

He was superior to all those passions and affections which attend vulgar minds, and was guilty of no other ambition than of knowledge, and to be reputed a lover of all good men; and that made him too much a contemner of those arts, which must be indulged in the transactions of human affairs. In the last short parliament, he was a burgess in the house of commons; and, from the debates which were then managed with all imaginable gravity and sobriety, he contracted such a reverence to parliaments, that he thought it really impossible they could ever produce mischief or inconvenience to the kingdom; or that the kingdom could be tolerably happy in the intermission of them. And from the unhappy and unseasonable dissolution of that convention, he harboured, it may be, some jealousy and prejudice to the court, towards which he was not before immoderately inclined; his father having wasted a full fortune there, in those offices and employments by which other men use to obtain a greater. He was chosen again this parliament to serve in the same place, and, in the beginning of it, declared himself very sharply and severely against those exorbitancies, which had been most grievous to the state; for he was so rigid an observer of established laws and rules, that he could not endure the least breach or deviation from them; and thought no mischief so intolerable as the presumption of ministers of state to break positive rules, for reasons of state; or judges to transgress known laws, upon the title of conveniency, or necessity; which made him so severe against the earl of Strafford and the lord Finch, contrary to his natural gentleness and temper: insomuch as they who did not know his composition to be as free from revenge, as it was from pride, thought that the sharpness to the former might proceed from the memory of some unkindnesses, not without a mixture of injustice, from him towards his father. But without doubt he was free from those temptations, and was only misled by the authority of those, who, he believed, understood the laws perfectly; of which himself was utterly ignorant; and if the assumption, which was scarce controverted, had been true, 'that an endeavour to overthrow the fundamental laws of the kingdom had been treason', a strict understanding might make reasonable conclusions to satisfy his own judgment, from the exorbitant parts of their several charges.

The great opinion he had of the uprightness and integrity of those persons who appeared most active, especially of Mr. Hambden, kept him longer from suspecting any design against the peace of the kingdom; and though he differed from them commonly in conclusions, he believed long their purposes were honest. When he grew better informed what was law, and discerned in them a desire to control that law by a vote of one or both houses, no man more opposed those attempts, and gave the adverse party more trouble by reason and argumentation; insomuch as he was, by degrees, looked upon as an advocate for the court, to which he contributed so little, that he declined those addresses, and even those invitations which he was obliged almost by civility to entertain. And he was so ealous of the least imagination that he should incline to preferment, that he affected even a morosity to the court, and to the courtiers; and left nothing undone which might prevent and divert the king's or queen's favour towards him, but the deserving it. For when the king sent for him once or twice to speak with him, and to give him thanks for his excellent comportment in those councils, which his majesty graciously termed 'doing him service', his answers were more negligent, and less satisfactory, than might be expected; as if he cared only that his actions should be just, not that they should be acceptable, and that his majesty should think that they proceeded only from the impulsion of conscience, without any sympathy in his affections; which, from a stoical and sullen nature, might not have been misinterpreted; yet, from a person of so perfect a habit of generous and obsequious compliance with all good men, might very well have been interpreted by the king as more than an ordinary averseness to his service: so that he took more pains, and more forced his nature to actions unagreeable, and unpleasant to it, that he might not be thought to incline to the court, than most men have done to procure an office there. And if any thing but not doing his duty could have kept him from receiving a testimony of the king's grace and trust at that time, he had not been called to his council; not that he was in truth averse to the court or from receiving public employ-ment; for he had a great devotion to the king's person, and had before used some small endeavour to be recommended to him for a foreign negociation, and had once a desire to be sent ambassador into France; but he abhorred an imagination or doubt should sink into the thoughts of any man, that, in the discharge of his trust and duty in parlia-ment, he had any bias to the court, or that the king himself should apprehend that he looked for a reward for being honest.

For this reason, when he heard it first whispered, 'that the king had a purpose to make him a counsellor', for which there was, in the beginning, no other ground, but because he was known sufficient, (*haud semper errat fama, aliquando et eligit,*) he resolved to decline it; and at last suffered himself only to be overruled, by the advice and persuasions of his friends, to submit to it. Afterwards, when he found that the king intended to make him secre-tary of state, he was positive to refuse it; declaring to his friends, 'that he was most unfit for it, and that he must either do that which would be great disquiet to his own nature, or leave that undone which was most necessary to be done by one that was honoured with that place; for

that the most just and honest men did, every day, that
which he could not give himself leave to do'. And indeed
he was so exact and strict an observer of justice and truth,
ad amussim, that he believed those necessary condescensions
and applications to the weakness of other men, and those
arts and insinuations which are necessary for discoveries,
and prevention of ill, would be in him a declension from
his own rules of life: which he acknowledged fit, and
absolutely necessary to be practised in those employments;
and was, in truth, so precise in the practic principles he
prescribed to himself, (to all others he was as indulgent,)
as if he had lived *in republica Platonis, non in faece Romuli.*

Two reasons prevailed with him to receive the seals,
and but for those he had resolutely avoided them. The
first, the consideration that it ⟨his refusal⟩ might bring
some blemish upon the king's affairs, and that men would
have believed, that he had refused so great an honour and
trust, because he must have been with it obliged to do
somewhat else not justifiable. And this he made matter of
conscience, since he knew the king made choice of him,
before other men, especially because he thought him more
honest than other men. The other was, lest he might be
thought to avoid it out of fear to do an ungracious thing
to the house of commons, who were sorely troubled at the
displacing sir Harry Vane, whom they looked upon as
removed for having done them those offices they stood in
need of; and the disdain of so popular an incumbrance
wrought upon him next to the other. For as he had a full
appetite of fame by just and generous actions, so he had an
equal contempt of it by any servile expedients: and he so
much the more consented to and approved the justice upon
sir Harry Vane, in his own private judgment, by how
much he surpassed most men in the religious observation
of a trust, the violation whereof he would not admit any
excuse for.

For these reasons, he submitted to the king's command,
and became his secretary, with as humble and devout an
acknowledgment of the greatness of the obligation, as
could be expressed, and as true a sense of it in his heart.
Yet two things he could never bring himself to, whilst he

continued in that office, that was to his death; for which
he was contented to be reproached, as for omissions in a
most necessary part of his place. The one, employing of
spies, or giving any countenance or entertainment to them.
I do not mean such emissaries, as with danger would venture to view the enemy's camp, and bring intelligence of
their number, or quartering, or such generals as such an
observation can comprehend; but those who by communication of guilt, or dissimulation of manners, wound themselves into such trusts and secrets, as enabled them to make
discoveries for the benefit of the state. The other, the
liberty of opening letters, upon a suspicion that they might
contain matter of dangerous consequence. For the first, he
would say, 'such instruments must be void of all ingenuity,
and common honesty, before they could be of use; and
afterwards they could never be fit to be credited: and that
no single preservation could be worth so general a wound,
and corruption of human society, as the cherishing such
persons would carry with it'. The last, he thought 'such
violation of the law of nature, that no qualification by
office could justify a single person in the trespass'; and
though he was convinced by the necessity and iniquity of
the time, that those advantages of information were not
to be declined, and were necessarily to be practised, he
found means to shift it from himself; when he confessed
he needed excuse and pardon for the omission: so unwilling he was to resign any thing in his nature to an
obligation in his office.

In all other particulars he filled his place plentifully,
being sufficiently versed in languages, to understand any
that are used in business, and to make himself again
understood. To speak of his integrity, and his high disdain
of any bait that might seem to look towards corruption,
in tanto viro, injuria virtutum fuerit. Some sharp expressions he
used against the archbishop of Canterbury, and his concurring in the first bill to take away the votes of bishops
in the house of peers, gave occasion to some to believe, and
opportunity to others to conclude, and publish, 'that he
was no friend to the church, and the established government of it'; and troubled his very friends much, who were

more confident of the contrary, than prepared to answer the allegations.

The truth is, he had unhappily contracted some prejudice to the archbishop; and having only known him enough to observe his passion, when, it may be, multiplicity of business, or other indisposition, had possessed him, did wish him less entangled and engaged in the business of the court, or state: though, I speak knowingly, he had a singular estimation and reverence of his great learning, and confessed integrity; and really thought his letting himself to those expressions, which implied a disesteem of him, or at least an acknowledgment of his infirmities, would enable him to shelter him from part of the storm he saw raised for his destruction; which he abominated with his soul.

The giving his consent to the first bill for the displacing the bishops, did proceed from two grounds: the first, his not understanding the original of their right and suffrage there: the other, an opinion, that the combination against the whole government of the church by bishops, was so violent and furious, that a less composition than the dispensing with their intermeddling in secular affairs, would not preserve the order. And he was persuaded to this by the profession of many persons of honour, who declared, 'they did desire the one, and would not then press the other'; which, in that particular, misled many men. But when his observation and experience made him discern more of their intentions, than he before suspected, with great frankness he opposed the second bill that was preferred for that purpose; and had, without scruple, the order itself in perfect reverence; and thought too great encouragement could not possibly be given to learning, nor too great rewards to learned men; and was never in the least degree swayed or moved by the objections which were made against that government, (holding them most ridiculous,) or affected to the other, which those men fancied to themselves.

He had a courage of the most clear and keen temper, and so far from fear, that he was not without appetite of danger; and therefore, upon any occasion of action, he always engaged his person in those troops, which he thought, by the forewardness of the commanders, to be most like to be farthest engaged; and in all such encounters he had about him a strange cheerfulness and companiableness, without at all affecting the execution that was then principally to be attended, in which he took no delight, but took pains to prevent it, where it was not, by resistance, necessary: insomuch that at Edge-hill, when the enemy was routed, he was like to have incurred great peril, by interposing to save those who had thrown away their arms, and against whom, it may be, others were more fierce for their having thrown them away: insomuch as a man might think, he came into the field only out of curiosity to see the face of danger, and charity to prevent the shedding of blood. Yet in his natural inclination he acknowledged he was addicted to the profession of a soldier; and shortly after he came to his fortune, and before he came to age, he went into the Low Countries, with a resolution of procuring command, and to give himself up to it, from which he was converted by the complete inactivity of that summer: and so he returned into England, and shortly after entered upon that vehement course of study we mentioned before, till the first alarm from the north; and then again he made ready for the field, and though he received some repulse in the command of a troop of horse, of which he had a promise, he went a volunteer with the earl of Essex.

From the entrance into this unnatural war, his natural cheerfulness and vivacity grew clouded, and a kind of sadness and dejection of spirit stole upon him, which he had never been used to; yet being one of those who believed that one battle would end all differences, and that there would be so great a victory on one side, that the other would be compelled to submit to any conditions from the victor, (which supposition and conclusion generally sunk into the minds of most men, and prevented the looking after many advantages, that might then have been laid hold of,) he resisted those indispositions, *et in luctu, bellum inter remedia erat*. But after the king's return from Brentford, and the furious resolution of the two houses not

to admit any treaty for peace, those indispositions, which
had before touched him, grew into a perfect habit of un-
cheerfulness; and he, who had been so exactly unreserved
and affable to all men, that his face and countenance was
always present, and vacant to his company, and held
any cloudiness, and less pleasantness of the visage, a kind
of rudeness or incivility, became, on a sudden, less com-
municable; and thence, very sad, pale, and exceedingly
affected with the spleen. In his clothes and habit, which
he had intended before always with more neatness, and
industry, and expense, than is usual to so great a mind,
he was not now only incurious, but too negligent; and
in his reception of suitors, and the necessary or casual
addresses to his place, so quick, and sharp, and severe, that
there wanted not some men, (who were strangers to his
nature and disposition,) who believed him proud and
imperious, from which no mortal man was ever more
free.

The truth is, that as he was of a most incomparable
gentleness, application, and even demissiveness and submission to good, and worthy, and entire men, so he was
naturally (which could not but be more evident in his
place, which objected him to another conversation and
intermixture, than his own election had done) *adversus
malos injucundus*; and was so ill a dissembler of his dislike
and disinclination to ill men, that it was not possible for
such not to discern it. There was once, in the house of commons, such a declared acceptation of the good service an
eminent member had done to them, and, as they said, to
the whole kingdom, that it was moved, he being present,
'that the speaker might, in the name of the whole house,
give him thanks; and then, that every member might, as
a testimony of his particular acknowledgment, stir or
move his hat towards him'; the which (though not ordered) when very many did, the lord Falkland, (who
believed the service itself not to be of that moment, and
that an honourable and generous person could not have
stooped to it for any recompense,) instead of moving his
hat, stretched both his arms out, and clasped his hands
together upon the crown of his hat, and held it close down

to his head; that all men might see, how odious that flattery was to him, and the very approbation of the person,
though at that time most popular.

When there was any overture or hope of peace, he
would be more erect and vigorous, and exceedingly solicitous to press any thing which he thought might promote it;
and sitting among his friends, often, after a deep silence
and frequent sighs, would, with a shrill and sad accent,
ingeminate the word *Peace, Peace*; and would passionately profess, 'that the very agony of the war, and the view
of the calamities and desolation the kingdom did and must
endure, took his sleep from him, and would shortly break
his heart'. This made some think, or pretend to think,
'that he was so much enamoured on peace, that he would
have been glad the king should have bought it at any
price'; which was a most unreasonable calumny. As if a
man, that was himself the most punctual and precise in
every circumstance that might reflect upon conscience or
honour, could have wished the king to have committed a
trespass against either. And yet this senseless scandal made
some impression upon him, or at least he used it for an
excuse of the daringness of his spirit; for at the leaguer
before Gloucester, when his friends passionately reprehended him for exposing his person unnecessarily to
danger, (as he delighted to visit the trenches and nearest
approaches, and to discover what the enemy did,) as
being so much beside the duty of his place, that it might
be understood against it, he would say merrily, 'that his
office could not take away the privileges of his age; and
that a secretary in war might be present at the greatest
secret of danger;' but withal alleged seriously, 'that it
concerned him to be more active in enterprises of hazard,
than other men; that all might see, that his impatiency
for peace proceeded not from pusillanimity, or fear to
adventure his own person'.

In the morning before the battle, as always upon action,
he was very cheerful, and put himself into the first rank
of the lord Byron's regiment, who was then advancing
upon the enemy, who had lined the hedges on both sides
with musketeers; from whence he was shot with a musket

in the lower part of the belly, and in the instant falling from his horse, his body was not found till the next morning; till when, there was some hope he might have been a prisoner; though his nearest friends, who knew his temper, received small comfort from that imagination. Thus fell that incomparable young man, in the four and thirtieth year of his age, having so much despatched the business of life, that the oldest rarely attain to that immense knowledge, and the youngest enter not into the world with more innocence: whosoever leads such a life, needs not care upon how short warning it be taken from him.

[With Falkland Clarendon] had a most entire friendship without reserve, from his age of twenty years to the hour of his death, near twenty years after: upon which there will be occasion to enlarge when we come to speak of that time, and often before, and therefore we shall say no more of him in this place, than to shew his condition and qualifications, which were the first ingredients into that friendship, which was afterwards cultivated and improved by a constant conversation and familiarity, and by many accidents which contributed thereto. He had the advantage of a noble extraction, and of being born his father's eldest son, when there was a greater fortune in prospect to be inherited, (besides what he might reasonably expect by his mother,) than came afterwards to his possession. His education was equal to his birth, at least in the care, if not in the climate; for his father being deputy of Ireland, before he was of age fit to be sent abroad, his breeding was in the court, and in the university of Dublin; but under the care, vigilance, and direction of such governors and tutors, that he learned all those exercises and languages, better than most men do in more celebrated places; insomuch as when he came into England, which was when he was about the age of eighteen years, he was not only master of the Latin tongue, and had read all the poets, and other of the best authors with notable judgment for that age, but he understood, and spake, and writ French, as if he had spent many years in France.

He had another advantage, which was a great ornament to the rest, that was, a good, a plentiful estate, of which he

had the early possession. His mother was the sole daughter
and heir of the lord chief baron Tanfield, who having
given a fair portion with his daughter in marriage, had
kept himself free to dispose of his land, and his other estate,
in such manner as he should think fit; and he settled it in
such manner upon his grandson sir Lucius Carey, without
taking notice of his father, or mother, that upon his
grandmother's death, which fell out about the time that
he was nineteen years of age, all the land, with two excellent houses excellently furnished (worth above 2000l. per
annum,) in a most pleasant country, and the two most
pleasant places in that country, with a very plentiful
personal estate, fell into his hands and possession, and to
his entire disposal.

With these advantages, he had one great disadvantage
(which in the first entrance into the world is attended with
too much prejudice,) in his person and presence, which
was in no degree attractive or promising. His stature was
low, and smaller than most men; his motion not graceful;
and his aspect so far from inviting, that it had somewhat
in it of simplicity; and his voice the worst of the three,
and so untuned, that instead of reconciling, it offended
the ear, so that nobody would have expected music from
that tongue; and sure no man was less beholden to nature
for its recommendation into the world: but then no man
sooner or more disappointed this general and customary
prejudice; that little person and small stature was quickly
found to contain a great heart, a courage so keen, and a
nature so fearless, that no composition of the strongest
limbs, and most harmonious and proportioned presence
and strength, ever more disposed any man to the greatest
enterprise; it being his greatest weakness to be too solicitous for such adventures: and that untuned tongue and
voice easily discovered itself to be supplied and governed
by a mind and understanding so excellent, that the wit
and weight of all he said carried another kind of lustre
and admiration in it, and even another kind of acceptation from the persons present, than any ornament of
delivery could reasonably promise itself, or is usually
attended with; and his disposition and nature was so

gentle and obliging, so much delighted in courtesy, kindness, and generosity, that all mankind could not but admire and love him.

In a short time after he had possession of the estate his grandfather had left him, and before he was of age, he committed a fault against his father, in marrying a young lady, whom he passionately loved, without any considerable portion, which exceedingly offended him; and disappointed all his reasonable hopes and expectation of redeeming and repairing his own broken fortune, and desperate hopes in court, by some advantageous marriage of his son; about which he had then some probable treaty. Sir Lucius Carey was very conscious to himself of his offence and transgression, and the consequence of it, which though he could not repent, having married a lady of a most extraordinary wit and judgment, and of the most signal virtue and exemplary life, that the age produced, and who brought him many hopeful children, in which he took great delight; yet he confessed it, with the most sincere and dutiful applications to his father for his pardon that could be made; and in order to the prejudice he had brought upon his fortune, by bringing no portion to him, he offered to repair it, by resigning his whole estate to his disposal, and to rely wholly upon his kindness for his own maintenance and support; and to that purpose, he had caused conveyances to be drawn by council, which he brought ready engrossed to his father, and was willing to seal and execute them, that they might be valid: but his father's passion and indignation so far transported him, (though he was a gentleman of excellent parts,) that he refused any reconciliation, and rejected all the offers that were made him of the estate; so that his son remained still in the possession of his estate against his will; for which he found great reason afterwards to rejoice: but he was for the present so much afflicted with his father's displeasure, that he transported himself and his wife into Holland, resolving to buy some military command, and to spend the remainder of his life in that profession: but being disappointed in the treaty he expected, and finding no opportunity to accommodate himself with such a command, he returned again into England; resolving to retire to a country life, and to his books; that since he was not like to improve himself in arms, he might advance in letters.

In his resolution he was so severe, (as he was always naturally very intent upon what he was inclined to,) that he declared, he would not see London in many years, which was the place he loved of all the world; and that in his studies, he would first apply himself to the Greek, and pursue it without intermission, till he should attain to the full understanding of that tongue: and it is hardly to be credited, what industry he used, and what success attended that industry: for though his father's death, by an unhappy accident, made his repair to London absolutely necessary, in fewer years, than he had proposed for his absence; yet he had first made himself master of the Greek tongue, (in the Latin he was very well versed before,) and had read not only all the Greek historians, but Homer likewise, and such of the poets as were worthy to be perused.

Though his father's death brought no other convenience to him, but a title to redeem an estate, mortgaged for as much as it was worth, and for which he was compelled to sell a finer seat of his own; yet it imposed a burden upon him, of the title of a viscount, and an increase of expense, in which he was not in his nature too provident or restrained; having naturally such a generosity and bounty in him, that he seemed to have his estate in trust, for all worthy persons, who stood in want of supplies and encouragement, as Ben Johnson, and many others of that time, whose fortunes required, and whose spirits made them superior to, ordinary obligations; which yet they were contented to receive from him, because his bounties were so generously distributed, and so much without vanity and ostentation, that, except from those few persons from whom he sometimes received the characters of fit objects for his benefits, or whom he intrusted for the more secret deriving them to them, he did all he could, that the persons themselves who received them should not know from what fountain they flowed; and when that could not be concealed, he sustained any acknowledgment from the persons obliged with so much trouble and bashfulness, that they might well perceive, that he was even ashamed of the little he had given, and to receive so large a recompense for it.

As soon as he had finished all those transactions, which the death of his father had made necessary to be done, he retired again to his country life, and to his severe course of study, which was very delightful to him, as soon as he was engaged in it: but he was wont to say, that he never found reluctancy in any thing he resolved to do, but in his quitting London, and departing from the conversation of those he enjoyed there; which was in some degree preserved and continued by frequent letters, and often visits, which were made by his friends from thence, whilst he continued wedded to the country; and which were so grateful to him, that during their stay with him, he looked upon no book, except their very conversation made an appeal to some book; and truly his whole conversation was one continued *convivium philosophicum*, or *convivium theologicum*, enlivened and refreshed with all the facetiousness of wit, and good humour, and pleasantness of discourse, which made the gravity of the argument itself (whatever it was) very delectable. His house where he usually resided, (Tew, or Burford, in Oxfordshire,) being within ten or twelve miles of the university, looked like the university itself, by the company that was always found there. There were Dr. Sheldon, Dr. Morley, Dr. Hammond, Dr. Earles, Mr. Chillingworth, and indeed all men of eminent parts and faculties in Oxford, besides those who resorted thither from London; who all found their lodgings there, as ready as in the colleges; nor did the lord of the house know of their coming or going, nor who were in his house, till he came to dinner, or supper, where all still met; otherwise, there was no troublesome ceremony or constraint, to forbid men to come to the house, or to make them weary of staying there; so that many came thither to study in a better air, finding all the books they could desire in his library, and all the persons together, whose company they could wish, and not find in any other society. Here Mr. Chillingworth wrote, and formed, and modelled, his excellent book against the learned Jesuit Mr. Nott, after frequent debates upon the most important particulars; in many of which, he suffered himself to be overruled by the judgment of his friends, though in others he still adhered to his own fancy, which was sceptical enough, even in the highest points.

In this happy and delightful conversation and restraint, he remained in the country many years; and until he made so prodigious a progress in learning, that there were very few classic authors in the Greek or Latin tongue, that he had not read with great exactness. He had read all the Greek and Latin fathers; all the most allowed and authentic ecclesiastical writers; and all the councils, with wonderful care and observation; for in religion he thought too careful and too curious an inquiry could not be made, amongst those, whose purity was not questioned, and whose authority was constantly and confidently urged, by men who were furthest from being of one mind among themselves; and for the mutual support of their several opinions, in which they most contradicted each other; and in all those controversies, he had so dispassioned a consideration, such a candour in his nature, and so profound a charity in his conscience, that in those points, in which he was in his own judgment most clear, he never thought the worse, or in any degree declined the familiarity, of those who were of another mind; which, without question, is an excellent temper for the propagation and advancement of Christianity. With these great advantages of industry, he had a memory retentive of all that he had ever read, and an understanding and judgment to apply it seasonably and appositely, with the most dexterity and address, and the least pedantry and affectation, that ever man, who knew so much, was possessed with, of what quality soever. It is not a trivial evidence of his learning, his wit, and his candour, that may be found in that discourse of his, against the infallibility of the church of Rome, published since his death, and from a copy under his own hand, though not prepared and digested by him for the press, and to which he would have given some castigations.

But all his parts, abilities, and faculties, by art and industry, were not to be valued, or mentioned in comparison of his most accomplished mind and manners: his gentleness and affability was so transcendent and obliging, that it drew reverence, and some kind of compliance, from the roughest, and most unpolished, and stubborn constitutions; and made them of another temper in debate, in his presence, than they were in other places. He was in his nature so severe a lover of justice, and so precise a lover of truth, that he was superior to all possible temptations for the violation of either; indeed so rigid an exacter of perfection, in all those things which seemed but to border upon either of them, and by the common practice of men were not thought to border upon either, that many who knew him very well, and loved and admired his virtue, (as all who did know him must love and admire it,) did believe, that he was of a temper and composition fitter to live *in republica Platonis*, than *in faece Romuli*: but this rigidness was only exercised towards himself; towards his friend's infirmities no man was more indulgent. In his conversation, which was the most cheerful and pleasant that can be imagined, though he was young, (for all I have yet spoken of him doth not exceed his age of twenty-five or twenty-six years, what progress he made afterwards will be mentioned in its proper season in this discourse,) and of great gayety in his humour, with a flowing delightfulness of language, he had so chaste a tongue and ear, that there was never known a profane or loose word to fall from him, nor in truth in his company; the integrity, and cleanliness of the wit of that time, not exercising itself in that license, before persons for whom they had any esteem.

10. *A View of the Early Part of the Reign of Charles I*

KING JAMES in the end of March 1625 died, leaving his majesty that now is, engaged in a war with Spain, but unprovided with money to manage it; though it was undertaken by the consent and advice of parliament: the people being naturally enough inclined to the war (having surfeited with the uninterrupted pleasures and plenty of twenty-two years peace) and sufficiently inflamed against the Spaniard; but quickly weary of the charge of it: and therefore, after an unprosperous and chargeable attempt in a voyage by sea upon Cadiz, and an unsuccessful and more unfortunate a one upon France, at the Isle of Rhé, (for some difference had likewise at the same time begotten a war with that prince,) a general peace was shortly concluded with both kingdoms; the exchequer being so exhausted with the debts of king James, the bounty of his majesty that now is, (who, upon his first access to the crown, gave many costly instances of his favour to persons near him,) and the charge of the war upon Spain, and France, that both the known and casual revenue being anticipated, the necessary subsistence of the household was unprovided for; and the king on the sudden driven to those straits for his own support, that many ways were resorted to, and inconveniences submitted to, for supply; as selling the crown-lands, creating peers for money, and many other particulars, which no access of power or plenty since could repair.

Parliaments were summoned, and again dissolved: and that in the fourth year (after the dissolution of the two former) was determined with a profession and declaration that there should be no more assemblies of that nature expected, and all men inhibited upon the penalty of censure, so much as to speak of a parliament. And here I cannot but let myself loose to say, that no man can shew me a source, from whence these waters of bitterness we now taste have more probably flowed, than from these unseasonable, unskilful, and precipitate dissolutions of parliaments; in which, by an unjust survey of the passion, insolence, and ambition of particular persons, the court measured the temper and affection of the country; and by the same standard the people considered the honour, justice, and piety of the court; and so usually parted, at those sad seasons, with no other respect and charity one toward the other, than accompanies persons who never meant to meet but in their own defence. In which the king had always the disadvantage to harbour persons about him, who, with their utmost industry, information, and malice, improved the faults and infirmities of the court to the people; and again, as much as in them lay, rendered the people suspected, if not odious to the king.

I am not altogether a stranger to the passages of those parliaments, (though I was not a member of them,) having carefully perused the journals of both houses, and familiarly conversed with many who had principal parts in them. And I cannot but wonder at those counsels, which persuaded the courses then taken; the habit and temper of men's minds being, no question, very applicable to the public ends; and those ends being only discredited by the jealousies the people entertained from the manner of the prosecution, that they were other and worse than in truth they were. It is not to be denied, that there were, in all those parliaments, especially in that of the fourth year, several passages, and distempered speeches of particular persons, not fit for the dignity and honour of those places, and unsuitable to the reverence due to his majesty and his councils. But I do not know any formed act of either house (for neither the remonstrance or votes of the last day were such) that was not agreeable to the wisdom and justice of great courts, upon those extraordinary occasions. And whoever considers the acts of power and injustice in the intervals of parliament will not be much scandalized at the warmth and vivacity of those meetings.

In the second parliament there was a mention, and intention declared, of granting five subsidies, a proportion (how contemptible soever in respect of the pressures now every day imposed) never before heard of in parliament. And that meeting being, upon very unpopular and plausible reasons, immediately dissolved, those five subsidies were exacted, throughout the whole kingdom, with the same rigour, as if, in truth, an act had passed to that purpose. Very many gentlemen of prime quality, in all the several counties of England, were, for refusing to pay the same, committed to prison, with great rigour and extraordinary circumstances. And could it be imagined, that these men would meet again in a free convention of parliament, without a sharp and severe expostulation, and inquisition into their own right, and the power that had imposed upon that right? And yet all these provocations, and many other, almost of as large an extent, produced no other resentment, than the petition of right, (of no prejudice to the crown,) which was likewise purchased at the price of five subsidies more, and, in a very short time after that supply granted, that parliament was likewise, with strange circumstances of passion on all sides, dissolved.

The abrupt and ungracious breaking off the two first parliaments was wholly imputed to the duke of Buckingham; and the third, principally to lord Weston, then lord high treasurer of England; both in respect of the great power and interest they then had in the affections of his majesty, and for that the time of the dissolutions happened to be, when some charges and accusations were preparing, and ready to be preferred against those two great persons. And therefore the envy and hatred, that attended them thereupon, was insupportable, and was visibly the cause of the murder of the first, (stabbed to the heart by the hand of an obscure villain, upon the mere impious pretence of his being odious to the parliament,) and made, no doubt, so great an impression upon the understanding and nature of the other, that, by degrees, he lost that temper and serenity of mind he had been before master of, and which was most fit to have accompanied him in his weighty employments: insomuch as, out of indignation to find himself worse used than he deserved, he cared less to deserve well, than he had done; and insensibly grew into that public hatred, that rendered him less useful to the service that he only intended.

I wonder less at the errors of this nature in the duke of Buckingham; who, having had a most generous education in courts, was utterly ignorant of the ebbs and floods of popular councils, and of the winds that move those waters; and could not, without the spirit of indignation, find himself, in the space of a few weeks, without any visible cause intervening, from the greatest height of popular estimation that any person hath ascended to, (insomuch as sir Edward Coke blasphemously called him our Saviour,) by the same breath thrown down to the depth of calumny and reproach. I say, it is no marvel, (besides that he was naturally to follow such counsel as was given him,) that he could think of no better way to be freed of the inconveniences and troubles the passions of those meetings gave him, than to dissolve them, and prevent their coming together: and that, when they seemed to neglect the public peace, out of animosity to him, that he intended his own ease and security in the first place, and easily believed the public might be otherwise provided for, by more intent and dispassionate councils. But that the other, the lord Weston, who had been very much and very popularly conversant in those conventions, who exactly knew the frame and constitution of the kingdom, the temper of the people, the extent of the courts of law, and the jurisdiction of parliaments, which at that time had never committed any excess of jurisdiction, (modesty and moderation in words never was, nor ever will be, observed in popular councils, whose foundation is liberty of speech,) should believe, that the union, peace, and plenty of the kingdom could be preserved without parliaments, or that the passion and distemper gotten and received into parliaments could be removed and reformed by the more passionate breaking and dissolving them; or that that course would not inevitably prove the most pernicious to himself, is as much my wonder, as any thing that hath since happened. So that, very probably, those two noble persons had been happy, if they had stoutly submitted to the proceedings ⟨which⟩ were designed against them; and, without question, it had been of sovereign use to the king, if, in those peaceable times, parliaments had been taught to know their own bounds, by being suffered to proceed as far as they could go; by which the extent of their power would quickly have been manifested: from whence no inconvenience of moment could have proceeded; the house of commons never then pretending to the least part of judicature, or exceeding the known verge of their own privileges; the house of peers observing the rules of law and equity in their judgments, and proceeding deliberately upon clear testimony and evidence of matter of fact; and the king retaining the sole power of pardoning, and receiving the whole profit of all penalties and judgments; and indeed having so great an influence upon the body of the peerage, that it was never known that any person of honour was severely censured in that house, (before this present parliament,) who was not either immediately prosecuted by the court, or in evident disfavour there; in which, it may be, (as it usually falls out,) some doors were opened, at which inconveniences to the crown have got in, that were not then enough weighed and considered.

But the course of exempting men from prosecution, by dissolving of parliaments, made the power of parliaments much more formidable, as conceived to be without limit; since the sovereign power seemed to be compelled (as unable otherwise to set bounds to their proceeds) to that rough cure, and to determine their being, because it could not determine their jurisdiction. Whereas, if they had been frequently summoned, and seasonably dissolved, after their wisdom in applying medicines and cures, as well as their industry in discovering diseases, had been discerned, they would easily have been applied to the uses for which they were first instituted; and been of no less esteem with the crown, than of veneration with the people. And so I shall conclude this digression, which I conceived not unseasonable for this place, nor upon this occasion, and return to the time when that brisk resolution was taken of totally declining those conventions; all men being inhibited (as I said before) by proclamation at the dissolution of the parliament in the fourth year, so much as to mention or speak as if a parliament should be called.

This digression, much longer than it was intended, may not be thought altogether unnatural in this discourse. For as the mention of his [Buckingham's] death was very pertinent, in the place, and upon the occasion, it happened to be made; so upon that occasion, it seemed the more reasonable to enlarge upon the nature, and character, and fortune of the duke; as being the best mirror to discern the temper and spirit of that age, and the rather and because all the particulars before set down are to be found in the papers and memorials of the person, whose life is the subject of this discourse, who was frequently heard to relate the wonderful concurrence of many fatal accidents, to disfigure the government of two excellent kings; under whom their kingdoms in general prospered exceedingly, and enjoyed a longer peace, a greater plenty, and in fuller security, than had been in any former age; and who was so far from any acrimony to the memory of that great favourite, (whose death he had lamented at that time, and endeavoured to vindicate him from some libels and reproaches, which vented after his death,) that he took delight in remembering his many virtues, and to magnify his affability and most obliging nature.

And because there was so total a change of all counsels, and in the whole face of the court, upon the death of that omnipotent favourite; all thoughts of war being presently laid aside, (though there was a faint looking towards the relief of Rochelle by the fleet, that was ready under the command of the earl of Lindsey,) and the provisions for peace and plenty taken to heart; it will not be unuseful nor unpleasant to enlarge the digression, before a return to the proper subject of the discourse, by a prospect of the constitution of the court, after that bright star was shot out of the horizon; who were the chief ministers, that had the principal management of public affairs in church and state; and how equal their faculties and qualifications were for those high transactions; in which mention shall be only made of those who were then in the highest trust; there being at that time no ladies, who had disposed themselves to intermeddle in business: and hereafter, when that activity began, and made more progress, it will be again necessary to take a new survey of the court upon that alteration.

[Having shortly mentioned the events of the first four years of Charles's reign Clarendon enlarges on the difficulties the government found in raising money after the king had dismissed his third parliament on 10 March 1629.] Supplemental acts of state were made to supply defect of laws; and so tonnage, and poundage, and other duties upon merchandises, were collected by order of the board, which had been perversely refused to be settled by act of parliament, and new and greater impositions laid upon trade: obsolete laws were revived, and rigorously executed, wherein the subject might be taught how unthrifty a thing it was, by too strict a detaining of what was his, to put the king as strictly to inquire what was his own.

And by this ill husbandry the king received a vast sum of money from all persons of quality, or indeed of any reasonable condition throughout the kingdom, upon the law of knighthood; which, though it had a foundation in right, yet, in the circumstances of proceeding, was very grievous. And no less unjust projects of all kinds, many ridiculous, many scandalous, all very grievous, were set on foot; the envy and reproach of which came to the king, the profit to other men: insomuch as, of two hundred thousand pound drawn from the subject, by these ways, in a year, scarce fifteen hundred came to the king's use or account. To recompense the damage the crown sustained by the sale of old lands, and by the grant of new pensions, the old laws of the forest are revived, by which not only great fines are imposed, but great annual rents intended, and like to be settled by way of contract; which burden lighted most upon persons of quality and honour, who thought themselves above ordinary oppressions, and therefore like to remember it with more sharpness. Lastly, for a spring and magazine that should have no bottom, and for an everlasting supply of all occasions, a writ is framed in a form of law, and directed to the sheriff of every county of England, 'to provide a ship of war for the king's service, and to send it, amply provided and fitted, by such a day, to such a place; and with that writ were sent to each sheriff instructions, that, instead of a ship, he should levy upon his county such a sum of money, and return the same to the treasurer of the navy for his majesty's use, with direction, in what manner he should proceed against such as refused': and from hence that tax had the denomination of ship-money; a word of a lasting sound in the memory of this kingdom; by which for some years really accrued the yearly sum of two hundred thousand pounds to the king's coffers: and was in truth the only project that was accounted to his own service. And, after the continued receipt of it for four years together, was at last (upon the refusal of a private gentleman to pay thirty shillings as his share) with great solemnity publicly argued before all the judges of England in the exchequer-chamber, and by the major part of them, the king's right to impose asserted, and the tax adjudged lawful; which judgment proved of more advantage and credit to the gentleman condemned (Mr. Hambden) than to the king's service.

For the better support of these extraordinary ways, and to protect the agents and instruments, who must be employed in them, and to discountenance and suppress all bold inquirers and opposers, the council-table and star-chamber enlarge their jurisdictions to a vast extent, 'holding' (as Thucydides said of the Athenians) ' for honourable that which pleased, and for just that which profited'; and being the same persons in several rooms, grew both courts of law to determine right, and courts of revenue to bring money into the treasury; the council-table by proclamations enjoining this, that was not enjoined by the law, and prohibiting that which was not prohibited; and the star-chamber censuring the breach, and disobedience to those proclamations, by very great fines and imprisonment; so that any disrespect to acts of state, or to the persons of statesmen, was in no time more penal, and those foundations of right, by which men valued their security, to the apprehension and understanding of wise men, never more in danger to be destroyed.

And here I cannot but again take the liberty to say, that the circumstances and proceedings in those new extraordinary cases, stratagems, and impositions, were very unpolitic, and even destructive to the services intended. As if the business of ship-money, being an imposition by the state, under the notion of necessity, upon a prospect of danger, which private persons could not modestly think themselves qualified to discern, had been managed in the same extraordinary way as the royal loan (which was the imposing the five subsidies after the second parliament spoken of before) was, men would much easier have submitted to it; as it is notoriously known, that pressure was borne with much more cheerfulness before the judgment for the king, than ever it was after; men before pleasing themselves with doing somewhat for the king's service, as a testimony of their affection, which they were not bound to do; many really believing the necessity, and therefore thinking the burden reasonable; others observing, that the access to the king was of importance, when the damage to them was not considerable; and all assuring themselves, that when they should be weary, or unwilling to continue the payment, they might resort to the law for relief, and find it. But when they heard this demanded in a court of law as a right, and found it, by sworn judges of the law, adjudged so, upon such grounds and reasons as every stander-by was able to swear was not law, and so had lost the pleasure and delight of being kind and dutiful to the king; and, instead of giving, were required to pay, and by a logic that left no man anything which he might call his own; they no more looked upon it as the case of one man, but the case of the kingdom, nor as an imposition laid upon them by the king, but by the judges; which they thought themselves bound in conscience to the public justice not to submit to. It was an observation long ago by Thucydides, 'That men are much more passionate for injustice, than for violence; because (says he) the one coming as from an equal, seems rapine; when the other, proceeding from one stronger, is but the effect of necessity'. So, when ship-money was transacted at the council-board, they looked upon it as a work of that power they were always obliged to trust, and an effect of that foresight they were naturally to rely upon. Imminent necessity, and public safety, were convincing persuasions; and it might not seem of apparent ill consequence to them, that upon an emergent occasion the regal power should fill up an hiatus, or supply an impotency in the law. But when they saw in a court of law, (that law that gave them title and possession of all that they had) apothegms of state urged as elements of law, judges as sharp-sighted as secretaries of state, and in the mysteries of state; judgment of law grounded upon matter of fact, of which there was neither inquiry or proof; and no reason given for the payment of the thirty shillings in question, but what concluded the estates of all the standers-by; they had no reason to hope that the doctrine, or the preachers of it, would be contained within any bounds; and it was no wonder that they, who had so little reason to be pleased with their own condition, were not less solicitous for, or apprehensive of, the inconveniences that might attend any alteration.

And here the damage and mischief cannot be expressed, that the crown and state sustained by the deserved reproach and infamy that attended the judges, by being made use of in this and the like acts of power; there being no possibility to preserve the dignity, reverence, and estimation of the laws themselves, but by the integrity and innocency of the judges. And no question, as the exorbitancy of the house of commons this parliament hath proceeded principally from their contempt of the laws, and that contempt from the scandal of that judgment; so the concurrence of the house of peers in that fury can be imputed to no one thing more, than to the irreverence and scorn the judges were justly in; who had been always before looked upon there as the oracles of the law, and the best guides and directors of their opinions and actions: and they now thought themselves excused for swerving from the rules and customs of their predecessors (who in altering and making laws, in judging of things and persons, had always observed the advice and judgment of those sages) in not asking questions of those whom they knew nobody would believe; and thinking it a just reproach upon them, (who out of their gentilesses had submitted the difficulties and mysteries of the law to be measured by the standard of general reason, and explained by the wisdom of state,) to see those men make use of the license they had taught, and determine that to be law, which they thought reasonable, or found to be convenient. If these men had preserved the simplicity of their ancestors, in severely and strictly defending the laws, other men had observed the modesty of theirs, in humbly and dutifully obeying them.

And upon this consideration it is very observable, that in the wisdom of former times, when the prerogative went highest, (as very often it hath been swoln above any pitch we have seen it at in our times,) never any court of law, very seldom any judge, or lawyer of reputation, was called upon to assist in an act of power; the crown well knowing the moment of keeping those the objects of reverence and veneration with the people: and that though it might sometimes make sallies upon them by the prerogative, yet the law would keep the people from any invasion of it, and that the king could never suffer, whilst the law and the judges were looked upon by the subject, as the asyla for their liberties, and security. And therefore you shall find the policy of many princes hath endured as sharp animadversions and reprehensions from the judges of the law, as their piety hath from the bishops of the church; imposing no less upon the people, under the reputation of justice, by the one, than of conscience and religion, by the other.

Now after all this (and I hope I cannot be accused of much flattery in this inquisition) I must be so just as to say, that, during the whole time that these pressures were exercised, and those new and extraordinary ways were run, that is, from the dissolution of the parliament in the fourth year, to the beginning of this parliament, which was above twelve years, this kingdom, and all his majesty's dominions, (of the interruption in Scotland somewhat shall be said in its due time and place,) enjoyed the greatest calm, and the fullest measure of felicity, that any people in any age, for so long time together, have been blessed with; to the wonder and envy of all the parts of Christendom.

And in this comparison I am neither unmindful of, nor ungrateful for, the happy times of queen Elizabeth, or for those more happy under king James. But for the former, the doubts, hazards, and perplexities, upon a total change and alteration of religion, and some confident attempts upon a farther alteration by those who thought not the reformation enough; the charge, trouble, and anxiety of a long continued war (how prosperous and successful so-ever) even during that queen's whole reign; and besides some domestic ruptures into rebellion, frequently into treason; and besides the blemish of an unparalleled act of blood upon the life of a crowned neighbour queen and ally) the fear and apprehension of what was to come (which is one of the most unpleasant kinds of melancholy) from an unknown, at least an unacknowledged, successor to the crown, clouded much of that prosperity then which now shines with so much splendour before our eyes in chronicle.

And for the other under king James, (which indeed were excellent times *bona si sua norint*,) the mingling with a stranger nation, formerly not very gracious with this, which was like to have more interest of favour: the subjection to a stranger prince, whose nature and disposition they knew not: the noise of treason, the most prodigious that had ever been attempted, upon his first entrance into the kingdom; the wants of the crown not inferior to what it hath since felt, (I mean whilst it sat right on the head of the king,) and the pressures upon the subject of the same nature, and no less complained of: the absence of the prince in Spain, and the solicitude that his highness might not be disposed in marriage to the daughter of that kingdom, rendered the calm and tranquillity of that time less equal and pleasant. To which may be added the prosperity and happiness of the neighbour kingdoms not much inferior to that of this, which, according to the pulse of states, is a great diminution of their health; at least their prosperity is much improved, and more visible, by the misery and misfortunes of their neighbours.

The happiness of the times I mentioned was enviously set off by this, that every other kingdom, every other province were engaged, some entangled, and some almost destroyed, by the rage and fury of arms; those which were ambitiously in contention with their neighbours, having the view and apprehensions of the miseries and desolation, which they saw other states suffer by a civil war; whilst the kingdoms we now lament were alone looked upon as the garden of the world; Scotland (which was but the wilderness of that garden) in a full, entire, undisturbed peace, which they had never seen; the rage and barbarism (that the blood, for of the charity we speak not) of their private feuds, being composed to the reverence, or to the awe, of public justice; in a competency, if not in an excess of plenty, which they had never hope to see, and in a temper (which was the utmost we desired and hoped to see) free from rebellion: Ireland, which had been a sponge to draw, and a gulph to swallow all that could be spared, and all that could be got from England, merely to keep the reputation of a kingdom, reduced to that good degree of husbandry and government, that it not only subsisted of itself, and gave this kingdom all that it might have expected from it; but really increased the revenue of the crown forty or fifty thousand pounds a year, besides much more to the people in the traffick and trade from thence; arts and sciences fruitfully planted there; and the whole nation beginning to be so civilized, that it was a jewel of great lustre in the royal diadem.

When these outworks were thus fortified and adorned, it was no wonder if England was generally thought secure, with the advantages of its own climate; the court in great plenty, or rather (which is the discredit of plenty) excess, and luxury; the country rich, and which is more, fully enjoying the pleasure of its own wealth, and so the easier corrupted with the pride and wantonness of it; the church flourishing with learned and extraordinary men, and (which other good times wanted) supplied with oil to feed those lamps; and the protestant religion more advanced against the church of Rome by writing, (without prejudice to other useful and godly labours,) especially by those two books of the late lord archbishop of Canterbury his grace, and of Mr. Chillingworth, than it had been from the reformation; trade increased to that degree, that we were the exchange of Christendom, (the revenue thereof to the crown being almost double to what it had been in the best times,) and the bullion of all other kingdoms brought to receive a stamp from the mint of England; all foreign merchants looking upon nothing as their own, but what they had laid up in the warehouses of this kingdom; the royal navy, in number and equipage much above former times, very formidable at sea; and the reputation of

the greatness and power of the king much more with
foreign princes than any of his progenitors; for those rough
courses, which made him haply less loved at home, made
him more feared abroad; by how much the power of kingdoms is more reverenced than their justice by their neighbours: and it may be, this consideration might not be the
least motive, and may not be the worst excuse for those
counsels. Lastly, for a complement of all these blessings,
they were enjoyed by, and under the protection of, a
king, of the most harmless disposition, and the most exemplary piety, the greatest example of sobriety, chastity, and
mercy, that any prince hath been endowed with, (and God
forgive those that have not been sensible of, and thankful
for, those endowments,) and who might have said that
which Pericles was proud of, upon his deathbed, 'that no
Englishman had ever worn a black gown through his
occasion'. In a word, many wise men thought it a time,
wherein those two miserable adjuncts, which Nerva was
deified for uniting, *imperium et libertas*, were as well reconciled as is possible.

But all these blessings could but enable, not compel us
to be happy: we wanted that sense, acknowledgment, and
value of our own happiness, which all but we had; and took
pains to make, when we could not find, ourselves miserable. There was in truth a strange absence of understanding in most, and a strange perverseness of understanding
in the rest: the court full of excess, idleness, and luxury;
and the country full of pride, mutiny, and discontent;
every man more troubled and perplexed at that they called
the violation of one law, than delighted or pleased with
the observation of all the rest of the charter: never imputing the increase of their receipts, revenue, and plenty,
to the wisdom, virtue, and merit of the crown, but ob-
jecting every small imposition to the exorbitancy and
tyranny of the government; the growth of knowledge
and learning being disrelished, for the infirmities of some
learned men, and the increase of grace and favour upon
the church more repined and murmured at, than the increase of piety and devotion in the church, which was
as visible, acknowledged, or taken notice of; whilst the

indiscretion and folly of one sermon at Whitehall was more bruited abroad, and commented upon, than the wisdom, sobriety, and devotion of a hundred.

[In exile the reign of Charles I appeared in even more glowing colours to the aged statesman who recalled his youth.] It was about the year 1639, when he was little more than thirty years of age, and when England enjoyed the greatest measure of felicity, that it had ever known; the two crowns of France and Spain worrying each other, by their mutual incursions and invasions of each other, whilst they had both a civil war in their own bowels; the former, by frequent rebellions from their own factions and animosities, the latter, by the defection of Portugal; and both laboured more to ransack and burn each other's dominions, than to extinguish their own fire. All Germany weltering in its own blood, and contributing to each other's destruction, that the poor crown of Sweden might grow great out of their ruins, and at their charge: Denmark and Poland being adventurers in the same destructive enterprises. Holland and the United Provinces wearied and tired with their long and chargeable war, how prosperous soever they were in it; and beginning to be more afraid of France their ally, than of Spain their enemy. Italy every year infested by the arms of Spain and France, which divided the princes thereof into the several factions.

Of all the princes of Europe, the king of England alone seemed to be seated upon that pleasant promontory, that might safely view the tragic sufferings of all his neighbours about him, without any other concernment than what arose from his own princely heart and Christian compassion, to see such desolation wrought by the pride, and passion, and ambition of private persons, supported by princes who knew not what themselves would have. His three kingdoms flourishing in entire peace and universal plenty, in danger of nothing but their own surfeits; and his dominions every day enlarged, by sending out colonies upon large and fruitful plantations; his strong fleets commanding all seas; and the numerous shipping of the nation bringing the trade of the world into his ports; nor could it with unquestionable security be carried any whither else; and all these blessings enjoyed under a prince of the greatest clemency and justice, and of the greatest piety and devotion, and the most indulgent to his subjects, and most solicitous for their happiness and prosperity.

O fortunati nimium, bona si sua norint!

In this blessed conjuncture, when no other prince thought he wanted any thing to compass what he most desired to be possessed of, but the affection and friendship of the king of England, a small, scarce discernible cloud arose in the north, which was shortly after attended with such a storm, that never gave over raging till it had shaken, and even rooted up, the greatest and tallest cedars of the three nations; blasted all its beauty and fruitfulness; brought its strength to decay, and its glory to reproach, and almost to desolation; by such a career and deluge of wickedness and rebellion, as by not being enough foreseen, or in truth suspected, could not be prevented.

11. *The Earl of Carlisle*

*James Hay, born ?; first earl 1622; married Honora
Denny 1607 and Lucy Percy 1617; died 1636*

[In 1628] There were two other persons of much authority in the council, because of great name in the court; as they deserved to be, being, without doubt, two as accomplished courtiers as were found in the palaces of all the princes in Europe; and the greatest (if not too great) improvers of that breeding, and those qualifications, with which courts use to be adorned; the earl of Carlisle, and ⟨the⟩ earl of Holland: both (though men of pleasure,) by their long experience in court, well acquainted with the affairs of the kingdom, and better versed in those abroad, than any other who sat then at that board.

The former, a younger brother of a noble family in Scotland, came into the kingdom with king James, as a gentleman; under no other character, than a person well qualified by his breeding in France, and by study in human learning, in which he bore a good part in the entertainment of the king, who much delighted in that exercise; and by these means, and notable gracefulness in his behaviour, and affability, in which he excelled, he had wrought himself into a particular interest with his master, and into greater affection and esteem with the whole English nation, than any other of that country; by choosing their friendships and conversation, and really preferring it to any of his own: insomuch as upon the king's making him gentleman of his bedchamber and viscount Doncaster, and by his royal mediation (in which office he was a most prevalent prince) he obtained the sole daughter and heir of the lord Denny to be given him in marriage; by which he had a fair fortune in land provided for any issue he should raise, and which his son by that lady lived long to enjoy.

He ascended afterwards, and with the expedition he desired, to the other conveniences of the court. He was groom of the stole, and an earl, and knight of the garter; and married a beautiful young lady, daughter to the earl of Northumberland, without any other approbation of her father, or concernment in it, than suffering him and her to come into his presence after they were married. He lived rather in a fair intelligence than any friendship with the favourites; having credit enough with his master to provide for his own interest, and he troubled not himself for that of other men; and had no other consideration of money, than for the support of his lustre; and whilst he could do that, he cared not for money, having no bowels in the point of running in debt, or borrowing all he could.

He was surely a man of greatest expense in his own person, of any in the age he lived; and introduced more of that expense in the excess of clothes and diet, than any other man; and was indeed the original of all those inventions from which others did but transcribe copies. He had a great universal understanding, and could have taken as much delight in any other way, if he had thought any other as pleasant, and worth his care. But he found business was attended with more rivals and vexation; and, he thought, with much less pleasure, and not more innocence.

He left behind him the reputation of a very fine gentleman, and a most accomplished courtier; and after having spent, in a very jovial life, above four hundred thousand pounds, which, upon a strict computation, he received from the crown, he left not a house, nor acre of land, to be remembered by. And when he had in his prospect (for he was very sharp-sighted, and saw as far before him as most men) the gathering together of that cloud in Scotland, which shortly after covered both kingdoms, he died with as much tranquillity of mind to all appearance, as used to attend a man of more severe exercise of virtue, and as little apprehension of death, which he expected many days.

12. *The Earl of Portland*

*Sir Richard Weston, born 1577; Baron Weston 1628;
earl 1633. Chancellor of the Exchequer 1621; Lord
Treasurer 1628; died 1635*

HE was a gentleman of a very good and ancient extraction by father and mother. His education had been very good amongst books and men. After some years study of the law in the Middle Temple, he travelled into foreign parts, and at an age fit to make observations and reflections; out of which, that which is commonly called experience is constituted. After this he betook himself to the court, and lived there some years; at that distance, and with that awe, as was agreeable to the modesty of the age, when men were seen some time before they were known; and well known before they were preferred, or durst pretend to be preferred.

He spent the best part of his fortune (a fair one, that he inherited from his father) in his attendance at court, and involved his friends in securities with him, who were willing to run his hopeful fortune, before he received the least fruit from it, but the countenance of great men and those in authority, the most natural and most certain stairs to ascend by.

He was then sent ambassador to the archdukes, Albert and Isabella, into Flanders; and to the diet in Germany, to treat about the restitution of the palatinate; in which negotiation he behaved himself with great prudence, and with the concurrent testimony of a wise man, from all those with whom he treated, princes and ambassadors, and upon his return was made a privy counsellor, and chancellor of the exchequer, in the place of lord Brooke, who was either persuaded, or put out of the place; which, being an office of honour and trust, is likewise an excellent stage for men of parts to tread, and expose themselves upon; and where they have occasion of all natures to lay out and spread all their faculties and qualifications most for their advantage. He behaved himself very well in this function, and appeared equal to it; and carried himself so luckily in parliament, that he did his master much service, and preserved himself in the good opinion and acceptation of the house; which is a blessing not indulged to many by those high powers. He did swim in those troubled and boisterous waters, in which the duke of Buckingham rode as admiral, with a good grace, when very many who were about him were drowned, or forced on shore with shrewd hurts and bruises: which shewed he knew well how and when to use his limbs and strength to the best advantage; sometimes only to avoid sinking, and sometimes to advance and get ground: and by this dexterity he kept his credit with those who could do him good, and lost it not with others, who desired the destruction of those upon whom he most depended.

He was made lord Treasurer in the manner and at the time mentioned before, upon the removal of the earl of Marlborough, and few months before the death of the duke. The former circumstance, which is often attended by compassion towards the degraded, and prejudice towards the promoted, brought him no disadvantage: for besides the delight that season had in changes, there was little reverence towards the person removed; and the extreme visible poverty of the exchequer sheltered that province from the envy it had frequently created, and opened a door for much applause to be the portion of a wise and provident minister. For the other, of the duke's death, though some, who knew the duke's passions and prejudice, (which often produced rather sudden indisposition, than obstinate resolution,) believed he would have been shortly cashiered, as so many had lately been; and so that the death of his founder was a greater confirmation of him in the office, than the delivery of the white staff had been: many other wise men, who knew the treasurer's talent in removing prejudice, and reconciling himself to wavering and doubtful affections, believed, that the loss of the duke was very unseasonable; and that the awe or apprehension of his power and displeasure was a very necessary allay for the impetuosity of the new officer's nature, which needed some restraint and check, for some time, to his immoderate pretences and appetite of power.

He did indeed appear on the sudden wonderfully elated, and so far threw off his old affectation to please some very much, and to displease none, in which art he had excelled, that in few months after the duke's death, he found himself to succeed him in the public displeasure, and in the malice of his enemies, without succeeding him in his credit at court, or in the affection of any considerable dependants. And yet, though he was not superior to all other men in the affection, or rather resignation, of the king, so that he might dispense favours and disfavours according to his own election, he had a full share in his master's esteem, who looked upon him as a wise and able servant, and worthy of the trust he reposed in him, and received no other advice in the large business of his revenue; nor was any man so much his superior, as to be able to lessen him in the king's affection by his power. So that he was in a post, in which he might have found much ease and delight, if he could have contained himself within the verge of his own province, which was large enough, and of such an extent, that he might, at the same time, have drawn a great dependence upon him of very considerable men, and appeared a very useful and profitable minister to the king; whose revenue had been very loosely managed during the late years, and might by industry and order, have been easily improved: and no man better understood what method was necessary towards that good husbandry, than he.

But I know not by what frowardness in his stars, he took

more pains in examining and inquiring into other men's offices, than in the discharge of his own; and not so much joy in what he had, as trouble and agony for what he had not. The truth is, he had so vehement a desire to be the sole favourite, that he had no relish of the power he had: and in that contention he had many rivals, who had credit enough to do him ill offices, though not enough to satisfy their own ambition; the king himself being resolved to hold the reins in his own hands, and to put no further trust in others than was necessary for the capacity they served in. Which resolution in his majesty was no sooner believed, and the treasurer's pretence taken notice ⟨of,⟩ than he found the number of his enemies exceedingly increased, and others to be less eager in the pursuit of his friendship; and every day discovered some infirmities in him, which being before known to few, and not taken notice of, did now expose him both to public reproach, and to private animosities; and even his vices admitted those contradictions in them, that he could hardly enjoy the pleasant fruit of any of them. That which first exposed him to the public jealousy, which is always attended with public reproach, was the concurrent suspicion of his religion. His wife and all his daughters were declared of the Romish religion: and though himself, and his sons, sometimes went to church, he was never thought to have zeal for it; and his domestic conversation and dependants, with whom only he used entire freedom, were all known catholics, and were believed to be agents for the rest. And yet, with all this disadvantage to himself, he never had reputation and credit with that party, who were the only people of the kingdom who did not believe him to be of their profession. For the penal laws (those only excepted which were sanguinary, and even those sometimes let loose) were never more rigidly executed, nor had the crown ever so great a revenue from them, as in his time; nor did they ever pay so dear for the favours and indulgences of his office towards them.

No man had greater ambition to make his family great, or stronger designs to leave a great fortune to it. Yet his expenses were so prodigiously great, especially in his house, that all the ways he used for supply, which were all that

occurred, could not serve his turn; insomuch that he contracted so great debts, (the anxiety whereof, he pretended,
broke his mind, and restrained that intentness and industry, which was necessary for the due execution of his
office,) that the king was pleased twice to pay his debts;
at least, towards it, to disburse forty thousand pounds in
ready money out of his exchequer. Besides, his majesty
gave him a whole forest (Chute forest in Hampshire) and
much other land belonging to the Crown; which was the
more taken notice of, and murmured against, because,
being the chief minister of the revenue, he was particularly
obliged, as much as in him lay, to prevent, and even
oppose, such disinherison; and because, under that obligation, he had, avowedly and sourly, crossed the pretences
of other men, and restrained the king's bounty from being
exercised almost to any. And he had that advantage, (if
he had made the right use of it,) that his credit was ample
enough (seconded by the king's own experience, and observation, and inclination) to retrench very much of the
late unlimited expenses, and especially those of bounties;
which from the death of the duke ran in narrow channels,
which never so much overflowed as towards himself, who
stopped the current to other men.

He was of an imperious nature, and nothing wary in
disobliging and provoking other men, and had too much
courage in offending and incensing them: but after having
offended and incensed them, he was of so unhappy a
feminine temper, that he was always in a terrible fright
and apprehension of them.

He had not that application, and submission, and reverence for the queen, as might have been expected from his
wisdom and breeding, and often crossed her pretences and
desires, with more rudeness than was natural to him. Yet
he was impertinently solicitous to know what her majesty
said of him in private, and what resentments she had
towards him. And when by some confidants, who had
their ends upon him from those offices, he was informed of
some bitter expressions fallen from her majesty, he was so
exceedingly afflicted and tormented with the sense of it,
that sometimes by passionate complaints and representa-

tions to the king; sometimes by more dutiful addresses and expostulations with the queen, in bewailing his misfortunes; he frequently exposed himself, and left his condition worse than it was before: and the eclaircissement commonly ended in the discovery of the persons from whom he had received his most secret intelligence.

He quickly lost the character of a bold, stout, and magnanimous man, which he had been long reputed to be in worse times; and, in his most prosperous season, fell under the reproach of being a man of big looks, and of a mean and abject spirit.

13. *The Duke of Buckingham*

George Villiers, born 1592; Viscount Villiers 1616;
Earl of Buckingham 1617; marquis 1618; Lord
High Admiral 1618–28; Duke of Buckingham 1623;
assassinated by John Felton 1628.

AND here it will give much light to that which follows, if we take a view of the state of the court and of the council at that time, by which, as in a mirror, we may best see the face of that time, and the affections and temper of the people in general.

And for the better taking this prospect, we will take a survey of the person of that great man, the duke of Buckingham, (who was so barbarously murdered at this time,) whose influence had been unfortunate in the public affairs, and whose death produced a change in all the counsels. The duke was indeed a very extraordinary person; and never any man, in any age, nor, I believe, in any country or nation, rose, in so short a time, to so much greatness of honour, fame, and fortune, upon no other advantage or recommendation than of the beauty and gracefulness and becomingness of his person. And I have not the least purpose of undervaluing his good parts, and qualities, (of which there will be occasion shortly to give some testimony,) when I say, that his first introduction into favour was purely from the handsomeness of his person.

He was the younger son of sir George Villiers, of Brookesby, in the county of Leicester; a family of ancient extraction, even from the time of the conquest, and transported then with the conqueror out of Normandy, where the family hath still remained, and still continues with lustre. After sir George's first marriage, in which he had two or three sons, and some daughters, who shared an ample inheritance from him; by a second marriage, with a young lady of the family of the Beaumonts, he had this gentleman, and two other sons and a daughter, who all came afterwards to be raised to great titles and dignities. George, the eldest son of this second bed, was, after the death of his father, by the singular affection and care of his mother, who enjoyed a good jointure in the account of that age, well brought up; and, for the improvement of his education, and giving an ornament to his hopeful person, he was by her sent into France; where he spent two or three years in attaining the language, and in learning the exercise of riding and dancing; in the last of which he excelled most men, and returned into England by the time he was twentyone years old.

King James reigned at that time; and though he was a prince of more learning and knowledge than any other of that age, and really delighted more in books, and in the conversation of learned men; yet of all wise men living, he was the most delighted and taken with handsome persons, and with fine clothes. He began to be weary of his favourite, the earl of Somerset, who was the only favourite that kept that post so long, without any public reproach from the people: and, by the instigation and wickedness of his wife, he became, at least, privy to a horrible murder, that exposed him to the utmost severity of the law, (the poisoning of sir Thomas Overbury,) upon which both he and his wife were condemned to die, after a trial by their peers; and many persons of quality were executed for the same.

Whilst this was in agitation, and before the utmost discovery was made, Mr. Villiers appeared in court, and drew the king's eyes upon him. There were enough in the court enough angry and incensed against Somerset, for being what themselves desired to be, and especially for

being a Scotsman, and ascending, in so short a time, from
being a page, to the height he was then at, to contribute
all they could to promote the one, that they they might
throw out the other: which being easily brought to pass,
by the proceeding of the law upon his crime aforesaid, the
other found very little difficulty in rendering himself
gracious to the king, whose nature and disposition was
very flowing in affection towards persons so adorned. Insomuch that, in few days after his first appearance in
court, he was made cupbearer to the king; by which he
was naturally to be much in his presence, and so admitted
to that conversation and discourse, with which that prince
always abounded at his meals.

And his inclination to his new cupbearer disposed him
to administer frequent occasions of discoursing of the court
of France, and the transactions there, with which he
had been so lately acquainted, that he could pertinently
enlarge upon that subject, to the king's great delight, and
to the reconciling the esteem and value of all the standers
by likewise to him: which was a thing the king was well
pleased with. He acted very few weeks upon this stage,
when he mounted higher; and, being knighted, without
any other qualification, he was at the same time made
gentleman of the bedchamber, and knight of the order of
the garter; and in a short time (very short for such a prodigious ascent) he was made a baron, a viscount, an earl, a
marquis, and became lord high admiral of England, lord
warden of the cinque ports, master of the horse, and
entirely disposed of all the graces of the king, in conferring
all the honours and all the offices of the three kingdoms,
without a rival; in dispensing whereof, he was guided
more by the rules of appetite than of judgment; and so
exalted almost all of his own numerous family and dependants, who had no other virtue or merit than their alliance
to him, which equally offended the ancient nobility, and
the people of all conditions, who saw the flowers of the
crown every day fading and withered; whilst the demesnes
and revenue thereof was sacrificed to the enriching a
private family, (how well soever originally extracted,) not
heard of before ever to the nation; and the expenses of

the court so vast and unlimited by the old good rules of economy, that they had a sad prospect of that poverty and necessity, which afterwards befell the crown, almost to the ruin of it.

[The duke was murdered while supervising the fitting-out of the fleet at Portsmouth.] The court was too near Portsmouth, and too many courtiers upon the place, to have this murder (so wonderful in the nature and circumstances, the like whereof had not been known in England in many ages) long concealed from the king. His majesty was at the public prayers of the church, when sir John Hippesly came into the room, with a troubled countenance, and, without any pause in respect of the exercise they were performing, went directly to the king, and whispered in his ear what had fallen out. His majesty continued unmoved, and without the least change in his countenance, till prayers were ended; when he suddenly departed to his chamber, and threw himself upon his bed, lamenting with much passion, and with abundance of tears, the loss he had of an excellent servant, and the horrid manner in which he had been deprived of him; and he continued in this melancholic and discomposure of mind many days.

Yet the manner of his receiving the news in public, when it was first brought to him in the presence of so many, (who knew or saw nothing of the passion he expressed upon his retreat), made many men to believe that the accident was not very ungrateful; at least, that it was very indifferent to him; as being rid of a servant very ungracious to the people, and the prejudice to whose person exceedingly obstructed all overtures made in parliament for his service.

And, upon this observation, persons of all conditions took great license in speaking of the person of the duke, and dissecting all his infirmities, believing they should not thereby incur any displeasure of the king. In which they took very ill measures; for from that time almost to the time of his own death, the king admitted very few into any degree of trust, who had ever discovered themselves to be enemies to the duke, or against whom he had ever manifested a notable prejudice. And sure never any prince manifested a more lively regret for the loss of a servant, than his majesty did for this great man, in his constant favour and kindness to his wife and children, in a wonderful solicitous care for the payment of his debts, (which, it is very true, were contracted for his service; though in such a manner, that there remained no evidence of it, nor was any of the duke's officers intrusted with the knowledge of it, nor was there any record of it, but in his majesty's own generous memory,) and all offices of grace towards his servants.

After all this, and such a transcendent mixture of ill fortune, of which as ill conduct and great infirmities seem to be the foundation and source, this great man was a person of a noble nature, and generous disposition, and of such other endowments, as made him very capable of being a great favourite to a great king. He understood the arts and artifices of a court, and all the learning that is professed there, exactly well. By long practice in business, under a master that discoursed excellently, and surely knew all things wonderfully, and took much delight in indoctrinating his young unexperienced favourite, who, he knew, would be always looked upon as the workmanship of his own hands, he had obtained a quick conception, and apprehension of business, and had the habit of speaking very gracefully and pertinently. He was of a most flowing courtesy and affability to all men who made any address to him; and so desirous to oblige them, that he did not enough consider the value of the obligation, or the merit of the person he chose to oblige; from which much of his misfortune resulted. He was of a courage not to be daunted, which was manifested in all his actions, and his contests with particular persons of the greatest reputation; and especially in his whole demeanour at the Isle of Rhé, both at the landing and upon the retreat; in both which no man was more fearless, or more ready to expose himself to the brightest dangers. His kindness and affection to his friends was so vehement, that it was as so many marriages for better and worse, and so many leagues offensive and defensive; as if he thought himself obliged to love all his friends, and to make war upon all they were angry with, let the cause be what it would. And it cannot be denied that he was an enemy in the same excess, and prosecuted those he looked upon as his enemies with the utmost rigour and animosity, and was not easily induced to a reconciliation. And yet there were some examples of his receding in that particular. And in the highest passion, he was so far from stooping to any dissimulation whereby his displeasure might be concealed and covered till he had attained his revenge, (the low method of courts), that he never endeavoured to do any man an ill office, before he first told him what he was to expect from him, and reproached him with the injuries he had done, with so much generosity, that the person found it in his power to receive further satisfaction, in the way he would choose for himself.

His single misfortune was, (which indeed was productive of many greater,) that he never made a noble and a worthy friendship with a man so near his equal, that he would frankly advise him for his honour and true interest, against the current, or rather the torrent, of his impetuous passion; which was partly the vice of the time, when the court was not replenished with great choice of excellent men; and partly the vice of the persons who were most worthy to be applied to, and looked upon his youth, and his obscurity, as obligations upon him to gain their friendships by extraordinary application. Then his ascent was so quick, that it seemed rather a flight than a growth; and he was such a darling of fortune, that he was at the top before he was seen at the bottom, for the gradation of his titles was the effect, not cause, of his first promotion: and, as if he had been born a favourite, he was supreme the first month he came to court; and it was want of confidence, not of credit, that he had not all at first which he obtained afterwards; never meeting with the least obstruction from his setting out, till he was as great as he could be: so that he wanted dependants before he thought he could want coadjutors. Nor was he very fortunate in the election of those dependants, very few of his servants having been ever qualified enough to assist or advise him, and were intent only upon growing rich under him, not upon their master's growing good as well as great: insomuch as he was throughout his fortune a much wiser man than any servant or friend he had.

Let the fault or misfortune be what or whence it will, it may very reasonably be believed, that, if he had been blessed with one faithful friend, who had been qualified with wisdom and integrity, that great person would have committed as few faults, and done as transcendent worthy actions, as any man who shined in such a sphere in that age in Europe. For he was of an excellent nature, and of a capacity very capable of advice and counsel. He was in his nature just and candid, liberal, generous, and bountiful; nor was it ever known, that the temptation of money swayed him to do an unjust or unkind thing. And though he left a very great inheritance to his heirs; considering the vast fortune he inherited by his wife, the sole daughter and heir of Francis earl of Rutland, he owed no part of it to his own industry or solicitation, but to the impatient humour of two kings his masters, who would make his fortune equal to his titles, and the one ⟨as much⟩ above other men, as the other was. And he considered it no otherwise than as theirs, and left it at his death engaged for the crown, almost to the value of it, as is touched upon before.

If he had an immoderate ambition, with which he was charged, and is a weed (if it be a weed) apt to grow in the best soils; it doth not appear that it was in his nature, or that he brought it with him to the court, but rather found it there, and was a garment necessary for that air. Nor was it more in his power to be without promotion, and titles, and wealth, than for a healthy man to sit in the sun in the brightest dog-days and remain without any warmth. He needed no ambition, who was so seated in the hearts of two such masters.

14. *Charles I and Henrietta Maria*

[The influence which the queen gained over her husband after the birth of the Prince of Wales in 1630 has been noticed in an unfavourable way both by their contemporaries and later historians. It would appear that her behaviour was moulded by her early experiences at court, particularly of the power and behaviour of Buckingham after he had determined Charles to make war against France in 1628.] And, which was worse than all this, he took great pains to lessen the king's affection towards his young queen, being exceedingly jealous, lest her interest might be of force enough to cross his other designs: and in this stratagem, he so far swerved from the instinct of his nature and his proper inclinations, that he, who was compounded of all the elements of affability, and courtesy towards all kind of people, had brought himself to a habit of neglect, and even of rudeness, towards the queen.

One day, when he unjustly apprehended that she had shewed some disrespect to his mother, in not going to her lodging at an hour she had intended to do, and was hindered by a very accident, he came into her chamber in much passion, and, after some expostulations rude enough, he told her, 'she should repent it'. And her majesty answering with some quickness, he replied insolently to her, 'that there had been queens in England who had lost their heads'. And it was universally known, that, during his life, the queen never had any credit with the king, with reference to any public affairs, and so could not divert the resolution of making a war with France.

[Clarendon considers the influence of the queen particularly in connexion with the proposed treaty of Oxford, April 1643.] Many were of opinion, that the king was too severe in this treaty, and insisted too much upon what is his own by right and law; and that if he would have distributed offices and places liberally to particular men, which had been a condescension in policy to be submitted to, he might have been repossessed of his own power. And I have heard this alleged by many, who at that time were extremely violent against all such artifices. The committee themselves (who at that time perfectly abhorred the proceedings of the parliament, or rather the power and superiority of the earl of Essex) seemed exceedingly desirous of such an accommodation, as all good men desired; and to believe, that if the king would have condescended so far, as to nominate the earl of Northumberland to be lord high admiral, that it would have made so great a division in the houses, that the treaty would have been continued, and his majesty been satisfied in all the other propositions. And the earl of Northumberland, to private friends, did make as full professions of future service to his majesty, and as ample recognitions of past errors and mistakes, as could reasonably be expected from a wary nature, before he could be sure what reception such professions and vows would find. But the king thought the power and interest of that committee would be able to do little, if it could not prevail for the enlarging the time of the treaty, in which they seemed heartily to engage themselves. And he was resolved at least to have a probable assurance of the conclusion, before he would offer such concessions, as taking no effect might prove prejudicial to him: as the nominating the earl of Northumberland to be admiral (though he would willingly have done it, as the price and pledge of an honourable peace) would have discontented all who had, how unreasonably soever, promised themselves that preferment; and many would have imputed it to an unseasonable easiness, (from which imputation it concerned the king, at that time, as much to purge himself, as of unmercifulness and revenge,) upon promises and hopes, to have readmitted a man to a charge and trust, he had so fatally betrayed and broken, against more solemn promises and obligations, than he could now enter into; and therefore it concerned the king to be sure of some advantage, in lieu of this visible hazard.

I am one of those, who do believe that this obligation at this time, laid upon the earl of Northumberland, with such other circumstances of kindness as would have been fit to accompany it, would have met real gratitude and faithfulness in him, (for as, originally, he had, I am persuaded, no evil purposes against the king; so he had now sufficient disdain and indignation against those who got him to tread their ways, when he had not their ends,) and that it would have made some rent and division in the two houses, (which could not but have produced some benefit to the king,) and that it might probably have procured some few days' addition for the continuance of the treaty; the avowed ground of denying it being, because the king had not, in the least degree, consented to any one thing proposed by them: but, I confess, I cannot entertain any imagination, that it would have produced a peace, or given the king any advantage, or benefit in the war: what inconvenience it might have produced hath been touched before. For, besides that the stirring and active party, who carried on the war, were neither gracious to the earl of Northumberland, nor he to them, their favourite at sea being then the earl of Warwick, who had the possession of the fleet, and the navy; whoever calls to mind what was done in the houses, during the time of the treaty, and by their directions; I say, whosoever remembers and considers all this . . . cannot, I conceive, believe that the king's consenting to make one person among them high admiral of England, would have been a means to have restored the kingdom to a present peace and the king to his just authority and rights.

If this secret underhand proposition had succeeded, and received, that encouragement from the king that was desired, and more application of the same remedies had been then made to other persons, (for alone it could never have proved effectual,) it is probable, that those violent and abominable counsels, which were but then in projection between very few men of any interest, and which were afterwards miserably put in practice, had been prevented. And it was exceedingly wondered at, by those who were then privy to this overture, and by all who afterwards came to hear of it, that the king should in that conjuncture decline so advantageous a proposition; since he did already discern many ill humours and factions, growing and nourished, both in his court and army, which would every day be uneasy to him; and did with all his soul desire an end of the war. And there was nothing more suitable and agreeable to his magnanimous nature, than to forgive those, who had in the highest degree offended him: which temper was notorious throughout his whole life. It will not be therefore amiss, in this discourse, which is never to see light, and so can reflect upon nobody's character with prejudice, to enlarge upon this fatal rejection, and the true cause and ground thereof.

The king's affection to the queen was of a very extraordinary alloy; a composition of conscience, and love, and generosity, and gratitude, and all those noble affections which raise the passion to the greatest height; insomuch as he saw with her eyes, and determined by her judgment; and did not only pay her this adoration, but desired that all men should know that he was swayed by her: which was not good for either of them. The queen was a lady of great beauty, excellent wit and humour, and made him a just return of noblest affections; so that they were the true idea of conjugal affection, in the age in which they lived. When she was admitted to the knowledge and participation of the most secret affairs, (from which she had been carefully restrained by the duke of Buckingham whilst he lived,) she took delight in the examining and discussing them, and from thence in making judgment of them; in which her passions were always strong.

She had felt so much pain in knowing nothing, and meddling with nothing, during the time of that great favourite, that now she took pleasure in nothing but knowing all things, and disposing all things; and thought it but just, that she should dispose of all favours and preferments, as he had done; at least, that nothing of that kind might be done without her privity: not considering that the universal prejudice that great man had undergone, was not with reference to his person, but his power; and that the same power would be equally obnoxious to murmur and complaint, if it resided in any other person than the king himself. And she so far concurred with the king's inclination, that she did not more desire to be possessed of this unlimited power, than that all the world should take notice that she was the entire mistress of it: which in truth (what other unhappy circumstances soever concurred in the mischief) was the foundation upon which the first and the utmost prejudices to the king and his government were raised and prosecuted. And it was her majesty's and the kingdom's misfortune, that she had not any person about her, who had either ability or affection, to inform and

advise her of the temper of the kingdom, or humour of the
people; or who thought either worth the caring for.

When the disturbances grew so rude as to interrupt this
harmony, and the queen's fears, and indisposition, which
proceeded from those fears, disposed her to leave the kingdom, which the king, to comply with her, consented to;
(and if that fear had not been predominant in her, her
jealousy and apprehension, that the king would at some
time be prevailed with to yield to some unreasonable
conditions, would have dissuaded her from that voyage;)
to make all things therefore as sure as might be, that her
absence should not be attended with any such inconvenience, his majesty made a solemn promise to her at parting,
that he would receive no person into any favour or trust,
who had disserved him, without her privity and consent;
and that, as she had undergone so many reproaches and
calumnies at the entrance into the war, so he would never
make any peace, but by her interposition and mediation, that the kingdom might receive that blessing only
from her.

This promise (of which his majesty was too religious an
observer) was the cause of his majesty's rejection, or not
entertaining this last overture; and this was the reason
that he had that aversion to the cessation, which he
thought would inevitably oblige him to consent to the
peace, as it should be proposed; and therefore he had
countenanced an address, that had been made to him
against it, by the gentlemen of several counties attending
the court: and in truth they were put upon that address by
the king's own private direction. Upon which the chancellor of the exchequer told him, when the business was
over, that he had raised a spirit he would not be able to
conjure down; and that those petitioners had now appeared in a business that pleased him, but would be as
ready to appear, at another time, to cross what he desired;
which proved true. For he was afterwards more troubled
with application and importunity of that kind, and the
murmurs that arose from that liberty, when all men would
be counsellors, and censure all that the council did, than
with the power of the enemy.

About the time that the treaty began, the queen landed
in the north, having been chased by the parliament ships
into Burlington bay, their ships discharging all their cannon upon a small village where she lodged after her landing, and she was glad to resort for shelter to some banks in
the field, where she spent most part of the night, and was
the next day received by the earl of Newcastle, with some
troops of his army, and was by him conveyed to York.
Her majesty had brought with her a good supply of arms
and ammunition, which was exceedingly wanted in the
king's quarters; and she resolved, with a good quantity of
ammunition and arms, to make what haste she could to
the king; having at her first landing expressed, by a letter
to his majesty, her apprehension of an ill peace by that
treaty: and declared, that she would never live in England,
if she might not have a guard for the security of her person: which letter came accidentally afterwards into the
hands of the parliament; of which they made use to the
queen's disadvantage. And the expectation of her majesty's
arrival at Oxford, was the reason that the king so much
desired the prolongation of the treaty. And if it had
pleased God that she had come thither time enough, as
she did shortly after, she would have probably condescended to many propositions for the gratifying particular
persons, as appeared afterwards, if thereby a reasonable
peace might have been obtained.

15. *William Laud*

*Born 1573; Bishop of St. David's 1621; of Bath and
Wells 1626; of London 1628; Archbishop of Canterbury 1633. Imprisoned 1641; executed 1645*

IT was within one week after the king's return from Scotland [in August 1633], that Abbot died at his house at
Lambeth. And the king took very little time to consider
who should be his successor, but the very next time the
bishop of London (who was longer upon his way home
than the king had been) came to him, his majesty entertained him very cheerfully with this compellation, *My*

lord's grace of Canterbury, you are very welcome; and gave
order the same day for the dispatch of all the necessary
forms for the translation: so that within a month or
thereabouts after the death of the other archbishop, he
was completely invested in that high dignity, and settled
in his palace at Lambeth. This great prelate had been
before in great favour with the duke of Buckingham, whose
great confidant he was, and by him recommended to the
king, as fittest to be trusted in the conferring all ecclesiastical preferments, when he was but bishop of St. David's,
or newly preferred to Bath and Wells; and from that time
he entirely governed that province without a rival: so
that his promotion to Canterbury was long foreseen and
expected; nor was it attended with any increase of envy
or dislike.

He was a man of great parts, and very exemplary virtues,
allayed and discredited by some unpopular natural infirmities; the greatest of which was (besides a hasty, sharp
way of expressing himself,) that he believed innocence of
heart, and integrity of manners, was a guard strong enough
to secure any man in his voyage through this world, in
what company soever he travelled, and through what ways
soever he was to pass: and sure never any man was
better supplied with that provision. He was born of honest
parents, who were well able to provide for his education
in the schools of learning, from whence they sent him to
St. John's college in Oxford, the worst endowed at that
time of any in that famous university. From a scholar he
became a fellow, and then the president of that college,
after he had received all the graces and degrees (the proc-
torship and the doctorship) could be obtained there. He
was always maligned and persecuted by those who were
of the Calvinian faction, which was then very powerful,
and who, according to their useful maxim and practice,
call every man they do not love, papist; and under this
senseless appellation they created him many troubles and
vexations; and so far suppressed him, that though he was
the king's chaplain, and taken notice of for an excellent
preacher, and a scholar of the most sublime parts, he had
not any preferment to invite him to leave his poor college,

which only gave him bread, till the vigour of his age was past: and when he was promoted by king James, it was but to a poor bishopric in Wales, which was not so good a support for a bishop, as his college was for a private scholar, though a doctor.

Parliaments in that time were frequent, and grew very busy; and the party under which he had suffered a continual persecution, appeared very powerful, and full of design, and they who had the courage to oppose them, began to be taken notice of with approbation and countenance: and under this style he came to be first cherished by the duke of Buckingham, after he had made some experiments of the temper and spirit of the other people, nothing to his satisfaction. From this time he prospered at the rate of his own wishes, and being transplanted out of his cold barren diocese of St. David's, into a warmer climate, he was left, as was said before, by that omnipotent favourite in that great trust with the king, who was sufficiently indisposed towards the persons or the principles of Mr. Calvin's disciples.

When he came into great authority, it may be, he retained too keen a memory of those who had so unjustly and uncharitably persecuted him before; and, I doubt, was so far transported with the same passions he had reason to complain of in his adversaries, that, as they accused him of popery, because he had some doctrinal opinions which they liked not, though they were nothing allied to popery; so he entertained too much prejudice to some persons, as if they were enemies to the discipline of the church, because they concurred with Calvin in some doctrinal points; when they abhorred his discipline, and reverenced the government of the church, and prayed for the peace of it with as much zeal and fervency as any in the kingdom; as they made manifest in their lives, and in their sufferings with it, and for it. He had, from his first entrance into the world, without any disguise or dissimulation, declared his own opinion of that classis of men; and, as soon as it was in his power, he did all he could to hinder the growth and increase of that faction, and to restrain those who were inclined to it, from doing the mischief they desired to do. But his power at court could not enough qualify him to go through with that difficult reformation, whilst he had a superior in the church, who, having the reins in his hand, could slacken them according to his own humour and indiscretion; and was thought to be the more remiss, to irritate his choleric disposition. But when he had now the primacy in his own hand, the king being inspired with the same zeal, he thought he should be to blame, and have much to answer, if he did not make haste to apply remedies to those diseases, which he saw would grow apace.

In the end of September of the year 1633, he was invested in the title, power, and jurisdiction of archbishop of Canterbury, and entirely in possession of the revenue thereof, without a rival in church or state; that is, no man professed to oppose his greatness; and he had never interposed or appeared in matter of state to this time. His first care was, that the place he was removed from might be supplied with a man who would be vigilant to pull up those weeds, which the London soil was too apt to nourish, and so drew his old friend and companion Dr. Juxon as near to him as he could. They had been fellows together in one college in Oxford, and, when he was first made bishop of saint David's, he made him president of that college: when he could no longer keep the deanery of the chapel royal, he made him his successor in that near attendance upon the king: and now he was raised to archbishop, he easily prevailed with the king to make the other, bishop of London, before, or very soon after, he had been consecrated bishop of Hereford, if he were more than elect of that church.

It was now a time of great ease and tranquillity; the king (as hath been said before) had made himself superior to all those difficulties and straits he had to contend with the four first years he came to the crown at home; and was now reverenced by all his neighbours who all needed his friendship, and desired to have it; the wealth of the kingdom notorious to all the world, and the general temper and humour of it little inclined to the papists, and less to the puritan. There were some late taxes and impositions introduced, which rather angered than grieved the people, who were more than repaired by the quiet, peace, and prosperity they enjoyed; and the murmur and discontent that was, appeared to be against the excess of power exercised by the crown, and supported by the judges in Westminster-hall. The church was not repined at, nor the least inclination to alter the government and discipline thereof, or to change the doctrine. Nor was there at that time any considerable number of persons of any valuable condition throughout the kingdom, who did wish either; and the cause of so prodigious a change in so few years after was too visible from the effects. The archbishop's heart was set upon the advancement of the church, in which he well knew he had the king's full concurrence, which he thought would be too powerful for any opposition; and that he should need no other assistance.

Though the nation generally, as was said before, was without any ill talent to the church, either in the point of the doctrine, or the discipline, yet they were not without a jealousy that popery was not enough discountenanced, and were very averse from admitting any thing they had not been used to, which they called innovation, and were easily persuaded, that any thing of that kind was but to please the papists. Some doctrinal points in controversy had been, in the late years, agitated in the pulpits with more warmth and reflections, than had used to be; and thence the heat and animosity increased in books pro and con upon the same arguments: most of the popular preachers, who had not looked into the ancient learning, took Calvin's word for it, and did all they could to propagate his opinions in those points: they who had studied more, and were better versed in the antiquities of the church, the fathers, the councils, and the ecclesiastical histories, with the same heat and passion in preaching and writing defended the contrary.

The archbishop had, all his life, eminently opposed Calvin's doctrine in those controversies, before the name of Arminius was taken notice of, or his opinions heard of; and thereupon, for want of another name, they had called him a papist, which nobody believed him to be, and he had more manifested the contrary in his disputations and writings, than most men had done; and it may be the other found the more severe and rigorous usage from him, for their propagating that calumny against him. He was a man of great courage and resolution, and being most assured within himself, that he proposed no end in all his actions or designs, than what was pious and just, (as sure no man had ever a heart more entire to the king, the church, or his country,) he never studied the best ways to those ends; he thought, it may be, that any art or industry that way would discredit, at least make the integrity of the end suspected, let the cause be what it will. He did court persons too little; nor cared to make his designs and purposes appear as candid as they were, by shewing them in any other dress than their own natural beauty and roughness; and did not consider enough what men said, or were like to say of him. If the faults and vices were fit to be looked into, and discovered, let the persons be who they would that were guilty of them, they were sure to find no connivance or favour from him. He intended the discipline of the church should be felt, as well as spoken of, and that it should be applied to the greatest and most splendid transgressors, as well as to the punishment of smaller offences, and meaner offenders; and thereupon called for or cherished the discovery of those who were not careful to cover their own iniquities, thinking they were above the reach of other men's, or their power or will to chastise. Persons of honour and great quality, of the court, and of the country, were every day cited, into the high-commission court, upon the fame of their incontinence, or other scandal in their lives, and were there prosecuted to their shame and punishment: and as the shame (which they called an insolent triumph upon their degree and quality, and levelling them with the common people) was never forgotten, but watched for revenge; so the fines imposed there were the most questioned, and repined against, because they were assigned to the rebuilding and repairing St. Paul's church; and thought therefore to be the more severely imposed, and the less compassionately reduced and excused; which likewise made the jurisdiction and rigour of the star-chamber more felt, and murmured against, which sharpened many men's humours against the bishops, before they had any ill intention towards the church.

The archbishop had not been long at Canterbury, when there was another great alteration in the court by the death of the earl of Portland, high treasurer of England; a man so jealous of the archbishop's credit with the king, that he always endeavoured to lessen it by all the arts and ways he could; which he was so far from effecting, that, as it usually falls out, when passion and malice make accusation, by suggesting many particulars which the king knew to be untrue, or believed to be no faults, he rather confirmed his majesty's judgment of him, and prejudiced his own reputation. His death caused no grief to the archbishop; who was upon it made one of the commissioners of the treasury and revenue, which he had reason to be sorry for, because it engaged him in civil business and matters of state, in which he had little experience, and which he had hitherto avoided. But being obliged to it now by his trust, he entered upon it with his natural earnestness and warmth, making it his principal care to advance and improve the king's revenue by all the ways which were offered, and so hearkened to all informations and propositions of that kind; and having not had experience of that tribe of people who deal in that traffick, (a confident, senseless, and for the most part a naughty people,) he was sometimes misled by them to think better of some projects than they deserved: but when he was so entirely devoted to what would be beneficial to the king, that all propositions and designs, which were for the profit (only or principally) of particular persons how great soever, were opposed and crossed, and very often totally suppressed and stifled in their birth, by his power and authority; which created him enemies enough in the court, and many of ability to do mischief, who knew well how to recompense discourtesies, which they always called injuries.

And the revenue of too many of the court consisted principally in enclosures, and improvement of that nature, which he still opposed passionately, except they were founded upon law; and then, if it would bring profit to the king, how old and obsolete soever the law was, he thought he might justly advise the prosecution. And so he did a little too much countenance the commission for depopulation, which brought much charge and trouble upon the people, which was likewise cast upon his account.

He had observed, and knew it must be so, that the principal officers of the revenue, who governed the affairs of money, had always access to the king, and spent more time with him in private than any of his servants or counsellors, and had thereby frequent opportunities to do good or ill offices to many men; of which he had had experience, when the earl of Portland was treasurer, and the lord Cottington chancellor of the exchequer; neither of them being his friends; and the latter still enjoying that place, and having his former access, and so continuing a joint commissioner of the treasury with him, and understanding that province much better, he still opposed, and commonly carried everything against him: so that he was weary of the toil and vexation of that business; as all other men were, and still are of the delays which are in dispatches, whilst that office is executed by commission.

The treasurer's is the greatest office of benefit in the kingdom, and the chief in precedence next the archbishop's, and the great seal: so that the eyes of all men were at gaze who should have this great office; and the greatest of the nobility, who were in the chiefest employments, looked upon it as the prize of one of them; such offices commonly making way for more removes and preferments: when on a sudden the staff was put into the hands of the bishop of London, a man so unknown, that his name was scarce heard of in the kingdom, who had been within two years before but a private chaplain to the king, and the president of a poor college in Oxford. This inflamed more men than were angry before, and no doubt did not only sharpen the edge of envy and malice against the archbishop, (who was the known architect of this new fabric,) but most unjustly indisposed many towards the church itself; which they looked upon as the gulph ready to swallow all the great offices, there being others in view, of that robe, who were ambitious enough to expect the rest.

In the meantime the archbishop himself was infinitely pleased with what was done, and unhappily believed he had provided a stronger support for the church; and never abated any thing of his severity and rigour towards men of all conditions, or in the sharpness of his language and expressions, which was so natural to him, that he could not debate any thing without some commotion, when the argument was not of moment, nor bear contradiction in debate, even in the council, where all men are equally free, with that patience and temper that was necessary; of which they who wished him not well took many advantages, and would therefore contradict him, that he might be transported with some indecent passion; which, upon a short recollection, he was always sorry for, and most readily and heartily would make acknowledgment. No man so willingly made unkind use of all those occasions, as the lord Cottington, who being a master of temper, and of the most profound dissimulation, knew too well how to lead him into a mistake, and then drive him into choler, and then expose him upon the matter, and the manner, to the judgment of the company; and he chose to do this most when the king was present; and then he would dine with him the next day.

[After he had been made a member of the Treasury commission] The archbishop of Canterbury, who till now had only intended the good government of the church, without intermeddling in secular affairs, otherwise than when the discipline of the church was concerned, in which he was very strict, both in the high commission, and in all other places, where he sat as a privy counsellor, well foreseeing, as he made manifest upon several occasions, the growth of the schismatics, and that if they were not with rigour suppressed, they would put the whole kingdom into a flame, which shortly after fell out to be too confessed a truth; though for the present his providence only served to increase the number of his enemies, who had from that his zeal contracted all the malice against him that can be imagined, and which he, out of the conscience of his duty,

and the purity of his intentions, and his knowledge of the
king's full approbation of his vigilance and ardour, too
much undervalued; I say, as soon as he was made commissioner of the treasury, he thought himself obliged to
take all the pains he could to understand that employment, and the nature of the revenue, and to find out all
possible ways for the improvement thereof, and for the
present managery of the expense. Many were of the opinion
that he was the more solicitous in that disquisition, and the
more inquisitive into what had been done, that he might
make some discovery of past actions, which might reflect
upon the memory of the late treasurer, the earl of Portland, and call his wisdom and integrity in question, who
had been so far from being his friend, that he had always
laboured to do him all the mischief he could; and it was
no small grief of heart to him, and much occasion of his
ill humour, to find that the archbishop had too much credit
with the king, to be shaken by him: and the archbishop
was not in his affections behindhand with him, looking
always upon him as a Roman catholic, though he dissembled it by going to church; and as the great counten-
ancer and support of that religion; all his family being of
that profession, and very few resorting to it, or having any
credit with him but such. It is very true, the archbishop
had no great regard for his memory, or for his friends,
and was willing enough to make any discovery of his
miscarriages, and to inform his majesty of them, who he
believed had too good an opinion of him and his integrity.
The truth is, the archbishop had laid down one principle
to himself, which he believed would much advance the
king's service, and was without doubt very prudent; that
the king's duties being provided for, and cheerfully paid,
the merchants should receive all the countenance and protection from the king that they could expect, and not be
liable to the vexation particular men gave them for their
private advantage; being forward enough to receive propositions which tended to the king's profit, but careful that
what accrued of burden to the subject, should redound
entirely to the benefit of the crown, and not enrich projectors at the charge of the people: and there is reason to

believe that if this measure had been well observed, much of that murmur had been prevented, which contributed to that jealousy and discontent which soon after brake out. This vigilance and inclination in the archbishop opened a door to the admission of any merchants or others to him, who gave him information of this kind; and who being ready to pay any thing to the king, desired only to be protected from private oppressions. The archbishop used to spend as much time as he could get at his country house at Croydon; and then his mind being unbent from business, he delighted in the conversation of his neighbours, and treated them with great urbanity.

The person whose life this discourse is to recollect (and who had so great an affection and reverence for the memory of that prelate, ⟨archbishop Laud,⟩ that he never spake of him without extraordinary esteem, and believed him to be a man of the most exemplar virtue and piety of any of that age) was wont to say, the greatest want the archbishop had was of a true friend, who would seasonably have told him of his infirmities, and what people spake of him; and he said, he knew well that such a friend would have been very acceptable to him; and upon that occasion he used to mention a story of himself: that when he was a young practiser of the law, being in some favour with him, (as is mentioned before,) he went to visit him in the beginning of a Michaelmas term, shortly after his return from the country, where he had spent a month or two of the summer.

He found the archbishop early walking in the garden; who received him according to his custom, very graciously; and continuing his walk, asked him, 'What good news in the country?' to which he answered, 'there was none good; the people were universally discontented; and (which troubled him most) that every ⟨one⟩ spoke extreme ill of his grace, as the cause of all that was amiss'. He replied, 'that he was sorry for it; he knew he did not deserve it; and that he must not give over serving the king and the church, to please the people, who otherwise would not speak well of him'. Mr. Hyde told him, 'he thought he need not lessen his zeal for either; and that it grieved him to find persons of the best condition, and who loved both king and church, exceedingly indevoted to him; complaining of his manner of treating them, when they had occasion to resort to him, it may be, for his directions'. And then named him two persons of the most interest and credit in Wiltshire, who had that summer attended the council board in some affairs which concerned the king and the county: that all the lords present used them with great courtesy, knowing well their quality and reputation; but that he alone spake very sharply to them, and without any thing of grace, at which they were much troubled; and one of them, supposing that somebody had done him ill offices, went the next morning to Lambeth, to present his service to him, and to discover, if he could, what misrepresentation had been made of him: that after he had attended very long, he was admitted to speak with his grace, who scarce hearing him, sharply answered him, that 'he had no leisure for compliments'; and so turned away; which put the other gentleman much out of countenance: and that this kind of behaviour of his was the discourse of all companies of persons of quality; every man continuing any such story with another like it, very much to his disadvantage, and to the trouble of those who were very just to him.

He heard the relation very patiently and attentively, and discoursed over every particular with all imaginable condescension; and said, with evident shew of trouble, that 'he was very unfortunate to be so ill understood; that he meant very well; that he remembered the time when those two persons were with the council; that upon any deliberations, when any thing was resolved, or to be said to any body, the council enjoined him to deliver their resolutions; which he did always according to the best of his understanding: but by the imperfection he had by nature, which he said often troubled him, he might deliver it in such a tune, and with a sharpness of voice, that made men believe he was angry, when there was no such thing; that when those gentlemen were there, and he had delivered what he was to say, they made some stay, and spake with some of the lords, which not being according to order, he thought he gave them some reprehension; they having at that time very much other business to do: that he did well remember that one of them (who was a person of honour) came afterwards to him at a time he was shut up about an affair of importance, which required his full thoughts; but that as soon as he heard of the other's being without, he sent for him, himself going into the next room, and receiving him very kindly, as he thought; and supposing that he came about business, asked him what his business was; and the other answering, that he had no business, but continuing his address with some ceremony, he had indeed said, that he had not time for compliments: but he did not think that he went out of the room in that manner: and concluded, that it was not possible for him, in the many occupations he had, to spend any time in unnecessary compliments; and that if his integrity and uprightness, which never should be liable to reproach, could not be strong enough to preserve him, he must submit to God's good pleasure'.

He was well contented to hear Mr. Hyde reply very freely upon the subject, who said, 'he observed by what his grace himself had related, that the gentlemen had too much reason for the report they made; and he did not wonder that they had been much troubled at his carriage towards them; that he did exceedingly wish that he would more reserve his passion towards all persons, how faulty soever; and that he would treat persons of honour, and quality, and interest in their country, with more courtesy and condescension; especially when they came to visit him, and make offer of their service'. He said, smiling, that 'he could only undertake for his heart; that he had very good meaning; for his tongue, he could not undertake, that he would not sometimes speak more hastily and sharply than he should do, (which oftentimes he was sorry for and reprehended himself for,) and in a tune which might be liable to misinterpretation with them who were not very well acquainted with him, and so knew that it was an infirmity, which his nature and education had so rooted in him, that it was in vain to contend with it'. For the state and distance he kept with men, he said, 'he thought it was not more than was suitable to the place and degree he held in the church and state; or so much as others had assumed to themselves who had sat in his place; and thereupon he told him some behaviour and carriage of his predecessor, Abbot, (who he said was not better born than himself,) towards the greatest nobility of the kingdom, which he thought was very insolent and inexcusable'; and was indeed very ridiculous.

After this bold enterprise, ⟨Mr. Hyde⟩ ever found himself more graciously received by him, and treated with more familiarity; upon which he always concluded, that if the archbishop had had any true friend, who would, in proper seasons, have dealt frankly with him in the most important matters, and wherein the errors were like to be most penal, he would not only have received it very well, but have profited himself by it. But it is the misfortune of most persons of that education, (how worthy soever,) that they have rarely friendships with men above their own condition; and that their ascent being commonly sudden, from low to high, they have afterwards rather dependants than friends, and are still deceived by keeping somewhat in reserve to themselves, even from those with whom they seem most openly to communicate; and which is worse, receive for the most part their informations and advertisements from clergymen who understand the least, and take the worst measure of human affairs, of all mankind that can write and read.

The archbishop of Canterbury had lain prisoner in the Tower, from the beginning of the parliament, full four years, without any prosecution till this time, when they brought him to the bars of both houses; charging him with several articles of high treason; which, if all that was alleged against him had been true, could not have made him guilty of treason. They accused him 'of a design to bring in popery, and of having correspondence with the pope', and of such like particulars, as the consciences of his greatest enemies absolved him from. No man was a greater or abler enemy to popery; no man a more resolute and devout son of the church of England. He was prosecuted by lawyers, assigned to that purpose, out of those, who from their own antipathy to the church and bishops, or from some disobligations received from him, were sure to bring passion, animosity, and malice enough of their own; what evidence soever they had from others. And they did treat him with all the rudeness, reproach, and barbarity imaginable; with which his judges were not displeased.

He defended himself with great and undaunted courage, and less passion than was expected from his constitution; answered all their objections with clearness and irresistible reason; and convinced all men of his integrity, and his detestation of all treasonable intentions. So that though few excellent men have ever had fewer friends to their persons, yet all reasonable men absolved him from any foul crime that the law could take notice of, and punish. However, when they had said all they could against him, and he all for himself that need to be said, and no such crime appearing, as the lords, as the supreme court of judicatory, would take upon them to judge him to be worthy of death, they resorted to their legislative power, and by ordinance of parliament, as they called it, that is, by a determination of those members who sat in the houses, (whereof in the house of peers there were not above twelve,) they appointed him to be put to death, as guilty of high treason. The first time that two houses of parliament had ever assumed that jurisdiction, or that ever ordinance had been made to such a purpose, nor could any rebellion be more against the law, than that murderous act.

When the first mention was made of their monstrous purpose, of bringing the archbishop to a trial for his life, the chancellor of the exchequer, who had always a great reverence and affection for him, had spoken to the king of it, and proposed to him, 'that in all events, there might be a pardon prepared, and sent to him, under the great seal of England; to the end, if they proceeded against him in any form of law, he might plead the king's pardon; which must be allowed by all who pretended to be governed by the law; but if they proceeded in a martial, or any other extraordinary way, without any form of law, his majesty should declare his justice and affection to an old faithful servant, whom he much esteemed, in having done all towards his preservation that was in his power to do'. The king was wonderfully pleased with the proposition; and took from thence occasion to commend the piety and virtue of the archbishop with extraordinary affection; and commanded the chancellor of the exchequer to cause the pardon to be drawn, and his ma·esty would sign and seal it with all possible secrecy; which at that time was necessary. Whereupon the chancellor sent for sir Thomas Gardiner, the king's solicitor, and told him the king's pleasure; upon which he presently prepared the pardon, and it was signed and sealed with the great seal of England, and carefully sent, and delivered into the archbishop's own hand, before he was brought to his trial; who received it with great joy, as it was a testimony of the king's gracious affection to him, and care of him, without any opinion that they who endeavoured to take away the king's life would preserve his by his majesty's authority.

When the archbishop's council had perused the pardon, and considered that all possible exceptions would be taken to it, though they should not reject it, they found, that the impeachment was not so distinctly set down in the pardon as it ought to be; which could not be helped at Oxford, because they had no copy of it; and therefore had supplied it with all those general expressions, as, in any court of law, would make the pardon valid against any exceptions the king's own council could make against it. Hereupon, the archbishop had, by the same messenger, returned the pardon again to the chancellor, with such directions and copies as were necessary; upon which it was perfected accordingly, and delivered safely again to him, and was in his hands during the whole time of his trial. So when his trial was over, and the ordinance passed for the cutting off his head, and he called and asked, according to custom in criminal proceedings, 'what he could say more, why he should not suffer death?' he told them, 'that he had the king's gracious pardon, which he pleaded, and tendered to them, and desired that it might be allowed'.

Whereupon he was sent to the Tower, and the pardon read in both Houses; where, without any long debate, it was declared 'to be of no effect, and that the king could not pardon a judgment of parliament'. And so, without troubling themselves farther, they gave order for his execution; which he underwent with all Christian courage and magnanimity, to the admiration of the beholders, and confusion of his enemies. Much hath been said of the person of this great prelate before, of his great endowments, and natural infirmities; to which shall be added no more in this place, (his memory deserving a particular celebration,) than that his learning, piety, and virtue, have been attained by very few, and the greatest of his infirmities are common to all, even to the best men.

16. *Lord Cottington*

Born 1578?; knighted 1623; at various times ambassador in Spain; P.C. 1628; baron 1631; Master of the Court of Wards 1635–41

HE was a very wise man, by the great and long experience he had in business of all kinds; and by his natural temper, which was not liable to any transport of anger, or any other passion, but could bear contradiction, and even reproach, without being moved, or put out of his way: for he was very steady in pursuing what he proposed to himself, and had a courage not to be frighted or amazed with any opposition. It is true he was illiterate as to the grammar of any language, or the principles of any science: but by his perfectly understanding the Spanish, (which he spoke as a Spaniard,) the French, and Italian languages, and having read very much in all, he could not be said to be ignorant in any part of learning, divinity only excepted. He had a very fine and extraordinary understanding in the nature of beasts and birds, and above all in all kind of plantations and arts of husbandry. He was born a gentleman both by father and mother, his father having a pretty entire seat near Bruton in Somersetshire, worth above two hundred pounds a year, which had descended from father to son for many hundred years, and is still in the possession of his elder brother's children, the family having been always Roman Catholic. His mother was a Stafford, nearly allied to sir Edward Stafford; who was vice-chamberlain to queen Elizabeth, and had been ambassador in France; by whom this gentleman was brought up, and was gentleman of his horse, and left one of his executors of his will, and by him recommended to sir Robert Cecil, then principal secretary of state; who preferred him to sir Charles Cornwallis, when he went ambassador into Spain, in the beginning of the reign of king James; where he remained, for the space of eleven or twelve years, in the condition of secretary or agent, without ever returning into England in all that time. He raised by his own virtue and industry, a very fair estate, of which though the revenue did not exceed above four thousand pounds by the year; yet he had four very good houses, and three parks, the value whereof was not reckoned into that computation. He lived very nobly, well served and attended in his house; had a better stable of horses, better provisions for sports, (especially of hawks, in which he took great delight,) than most of his quality, and lived always with great splendour; for though he loved money very well, and did not warily enough consider the circumstances of getting it, he spent it well all ways but in giving, which he did not affect. He was of an excellent humour, and very easy to live with; and, under a grave countenance, covered the most of mirth, and caused more, than any man of the most pleasant disposition. He never used any body ill, but used many very well for whom he had no regard: his greatest fault was, that he could dissemble, and make men believe that he loved them very well, when he cared not for them. He had not very tender affections, nor bowels apt to yearn at all objects which deserved compassion: he was heartily weary of the world, and no man was more willing to die; which is an argument that he had peace of conscience. He left behind him a greater esteem of his parts, than love to his person.

17. *The Short Parliament, 13 April 1640 to 5 May 1640, and the Long Parliament, 3 November 1640; 'purged' 1648*

[LAUD's policy had roused the Scottish Presbyterians to action and Charles had opposed them with an English army. But as part of the nobility proved refractory and the Scottish army was much better organized, the king had to conclude with the Covenanters the treaty of Berwick, 1639. Its provisions, however, were not well kept and the king therefore prepared for a renewal of military measures in 1640.] That summer's action had wasted all the money that had been carefully laid up; and, to carry on that vast expense, the revenue of the crown had been anticipated; so that, though the raising of an army was visibly necessary, there appeared no means how to raise that army. No expedient occurred to them so proper as a parliament, and which had been now intermitted near twelve years. And though those meetings had of late been attended by some disorders, the effects of mutinous spirits; and the last had been dissolved (as hath been said before) with some circumstances of passion, and undutifulness, which so far incensed the king, that he was less inclined to those assemblies; yet this long intermission, and the general composure of men's minds in a happy peace, and universal plenty over the whole nation, (superior sure to what any other nation ever enjoyed,) made it reasonably believed, notwithstanding the murmurs of the people against some exorbitancies of the court, that sober men, and such as loved the peace and plenty they were possessed of, would be made choice of to serve in the house of commons; and then the temper of the house of peers was not to be apprehended: but especially the opinion of the prejudice and general aversion over the whole kingdom to the Scots, and the indignation they had at their presumption in their thought of invading England, made it believed, that a parliament would express a very sharp sense of their insolence and carriage towards the king, and provide remedies proportionable.

Upon these motives and reasons, with the unanimous consent and advice of the whole committee, the king resolved to call a parliament; which he communicated the same day, or rather took the resolution that day, in his full council of state, which expressed great joy upon it; and directed the lord keeper to issue out writs for the meeting of a parliament upon the 13th day of April then next ensuing; it being now in the month of December; and all expedition was accordingly used in sending out the said writs, the notice of it being most welcome to the whole kingdom.

That it might appear that the court was not at all apprehensive of what the parliament would or could do; and that it was convened by his majesty's grace and inclination, not by any motive of necessity; it proceeded in all respects in the same unpopular ways it had done: ship-money was levied with the same severity; and the same rigour used in ecclesiastical courts, without the least compliance with the humour of any man; which was great steadiness; and, if it were then well pursued, it degenerated too soon afterwards.

[The Short Parliament disagreed with the king's council as to the best way in which to raise supply and was dissolved.] There could not a greater damp have seized upon the spirits of the whole nation, than this dissolution caused; and men had much of the misery in view, which shortly after fell out. It could never be hoped, that more sober and dispassionate men would ever meet together in that place, or fewer who brought ill purposes with them; nor could any man imagine what offence they had given, which put the king to that resolution. But it was observed, that in the countenances of those who had most opposed all that was desired by his majesty, there was a marvellous serenity; nor could they conceal the joy of their hearts: for they knew enough of what was to come, to conclude that the king would be shortly compelled to call another parliament; and they were as sure, that so many grave and unbiassed men would never be elected again.

Within an hour after the dissolving, Mr. Hyde met Mr. Saint-John, who had naturally a great cloud in his face, and very seldom was known to smile, but then had a most cheerful aspect, and seeing the other melancholic, as in truth he was from his heart, asked him, 'What troubled him?' who answered, 'That the same that troubled him, he believed, troubled most good men; that in such a time of confusion, so wise a parliament, which could only have found remedy for it, was so unseasonably dismissed': the other answered with a little warmth, 'That all was well: and that it must be worse, before it could be better; and that this parliament would never have done what was necessary to be done'; as indeed it would not, what he and his friends thought necessary. [In the meantime the Scots had succeeded in routing the king's army at Newburn but were willing to negotiate. Thus a cessation of hostilities was arranged at Ripon and the government undertook to pay both armies until the final settlement which was to be negotiated in London.] It is not to be denied, the king was in very great straits, and had it not in his power absolutely to choose which way he would go; and well foresaw, that a parliament in that conjuncture of affairs would not apply natural and proper remedies to the disease; for though it was not imaginable it would have run the courses it afterwards did, yet it was visible enough he must resign very much to their affections, and appetite, (which were not like to be contained within any modest bounds,) and therefore no question his majesty did not think of calling a parliament at first, but was wrought to it by degrees: yet the great council could not but produce the other; where the unskilfulness and passion of some for want of discerning consequences, and a general sharpness and animosity against persons, did more mischief than the power or malice of those who had a formed design of confusion; for without doubt that fire at that time (which did shortly after burn the whole kingdom) might have been covered under a bushel. So as in truth there was no counsel so necessary then, as for the king to have continued in his army, and to have drawn none thither, but such as were more afraid of dishonour than danger; and to have trusted the justice and power of the law with suppressing of tumults, and quieting disorders in his rear.

It is strange, and had somewhat of a judgment from Heaven in it, that all the industry and learning of the late years had been bestowed in finding out and evincing, that in case of necessity any extraordinary way for supply was lawful; and upon that ground had proceeded when there was no necessity; and now, when the necessity was apparent, money must be levied in the ordinary course of parliament, which was then more unnatural and extraordinary than the other had been; as York must be defended from an enemy within twenty-five miles of it, by money to be given at London six weeks after, and to be gathered in six months. It had been only the season and evidence of necessity that had been questioned; and the view of it in a perspective of state at a distance that no eyes could reach, denied to be ground enough for an imposition: as no man could pull down his neighbour's house, because it stood next furze, or thatch, or some combustible matter which might take fire; though he might do it when that combustible matter was really a-fire. But it was never denied that *flagrante bello*, when an enemy had actually invaded the kingdom, and so the necessity both seen and felt, that all men's goods are the goods of the public, to be applied to the public safety, and as carefully to be repaired by the public stock. And it is very probable, (since the factions within, and the correspondence abroad was so apparent, that a parliament then called would do the business of the Scots, and of those who invited them hither,) that if the king had positively declared, that he would have no parliament as long as that army stayed in England, but as soon as they were retired into their own country he would summon one, and refer all matters to their advice, and even be advised by them in the composing the distractions of Scotland: I say, it is probable, that they would either willingly have left the kingdom, or speedily have been compelled; there being at that time an army in Ireland (as was said before) ready to have visited their own country.

In all conspiracies, there must be great secrecy, consent, and union; yet it can hardly be conceived, with what entire confidence in each other the numerous proud and indigent nobility of Scotland (for of the common people, who are naturally slaves to the other, there can be no wonder) concurred in the carrying on this rebellion: their strange condescension and submission to their ignorant and insolent clergy, who were to have great authority, because they were to inflame all sorts of men upon the obligations of conscience; and in order thereunto, and to revenge a little indiscretion and ill manners of some of the bishops, had liberty to erect a tribunal the most tyrannical over all sorts of men, and in all the families of the kingdom: so that the preacher reprehended the husband, governed the wife, chastised the children, and insulted over the servants, in the houses of the greatest men. They referred the managery and conduct of the whole affair to a committee of a few, who had never before exercised any office or authority in the public, with that perfect resignation and obedience that nobody presumed to inquire what was to be done, or to murmur at or censure any thing that was done; and the general himself, and the martial affairs, were subject to this regimen and discipline as well as the civil: yet they who were intrusted with this superiority, paid all the outward respect and reverence to the person of the general, as if the sole power and disposal had been in him alone.

The few English (for there were yet but very few who were intrusted from the beginning of the enterprise, and with all that was then projected) were men of reserved and dark natures, of great industry and address, and of much reputation for probity and integrity of life, and who trusted none but those who were contented to be trusted to that degree as they were willing to trust them, without being inquisitive into more than they were ready to communicate, and for the rest depended upon their discretion and judgment; and so prepared and disposed, by second and third hands, many to concur and contribute to many preparatory actions, who would never have consented to those conclusions which naturally resulted from those premises.

This united strength, and humble and active temper, was not encountered by an equal providence and circumspection in the king's councils, or an equal temper and dutiful disposition in the court; nor did they, who resolved honestly and stoutly to discharge the offices of good servants and good subjects to the utmost opposition of all unlawful attempts, communicate their purposes to men of the same integrity, that só they might unite their counsels as well in the manner and way, as their resolutions in the end. But every one thought it enough to preserve his own innocence, and to leave the rest to those who should have authority to direct. The king was perplexed and irresolute, and, according to his natural constitution, (which never disposed him to jealousy of any man of whom he had once thought well,) was full of hope, that his condition was not so bad as it seemed to be. The queen, how much troubled soever, wished much better to the earl of Holland, than to the archbishop, or the earl of Strafford, neither of them being in any degree acceptable to her; so that she was little concerned for the danger that threatened them: but when she saw the king's honour and dignity invaded in the prosecution, she withdrew her favour from the earl of Holland: but then she was persuaded, by those who had most credit with her, to believe that, by the removal of the great ministers, her power and authority would be increased, and that the prevailing party would be willing to depend upon her; and that, by gratifying the principal persons of them with such preferments as they affected, she would quickly reconcile all ill humours; and so she hearkened to any overtures of that kind; which were always carried on without the consent or privity of those who were concerned, who in truth more disliked her absolute power with the king, than any other excess of the court, and looked upon it as the greatest grievance. Every man there considered only what application would be most like to raise his own fortune, or to do him harm with whom he was angry, and gave himself wholly up to those artifices which might promote either. To preserve themselves from the displeasure and censure of the parliament, and to render themselves gracious to those who were like to be powerful in it, was all men's business and solicitude. And in this very unequal and disproportioned condition and temper, was the king's and the Scottish army, the court and the country, when the parliament met.

The parliament met upon the third of November, 1640, with a fuller appearance than could be reasonably expected, from the short time for elections after the issuing out of the writs; insomuch as at the first ⟨not⟩ many members were absent. It had a sad and a melancholic aspect upon the first entrance, which presaged some unusual and unnatural events. The king himself did not ride with his accustomed equipage nor in his usual majesty to Westminster, but went privately in his barge to the parliament stairs, and so to the church, as if it had been to a return of a prorogued or adjourned parliament. And there was likewise an untoward, and in truth an unheard of accident, which brake many of the king's measures, and infinitely disordered his service, beyond a capacity of reparation. From the time the calling a parliament was resolved upon, the king designed sir Thomas Gardiner, who was recorder of London, to be speaker in the house of commons; a man of gravity and quickness, that had somewhat of authority and gracefulness in his person and presence, and in all respects equal to the service. There was little doubt but that he would be chosen to serve in one of the four places for the city of London, which have very rarely rejected their recorder upon that occasion; and lest that should fail, diligence was used in one or two other places that he might be elected. The opposition was so great, and the faction so strong, to hinder his being elected in the city, that four others were chosen for that service, without hardly mentioning his name: nor was there less industry used to prevent his being chosen in other places; clerks were corrupted not to make out the writs for one place, and ways were found to hinder the writ from being executed in another, time enough for the return before the meeting: so great a fear there was, that a man of entire affections to the king, and of prudence enough to manage those affections, and to regulate the contrary, should be put into that chair. So that the very morning the parliament was to meet, and when the king intended to go thither, he was informed that sir Thomas Gardiner was not returned to serve as a member in the house of commons, and so was not capable of being chosen to be a speaker; so that his majesty deferred his going to the house till the afternoon, by which time he was to think of another speaker.

Upon the perusal of all the returns into the crown office, there were not found many lawyers of eminent name, (though many of them proved very eminent men afterwards,) or who had served long in former parliaments, the experience whereof was to be wished; and men of that profession had been always thought the most proper for that service, and the putting it out of that channel at that time was thought too hazardous; so that after all the deliberation that time would admit, Mr. Lenthall, a bencher of Lincoln's Inn, (a lawyer of competent practice, and no ill reputation for his affection to the government both of church, and state,) was pitched upon by the king, and with very great difficulty rather prevailed with than persuaded to accept the charge. And no doubt a worse could not have been deputed of all that profession who were then returned; for he was a man of a very narrow, timorous nature, and of no experience or conversation in the affairs of the kingdom, beyond what the very drudgery in his profession (in which all his design was to make himself rich) engaged him in. In a word, he was in all respects very unequal to the work; and not knowing how to preserve his own dignity, or to restrain the license and exorbitance of others, his weakness contributed as much to the growing mischiefs, as the malice of the principal contrivers. However, after the king had that afternoon commended the distracted condition of the kingdom (with too little majesty) to the wisdom of the two houses of parliament, to have such reformation and remedies applied as they should think fit, proposing to them, as the best rule for their counsels, 'that all things should be reduced to the practice of the time of queen Elizabeth:' the house of commons no sooner returned to their house, than they chose Mr. Lenthall to be their speaker; and two days after, with the usual ceremonies and circumstances, presented him to the king, who declared his acceptation; and so both houses were ready for their work.

There was observed a marvellous elated countenance in most of the members of parliament before they met together in the house; the same men who six months before were observed to be of very moderate tempers, and to wish that gentle remedies might be applied, without opening the wound too wide, and exposing it to the air, and rather to cure what was amiss than too strictly to make inquisition into the causes and original of the malady, talked now in another dialect both of things and persons. Mr. Hyde, who was returned to serve for a borough in Cornwall, met Mr. Pym in Westminster-hall some days before the parliament, and conferring together upon the state of affairs, the other told him, Mr. Hyde, 'that they must now be of another temper than they were the last parliament; that they must not only sweep the house clean below, but must pull down all the cobwebs which hung in the top and corners, that they might not breed dust, and so make a foul house hereafter; that they had now an opportunity to make their country happy, by removing all grievances, and pulling up the causes of them by the roots, if all men would do their duties'; and used much other sharp discourse to him to the same purpose: by which it was discerned, that the warmest and boldest counsels and overtures would find a much better reception than those of a more temperate allay; which fell out accordingly: and the very first day they met together, in which they could enter upon business, Mr. Pym, in a long, formed discourse, lamented the miserable state and condition of the kingdom, aggravated all the particulars which had been done amiss in the government, as 'done and contrived maliciously ,and upon deliberation, to change the whole frame, and to deprive the nation of all the liberty and property which was their birthright by the laws of the land, which were now no more considered, but subjected to the arbitrary power of the privy-council, which governed the kingdom according to their will and pleasure; these calamities falling upon us in the reign of a pious and virtuous king, who loved his people, and was a great lover of justice'. And thereupon enlarging in some specious commendation of the nature and goodness of the king, that he might wound him with less suspicion, he said, 'We must inquire from what fountain these waters of bitterness flowed;

what persons they were who had so far insinuated themselves into his royal affections, as to be able to pervert his excellent judgment, to abuse his name, and wickedly apply his authority to countenance and support their own corrupt designs. Though he doubted there would be many found of this classis, who had contributed their joint endeavours to bring this misery upon the nation; yet he believed there was one more signal in that administration than the rest, being a man of great parts and contrivance, and of great industry to bring what he designed to pass; a man, who in the memory of many present had sat in that house an earnest vindicator of the laws, and a most zealous assertor and champion for the liberties of the people; but that it was long since he turned apostate from those good affections, and, according to the custom and nature of apostates, was become the greatest enemy to the liberties of his country, and the greatest promoter of tyranny that any age had produced'; and then named 'the earl of Strafford, lord lieutenant of Ireland, and lord president of the council established in York, for the Northern parts of the kingdom: who', he said, 'had in both places, and in all other provinces wherein his service had been used by the king, raised ample monuments of his tyrannical nature'; and that he believed, 'if they took a short survey of his actions and behaviour, they would find him the principal author and promoter of all those counsels, which had exposed the kingdom to so much ruin': and so instanced some high and imperious actions done by him in England and in Ireland, some proud and over-confident expressions in discourse, and some passionate advices he had given in the most secret councils, and debates of the affairs of state; adding some lighter passages of his vanity and amours; that they who were not inflamed with anger and detestation against him for the former, might have less esteem and reverence for his prudence and discretion: and so concluded, 'That they would well consider how to provide a remedy proportionable to the disease, and to prevent the farther mischiefs which they were to expect from the continuance of this great man's power and credit with the king, and his influence upon his counsels.'

[After long debates Strafford was impeached by the House of Commons, Pym being the main manager of the accusation. Clarendon's account is somewhat too favourable to the peers. For the earl was sent for though ill but not allowed to talk in his own defence.] And with very little debate the peers resolved 'that he should be committed to the custody of the gentleman usher of the black-rod, there to remain until the house of commons should bring in a particular charge against him': which determination of the house was pronounced to him at the bar upon his knees, by the lord keeper of the great seal, upon the wool-sack: and so being taken away by Maxwell, gentleman usher, Mr. Pym was called in, and informed what the house had done; after which (it being then about four of the clock) both houses adjourned till the next day.

When this work was so prosperously over, they began to consider, that notwithstanding all the industry that had been used to procure such members to be chosen, or returned though not chosen, who had been most refractory to the government of the church and state; yet that the house was so constituted, that when the first heat (which almost all men brought with them) should be a little allayed, violent counsels could not be long hearkened to: and therefore, as they took great care by their committee of elections to remove as many of those members as they suspected not to be inclinable to their passions upon pretence 'that they were not regularly chosen', that so they might bring in others more compliable in their places; in which no rules of justice was so much as pretended to be observed by them; insomuch as it was often said by leading men amongst them, 'That they ought in those cases of elections to be guided by the fitness and worthiness of the person, whatever the desire of those was, in whom the right of election remained'; and therefore one man hath been admitted upon the same rule by which another hath been rejected: so they declared, 'That no person, how lawfully and regularly soever chosen and returned, should be and sit as a member with them, who had been a party or a favourer of any project, or who had been employed in any illegal commission.' And by this means, (contrary to the custom and rights of parliament) many gentlemen of good quality were removed, in whose places commonly others were chosen of more agreeable dispositions: but in this likewise there was no rule observed; for no person was hereby removed, of whom there was any hope that he might be applied to the violent courses which were intended. Upon which occasion the king charged them in one of his declarations, 'that when, under that notion of projectors, they expelled many, they yet never questioned sir Henry Mildmay, or Mr. Laurence Whitaker'; who had been most scandalously engaged in those pressures, though since more scandalously in all enterprises against his majesty; to which never any answer or reply was made.

The next art was to make the severity and rigour of the house as formidable as was possible, and to make as many men apprehend themselves obnoxious to the house, as had been in any trust or employment in the kingdom. Thus they passed many general votes concerning ship-money, in which all who had been high-sheriffs, and so collected it, were highly concerned. The like sharp conclusions ⟨were made⟩ upon all lords lieutenants and their deputies, which were the prime gentlemen of quality in all the counties of England. Then upon some disquisition of the proceedings in the star-chamber, and at the council-table, all who concurred in such a sentence, and consented to such an order, were declared criminous, and to be proceeded against. So that, in a moment, all the lords of the council, all who had been deputy lieutenants, or high sheriffs, during the late years, found themselves within the mercy of these grand inquisitors: and hearing new terms of art, that a complication of several misdemeanours might grow up to treason, and the like, it was no wonder if men desired by all means to get their favour and protection.

When they had sufficiently startled men by these proceedings, and upon half an hour's debate sent up an accusation against the lord archbishop of Canterbury of high treason, and so removed him likewise from the king's council, they rested satisfied with their general rules, votes, and orders, without making haste to proceed either against things or persons; being willing rather to keep men in suspense, and to have the advantage of their fears, than, by letting them see the worst that could befall them, lose the benefit of their application.

This was the present temper and constitution of both houses of parliament upon their first coming together, when (as Tacitus says of the Jews, 'that they exercised the highest offices of kindness and friendship towards each other, *et adversus omnes alios hostile odium*') they watched all those who they knew were not of their opinions, nor like to be, with all possible jealousy; and if any of their elections could be brought into question, they were sure to be voted out of the house, and then all the artifices were used to bring in more sanctified members; so that every week increased the number of their party, both by new elections, and the proselytes they gained upon the old. Nor was it to be wondered at, for they pretended all public thoughts, and only the reformation of disapproved and odious enormities, and dissembled all purposes of removing foundations, which, though it was in the hearts of some, they had not the courage and confidence to communicate it.

In the house of commons were many persons of wisdom and gravity, who being possessed of great and plentiful fortunes, though they were undevoted enough to the court, had all imaginable duty for the king, and affection to the government established by law or ancient custom: and without doubt, the major part of that body consisted of men who had no mind to break the peace of the kingdom, or to make any considerable alteration in the government of church or state: and therefore all inventions were set on foot from the beginning to work on them, and corrupt them, by suggestions 'of the dangers which threatened all that was precious to the subject in their liberty and their property by overthrowing or overmastering the law, and subjecting it to an arbitrary power, and by countenancing popery to the subversion of the protestant religion'; and then, by infusing terrible apprehensions into some, and so working upon their fears 'of being called in question for somewhat they had done', by which they would stand in need of their protection; and raising the hopes of others, 'that, by concurring with them, they should be sure to obtain offices, and honours, and any kind of preferment'. Though there were too many corrupted and misled by these several temptations, and others who needed no other temptations than from the fierceness and barbarity of their own natures, and the malice they had contracted against the church and against the court; yet the number was not great of those in whom the government of the rest was vested, nor were there many who had the absolute authority to lead, though there were a multitude that was disposed to follow.

Mr. Pym was looked upon as the man of greatest experience in parliament, where he had served very long, and was always a man of business, being an officer in the exchequer, and of a good reputation generally, though known to be inclined to the puritan party; yet not of those furious resolutions against the church as the other leading men were, and wholly devoted to the earl of Bedford, who had nothing of that spirit.

The earl of Bedford [was] a wise man, and of too great and plentiful a fortune to wish a subversion of the government; and it quickly appeared, that he only intended to make himself and his friends great at court, not at all to lessen the court itself. [Clarendon repeats the same opinion after the king's retreat to York.] And I am persuaded, that even then, and I was at that time no stranger to the persons of most that governed, and a diligent observer of their carriage, they had rather a design of making themselves powerful with the king, and great at court, than of lessening the power of the one or reforming the discipline of the other: but, no doubt, there were some few in the number that looked further.

The earl of Bedford secretly undertook to his majesty, that the earl of Strafford's life should be preserved; and to procure his revenue to be settled, as amply as any of his progenitors; the which he intended so really, that, to my knowledge, he had it in design to endeavour the setting up the excise in England, as the only natural means to advance the king's profit. He fell sick within a week after the bill of attainder was sent up to the lords' house; and

died shortly after, much afflicted with the passion and
fury which he perceived his party inclined to: insomuch
as he declared, to some of near trust with him, 'that he
feared the rage and madness of this parliament would
bring more prejudice and mischief to the kingdom, than
it had ever sustained by the long intermission of parliaments'. He was a wise man, and would have proposed and
advised moderate courses; but was not incapable, for want
of resolution, of being carried into violent ones, if his
advice would not have been submitted to: and therefore
many, who knew him well, thought his death not unseasonable, as well to his fame, as his fortune; and that it rescued
him as well from some possible guilt, as from those visible
misfortunes, which men of all condition have since undergone.

[After the king had left London, Parliament was the
prey of fears and rumours and made many orders to deal
with them.] Though seldom any thing was after done,
or no matter of moment, yet it served to keep up the
fears and apprehensions in the people, of dangers and
designs, and to disincline them from any reverence or
affection to the queen, whom they began every day more
implacably to hate, and consequently to disoblige. And,
as upon those and the like light occasions, they grew to a
licence of language, without the least respect of persons, of
how venerable estimation whatsoever; so they departed
from any order or regularity in debate; or rules and
measure in judging; the chief rulers among them first
designing what they thought fit to be done, and the rest
concluding any thing lawful, that they thought in order
to the doing or compassing the same: in which neither
laws nor customs could be admitted to signify any thing
against their sense.

It is not to be believed how many sober, well-minded
men, who were real lovers of the peace of the kingdom,
and had the known laws in full submission and reverence,
were imposed upon, and had their understandings confounded, and so their wills perverted, by the mere mention
of privilege of parliament; which, from the most defined,
limited notion, was, by the dexterity of those boutefeus,

and their under-agents of the law, and the supine sottish-
ness of the people, rendered such a mystery, as could be
only explained by themselves, and extended as far as they
found necessary for their occasions, and was to be acknowledged a good reason for any thing that no other reason
could be given for. 'We are,' say they, 'and have been
always confessed, the only judges of our own privileges;
and therefore whatsoever we declare to be our privilege,
is such: otherwise whosoever determines that it is not so,
makes himself judge of that, whereof the cognizance only
belongs to us.' And this sophistical riddle hath perplexed
many, who, notwithstanding the desperate consequence
they saw must result from such logic, taking the first proposition for true, which, being righly understood, is so,
have not been able to wind themselves out of the labyrinth
of the conclusion: I say the proposition rightly understood:
they are the only judges of their own privileges, that is,
upon the breach of those privileges, which the law hath
declared to be their own, and what punishment is to be
inflicted upon such breach. But there can be no privilege,
of which the law doth not take notice, and which is not
pleadable by, and at law.

And indeed these two, of freedom from arrests for their
persons, (which originally hath not been of that latitude
to make a parliament a sanctuary for bankrupts, where
any person outlawed hath been declared incapable of
being returned thither a member,) and of liberty of speech,
were accounted their chiefest, if not their only privileges
of parliament: for their other, of access to the king, and
correspondence by conference with the lords, are rather of
the essence of their councils, than privileges belonging to it.
But that their being judges of their privileges should qualify
them to make new privileges, or that their judgment
should create them such, as it was a doctrine never before
now heard of, so it could not but produce all those monstrous effects we have seen: when they have assumed to
swallow all the rights and prerogative of the crown, the
liberties and lands of the church, the power and jurisdiction of the peers, in a word, the religion, laws, and liberties
of England, in the bottomless and insatiable gulph of

their own privileges: and no doubt will determine this digression to be the most unparalleled and capital breach of those privileges, that had ever yet been attempted.

18. *The Trial and Character of the Earl of Strafford*

Thomas Wentworth, born 1593; knighted 1611; second baronet 1614; Viscount Wentworth 1628; Earl of Strafford 1640; President of the Council of the North 1628; Lord Deputy of Ireland 1632; executed 1641

ALL things being thus prepared and settled; on Monday, the twenty-second of March, the earl of Strafford was brought to the bar in Westminster-hall; the lords sitting in the middle of the hall in their robes; and the commoners, and some strangers of quality, with the Scottish commissioners, and the committee of Ireland, on either side: there being a close box made at one end, at a very convenient distance for hearing, in which the king and queen sat untaken notice of; his majesty, out of kindness and curiosity, desiring to hear all that could be alleged: of which, I believe, he afterwards repented himself; when 'his having been present at the trial' was alleged and urged to him, as an argument for the passing the bill of attainder.

After his charge was read, and an introduction made by Mr. Pym, in which he called him the wicked earl; some member of the house of commons according to their parts assigned, being a lawyer, applied and pressed the evidence with great license and sharpness of language; and, when the earl had made his defence, replied with the same liberty upon whatsoever he said; taking all occasions of bitterly inveighing against his person: which reproachful way of carriage was looked upon with so much approbation, that one of the managers (Mr. Palmer) lost all his credit and interest in them, and never recovered it, for using a decency and modesty in his carriage and language towards him; though the weight of his arguments pressed more upon the earl, than all the noise of the rest.

The trial lasted eighteen days; in which, 'all the hasty or proud expressions, or words, he had uttered at any time since he was first made a privy-counsellor; all the acts of passion or power that he had exercised in Yorkshire, from the time that he was first president there; his engaging himself in projects in Ireland, as the sole making of flax, and selling tobacco in that kingdom; his billeting of soldiers, and exercising of martial law in that kingdom; his extraordinary proceeding against the lord Mount-norris, and the lord chancellor ⟨Loftus⟩; his assuming a power of judicature at the council-table to determine private interest, and matter of inheritance; some rigorous and extrajudicial determinations in cases of plantations; some high discourses at the council-table in Ireland; and some casual and light discourses at his own table, and at public meetings; and lastly, some words spoken in secret council in this kingdom after the dissolution of the last parliament', were urged and pressed against him, to make good the general charge, of 'an endeavour to overthrow the fundamental government of the kingdom, and to introduce an arbitrary power'.

The earl behaved himself with great show of humility and submission; but yet, with such a kind of courage, as would lose no advantage; and in truth, made his defence with all imaginable dexterity; answering this, and evading that, with all possible skill and eloquence; and though he knew not, till he came to the bar, upon what parts of his charge they would proceed against him, or what evidence they would produce, he took very little time to recollect himself, and left nothing unsaid that might make for his own justification.

[The impeachment having failed, the Commons proceeded by bill of attainder. And on 2 April 1641] the bill of attainder in few days passed the house of commons; though some lawyers, of great and known learning, declared, 'that there was no ground or colour in law, to judge him guilty of high treason': and the lord Digby (who had been, from the beginning, of that committee for the prosecution, and had much more prejudice than kindness to the earl) in a very pathetical speech declared, 'that he could not give his consent to the bill: not only, for that he was unsatisfied in the matter of law, but, for that he was more unsatisfied in the matter of fact; those words, upon which the impeachment was principally grounded, being so far from being proved by two witnesses, that he could not acknowledge it to be by one; since he could not admit sir Harry Vane to be a competent witness, who being first examined, denied that the earl spake those words; and upon his second examination, remembered some; and at his third the rest of the words': and thereupon related many circumstances, and made many sharp observations upon what had passed; which none but one of the committee could have done: for which he was presently after questioned in the house; but made his defence so well, and so much to the disadvantage of those who were concerned, that from that time they prosecuted him with an implacable rage and uncharitableness upon all occasions. The bill passed with only fifty-nine dissenting voices, there being near two hundred in the house; and was immediately sent up to the lords, with this addition, 'that the commons would be ready the next day in Westminster-hall, to give their lordships satisfaction in the matter of law, upon what had passed at the trial'.

The earl was then again brought to the bar; the lords sitting as before, in their robes; and the commons as they had done; amongst them, Mr. Saint-John, (whom his majesty had made his solicitor general since the beginning of parliament), from his place, argued for the space of near an hour the matter of law. Of the argument itself I shall say little, it being in print, and in many hands; I shall only remember two notable propositions, which are sufficient characters of the person and the time. Lest what had been said on the earl's behalf, in point of law, and upon the want of proof, should have made any impression in their lordships, he averred, 'That, in that way of bill, private satisfaction to each man's conscience was sufficient, although no evidence had been given in at all': and as to the pressing the law, he said, 'It was true, we give law to hares and deer, because they be beasts of chase; but it was never accounted either cruelty, or foul play, to knock foxes and wolves on the head as they can be found, because they be beasts of prey.' In a word, the law and the humanity were alike; the one being more fallacious, and the other more barbarous, than in any age had been vented in such an auditory.

The same day, as a better argument to the lords speedily to pass the bill, the nine and fifty members of the house of commons, who (as is said before) had dissented from that act, had their names written in pieces of parchment or paper, under this superscription, Straffordians, or enemies to their country; and those papers fixed upon posts, and other of the most visible places about the city; which was as great and destructive a violation of the privileges and freedom of parliament, as can be imagined; yet, being complained of in the house, not the least countenance was given to the complaint, or the least care taken for the discovery.

In the afternoon of the same day (when the conference had been in the painted chamber upon the court of York) Mr. Hyde going to a place called Piccadilly, (which was a fair house for entertainment and gaming, and handsome gravel walks with shade, and where were an upper and lower bowling green, whither very many of the nobility, and gentry of the best quality, resorted, both for exercise and conversation,) as soon as ever he came into the ground, the earl of Bedford came to him; and after some short compliments upon what had passed in the morning, he told him, 'He was glad he was come thither, for there was a friend of his in the lower ground, who needed his counsel.' He then lamented 'the misery the kingdom was like to fall into, by their own violence, and want of temper, in the prosecution of their own happiness'. He said, 'This business concerning the earl of Strafford was a rock, upon which we should all split, and that the passion of the parliament would destroy the kingdom: that the king was ready to do all they could desire, if the life of the earl of Strafford might be spared: that he was satisfied, that he had proceeded with more passion in many things, than he ought to have done, by which he had rendered himself useless to his service for the future; and therefore he was well contented, that he might be made incapable of any employment for the time to come; and that he should be banished, or imprisoned for his life, as they should choose: that if they would take his death upon them, by their own judicatory, he would not interpose any act of his own conscience: but since they had declined that way, and meant to proceed by an act of parliament, to which he himself must be a party, that it could not consist with his conscience, ever to give his royal assent to that act; because, having been present at the whole trial', (as he had been, in a box provided on purpose, *incognito*, though conspicuous enough,) 'and heard all the testimony they had given against him, and he had heard nothing proved, by which he could believe that he was a traitor, either in fact or in intention: and therefore his majesty did most earnestly desire, that the two houses would not bring him a bill to pass, which in conscience he could not, and therefore would not consent'.

The earl said: 'Though he yet was satisfied so well in his own conscience, that he believed he should have no scruple in giving his own vote for the passing it', (for it yet depended in the lords' house,) 'he knew not how the king could be pressed to do an act so contrary to his own conscience; and that, for his part, he took all the pains he could to persuade his friends to decline their violent prosecution, and to be contented with the remedy proposed by the king; which he thought might be rendered so secure, that there need remain no fears of that man's ever appearing again in business: and that how difficult a work soever he found it to be, he should not despair of it, if he could persuade the earl of Essex to comply; but that he found him so obstinate, that he could not in the least degree prevail with him; that he had left his brother, the earl of Hertford, (who was that day made a marquis,) in the lower ground, walking with him, who he knew would do all he could; and he desired Mr. Hyde to walk down into that place, and take his turn, to persuade him to what was reasonable'; which he was very willing to do.

He found the marquis and the earl walking there

together, and no other persons there; and as soon as
they saw him, they both came to him; and the marquis,
after a short salutation, departed, and left the other two
together; which he did purposely. The earl began merrily,
in telling him, 'That he had that morning performed
a service, which he knew he did not intend to do; that
by what he had said against the court of York, he had
revived their indignation against the earl of Strafford;
so that he now hoped, they should proceed in their bill
against him with vigour, (whereas they had slept so long
upon it,) which he said was the effect, of which he was sure
he had no mind to be the cause.' Mr. Hyde confessed, 'he
had indeed no such purpose; and hoped, that somewhat
he had said might put other thoughts into them, to proceed in another manner upon his crimes: that he knew
well, that the cause of their having slept so long upon the
bill, was their disagreement upon the point of treason,
which the longer they thought of, would administer the
more difficulties: but that, if they declined that, they
should all agree, that there were crimes and misdemeanours evidently enough proved, to deserve so severe a
censure, as would determine all the activity hereafter of
the earl of Strafford, that might prove dangerous to the
kingdom; or mischievous to any particular person, to
whom he was not a friend'.

He shook his head, and answered, 'Stone-dead hath no
fellow: that if he were judged guilty in a premunire,
according to the precedents cited by him; or fined in any
other way; and sentenced to be imprisoned during his life;
the king would presently grant him his pardon and his
estate, release all fines, and would likewise give him his
liberty, as soon as he had a mind to receive his service;
which would be as soon as the parliament should be
ended.' And when he was ready to reply to him the earl
told him familiarly, 'that he had been tired that afternoon
upon that argument, and therefore desired him to continue the discourse no longer then; assuring him, he would
be ready to confer with him upon it at any other time'.

And shortly after, Mr. Hyde took another opportunity
to speak freely with him again concerning it, but found

him upon his guard; and though he heard all the other would say, with great patience, yet he did not at all enlarge in his answers, but seemed fixed in his resolution; and when he was pressed, 'how unjustifiable a thing it was, for any man to do anything which his conscience informed him was sinful; that he knew him so well, that if he were not satisfied in his own conscience, of the guilt of the earl of Strafford, the king could never be able to oblige him to give his vote for that bill; and therefore he wondered, how he could urge the king to do an act which he declared to be so much against his conscience, that he neither could, nor would, ever give his royal assent to that bill?' to which he answered more at large, and with some commotion, (as if he were in truth possessed with that opinion himself,) 'That the king was obliged in conscience to conform himself, and his own understanding, to the advice and conscience of his parliament:' which was a doctrine newly resolved by their divines, and of great use to them for the pursuing their future counsels.

[While the Bill was pending rumours of the army plot, the death of the Earl of Bedford, and the king's attempt personally to influence the House of Lords had increased the tension.] The next day great multitudes of people came down to Westminster, and crowded about the house of peers, exclaiming with great outcries, 'that they would have justice'; and publicly reading the names of those who had dissented from that bill in the house of commons, as enemies to their country; and as any lord passed by, called, Justice, justice! and with great rudeness and insolence, pressing upon, and thrusting, those lords whom they suspected not to favour that bill; professing aloud, 'that they would be governed and disposed by the honourable house of commons, and would defend their privileges according to their late protestation'. This unheard of act of insolence and sedition continued so many days, till many lords grew so really apprehensive of having their brains beaten out, that they absented themselves from the house; and others, finding what seconds the house of commons was like to have to compass whatever they desired, changed their minds; and so in an afternoon, when of the fourscore who had been present at the trial, there were only six and forty lords in the house, (the good people still crying at the doors for justice,) they put the bill to the question, and eleven lords only dissenting, it passed that house, and was ready for the king's assent.

The king continued as resolved never to give his consent. The same oratory then attended him at Whitehall, which had prevailed at Westminster; and a rabble of many thousand people besieged that place, crying out, *Justice, justice; that they would have justice*; not without great and insolent threats and expressions, what they would do, if it were not speedily granted. The privy-council was called together, to advise what course was to be taken to suppress these traitorous riots. Instead of considering how to rescue their master's honour and his conscience from this infamous violence and constraint, they press the king to pass the bill of attainder, saying, 'there was no other way to preserve himself and his posterity, than by so doing; and therefore that he ought to be more tender of the safety of the kingdom, than of any one person how innocent soever': not one counsellor interposing his opinion, to support his master's magnanimity and innocence: they who were of that mind, either suppressing their thoughts through fear, upon the new doctrine established then by the new counsellors, 'that no man ought to presume to advise any thing in that place contrary to the sense of both houses'; others sadly believing, the force and violence offered to the king would be, before God and man, a just excuse for whatsoever he should do.

His majesty told them, 'that what was proposed to him to do, was in a diameter contrary to his conscience, and that being so, he was sure they would not persuade him to it, though themselves were never so well satisfied'. To that point, they desired him 'to confer with his bishops, who, they made no question, would better inform his conscience'. The archbishop of York was at hand; who to his argument of conscience, told him, 'that there was a private and a public conscience; that his public conscience as a king might not only dispense with, but oblige him to do that which was against his private conscience as a man: and that the question was not, whether he should save the earl of Strafford, but, whether he should perish with him: that the conscience of a king to preserve his kingdom, the conscience of a husband to preserve his wife, the conscience of a father to preserve his children, (all which were now in danger,) weighed down abundantly all the considerations the conscience of a master or a friend could suggest to him, for the preservation of a friend, or servant'. And by such unprelatical, ignominious arguments, in plain terms advised him, 'even for conscience sake, to pass that act'.

Though this bishop acted his part with more prodigious boldness and impiety, the other of the same function (of whose learning and sincerity the king and the world had greater reverence) did not what might have been expected from their calling or their trust; but at least forbore to fortify and confirm a conscience, upon the courage and piety of which, themselves and their order did absolutely depend.

During these perplexities, the earl of Strafford, taking notice of the straits the king was in, the rage of the people still increasing, (from whence he might expect a certain outrage and ruin, how constant soever the king continued to him; and, it may be, knowing of an undertaking (for such an undertaking there was) by a great person, who had then a command in the Tower, 'that if the king refused to pass the bill, to free the kingdom from the hazard it seemed to be in, he would cause his head to be stricken off in the Tower',) writ a most pathetical letter to the king, full of acknowledgment of his favours; but lively presenting 'the dangers, which threatened himself and his posterity, by his obstinacy in those favours'; and therefore by many arguments conjuring him 'no longer to defer his assent to the bill, that so his death might free the kingdom from the many troubles it apprehended'.

The delivery of this letter being quickly known, new arguments were applied; 'that this free consent of his own clearly absolved the king from any scruple that could remain with him'; and so in the end they extorted from him, to sign a commission to some lords to pass the bill:

which was as valid as if he had signed it himself; though they comforted him even with that circumstance, 'that his own hand was not in it'.

It may easily be said, that the freedom of the parliament, and his own negative voice, being thus barbarously invaded, if his majesty had, instead of passing that act, come to the house and dissolved the parliament; or if he had withdrawn himself from that seditious city, and put himself in the head of his own army; much of the mischief, which hath since happened, would have been prevented. But whoever truly considers the state of affairs at that time; the prevalency of that faction in both houses; the rage and fury of the people; the use that was made by the schismatical preachers (by whom all the orthodox were silenced) of the late protestation in their pulpits; the fears and jealousies they had infused into the minds of many sober men, upon the discourse of the late plot; the consti tution of the council-table, that there was not an honest man durst speak his conscience to the king, for fear of his ruin; and that those, whom he thought most true to him, betrayed him every hour, insomuch as his whispers in his bedchamber were instantly conveyed to those against whom those whispers were; so that he had very few men to whom he could breathe his conscience and complaint, that were not suborned against him, or averse to his opinions: that on the other side, if some expedient were not speedily found out, to allay that frantic rage and combination in the people, there was reason enough to believe, their impious hands would be lifted up against his own person, and (which he much more apprehended) against the person of his royal consort: and lastly, that (besides the difficulty of getting thither except he would have gone alone) he had no ground to be very confident of his own army: I say, whoever contemplates this, will find cause to confess, the part which the king had to act was not only harder than any prince, but than any private gentleman, had been incumbent to; and that it is much easier, upon the accidents and occurrences which have since happened, to determine what was not to have been done, than at that time to have foreseen, by what means to have freed himself from the labyrinth in which he was involved.

All things being thus transacted, to conclude the fate of this great person, he was on the twelfth day of May brought from the Tower of London (where he had been a prisoner near six months) to the scaffold on Tower-hill; where, with a composed, undaunted courage, he told the people, 'he was come thither to satisfy them with his head; but that he much feared, the reformation which was begun in blood would not prove so fortunate to the kingdom, as they expected, and he wished': and after great expressions 'of his devotion to the church of England, and the protestant religion, established by law, and professed in that church; of his loyalty to the king, and affection to the peace and welfare of the kingdom'; with marvellous tranquillity of mind, he delivered his head to the block, where it was severed from his body at a blow: many of the standers by, who had not been over charitable to him in his life, being much affected with the courage and Christianity of his death.

Thus fell the greatest subject in power, and little inferior to any in fortune, that was at that time in any of the three kingdoms; who could well remember the time, when he led those people, who then pursued him to his grave. He was a man of great parts, and extraordinary endowments of nature; not unadorned with some addition of art and learning, though that again was more improved and illustrated by the other; for he had a readiness of conception, and sharpness of expression, which made his learning thought more than in truth it was. His first inclinations and addresses to the court were only to establish his greatness in the country; where he apprehended some acts of power from the old lord Savile, who had been his rival always there, and of late had strengthened himself by being made a privy-counsellor, and officer at court: but his first attempts were so prosperous, that he contented not himself with being secure from his power in the country, but rested not, till he had bereaved him of all power and place in court; and so sent him down, a most abject, disconsolate old man, to his country, where he was to have the superintendency over him too, by getting himself at that time made lord president of the north. These successes, applied to a nature too elate and arrogant of itself, and a quicker progress into the greatest employments and trust, made him more transported with disdain of other men, and more contemning the forms of business, than happily he would have been, if he had met with some interruptions in the beginning, and had passed in a more leisurely gradation to the office of a statesman.

He was, no doubt, of great observation, and a piercing judgment, both into things and persons; but his too good skill in persons made him judge the worse of things: for it was his misfortune to be of a time wherein very few wise men were equally employed with him; and scarce any (but the lord Coventry, whose trust was more confined) whose faculties and abilities were equal to his: so that upon the matter he wholly relied upon himself; and discerning many defects in most men, he too much neglected what they said or did. Of all his passions, his pride was most predominant: which a moderate exercise of ill fortune might have corrected and reformed; and which was by the hand of Heaven strangely punished, by bringing his destruction upon him by two things that he most despised, the people and sir Harry Vane. In a word, the epitaph, which Plutarch records that Sylla wrote for himself, may not be unfitly applied to him; 'that no man did ever pass him, either in doing good to his friends, or in doing mischief to his enemies'; for his acts of both kinds were most exemplary and notorious.

19. *Sir Henry Vane, the younger*

Born 1613; in Massachusetts 1635–7; joint treasurer of the navy 1639–41; member of the Long Parliament and Councillor of State during the Interregnum; executed 1662

SIR HARRY VANE was a man of great natural parts, and of very profound dissimulation, of a quick conception, and very ready, sharp, and weighty expression. He had an unusual aspect, which, though it might naturally proceed both from his father and mother, neither of which were beautiful persons, yet made men think there was somewhat in him of extraordinary; and his whole life made good that imagination. Within a very short time after he returned from his studies in Magdalen college in Oxford, where, though he was under the care of a very worthy tutor, he lived not with great exactness, he spent some little time in France, and more in Geneva, and, after his return into England, contracted a full prejudice and bitterness against the church, both against the form of the government, and the liturgy, which was generally in great reverence, even with many of those who were not friends to the other. In this giddiness, which then much displeased, or seemed to displease, his father, who still appeared highly conformable, and exceedingly sharp against those who were not, he transported himself into New England, a colony, within few years before planted by a mixture of all religions, which disposed the professors to dislike the government of the church; who were qualified by the king's charter to choose their own government and governors, under the obligation, 'that every man should take the oaths of allegiance and supremacy'; which all the first planters did, when they received their charter, before they transported themselves from hence, nor was there in many years after the least scruple amongst them of complying with those obligations; so far men were, in the infancy of their schism, from refusing to take lawful oaths. He was no sooner landed there, but his parts made him quickly taken notice of, and very probably his quality, being the eldest son of a privy-counsellor, might give him some advantage; insomuch that, when the next season came for the election of their magistrates, he was chosen their governor: in which place he had so ill fortune (his working and unquiet fancy raising and infusing a thousand scruples of conscience, which they had not brought over with them, nor heard of before) that he unsatisfied with them, and they with him, he transported himself into England; having sowed such seed of dissension there, as grew up too prosperously, and miserably divided the poor

colony into several factions, and divisions, and persecu-
tions of each other, which still continue to the great prejudice of that plantation: insomuch as some of them, upon
the ground of their first expedition, liberty of conscience,
have withdrawn themselves from their jurisdiction, and
obtained other charters from the king, by which, in other
forms of government, they have enlarged their plantation,
within new limits adjacent to the other. He was no sooner
returned to England, than he seemed to be much reformed
in those extravagancies, and, with his father's approbation
and direction, married a lady of a good family, and by his
father's credit with the earl of Northumberland, who was
high admiral of England, was joined presently and jointly
with sir William Russel in the office of treasurer of the
navy, (a place of great trust and profit,) which he equally
shared with the other, and seemed a man well satisfied
and composed to the government. When his father received the disobligation from the lord Strafford, by his
being created baron of Raby, the house and land of Vane,
(and which title he had promised himself, which was
unluckily cast upon him, purely out of contempt,) they
sucked in all the thoughts of revenge imaginable; and
from thence he betook himself to the friendship of Mr.
Pym, and all other discontented or seditious persons, and
contributed all that intelligence (which will be hereafter
mentioned, as he himself will often be) that designed the
ruin of the earl, and which grafted him in the entire confidence of those who promoted the same; so that nothing
was concealed from him, though it is believed that he
communicated his own thoughts to very few.

[In 1643 Sir Henry was one of the English commissioners sent to Scotland to make an alliance between
Parliament and the Scots. He was successful and both
nations were joined in the so-called Solemn League and
Covenant.] Sir Harry Vane was one of the commissioners,
and therefore the other need not be named, since he was
all in any business where others were joined with him.
(But they were not a little startled, when they found this
message had obliged them to a present expense of a
hundred thousand pounds, before there was any visible

relief given them; and saw themselves involved in new obligations of guilt, and to purposes they really abhorred.⟩

There hath been scarce any thing more wonderful throughout the progress of these distractions, than that this covenant did with such extraordinary expedition pass the two houses, when all the leading persons in those councils were at the same time known to be as great enemies to presbytery, (the establishment whereof was the sole end of this covenant,) as they were to the king or the church. And he who contributed most to it, and who, in truth, was the principal contriver of it, and the man by whom the committee in Scotland was entirely and stupidly governed, sir Harry Vane the younger, was not afterwards more known to abhor the covenant, and the presbyterians, than he was at that very time known to do, and laughed at them then, as much as ever he did afterwards.

He was indeed a man of extraordinary parts, a pleasant wit, a great understanding, which pierced into and discerned the purposes of other men with wonderful sagacity, whilst he had himself *vultum clausum*, that no man could make a guess of what he intended. He was of a temper not to be moved, and of rare dissimulation, and could comply when it was not seasonable to contradict, without losing ground by the condescension; and if he were not superior to Mr. Hambden, he was inferior to no other man, in all mysterious artifices. There need no more be said of his ability, than he was chosen to cozen and deceive a whole nation, which excelled in craft and cunning; which he did with notable pregnancy and dexterity, and prevailed with a people, that could not otherwise be prevailed upon than by advancing their interest, and their faith, to the erecting a power and authority that resolved to persecute presbytery to an extirpation; and very near brought their purpose to pass.

Vane was not a man to be described by any character of religion; in which he had swallowed some of the fancies and extravagancies of every sect or faction; and was become (which cannot be expressed by any other language than was peculiar to that time) *a man above ordinances*, un-

limited and unrestrained by any rules or bounds prescribed to other men, by reason of his perfection. He was
a perfect enthusiast; and, without doubt, did believe
himself inspired; which so far corrupted his reason and
understanding, (which in all matters without the verge
of religion was inferior to that of few men,) that he did
at some time believe, he was the person deputed to reign
over the saints upon earth for a thousand years.

20. *The Law and the Church*

[After the dissolution of the Short Parliament Laud had
kept Convocation in sitting; it had voted 17 canons and
6 subsidies, under the circumstances both measures of
doubtful legality. The anti-Laudian party used this to
agitate for the removal of the bishops from the House of
Lords. The debate on this question saw the only diver-
gence of opinion recorded between Lord Falkland and
his friend.] When he had done, the lord Falkland, who
always sat next to him, (which was so much taken notice
of, that, if they came not into the house together, as usually
they did, every body left the place for him that was absent,)
suddenly stood up, and declared himself 'to be of another
opinion; and that, as he thought the thing itself to be
absolutely necessary for the benefit of the church, which
was in so great danger; so he had never heard, that the
constitution of the kingdom would be violated by the
passing that act; and that he had heard many of the clergy
protest, that they could not acknowledge that they were
represented by the bishops. However we might presume,
that if they could make that appear, that they were a third
estate, that the house of peers (amongst whom they sat,
and had yet their votes) would reject it.' And so, with
some facetiousness, answering some other particulars,
concluded, 'for the passing the act'.

The house was so marvellously delighted, to see the two
inseparable friends divided in so important a point, that
they could not contain from a kind of rejoicing; and the
more, because they saw Mr. Hyde was much surprised

with the contradiction; as in truth he was; having never discovered the least inclination in the other towards such a compliance: and therefore they entertained an imagination and hope that they might work the lord Falkland to a farther concurrence with them. But they quickly found themselves disappointed, and that, as there was not the least interruption of close friendship between the other two; so, when the same argument came again into debate, about six months after, the lord Falkland changed his opinion, and gave them all the opposition he could: nor was he reserved in acknowledging, 'that he had been deceived, and by whom'; and confessed to his friends, with whom he would deal freely, 'that Mr. Hambden had assured him, that if that bill might pass, there would be nothing more attempted to the prejudice of the church': which he thought, as the world then went, would be no ill composition.

In all debates of this nature, where the law, reason and common sense, were in a diameter opposite to what they [the leaders of the opposition] proposed, they suffered those who differed from them in opinion, and purposes, to say what they thought fit in opposition; and then, without vouchsafing to endeavour their satisfaction, called importunately for the question; well knowing that they had a plurality of voices to concur with them, in whatsoever they desired. And for this, without any shame, they found lawyers in their house, who, prostituting the dignity and learning of their profession, to the cheap and vile affectation of popular applause, were not ashamed to aver custom and law for their senseless proposition. But the house of peers was not yet deluded enough, or terrified, (though too many amongst them paid an implicit devotion to the house of commons,) to comply in this unreasonable demand.

And here I cannot but with grief and wonder remember the virulency and animosity expressed upon all occasions, from many of good knowledge in the excellent and wise profession of the common law, towards the church and churchmen; taking all opportunities, uncharitably, to improve mistakes into crimes; and, unreasonably, to transfer

THE LAW AND THE CHURCH

and impute the follies and faults of particular men
(swollen with ambition or corrupted with avarice) to the
malignity of their order and function; and so whet and
sharpen the edge of the law, to wound the church in its
jurisdiction; and at last to cut it up by the roots, and
demolish its foundation. It cannot be denied, that the
peevish and petulant spirits of some clergymen have taken
great pains to irreconcile that profession to them; and
others as unskilfully (finding that in former times, when
the religion of the state was a vital part of its policy,
many churchmen were employed eminently in the civil
government of the kingdom) imputed their wanting those
ornaments their predecessors wore, to the power and prevalency of the lawyers; some principal men whereof, in
all times, they could not but remember as avowed enemies
of the church: and so believed the straitening and con-
fining their profession must naturally extend and enlarge
their own jurisdiction. Thence proceeded their bold and
unwarrantable opposing and protesting against prohibitions, and other proceedings at law, on the behalf of
ecclesiastical courts; and the procuring some orders and
privileges from the king, on the behalf of that faculty;
even with an exclusion of the other; as the archbishop of
Canterbury prevailed with the king to direct, 'that half
the masters of the chancery should be always civil lawyers'; and to declare, 'that no others, of what condition
soever, should serve him as masters of request'. Which was a
great mistake: for, besides the stopping prohibitions was
an envious breach upon the justice of the kingdom; which,
at some time or other, will still be too hard for the strongest
opposers and oppressors of it: I could never yet know,
why the doctors of the civil laws were more of a kin to the
bishops, or the church, than the common lawyers were.
To say that their places were in their disposal, as chan-
cellors, commissaries, and the like; and, therefore, that
their persons were more like to be at their disposal too, at
least, to pay them greater reverence, concludes nothing:
for they had all opportunity enough, and I think equal to
oblige and create a dependence from the other profession;
and I am persuaded, the stewardship to bishops, and of

the lands of the church, which were to be managed by the rules of the common law, were not much inferior in profit to all the chancellorships in England. And for their affection and respect to their patrons, I believe, experience hath now manifested, that though many of the common lawyers have much indiscretion, injustice, and malice to repent of towards the church, the professors of the civil law have not been less active, to their skill and power, in the unnatural destruction of their mother; and then, where their policy may consist with justice, it will be no ill measure in making friendship, to look into the power of doing hurt and doing good, as well as into the faculty of judging; and it was apparent, that the civil law in this kingdom could neither help or hurt the church in any exigent, it being neither of reputation enough to advance it, or power to oppress it; whereas the professors of the other had always, by their interests, experience, abilities, and reputation, so great an influence upon the civil state, upon court and country, that they were notable friends or enemies; and then the dependence of the church was entirely upon that law, all their inheritance and estates (except their minute tithes) being only determinable by those rules; and by which they have seldom received eminent injustice. And truly, I have never yet spoken with one clergyman, who hath had the experience of both litigations, that hath not ingenuously confessed, 'he had rather, in the respect of his trouble, charge, and satisfaction to his understanding, have three suits depending in Westminster-hall, than one in the arches, or any ecclesiastical court'.

The particulars above mentioned were, I confess, to vulgar minds, great provocations and temptations to revenge; and, therefore, I do not at all wonder, that, in the great herd of the common lawyers, many pragmatical spirits, whose thoughts and observations have been contracted to the narrow limits of the few books of that profession, or within the narrower circle of the bar-oratory, should side with the others, in the womanish art of inveighing against persons, when they should be reforming things: and that some, by degrees, having found the benefit of being of that opinion, (for we all remember, when papist and puritan lawyers got more money than their neighbours, for the opinions they had; not which they delivered,) grew, at last, to have fits of conscience in earnest; and to believe, that a parity in the church was necessary to religion, and not like to produce a parity in the state; the suspicion of which would quickly have wrought upon their divinity.

But, that learned and unbiassed (I mean unprovoked) men, in that science, who knew the frame and constitution of the kingdom, and that the bishops were no less the representative body of the clergy, than the house of commons was of the people; and, consequently, that the depriving them of voice in parliament, was a violence, and removing landmarks, and not a shaking (which might settle again) but dissolving foundations; which must leave the building unsafe for habitation: ⟨that such men⟩ who knew the ecclesiastical and civil state was so wrought and interwoven together, and, in truth, so incorporated in each other, that like Hippocrates' twins, they cannot but laugh and cry together; and that the professors of the law were never at so great a height, as even in this time that they so unjustly envied the greatness of the church: and, lastly, ⟨that they,⟩ who might well know, that the great and unwieldy body of the clergy, consisting of such different tempers, humours, inclinations, and abilities, and which inevitably will have so strong an influence upon the natures and affections of the people, could ever be regulated and governed by any magistrates, but of themselves; nor by any rules, but such power which the bishops exercised; whom (besides all arguments of piety, and submission to antiquity) experience of that blessed time since the reformation, not to be paralleled in any nation under heaven, declared to be the most happy managers of that power, whatsoever rankness and excrescence had proceeded from some branches: I say, that these knowing and discerning men (for such I must confess there have been) should believe it possible for them to flourish, and that the law itself would have the same respect and veneration from the people, when the well disposed fabric of the church should be rent asunder (which, without their activity and skill in confusion, could never have been compassed,) hath been to me an instance of the Divine anger against the pride of both, in suffering them to be the fatal engines to break one another: which could very hardly have been oppressed by any other strength or power than their own.

And I cannot but say, to the professors of that great and admirable mystery, the law, (upon which no man looks with more affection, reverence, and submission,) who seem now, by the fury and iniquity of the time, to stand upon the ground they have won, and to be masters of the field; and, it may be, wear some of the trophies and spoils they have ravished from the oppressed; that they have yet sharpened weapons for others to wound themselves; and that their own eloquence shall be applied to their own destruction. And, therefore, if they have either piety to repent and redeem the ill that they have wrought, or policy to preserve their own condition from contempt, and themselves from being slaves to the most abject of the people, they will wind up the church and the law into one bottom; and, by a firm combination and steady pursuit, endeavour to fix both to the same pinnacle, from whence they have been so violently ravished.

The bill for the taking away the votes of bishops out of the house of peers, which was called a bill for taking away all temporal jurisdiction from those in holy orders, was no sooner passed the house of peers, than the king was earnestly desired 'to give his royal assent to it'. The king returned, 'that it was a matter of great concernment; and therefore he would take time to advise, and would return an answer in convenient time'. But this delay pleased not their appetite; they could not attempt their perfect reformation in church and state, till those votes were utterly abolished; therefore they sent the same day again to the king, who was yet at Windsor, and gave him reasons to persuade him 'immediately to consent to it; one of which was the grievances the subjects suffered by their exercising of temporal jurisdiction, and their making a party in the lords' house: a second, the great content of all sorts by the happy conjunction of both houses in their absence: and a third, that the passing of that bill would be a comfortable pledge of his majesty's gracious assent to the future remedies of those evils, which were to be presented to him, this once being passed'.

Reasons sufficient to have converted him, if he had the least inclination or propensity to have concurred with them. For it was, upon the matter, to persuade him to join with them in this, because, that being done, he should be able to deny them nothing.

However those of greatest trust about the king, and who were very faithful to his service, though in this particular exceedingly deceived in their judgments, and not sufficiently acquainted with the constitution of the kingdom, persuaded him 'that the passing this bill was the only way to preserve the church, there being so united a combination in this particular, that he would not be able to withstand it. Whereas, by the passing this bill, so many persons in both houses would be fully satisfied, that they would join in no further alteration: but, on the other hand, if they were crossed in this, they would violently endeavour an extirpation of bishops, and a demolishing of the whole fabric of the church.'

They alleged 'that he was, upon the matter, deprived of their votes already, they being not suffered to come to the house, and the major part in prison under an accusation of high treason, of which there was not like to be any reformation, till these present distempers were composed; and then that by his power, and the memory of the indirect means that had been used against them, it would be easier to bring them in again, than to keep them in now.' They told him, 'there were two matters of great importance pressed upon him for his royal assent, but they were not of equal consequence and concernment to his sovereign power; the first, that bill for the bishops' votes; the other, the whole militia of the kingdom, the granting of which would absolutely divest him of all regal power; that he would not be able to deny both; but by granting the former, in which he parted with no matter of moment, he would, it may be, not be pressed in the second; or if he were, that as he could not have a more popular quarrel to take up arms, than to defend himself, and preserve that power in his hands, which the law had vested in him, and without which he could not be a king; so he could not have a more unpopular argument for that contention, than the preservation of the bishops in the house of peers, which few men thought essential, and most men believed prejudicial, to the peace and happiness of the kingdom.'

These arguments, though used by men whom he most trusted, and whom he knew to have opposed that bill in its passage, and to be cordially friends to the church of England in discipline and doctrine, prevailed not so much with his majesty, as the persuasions of the queen; who was not only persuaded to think those reasons valid, and that indeed the church could be only that way preserved, (and there are that believe that infusion to have been made in her by her own priests, by instructions from France, and for reasons of state in that kingdom,) but that her own safety very much depended upon the king's consent to that bill; and that, if he should refuse it, her journey into Holland would be crossed by the parliament, and possibly her person in danger either by the tumults, which might easily be brought to Windsor from Westminster, or by the insurrection of the counties in her passage from thence to Dover, where she intended to take shipping. Whereas by her intercession with the king to do it, she would lay a most seasonable and popular obligation upon the whole nation, and leave a pleasant odour of her grace and favour to the people behind her, which would prove much to her advantage in her absence; and she should have the thanks for that act, as acquired by her goodness, which otherwise would be extorted from the king, when she was gone.

These insinuations and discourses so far satisfied the queen, and she the king, that, contrary to his most positive resolution, the king consented, and sent a commission for the enacting both that bill, and the other for pressing; which was done accordingly, to the great triumph of the boutefeus, the king sending the same day that he passed those bills, which was the fourteenth of February, a message to both houses; 'That he was assured his having passed those two bills, being of so great importance, so suddenly, would serve to assure his parliament, that he desired nothing more than the satisfaction of his kingdom.' For Ireland, he said, 'as he had concurred in all propositions made for that service by his parliament, so he was resolved to leave nothing undone for their relief, which should fall within his possible power, nor would refuse to venture his own person in that war, if the parliament should think it convenient, for the reduction of that miserable kingdom'.

The passing that bill for taking away the bishops' votes, exceedingly weakened the king's party; not only as it perpetually swept away so considerable a number out of the house of peers, which were constantly devoted to him; but as it made impression on others, whose minds were in suspense, and shaken, as when foundations are dissolved. Besides, they that were best acquainted with the king's nature, opinions, and resolutions, had reason to believe, that no exigence could have wrought upon him to have consented to so antimonarchical an act; and therefore never after retained any confidence, that he would deny what was importunately asked; and so, either absolutely withdrew themselves from those consultations, thereby avoiding the envy, and the danger of opposing them, or quietly suffered themselves to be carried by the stream, and consent to any thing that was boldly and lustily attempted.

And then it was so far from dividing the other party, that I do not remember one man, who furiously insisted on, indeed heartily wished, the passing of that bill, that ever deserted them, till the kingdom was in a flame: but, on the contrary, very many, who cordially and constantly opposed that act, as friends rather to monarchy than religion, after that bill, never considered or resisted any attempt, or further alteration, in the church, looking upon the bishops as useless to sovereignty, and so not of importance enough to defend by the sword. And I have heard the same men, who urged before, 'that their places in that house had no relation to the discipline of the church, and their spiritual jurisdiction, and therefore ought to be sacrificed to the preservation of the other, upon which the peace and unity of religion so much depended', since argue, 'that since their power in that house, which was a good outwork to defend the king's from invasion, was taken away, any other form of government would be equally advantageous to his majesty; and therefore, that he ought not to insist on it, with the least inconvenience to his condition'.

That which was above, or equal to all this, ⟨was,⟩ that, by his majesty's enacting those two bills, he had, upon the matter, approved the circumstances of their passage, which had been by direct violence, and force of arms; in which case, he ought not to have confirmed the most politic, or the most pious constitutions: *Male posita est lex, quae tumultuarie posita est*, was one of those positions of Aristotle, which hath never been since contradicted; and was an advantage, that, being well managed, and stoutly insisted upon, would, in spite of all their machinations, which were not yet firmly and solidly formed, have brought them to a temper of being treated with. But I have some cause to believe, that even this argument, which was answerable for the rejecting of that bill, was applied for the confirming it; and an opinion that the violence and force, used in procuring it, rendered it absolutely invalid, and void, made the confirmation of it less considered, as not being of strength to make that act good, which was in itself null. And I doubt this logic had an influence upon other acts of no less moment than these: but it was an erroneous and unskilful suggestion; for an act of parliament, what circumstances soever concurred in the contriving and framing it, will be always of too great reputation to be avoided, or to be declared void, by the sole authority of any private persons, ⟨or⟩ the single power of the king himself. And though the wisdom, sobriety, and power, of a future parliament, if God shall ever bless the kingdom with another regularly constituted, may find cause to declare this or that act of parliament void; yet there will be the same temper requisite to such a declaration, as would serve to repeal it. And it may be then, many men, who abhorred the thing when it was done, for the manner of doing it, will be of the civilian's opinion, *fieri non debuit, factum valet*; and never consent to the altering of that, which they would never have consented to the establishing: neither will that single precedent of the judges in the case of king Henry the Seventh, when they declared the act of attainder to be void by the accession of the crown, (though if he had in truth been the person, upon whom the crown had lineally and rightfully descended, it was good law,) find, or make, the judges of another age parallel to them, till the king hath as strong a sword in his hand, and the people as much at his devotion and disposal; and then the making, and declaring law, will be of equal facility, though, it may be, not of equal justice. How much soever the king's friends were, for the reasons aforesaid, dejected upon the passing those two acts, it is certain, they who thought they got whatever he lost, were mightily exalted, and thought themselves now superior to any opposition: and what returns of duty and acknowledgment they made to the king for that grace and favour, is to be remembered in the next place.

To confirm and encourage the factious and schismatical party of the kingdom, which thought the pace towards the reformation was not brisk and furious enough, and was with great difficulty contained in so slow a march, they had, a little before, published a declaration:

'That they intended a due and necessary reformation of the government and liturgy of the church, and to take away nothing in the one or the other, but what should be evil, and justly offensive, or at least unnecessary and burdensome: and, for the better effecting thereof, speedily to have consultation with godly and learned divines: and, because that would never of itself attain the end sought therein, they would therefore use their utmost endeavours to establish learned and preaching ministers, with a good and sufficient maintenance throughout the whole kingdom, wherein many dark corners were miserably destitute of the means of salvation, and many poor ministers wanted necessary provision.'

This declaration, printed and appointed to be published by the sheriffs in their several counties, in all the market-towns within the kingdom of England and dominion of Wales, was not more intended to the heartening of those who were impatient for a reformation, (who in truth had so implicit a faith in their leaders, that they expected another manner of reformation than was publicly promised,) than to the lulling those asleep, who began to be awake with the apprehension of that confusion, they apprehended from the practice and license, they saw practised against the received government, and doctrine of the church; and to be persuaded, that it was time to oppose that current. And in this project they were not disappointed: for though this warily worded declaration was evidence enough to wise men, what they intended, and logically comprehended, an alteration as great as hath been since attempted and made; yet to lazy and quiet men, who could not discern consequences, and were not willing to antedate their miseries, by suspecting worse was to come than they felt, or saw in their view, their fears were much abated, and the intentions of the parliament seemed not so bad as they had been told by some that they were: and as this very declaration of a due reformation to be made of the government of the church, and the liturgy, would, a year before, have given great umbrage and scandal to the people, when, generally, there was a due submission to the government, and a singular reverence of the liturgy of the church of England; so now, when there was a general fear and apprehension inculcated into them, of a purpose utterly to subvert the government, and utterly to abolish the liturgy, they thought the taking away nothing in the one or the other, but what should be evil, and justly offensive, or, at least, unnecessary and burdensome, was an easy composition; and so, by degrees, they suffered themselves to be still prevailed on towards ends they extremely abhorred; and what at first seemed profane and impious to them, in a little time appeared only inconvenient; and what, in the beginning, they thought matter of conscience and religion, shortly after they looked upon as somewhat rather to be wished than positively insisted on; and consequently not to be laid in the balance with the public peace, which they could imagine to be endangered by opposing the sense that then prevailed; and so, by undervaluing many particulars, (which they truly esteemed,) as rather to be consented to, than that the general should suffer, they brought, or suffered the public to be brought to all the sufferings it since underwent.

And now they shewed what consultation they meant to have with godly and learned divines, and what reformation they intended, by appointing the knights and burgesses to bring in the names of such divines for the several counties, as they thought fit to constitute an assembly for the framing a new model for the government of the church, which was done accordingly; those who were true sons of the church, not so much as endeavouring the nomination of sober and learned men, abhorring such a reformation, as begun with the invasion and suppression of the church's rights in calling a synod, as well known as Magna Charta: and if any well affected member, not enough considering the scandal and the consequences of that violation, did name an orthodox and well reputed divine, to assist in that assembly, it was argument enough against him, that he was nominated by a person in whom they had no confidence; and they only had reputation enough to commend to this consultation, who were known to desire the utter demolishing of the whole fabric of the church: so that of about one hundred and twenty, of which that assembly was to consist, (though, by the recommendation of two or three members of the commons, whom they were not willing to displease, and by the authority of the lords, who added a small number to those named by the house of commons, a few reverend and worthy men were inserted; yet of the whole number) they were not above twenty, who were not declared and avowed enemies to the doctrine or discipline of the church of England; many of them infamous in their lives and conversations; and most of them of very mean parts in learning, if not of scandalous ignorance; and of no other reputation, than of malice to the church of England; so that that convention hath not since produced any thing, that might not then reasonably have been expected from it.

But that which gave greatest power and strength to

their growing faction, was the severity they used against all those, of what quality or degree soever, who opposed their counsels and proceedings. If any lord, who had any place of honour or trust from the king, concurred not with them, they made an inquisition into the whole passages of his life; and if they could find no fault, or no folly (for any levity, or indiscretion, served for a charge) to reproach him with, it was enough, 'that they could not confide in him': so they threatened the earl of Portland, who with extraordinary vivacity crossed their consultations, 'that they would remove him from his charge and government of the Isle of Wight', (which, at last, they did *de facto*, by committing him to prison, without so much as assigning a cause,) and to that purpose objected all the acts of good fellowship; all the waste of powder, and all the waste of wine, in the drinking of healths; and other acts of jollity, whenever he had been at his government, from the first hour of his entering upon it: so that the least inconvenience a man in their disfavour was to expect, was to have his name and reputation used, for two or three hours, in the house of commons, with what license and virulency they pleased. None were persecuted with more rigour than the clergy; whereof whosoever publicly, or privately, censured their actions, or suspected their intentions, was either committed to prison, or compelled to a chargeable and long attendance, as inconvenient as imprisonment. And this measure of proceeding was equally, if not with more animosity, applied to those, who, in former times, had been looked upon by that party with most reverence. On the contrary, whoever concurred, voted, and sided with them, in their extravagant conclusions, let the infamy of his former life, or present practice, be what it would, his injustice and oppression never so scandalous and notorious, he was received, countenanced, and protected, with marvellous demonstrations of affection: so that, between those that loved them, and those that feared them, those that did not love the church, and those that did not love some churchmen; those whom the court had oppressed, and those who had helped the court to oppress others; those who feared their power, and those who feared their justice; their party was grown over the king-dom, but especially in the city, justly formidable.

In the mean time, the king omitted no opportunity to provide against the storm he saw was coming; and, though he might not yet own the apprehension of that danger he really found himself in, he neglected not the provision of what he thought most necessary for his defence; he caused all his declarations, messages, and answers, to be industriously communicated throughout his dominions; of which he found good effects; and, by their reception, discovered that the people universally were not so irre-coverably poisoned, as he before had cause to fear. [Most of the king's declarations were drawn up by Hyde; the first being the answer to the Grand Remonstrance, Decem-ber 1641. It was sometimes objected 'that the style was not answerable to the provocation, nor princely enough for such a contest'. But, Clarendon answers] though it might be presumed, that the exorbitancy of the parlia-ment might be very offensive to some sober and discerning men, yet his majesty had no reason to presume of their eminent and vehement zeal on his behalf, since he saw all those (two or three only excepted) from whom he might challenge the duty, and faith of servants *usque ad aras*, and for whose sake he had undergone many diffi-culties, either totally aliened from his service, and engaged against him, or, like men in a trance, unapplicable to it: he will conclude that it concerned his majesty, by all gentleness and condescension, to undeceive and recover men to their sobriety and understanding, before he could hope to make them apprehensive of their own duty, or the reverence that was due to him; and therefore, that he was to descend to all possible arts and means to that purpose, it being very evident, that men would no sooner discern his princely justice and clemency, than they must be sensible of the indignities which were offered to him, and incensed against those who were the authors of them.

And the truth is, (which I speak knowingly,) at that time, the king's resolution was to shelter himself wholly under the law; to grant any thing, that by the law he was obliged to grant; and to deny what by the law was in his own power, and which he found inconvenient to consent to; and to oppose and punish any extravagant attempt by the force and power of the law, presuming that the king and the law together would have been strong enough for any encounter that could happen; and that the law was so sensible a thing, that the people would easily perceive who endeavoured to preserve, and who to suppress it, and dispose themselves accordingly.

21. *John Hampden*

Born *1594; died 1643*

MR. HAMBDEN was a man of much greater cunning, and it may be of the most discerning spirit, and of the greatest address and insinuation to bring any thing to pass which he desired, of any man of that time, and who laid the design deepest. He was a gentleman of a good extraction, and a fair fortune, who, from a life of great pleasure and license, had on a sudden retired to extraordinary sobriety and strictness, and yet retained his usual cheerfulness and affability; which, together with the opinion of his wisdom and justice, and the courage he had shewed in opposing the ship-money, raised his reputation to a very great height, not only in Buckinghamshire, where he lived, but generally throughout the kingdom. He was not a man of many words, and rarely begun the discourse, or made the first entrance upon any business that was assumed; but a very weighty speaker, and after he had heard a full debate, and observed how the house was like to be inclined, took up the argument, and shortly, and clearly, and craftily, so stated it, that he commonly conducted it to the conclusion he desired; and if he found he could not do that, he never was without the dexterity to divert the debate to another time, and to prevent the determining any thing in the negative, which might prove inconvenient in the future. He made so great a show of civility, and modesty, and humility, and always of mistrusting his own judgment, and of esteeming his with whom he conferred for the present, that he seemed to have no opinions or resolutions, but such as he contracted from the information and instruction he received upon the discourses of others, whom he had a wonderful art of governing, and leading into his principles and inclinations, whilst they believed that he wholly depended upon their counsel and advice. No man had ever a greater power over himself, or was less the man that he seemed to be, which shortly after appeared to every body, when he cared less to keep on the mask. [Prince Rupert had been victorious at Chalgrove Field, 1643.] But that which would have been looked upon as a considerable recompence for a defeat, could not but be thought a glorious crown of victory, which was the death of Mr. Hambden; who, being shot into the shoulder with a brace of bullets, which brake the bone, within three weeks after died with extraordinary pain; to as great a consternation of all that party, as if their whole army had been defeated, or cut off.

Many men observed (as upon signal turns of great affairs, as this was, such observations are frequently made) that the field in which the late skirmish was, and upon which Mr. Hambden received his death's wound, Chalgrave field, was the same place in which he had first executed the ordinance of the militia, and engaged that county, in which his reputation was very great, in this rebellion: and it was confessed by the prisoners that were taken that day, and acknowledged by all, that upon the alarm that morning, after their quarters were beaten up, he was exceedingly solicitous to draw forces together to pursue the enemy; and, being himself a colonel of foot, put himself among those horse as a volunteer, who were first ready; and that when the prince made a stand, all the officers were of opinion to stay till their body came up, and he alone (being second to none but the general himself in the observance and application of all men) persuaded, and prevailed with them to advance, so violently did his fate carry him, to pay the mulct in the place where he had committed the transgression, about a year before.

He was a gentleman of good family in Buckinghamshire, and born to a fair fortune, and of a most civil and affable deportment. In his entrance into the world, he indulged to himself all the license in sports and exercises, and company, which was used by men of the most jolly conversation. Afterwards, he retired to a more reserved and melancholy society, yet preserving his own natural cheerfulness and vivacity, and above all, a flowing courtesy to all men; though they who conversed nearly with him, found him growing into a dislike of the ecclesiastical government of the church, yet most believed it rather a dislike of some churchmen, and of some introducements of theirs, which he apprehended might disquiet the public peace. He was rather of reputation in his own country, than of public discourse, or fame in the kingdom, before the business of ship-money; but then he grew the argument of all tongues, every man inquiring who and what he was, that durst, at his own charge, support the liberty and property of the kingdom, and rescue his country, as he thought, from being made a prey to the court. His carriage, throughout this agitation, was with that rare temper and modesty, that they who watched him narrowly to find some advantage against his person, to make him less resolute in his cause, were compelled to give him a just testimony. And the judgment that was given against him infinitely more advanced him, than the service for which it was given. When this parliament begun, (being returned knight of the shire for the county, where he lived,) the eyes of all men were fixed on him, as their *patriae pater*, and the pilot that must steer the vessel through the tempests and rocks which threatened it. And I am persuaded, his power and interest, at that time, was greater to do good or hurt, than any man's in the kingdom, or than any man of his rank hath had in any time: for his reputation of honesty was universal, and his affections seemed so publicly guided, that no corrupt or private ends could bias them.

He was of that rare affability and temper in debate, and of that seeming humility and submission of judgment, as if he brought no opinion with him, but a desire of information and instruction; yet he had so subtle a way of interrogating, and, under the notion of doubts, insinuating his objections, that he left his opinions with those from whom he pretended to learn and receive them. And even with them who were able to preserve themselves from his infusions, and discerned those opinions to be fixed in him, with which they could not comply, he always left the character of an ingenious and conscientious person. He was indeed a very wise man, and of great parts, and possessed with the most absolute spirit of popularity, that is, the most absolute faculties to govern the people, of any man I ever knew. For the first year of the parliament, he seemed rather to moderate and soften the violent and distempered humours, than to inflame them. But wise and dispassioned men plainly discerned, that that moderation proceeded from prudence, and observation that the season was not ripe, rather than that he approved of the moderation; and that he begat many opinions and motions, the education whereof he committed to other men; so far disguising his own designs, that he seemed seldom to wish more than was concluded: and in many gross conclusions, which would hereafter contribute to designs not yet set on foot, when he found them sufficiently backed by majority of voices, he would withdraw himself before the question, that he might seem not to consent to so much visible unreasonableness; which produced as great a doubt in some, as it did approbation in others, of his integrity. What combination soever had been originally with the Scots for the invasion of England, and what farther was entered into afterwards in favour of them, and to advance any alteration ⟨of the government⟩ in parliament, no man doubts was at least with the privity of this gentleman.

After he was among those members accused by the king of high treason, he was much altered; his nature and carriage seeming much fiercer than it did before. And without question, when he first drew his sword, he threw away the scabbard, for he passionately opposed the overture made by the king for a treaty from Nottingham, and as eminently, any expedients that might have produced any accommodations in this that was at Oxford; and was principally relied on, to prevent any infusions which might be made into the earl of Essex towards peace, or to render them ineffectual, if they were made; and was indeed much

more relied on by that party, than the general himself.
In the first entrance into the troubles, he undertook the
command of a regiment of foot, and performed the duty
of a colonel, on all occasions, most punctually. He was
very temperate in diet, and a supreme governor over all
his passions and affections, and had thereby a great power
over other men's. He was of an industry and vigilance not
to be tired out, or wearied by the most laborious; and of
parts not to be imposed upon by the most subtle or sharp;
and of a personal courage equal to his best parts; so that
he was an enemy not to be wished wherever he might have
been made a friend; and as much to be apprehended where
he was so, as any man could deserve to be. And therefore
his death was no less congratulated on the one party, than
it was condoled in the other. In a word, what was said of
Cinna might well be applied to him; 'he had a head to
contrive, and a tongue to persuade, and a hand to execute,
any mischief'. His death therefore seemed to be a great
deliverance to the nation.

22. *Oliver St. John and the Question of the Militia*

*Born 1598?; in Tower 1629; M.P. 1640; Solicitor-
General 1641–3; Chief Justice of Common Pleas
1648; died abroad 1673*

MR. SAINT-JOHN who was in a firm and entire conjunction with the other two, was a lawyer of Lincoln's
Inn, known to be of parts and industry, but not taken
notice of for practice in Westminster-hall, till he argued
at the exchequer-chamber the case of ship-money on the
behalf of Mr. Hambden; which gave him much reputation, and called him into all courts, and to all causes,
where the king's prerogative was most contested. He was a
man reserved, and of a dark and clouded countenance,
very proud, and conversing with very few, and those men
of his own humour and inclinations. He had been questioned, committed, and brought into the star-chamber,
many years before, with other persons of great name and
reputation, (which first brought his name upon the stage,)

for communicating some paper among themselves, which some men had a mind at that time to have extended to a design of sedition: but it being quickly evident that the prosecution would not be attended with success, they were all shortly after discharged; but he never forgave the court the first assault, and contracted an implacable displeasure against the church purely from the company he kept. He was of an intimate trust with the earl of Bedford, to whom he was allied, (being a natural son of the house of Bolingbroke,) and by him brought into all matters where himself was to be concerned.

[In 1641 several of the leaders of the opposition were to be taken into the king's service.] And, that this might be the better done, the earl of Bedford prevailed with the king, upon the removes mentioned before, to make Oliver Saint-John (who hath been often, and will be oftener mentioned in this discourse) his solicitor general; which his majesty readily consented to; hoping that, being a gentleman of an honourable extraction, (if he had been legitimate,) he would have been very useful in the present exigence to support his service in the house of commons, where his authority was then great; at least, that he would be ashamed ever to appear in any thing that might prove prejudicial to the crown. And he became immediately possessed of that office, of great trust; and was so well qualified for it, by his fast and rooted malignity against the government, that he lost no credit with his party, out of any apprehension or jealousy that he would change his side: and he made good their confidence; not in the least degree abating his malignant spirit, or dissembling it; but with the same obstinacy opposed every thing which might advance the king's service, when he was his solicitor, as ever he had done before.

[This became very clear after the king's return to Whitehall, winter 1641, in the debate on how to raise men for service against the Irish rebels.] However, for all this, and the better, it may be, for all this, the king, upon his arrival at Whitehall, found both his houses of parliament of a much better temper than they had been; many having great indignation to see his majesty so ill treated by his own servants, and those who were most obliged to his bounty and magnificence; and likewise to discern how much ambition and private interest was covered under public pretences. They who were in truth zealous for the preservation of the law, the religion, and true interest of the nation, were solicitous to preserve the king's honour from any indignity, and his regal power from violation; and so always opposed those who trenched upon either, and who could compass their ends by no other means than by trampling upon both. So that, in truth, that which was called the king's party, in both houses, was made up of persons who were strangers, or without any obligation, to the court; of the best fortunes, and the best reputation, in their several counties where they were known; as having always appeared very zealous in the maintenance of their just rights, and opposed, as much as in them lay, all illegal and grievous impositions: whilst his own privy-council, (two or three only excepted,) and much the greater number of all his own servants, either publicly opposed, or privately betrayed him; and so much the more virulently abhorred all those who now appeared to carry on his service, because they presumed to undertake, at least to endeavour, (for they undertook nothing, nor looked for any thanks for their labour,) to do that which they ought to have done; and so they were upon this disadvantage, that whenever they pressed any thing in the house which seemed immediately to advance the king's power and authority, some of the king's council, or his servants, most opposed it, under the notion 'of being prejudicial to the king's interest': whilst they who had used to govern and impose upon the house, made show of being more modest, and yet were more silent ⟨insolent⟩; and endeavoured, by setting new counsels on foot, to entangle, and engage, and indeed to overreach the house; by cozening them into opinions which might hereafter be applicable to their ends, rather than to pursue their old designs, in hope to obtain in the end a success by their authority. The night of the remonstrance had humbled them in that point: and from that time, they rather contrived ways to silence those who opposed them, by traducing them abroad, and taking any advantage against them in the house, for any expressions they used in debate which might be misinterpreted; and so calling them to the bar, or committing them to the Tower: which did in truth strike such terror into the minds of many, that they forbore to come to the house, rather than expose themselves to many uneasinesses there.

There was at this time, or thereabout, a debate started in the house, as if by mere chance, which produced many inconveniences after; and, if there had not been too many concurrent causes, might be thought the sole cause and ground of all the mischief which ensued. Upon some report, or discourse of some accident, which had happened upon or in the disbanding the late army, an obscure member moved, 'That the house would enter upon the consideration, whether the militia of the kingdom was so settled by law, that a sudden force, or army, could be drawn together, for the defence of the kingdom if it should be invaded, or to suppress an insurrection or rebellion, if it should be attempted.'

The house kept a long silence after the motion, the newness of it amusing most men, and few in truth understanding the meaning of it; until one and another of the members, who were least taken notice of, seeming to be moved by the weight of what had been said, enlarged upon the same argument: and in the end it was proposed, 'That a committee might be appointed, to consider of the present state of the militia, and the power of it; and to prepare such a bill for the settling it, as might provide for the public peace, and for the suppressing any foreign enemy, or domestic insurrection.'

And hereupon they were inclined to nominate a committee, to prepare such a bill as should be thought necessary: upon which Mr. Hyde spake against the making any such committee; said, 'There could be no doubt, that the power of the militia resided in the king, in whom the right of making war and peace was invested; that there had never yet appeared any defect of power, by which the kingdom had been in danger, and we might reasonably expect the same security for the future.' With which the house seemed well satisfied and composed, and inclined to resume some other debate, until Saint-John, who was then the king's solicitor, and the only man in the house of his learned council, stood up, and said, 'He could not suffer that debate, in which there had been so many weighty particularities mentioned, to be discontinued without some resolution: that he would be very glad there were that power in the king, (whose rights he was bound to defend,) as the gentleman who spake last seemed to imagine; which, for his part, he knew there was not; that the question was not about taking any power from the king, which was vested in him, (which was his duty always to oppose,) but to inquire, whether there be such a power in him, or any where else, as is necessary for the preservation of the king and the people, in many cases that may fall out; and if there be not, then to supply him with that power and authority;' and he said 'he did take upon him with confidence to say, that there was a defect of such power and authority': he put them in mind, 'how that power had been executed in the age in which we live; that the crown had granted commissions to great men, to be lord lieutenants of counties; and they to gentlemen of quality, to be their deputy lieutenants; and to colonels, and other officers, to conduct and list soldiers; and then he, wished them to consider, what votes they had passed, of the illegality of all those commissions, and the unjustifiableness of all the proceedings which had ⟨been⟩ by virtue of those commissions; so that let the occasion or necessity be what it would, he did presume, no man would hereafter execute any such commission; and if there were any men so hardy, that nobody would obey them; and therefore desired them to consider, whether there be not a defect of power, and whether it ought not to be supplied'.

It was now evident enough, that the debate had not begun by chance, but had been fully deliberated; and what use they would make, upon occasions, of those volumes of votes, they had often poured out upon all accidental debates; and no man durst take upon him to answer all that had been alleged, by saying, all those votes were of no validity; and that the king's right was, and would be, judged the same it had been before, notwithstanding those votes; which is very true: but this being urged by the king's own solicitor, they appointed him 'to bring in and prepare such a bill as he thought necessary'; few men imagining that such a sworn officer would not be very careful and tender of all his master's prerogatives, which he was expressly sworn to defend.

Within few days after, he brought in a very short bill, in which was mentioned by way of preface, 'That the power over the militia of the kingdom was not settled in any such manner, that the security of the kingdom was provided for, in case of invasion or insurrection, or such like accidents'; and then an enacting clause, 'That henceforward the militia, and all the power thereof, should be vested in—&c.' and then a large blank left for inserting names; and afterwards, the 'absolute authority to execute —&c.' The ill meaning whereof was easily understood; and with some warmth pressed, 'That by this bill all the power would be taken out of the crown, and put into the hands of commissioners.' To which the solicitor made answer, 'That the bill took no power from any body who had it, but was provided to give power where it was not; nor was there mention of any commissioners; but a blank was therefore left, that the house might fill it up as they thought fit, and put the power into such hands as they thought proper; which, for aught he knew, might be the king's; and he hoped it would be so.'

And with this answer the bill was received, notwithstanding all opposition, and read; all those persons who had formerly been deputy lieutenants, and lay under the terror of that vote, presuming, that this settlement would provide for the indemnity of all that had passed before; and the rest, who might still be exposed to the same hazards, if they should be required to act upon the like occasions, concurring in the desire, that somewhat might be done for a general security; and they who had contrived it, were well enough contented that it was once read; not desiring to prosecute it, till some more favourable conjuncture should be offered: and so it rested.

23. *Duties, Rights, and Tribulations of a Privy Councillor*

[In order to facilitate negotiations with the Scottish commissioners in 1640.] Hereupon in one day were sworn privy-counsellors, much to the public joy, the earl of Hertford, (whom the king shortly after made marquis,) the earl of Bedford, the earl of Essex, the earl of Bristol, the lord Say, the lord Savile, and the lord Kimbolton; and within two or three days after, the earl of Warwick: being all persons at that time very gracious to the people, or to the Scots, by whose election and discretion the people chose; and had been all in some umbrage at court, and most of them in visible disfavour there. This act the king did very cheerfully; heartily inclined to some of them, as he had reason; and not apprehending any inconvenience by that act from the other, whom he thought this light of his grace would reform, or at least restrain.

But the calling and admitting men to that board is not a work that can be indifferent; the reputation, if not the government, of the state so much depending on it. And though, it may be, there hath been too much curiosity heretofore used to discover men's particular opinions in particular points, before they have received that honour; whereas possibly such differences were rather to have been desired than avoided; yet there are certain opinions, certain propositions, and general principles, that whosoever does not hold, does not believe, is not, without great danger, to be accepted for a privy-counsellor. As, whosoever is not fixed to monarchical grounds, the preservation and upholding whereof is the chief end of such a council: whosoever does not believe that, in order to that great end, there is a dignity, a freedom, a jurisdiction most essential to be preserved in and to that place; and takes not the preservation thereof to heart; ought never to be received there. What in prudence is to be done towards that end, admits a latitude that honest and wise men may safely and profitably differ ⟨in⟩; and those differences (which I said before there was too much unskilful care to prevent) usually produce great advantages in knowledge and wisdom: but the end itself, that which the logicians call the *terminus ad quem*, ought always to be a *postulatum*, which whosoever doubts, destroys: and princes cannot be too strict, too tender, in this consideration, in the constituting the body of their privy-council; upon the prudent doing whereof much of their safety, more of their honour and reputation (which is the life itself of princes) both at home and abroad, necessarily depends; and the inadvertencies in this point have been, mediately or immediately, the root and the spring of all the calamities that have ensued.

Two reasons have been frequently given by princes for oversights, or for wilful breaches, in this important dispensation of their favours. The first, 'that such a man can do no harm'; when, God knows, few men have done more harm than those who have been thought to be able to do least; and there cannot be a greater error, than to believe, a man whom we see qualified with too mean parts to do good, to be therefore incapable of doing hurt: there is a supply of malice, of pride, of industry, and even oi folly, in the weakest, when he sets his heart upon it, that makes a strange progress in mischief. The second, 'when persons of ordinary faculties, either upon importunity, or other collateral respects, have been introduced thither, that it is but a place of honour, and a general testimony of the king's affection'; and so it hath been as it were reserved as a preferment for those, who were fit for no other preferment. As amongst the Jesuits they have a rule, that they who are unapt for greater studies, shall study cases of conscience. By this means the number hath been increased, which in itself breeds great inconveniences; since a less number are fitter both for counsel and despatch, in matters of the greatest moment, that depend upon a quick execution, than a greater number of men equally honest and wise: and for that and other reasons of unaptness and incompetency, committees of dexterous men have been appointed out of the table to do the business of the table; and so men have been no sooner exalted with the reverent title, and pleased with the obligation of being made privy counsellors, than they have checked that delight with discerning that they were not fully trusted; and so been more incensed with the reproachful distinction at, than obliged with the honourable admission to, that board, where they do not find all persons equally members. And by this kind of resentment, many sad inconveniences have befallen to the king, and to those men who have had the honour and misfortune of those secret trusts.

The truth is, the sinking and near desperate condition of monarchy in this kingdom can never be buoyed up, but by a prudent and steady council attending upon the virtue and vivacity of the king; nor be preserved and improved when it is up, but by cherishing and preserving the wisdom, integrity, dignity, and reputation of that council: the lustre whereof always reflects .pon the king himself; who is not thought a great monarch when he follows the reins of his own reason and appetite; but when, for the informing his reason, and guiding his actions, he uses the service, industry, and faculties of the wisest men. And though it hath been, and will be, always necessary to admit to those counsels some men of great power, who will not take the pains to have great parts; yet the number of the whole should not be too great; and the capacities and qualities of the most ⟨should be⟩ fit for business; that is, either for judgment and despatch; or for one of them at least; and integrity above all.

This digression (much longer than was intended) will not appear very impertinent, when the great disservice shall appear, which befell unto the king by the swearing those lords formerly mentioned (I speak but of some of them) privy-counsellors. For, instead of exercising themselves in their new province, an⁻ endeavouring to preserve and vindicate that jurisdiction, they looked upon themselves as preferred thither, by their reputation in parliament, not ⟨by the⟩ kindness and estimation of the king; and so resolved to keep up principally the greatness of that place, to which they thought they owed their greatness. And therefore, when the king required the advice of his privy-council, in those matters of the highest importance which were then every day incumbent on him, the new privy-counsellors positively declared, 'that they might not (that was, that nobody might) give his majesty any advice in matters depending in the two houses, and not agreeable to the sense of the two houses; which (forsooth) was his great council, by whose wisdom he was entirely to guide himself'. And as this doctrine was most insipidly and perniciously urged by them; so it was most supinely and stupidly submitted to by the rest: insomuch as the king in a moment found himself bereaved of any public assistance or advice, in a time when he needed it most; and his greatest, and, upon the matter, his only business, being prudently to weigh and consider what to consent to, and what to deny, of such things as should be proposed to him by the two houses, he was now told, 'that he was only to be advised by them'; which was as much as to ask, whether they had a mind he should do whatever they desired of him.

Whereas in truth, it is not only lawful for, but the duty of the privy-council, to give faithfully and freely their advice to the king upon all matters concluded in parliament, to which h s royal consent is necessary, as well as upon any other s bject whatsoever. Nay, as a counsellor, he is bound to dissuade the king to consent to that which is prejudicial to the crown; at least to make that prejudice manifest to him; though as a private person he could wish the matter consented to. And therefore, by the constitution of the kingdom, and the constant practice of all times, all bills, after they are passed both houses, and engrossed, are delivered by the clerk of the parliament to the clerk of the crown; and by him brought to the attorney-general; who presented the same to his majesty sitting in council, and having read them, declares what alterations are made by those bills in former laws, and what benefit or detriment, in profit or jurisdiction, will accrue thereby to the crown: and then, upon a full and free debate by his counsellors, the king resolves, and accordingly doth mark the bills that are to be enacted into laws, and respites the other that he thinks not fit to consent to. And methinks as this hath been the known practice, so the reason is very visible; that the royal assent being a distinct and essential part towards the making a law, there should be as much care taken to inform the understanding and conscience of the king upon those occasions, as theirs, who prepare the same for his royal stamp.

And I cannot but, on this occasion, continue this digression thus much farther, to observe, that they who avoid public debates in council, or think them of less moment, upon undervaluing the persons of some counsellors, and from the particular infirmities of the men, the heaviness of this man, the levity of that, the weakness and simplicity of a third, conclude, that their advice and opinions are not requisite to any great design, are exceedingly deceived; and will perniciously deceive others who are misled by those conclusions. For it is in wisdom, as it is in beauty, a face that, being taken in pieces, affords scarce one exact feature, an eye, or a nose, or a tooth, or a brow, or a mouth, against which a visible just exception cannot be taken, yet altogether, by gracefulness and vivacity in the whole, may constitute an excellent beauty, and be more catching than another, whose symmetry is more faultless; so there are many men, who in this particular argument may be unskilful, in that affected, who may seem to have levity, or vanity, or formality, in ordinary and cursory conversation, (a very crooked rule to measure any man's abilities, as giving a better measure of the humour, than of the understanding,) and yet in formed counsels, deliberations, and transactions, are men of great insight, and wisdom, and from whom excellent assistance may be contributed.

And no question, all great enterprises and designs, that are to be executed, have many parts, even in the projection, fit for the survey and disquisition of several faculties and abilities, and phlegmatic understandings. And we often hear, in debates of great moment, animadversions of more weight and consequence, from those whose ordinary conversation is not so delightful, than from men of more sublime parts. Certainly Solomon very well understood himself, when he said, *In the multitude of counsellors there is safety*. And though it were confessed, that reason would be better discovered, and stated, and conclusions easier made by a few, than by a greater number, yet when the execution depends on many, and the general interpretation so much depends on the success, and the success on the interpretation, we see those counsels most prosperous, whereof the considerations and deliberations have been measured by that standard which is most publicly acknowledged and received. And he hath had but small experience in the managing affairs, who is not able experimentally to name to himself some very good and useful conclusions, which have therefore only succeeded amiss, because they were not communicated to those, who had reason to believe themselves competent parties to the secret. There was seldom ever yet that public-heartedness sunk into the breasts of men, that they were long willing to be left out in those transactions, to the privacy whereof they had a right. And therefore men have been often willing enough, any single advice should miscarry, of whatsoever general concernment, rather than contribute to the fame of some one man, who has thought their approbation not worth the providing for. And though the objection of secrecy and despatch seems to favour a small number, and a reservation of communicating, yet (except in those few cases, which in their nature are to be consulted, and acted together, and the full execution whereof may be by a few) I am not sure that the inconveniency will be greater by a necessary delay, or even by such a discovery, as may be supposed to proceed from the levity of a counsellor, (futile and malicious natures ought not to be supposed to be admitted into that rank of men,) than by wanting the approbation and concurrence of those, (admitting there could be no benefit from their information,) who will unavoidably know it soon enough to add to, or take from, the success, at least the reputation. And from this root much of the negligence and disrespect towards the civil councils proceeded. For as all corporations, tribes, and fraternities, suffer most by the malignity of some of their own members; so the jealousy and indisposition of some counsellors contributed much to the disregard which fell upon the order; and in them, upon the king.

Amongst those who were nearest the king's trust, and

to whom he communicated the greatest secrets in his affairs, there were some, who from private, though very good, conditions of life, without such an application to court as usually ushered in those promotions, were ascended to that preferment; and were believed to have an equal interest with any, in their master's estimation. And these were sure to find no more charity from the court, than from the army; and having had lately so many equals, it was thought no presumption, freely to censure all they did, or spake; what effect soever such freedom had upon the public policy and transactions. It were to be wished, that persons of the greatest birth, honour, and fortune, would take that care of themselves by education, industry, literature, and a love of virtue, to surpass all other men in knowledge, and all other qualifications, necessary for great actions, as far as they do in quality and titles, that princes, out of them, might always choose men fit for all employments, and high trusts; which would exceedingly advance their service; when the reputation and respect of the person carries somewhat with it that facilitates the business. And it cannot easily be expressed, nor comprehended by any who have not felt the weight and burden of the envy, which naturally attends upon those promotions, which seem to be *per saltum*, how great straits and difficulties such ministers are forced to wrestle with, and by which the charges, with which they are intrusted, must proportionably suffer, let the integrity and wisdom of the men be what it can be supposed to be. Neither is the patience, temper and dexterity, to carry a man through those straits, easily attained; it being very hard, in the morning of preferment, to keep an even temper of mind, between the care to preserve the dignity of the place committed to him, (without which he shall expose himself to a thousand unchaste attempts, and dishonour the judgment that promoted him, by appearing too vile for such a trust,) and the caution, that his nature be not really exalted to an overweening pride and folly, upon the privilege of his place; which will expose him to much more contempt than the former; and therefore ⟨is⟩, with a more exact guard upon a man's self, to be avoided:

the errors of gentleness and civility being much more easily reformed, as well as endured, that the other of arrogance and ostentation.

The best provision that such men can make for their voyage, besides a stock of innocency that cannot be impaired, and a firm confidence in God Almighty, that he will never suffer that innocency to be utterly oppressed, or notoriously defamed, is, an expectation of those gusts and storms of rumour, detraction, and envy; and a resolution not to be over sensible of all calumnies, unkindness, or injustice; but to believe, that, by being preferred before other men, they have an obligation upon them, to suffer more than other men would do; and that the best way to convince scandals, and misreports, is, by neglecting them, to appear not to have deserved them. And there is not a more troublesome passion, or that often draws more inconveniences with it, than that which proceeds from the indignation of being unjustly calumniated, and from the pride of an upright conscience; when men cannot endure to be spoken ill of, if they have not deserved it: in which distemper, though they free themselves from the errors, or infirmities, with which they were traduced, they commonly discover others, of which they had never been suspected. In a word, let no man think, that is once entered into the list, he can by any skill, or comportment, prevent these conflicts and assaults; or by any stubborn or impetuous humour, suppress and prevail over them: but let him look upon it as purgatory he is unavoidably to pass through. and depend upon Providence, and time, for a vindication; and by performing all the duties of his place to the end with justice, integrity, and uprightness, give all men cause to believe, he was worthy of it the first hour, which is a triumph very lawful to be affected.

[Clarendon's opinion concerning the duties of the Privy Council did not change after the Restoration. Thus he says for instance with regard to the profligacy at court.] All men of virtue and sobriety, of which there were very many in the king's family, were grieved and heartbroken with hearing what they could not choose but hear, and seeing many things which they could not avoid the seeing.

There were few of the council that did not to one another lament the excesses, which must in time be attended with fatal consequences, and for the present did apparently lessen the reverence to the king, that is the best support of his royalty: but few of them had the courage to say that to his majesty, which was not so fit to be said to any body else. Nor can it be denied, that his majesty did, upon all occasions, receive those advertisements from those who presented them to him, with patience and benignity, and without the least show of displeasure; though the persons concerned endeavoured no one thing more than to persuade him, 'that it was the highest presumption imaginable in the privy-council to believe, that they had any jurisdiction in the court, or ought to censure the manners of it'.

Nor were all those endeavours without making some impression upon his majesty, who rather esteemed some particular members of it, than was inclined to believe that the body of it ought to receive a reverence from the people, or be looked upon as a vital part of the government: in which his majesty (as hath been often said before) by the ill principles he had received in France, and the accustomed liberty of his bedchamber, was exceedingly and unhappily mistaken. For by the constitution of the kingdom, and the very laws and customs of the nation, as the privy-council and every member of it is of the king's sole choice and election of him to that trust, (for the greatest office in the state, though conferred likewise by the king himself, doth not qualify the officer to be of the privy-council, or to be present in it, before by a new assignation that honour is bestowed on him, and that he be sworn of the council;) so the body of it is the most sacred, and hath the greatest authority in the government of the state, next the person of the king himself, to whom all other powers are equally subject: and no king of England can so well secure his own just prerogative, or preserve it from violation, as by a strict defending and supporting the dignity of his privy-council.

When it was too much taken notice of, that the king himself had not that esteem or consideration of the council that was due to it, what they did or ordered to be done was less valued by the people; and that disrespect every day improved by the want of gravity and justice and constancy in the proceedings there, the resolutions of one day being reversed or altered the next, either upon some whispers in the king's ear, or some new fancy in some of those counsellors, who were always of one mind against all former orders and precedents.

24. *The First and the Second Earls of Bristol*

The first earl, John Digby, born 1580; ambassador at Madrid during the reign of James I; Earl of Bristol 1622; P.C. 1641; died 1653

THE earl of Bristol was a man of grave aspect, of a presence that drew respect, and of long experience in affairs of great importance. He had been, by the extraordinary favour of king James to his person (for he was a very handsome man) and his parts, which were naturally great, and had been improved by a good education at home and abroad, sent ambassador into Spain, before he was thirty years of age; and afterwards in several other embassies; and at last, again into Spain; where he treated and concluded the marriage between the prince of Wales and that infanta; which was afterwards dissolved. He was by king James made of the privy-council, vice-chamberlain of the household, an earl, and a gentleman of the bed-chamber to the prince, and was then crushed by the power of the duke of Buckingham, and the prejudice the prince himself had contracted against him, during his highness's being in Spain; upon which he was imprisoned upon his return; and after the duke's death, the king retained so strict a memory of all his friendships and displeasures, that the earl of Bristol could never recover any admission to the court; but lived in the country, in ease, and plenty in his fortune, and in great reputation with all who had not an implicit reverence for the court; and before, and in the beginning of the parliament, appeared in the head of all the discontented party; but quickly left them, when they entered upon their unwarrantable violences, and

grew so much into their disfavour, that after the king was
gone to York, upon some expressions he used in the house
of peers in debate, they committed him to the Tower;
from whence being released, in two or three days, he made
haste to York to the king; who had before restored him
to his place in the council and the bedchamber. He was
with him at Edge-hill, and came with him from thence
to Oxford; and, at the end of the war, went into France;
where he died; that party having so great an animosity
against him, that they would not suffer him to live in
England, nor to compound for his estate, as they suffered
others to do, who had done them more hurt. Though he
was a man of great parts, and a wise man, yet he had been
for the most part single, and by himself, in business; which
he managed with good sufficiency; and had lived little in
consort, so that in council he was passionate, and super-
cilious, and did not bear contradiction without much
passion, and was too voluminous in discourse; so that he
was not considered there with much respect; to the lessening whereof no man contributed more than his son, the
lord Digby; who shortly after came to sit there as secretary of state, and had not that reverence for his father's
wisdom, which his great experience deserved, though he
failed not in his piety towards him.

The second earl, George Digby, born 1612; M.P.
1640; baron 1641; Secretary of State after Falkland's
death 1643; Earl of Bristol 1653; again Secretary of
State 1657 but loses office on conversion; impeaches
Clarendon 1663 unsuccessfully; in hiding for two years
but back in Parliament July 1667; died 1677

[In 1641] As soon as the [Grand] Remonstrance, so much
mentioned before, was printed, Mr. Hyde, only to give
vent to his own indignation, and without the least purpose of communicating it, or that any use should be made
of it, had drawn such a full answer to it, as the subject
would have enabled any man to have done who had
thought of it: and the lord Digby, who had much conversation and friendship with him, coming accidentally
and suddenly into the room, where he was alone amongst

his books and papers; conferring together of the extravagant proceedings of the parliament, he, upon the familiarity that was between them, and upon the argument that was then between them, read the answer to him which he had prepared to the remonstrance; with which he seemed much pleased, and desired him, that he would permit it to be made use of by the king, and that he might shew it to his majesty; who found it absolutely necessary to publish some answer in his own name to that remonstrance, which had so much poisoned the hearts of the people; and that his majesty was endeavouring to procure such an answer to be drawn. The other expressly and positively refused to give it him, or that any use should be made of it; and reproached him for proposing a thing to him which might prove ruinous to him, if the house should have the least imagination that he exercised himself in such offices; with which answer he seemed satisfied, and departed: no other person having seen it but the lord Falkland, from whom nothing was ever concealed.

[Digby, however, mentioned the paper to the king who asked to see it.] Mr. Hyde, though he was very unsatisfied with what the lord Digby had done, (whose affection to him he did not in any degree make question of, but did not like his over activity, to which his restless fancy always disposed him; and as he doubted not that himself had given the occasion to the king to send those commands, so he had likewise enlarged those commands, as he believed, in such a manner as he thought might most oblige him,) yet upon the real consideration that it might do the king much service, he did, without delay, deliver the papers; insisting upon the promise of secrecy, and, likewise, that his majesty would not publish without first communicating it to his council, and as done with their advice. And to that purpose he affixed that title to it, before he delivered the papers out of his hands; believing, that as it would be more for the king's service to carry such an authority in the front of it, as 'The king's answer with the advice of his council'; so it could not be refused by them, and yet might engage them in some displeasure with the house of commons, which probably might be offended at it. The king was very punctual in doing what was desired, and caused it to be read at a full council, where many of the lords commended it very much, and none spake against it; and so it was published and printed; and it was very apparent to all men, that the king's service was very much advanced by it; and it was not more evident to any than to the house of commons, who knew not how to make any expostulation upon it, it being in the king's own name, and published with the advice of his privy-council: so that all they could do was, to endeavour to discover who was the penner of it; to which discovery they were most intent by all their secret friends in court, who found means to discover most other secrets to them, but in this could do them no service.

By what hath been said before, it appears, that the lord Digby was much trusted by the king, and he was of great familiarity and friendship with the other three [Hyde, Falkland, Colepepper], at least with two of them; for he was not a man of that exactness, as to be in the entire confidence of the lord Falkland, who looked upon his infirmities with more severity than the other two did; and he lived with more frankness towards those two, than he did towards the other; yet between those two there was a free conversation and kindness to each other. He was a man of very extraordinary parts by nature and art, and had surely as good and excellent an education as any man of that age in any country: a graceful and beautiful person; of great eloquence and becomingness in his discourse, (save that sometimes he seemed a little affected,) and of so universal a knowledge, that he never wanted subject for a discourse: he was equal to a very good part in the greatest affair, but the unfittest man alive to conduct it, having an ambition and vanity superior to all his other parts, and a confidence peculiar to himself, which sometimes intoxicated, and transported, and exposed him. He had from his youth, by the disobligations his family had undergone from the duke of Buckingham, and the great men who succeeded him, and some sharp reprehension himself had met with, which obliged him to a country life, contracted a prejudice and ill-will to the court; and so had in the beginning of the parliament engaged himself with that party which discovered most aversion from it, with a passion and animosity equal to their own, and therefore very acceptable to them. But when he was weary of their violent counsels, and withdrew himself from them with some circumstances which enough provoked them, and made a reconciliation, and mutual confidence in each other for the future, manifestly impossible; he made private and secret offers of his service to the king, to whom, in so general a defection of his servants, it could not but be very agreeable: and so his majesty being satisfied, both in the discoveries he made of what had passed, and in his profession for the future, removed him from the house of commons, where he had rendered himself marvellously ungracious, and called him by writ to the house of peers, where he did visibly advance the king's service, and quickly rendered himself grateful to all those who had not thought too well of him before, when he deserved less; and men were not only pleased with the assistance he gave upon all debates, by his judgment and vivacity, but looked upon him as one, who could derive the king's pleasure to them, and make a lively representation of their good demeanour to the king, which he was very luxuriant in promising to do, and officious enough in doing as much as was just.

He had been instrumental in promoting the three persons above mentioned to the king's favour; and had himself, in truth, so great an esteem of them, that he did very frequently, upon conference together, depart from his own inclinations and opinions, and concurred in theirs; and very few men of so great parts are, upon all occasions, more counsellable than he; so that he would seldom be in danger of running into great errors, if he would communicate and expose all his own thoughts and inclinations to such a disquisition; nor is he uninclinable in his nature to such an entire communication in all things which he conceived to be difficult. But his fatal infirmity is, that he too often thinks difficult things very easy; and doth not consider possible consequences, when the proposition administers somewhat that is delightful to his fancy, and by pursuing whereof he imagines he shall reap some glory to himself, of which he is immoderately ambitious; so that, if the consultation be upon any action to be done, no man more implicitly enters into that debate, or more cheerfully resigns his own conceptions to a joint determination: but when it is once affirmatively resolved, (besides that he may possibly reserve some impertinent circumstance, as he thinks, the imparting whereof would change the nature of the thing,) if his fancy suggests to him any particular, which himself might perform in that action, upon the imagination that every body would approve it, if it were proposed to them, he chooses rather to do it, than to communicate, that he may have some signal part to himself in the transaction, in which no other person can claim a share.

And by this unhappy temper he did often involve himself in very unprosperous attempts. The king himself was the unfittest person alive to be served by such a counsellor, being too easily inclined to sudden enterprises, and as easily amazed when they were entered upon. And from this unhappy composition in the one, and the other, a very unhappy counsel was entered upon, and resolution taken, without the least communication with either of the three, ⟨who⟩ had been so lately admitted to an entire trust.

25. *The Earl of Holland*

Henry Rich, born 1590; M.P. 1610; Baron Kensington 1623; Earl of Holland 1624; K.G. 1625; Chief Justice in Eyre South of Trent 1631; General of Horse 1639; negotiates with the court 1643 and 1645; royal general in Second Civil War; executed 1649

THE earl of Holland was a younger son of a noble house, and a very fruitful bed, which divided a numerous issue between two great fathers; the eldest, many sons and daughters to the lord Rich; the younger, of both sexes, to Mountjoy earl of Devonshire, who had been more than once married to the mother. The reputation of his family gave him no great advantage in the world, though his eldest brother was earl of Warwick, and owner of a great fortune; and his younger earl of Newport, of a very plentiful revenue likewise. He, after some time spent in France, betook himself to the war in Holland, which he intended to have made his profession; where, after he had made two or three campaigns, according to the custom of the English volunteers, he came in the leisure of the winter to visit his friends in England, and the court, that shined then in the plenty and bounty of king James; and about the time of the infancy of the duke of Buckingham's favour, to whom he grew in a short time very acceptable. But his friendship was more entire to the earl of Carlisle, who was more of his nature and humour, and had a generosity more applicable at that time to his fortune and his ends. And it was thought by many who stood within view, that for some years he supported himself upon the familiarity and friendship of the other; which continued mutually between them very many years, with little interruption, to their death.

He was a very handsome man, of a lovely and winning presence, and gentle conversation; by which he got so easy an admission into the court, and grace of King James, that he gave over the thought of further intending the life of a soldier. He took all the ways he could to endear himself to the duke, and to his confidence, and wisely declined the receiving any grace or favour, but as his donation; above all, avoided the suspicion that the king had any kindness for him, upon any account but of the duke, whose creature he desired to be esteemed, though the earl of Carlisle's friend. And he prospered so well in that pretence, that the king scarce made more haste to advance the duke, than the duke did to promote the other.

He first preferred him to a wife, the daughter and heir of Cope, by whom he had a good fortune; and, amongst other things, the manor and seat of Kensington, of which he was shortly after made baron. And he had quickly so entire a confidence in him, that he prevailed with the king to put him about his son the prince of Wales, and to be a gentleman of his bedchamber, before the duke himself had reason to promise himself any proportion of his highness's grace and protection. He was then made earl of Holland, captain of the guard, knight of the order, and of the privy-council; sent the first ambassador into France to treat the marriage with the queen, or rather privately to treat about the marriage before he was ambassador. And when the duke went to the Isle of Rhé, he trusted the earl of Holland with the command of that army with which he was to be recruited and assisted.

And in this confidence, and in this posture, he was left by the duke when he died; and having the advantage of the queen's good opinion and favour, (which the duke neither had, nor cared for,) he made all possible approaches towards the obtaining his trust, and succeeding him in his power; or rather that the queen might have solely that power, and he only be subservient to her; and upon this account he made a continual war upon the earl of Portland the treasurer, and all others who were not gracious to the queen, or desired not the increase of her authority. And in this state, and under this protection, he received every day new obligations from the king, and great bounties, and continued to flourish above any man in the court, whilst the weather was fair: but the storm did no sooner arise, but he changed so much, and declined so fast from the honour he was thought to be master of, that he fell into that condition, which there will be hereafter too much cause to mention, and to enlarge upon.

[In 1641] The armies were at last disbanded: and, about the end of September, the earl of Holland, in great pomp, returned to his house at Kensington; where he was visited and caressed, with great application, by all the factious party: for he had now, whether upon the disobligation remembered before, of being denied the making a baron; or upon some information, of some sharp expressions used by the queen upon his letter; and the conscience of that letter: or the apprehensions of being questioned and prosecuted upon the enormities of his office of chief justice in eyre, and other transgressions, fully declared himself of their party. And that they might be better prepared to keep up the prejudice to the king, and the keenness against the court, till the coming together of both houses; when they had reason to believe the observation of their crooked and indirect courses, and their visible, unwarrantable breaches, upon the church, and the religion established by law, would render men less devoted to them; his lordship furnished them with many informations of what had passed in the late army, which might be wrested to the king's disadvantage; told them whatsoever the king himself had said to him, when he looked upon him as a person true to him; and when, it is very probable, he was not much delighted with the proceedings at Westminster; and of all the particulars, which sir Jacob Ashley, and sir John Coniers, had informed him, when they took him to be of entire trust with his majesty, and wholly under that consideration, (whereupon they were afterwards examined, and compelled to testify that in public, which they had before imparted to him in the greatest secrecy); and added to all this, whatever information he had received by the lady Carlisle, of words or actions, spoken or done by the queen, which might increase their jealousy and malice to her majesty. And himself (who had been always believed a creature of the queen's, and exceedingly obliged and protected by her immediate and single grace and favour, against the earl of Portland, the earl of Strafford, and the archbishop of Canterbury, in those high times when they had otherwise destroyed him) visited her majesty but once, from the time of his return out of the north, to the time of the king's return from Scotland, which was full six weeks. And yet, there were some men still at those private meetings at Kensington, who thought the Queen's favour a likelier means for their preferment, than the interest of the others; and therefore always gave advertisement to her of what passed in that company: which information, for want of due care in the managery, and by reason of the unfaithfulness of her nearest servants, commonly produced somewhat, of which the other side made greater advantage, than she could do by the knowledge of their counsels and resolutions.

[In 1642] When the King came to York, he found

himself at ease; the country had received him with great
expressions of joy and duty, and all persons of quality of
that great county, and of the counties adjacent, resorted
to him, and many persons of condition from London, and
those parts, who had not the courage to attend upon him
at Whitehall; so that the court appeared with some lustre.
And now he began to think of executing some of those
resolutions, which he had made with the queen before
her departure; one of which was, and to be first done,
the removing the earls of Essex and Holland from their
offices in the court, the one of chamberlain, the other of
groom of the stole, which hath the reputation and benefit
of being first gentleman of the bedchamber. Indeed no
man could speak in the justification of either of them, yet
no man thought them both equally culpable. The earl of
Holland was a person merely of the king's creation; raised
from the condition of a private gentleman, a younger
brother of an extraction that lay under a great blemish,
and without any fortune, to a great height by the king's
mere favour and bounty. And he had not only adorned
him with titles, honours, and offices, but enabled him to
support those in the highest lustre, and with the largest
expense: and had drawn many inconveniences, and great
disadvantages, upon himself and his service, by his preferring him to some trusts, which others did not only think
themselves, but really were, worthier of; but especially
by indulging him so far in the rigorous execution of his
office of chief justice in the eyre, in which he brought more
prejudice upon the court, and more discontent upon the
king, from the most considerable part of the nobility and
gentry in England, than any one action, that had its rise
from the king's will and pleasure, though it was not without some warrant from law; which having not been
practised for some hundreds of years, was looked upon
as a terrible innovation and exaction upon persons, who
knew not that they were in any fault; nor was any imputed to them, but the original sin of their forefathers,
even for which they were obliged to pay great penalties
and ransoms. That such a servant should suffer his zeal
to lessen and decay towards such a master, and that he

should keep a title to lodge in his bedchamber, from whose court he had upon the matter withdrawn himself, and adhered to and assisted those who affronted and contemned his majesty so notoriously, would admit of no manner of interposition and excuse.

[During the summer of 1642 messages had passed between the king and parliament, but to no effect.] And sure, from that time, the earl of Holland was more transported from his natural temper and gentleness of disposition, into passion and animosity against the king and his ministers; and, having been nothing pleased with his own condition at London, finding the earl of Essex (whom he did not secretly love, and indeed contemned) to draw all men's eyes towards him, and to have the greatest interest in their hearts, he had seriously intended, under colour of this message to the king, to discover if there were any sparks yet left in his royal breast, which might be kindled into affection or acceptation of his service; and hoped, if he could get any credit, to redeem his former trespasses: but when he found his majesty not only cold towards him, but easily enough discerned, by his reception, that all former inclinations were dead, and more than ordinary prejudices grown up towards him in their places, and that his advices were rejected, he returned with rancour equal to the most furious he went to; and heartily joined and concurred towards the suppressing that power, in the administration whereof he was not like to bear any part.

[In the summer of 1643 the three earls of Bedford, Holland, and Clare returned to the king's side. But when the court had gone into winter quarters in Oxford] there was no particular that gave the king more unquietness, than the presence of my lord of Holland. The three earls had attended the king before he rose from Gloucester, and had waited upon him throughout that march, and had charged the enemy, in the king's regiment of horse, at the battle of Newbury, very bravely; and had behaved themselves, throughout, very well; and returned to Oxford with his majesty; and now expected to be well looked upon: and the other two had no cause to complain; the king, upon all occasions, spoke very graciously to them, and sent the chancellor of the exchequer to the earl of Clare, 'that he had liberty, and might be present at the councils of war'; where the peers usually were, and where the general matters of contribution, and such things as concerned the country, were usually debated. But the earl of Holland was not pleased; he thought nothing of former miscarriages ought to be remembered; that all those were cancelled by the merit of coming to the king now, and bringing such considerable persons with him, and disposing others to follow; and expected, upon his first appearance, to have had his key restored to him; to have been in the same condition he was in the bedchamber, and in the council, and in the king's grace and countenance; of all which he had assurance from the queen before he came.

[Clarendon is the friend in question.] The earl had a friend, who did heartily desire to do him all the offices and services that would consist with the king's honour, and always apprehended the ill consequence of discouraging such revolutions, and who spake often to the earl of his own affairs. And when he complained of his usage, and repeated what promises and encouragement he had received to come to the king, and of what importance his good reception would have been; 'that there were many of considerable reputation and interest in the house of commons, (whom he named,) who intended to have followed, and that the earl of Northumberland expected only his advice'; his friend asked him, 'whether he had done all things, since he came to the king, which might reasonably be expected from him?' He said, 'he thought he had done all ⟨that⟩ could be expected from him, in bringing himself to the king; and, since his coming to him, in venturing his life for him; and in lieu thereof he had not received thanks, or one gracious word; and now, after his office had been kept unbestowed near two years, and a promise made to him, that he should be restored to it, it was to be bestowed upon another, to make his disgrace the more notorious; which he thought would not prove for his majesty's honour or advantage'.

His friend asked him, 'whether he had asked it of the

king, or informed him of the promise that was made to him?' He said 'he had done neither, nor ever would; he expected it of the king's grace, and would not extort it by a promise, which, it might be, his majesty was not privy to'. The other replied very plainly to him, 'that if he thought he had never committed any fault against the king, he had no reason to acknowledge it, or make excuse for it; but if he were guilty of any such, how unwarily soever it had been done, or how unmaliciously soever it had been intended, he ought to make some confession and apology to his majesty; nor could his majesty, with the safety of his honour, avow the receiving him into any trust without it; nor was he capable of receiving any offices from his friends, or the queen's own declared interposition on his behalf, till he had performed that necessary introduction'. He told him, 'if he would follow his advice, he believed he might receive some effect of it'; which was, 'that he should send to desire a private audience of his majesty in some room, where nobody might be present; which would not be refused him; and then he should (with all the excuses upon the terror the parliament gave to all men, who had exceeded the common rules, in their administration of the trust they had from his majesty; as he could not deny he had done in many particulars for the advancement of his majesty's service) confess, that he had not been hardy enough to contemn that power, but had been so much in awe of it, that he chose rather to presume upon his Majesty's goodness, than to provoke their jealousy and displeasure; and so had complied with them more, than in his duty and gratitude to his majesty he ought to have done; for which he begged his pardon upon his knees; and if he might obtain it, he made no doubt, he should wipe out the memory of past offences by some new services, which should be beneficial to his majesty'; and he told him, 'that he would do very well, if he would sue out his pardon, as the earl of Bedford had done; who had asked it of the king when he first kissed his hand, and had since wisely taken it out under the great seal of England'.

The earl of Holland seemed not at all pleased with this advice; said, 'He did not think, though he would not justify all that he had done, his transgressions were of that magnitude, that they required such a formality of asking pardon; that his case was very different from that of the earl of Bedford, who had been in arms, and a general officer in the field against the king; whereas he had only sat in the parliament, as lawfully he might do; and if he had failed in his attendance upon his majesty, and otherwise deserved his displeasure, he had received so many marks of it before he deserved it, that might well transport a very faithful servant into a discontent that would not become him. That as soon as he found himself restored to any proportion of his majesty's grace and confidence, his own inclinations would carry him to as humble apologies, and as deep acknowledgments of all his transgressions, as could be expected from him, and such as he believed would reconcile the king's goodness to him: but to make the first advance by such a kind of submission, he did not think he could prevail over himself to do it.' However, he took his advice very kindly, and spoke often with him after upon the same subject.

Being, upon conference with some other friends, advised the same, especially by his daughter, (whom he loved and esteemed exceedingly,) so that he seemed resolved to do it; but whether he thought worse of the king's affairs, or liked the court the less, because he saw the poverty of it, and that whatever place or favour he might obtain, he could not expect a support from it to defray his expenses, (nor could he draw from it any other place,) he delayed it so long, till the king found it reasonable to confer the office he had so long promised, upon the marquis of Hertford; and then withdrawing himself, for his convenience, to a neighbour village, where he had a private lodging; after a few days, with the help of a dark night and a good guide, he got himself into the enemy's quarters, and laid himself at the feet of the parliament; which, after a short imprisonment, gave him leave to live in his own house, without farther considering him, than as a man able to do little good or harm. And yet he did endeavour to render himself as grateful to them as he could, by an act very unsuitable to his honour, or his own generous nature: for he published a declaration in print, of the cause of his going to, and returning from Oxford; in which he endeavoured to make it believed, 'that his compassion and love to his country had only prevailed with him to go to the king, in hope to have been able, upon the long knowledge his majesty had of his fidelity, to persuade him to make a peace with his parliament; which, from the time of his coming thither, he had laboured to do; but that he found the court so indisposed to peace, and that the papists had so great a power there', (using many expressions dishonourable towards the king and his council,) 'that he resolved to make what haste he could back to the parliament, and to spend the remainder of his life in their service': which action, so contrary to his own natural discretion and generosity, lost him the affection of those few who had preserved some kindness for him, and got him credit with nobody; and may teach all men how dangerous it is to step aside out of the path of innocence and virtue, upon any presumption to be able to get into it again; since they usually satisfy themselves in doing any thing to mend the present exigent they are in, rather than think of returning to that condition of innocence, from whence they departed with a purpose of returning.

However, this unhappy ill carriage of the earl doth not absolve the king's council from oversight in treating him no better; which was a great error; and made the king, and all those about him, looked upon as implacable; and so diverted all men from farther thoughts of returning to their duty by such application, and made those who abhorred the war, and the violent counsels in the carrying it on, choose rather to acquiesce, and expect a conjuncture when a universal peace might be made, than to expose themselves by unseasonable and unwelcome addresses. The earl of Northumberland, who was gone to Petworth, as is said before, with a purpose of going to the king, if by the lord Conway's negociation, and the earl of Holland's reception, he found encouragement, returned to the parliament, where he was received with great respect, all men concluding, that he had never intended to do, what he had not done. And the other members, who had entertained the same resolutions, changed their minds with him, and returned to their former station: and the two earls who yet remained at Oxford, shortly after found means to make their peace; and returned again to their own habitations in London, without farther mark of displeasure, than a restraint, from coming to the house of peers, or being trusted in their counsels.

[In 1648] the earl of Holland, who had done twice very notoriously amiss, and had been, since his return from Oxford, notably despised by all persons of credit in the parliament and the army, had a mind to redeem his former faults by a new and thorough engagement. He had much credit by descent and by alliance with the presbyterian party and was privy to the undertakings of Scotland, and had constant intelligence of the advance that was made there. [But his plotting was unsuccessful and he was taken prisoner. And after the execution of the king, he too was beheaded together with Duke Hamilton and Lord Capel.]

The earl of Holland was brought next, who, by his long sickness, was so spent, that his spirits served not to entertain the people with long discourse. He spoke of 'his religion, as a matter unquestionable, by the education he had had in the religious family of which he was a branch': which was thought a strange discourse for a dying man, who, though a son, knew enough of the iniquity of his father's house, which should rather have been buried in silence, than, by such an unseasonable testimony, have been revived in the memory and discourse of men. He took more care to be thought a good friend to parliaments, than a good servant to his master, and was thought to say too little of his having failed so much in his duty to him, which most good men believed to be the source from whence his present calamity sprung. He was a very well bred man, and a fine gentleman in good times; but too much desired to enjoy ease and plenty, when the king could have neither; and did think poverty the most insupportable evil that could befall any man in this world. He was then so weak that he could not have lived long; and when his head was cut off, very little blood followed.

26. *The Earl of Manchester*

Edward Montagu, born 1602; Baron Montagu of
Kimbolton, 1626, and courtesy title Mandeville; second
Earl of Manchester 1642; P.C. 1660; F.R.S. 1667;
died 1671

THE lord Mandevile, eldest son to the lord Privy-seal,
was a person of great civility, and very well bred, and had
been early in the court under the favour of the duke of
Buckingham, a lady of whose family he had married: he
had attended upon the prince when he was in Spain, and
had been called to the house of peers in the lifetime of his
father, ⟨by the name of the lord Kimbolton,⟩ which was
a very extraordinary favour. Upon the death of the duke
of Buckingham, his wife being likewise dead, he married
the daughter of the earl of Warwick; a man in no grace
at court, and looked upon as the greatest patron of the
puritans, because of much the greatest estate of all who
favoured them, and so was esteemed by them with great
application and veneration: though he was of a life very
licentious, and unconformable to their professed rigour,
which they rather dispensed with, than to withdraw from
a house where they received so eminent a protection, and
such notable bounty. From this latter marriage the lord
Mandevile totally estranged himself from the court, and
upon all occasions appeared enough to dislike what was
done there, and engaged himself wholly in the conversation of those who were most notoriously of that party,
whereof there was a kind of fraternity of many persons of
good condition, who chose to live together in one family,
at a gentleman's house of fair fortune, near the place
where the lord Mandevile lived; whither others of that
classis likewise resorted, and maintained a joint and
mutual correspondence and conversation together with
much familiarity and friendship: that lord, to support
and the better to improve that popularity, living at a
much higher rate than the narrow exhibition allowed to
him by his wary father could justify, making up the rest

by contracting a great debt, which long lay heavy upon him; by which generous way of living, and by his natural civility, good manners, and good nature, which flowed towards all men, he was universally acceptable and beloved; and no man more in the confidence of the discontented and factious party than he, and ⟨none⟩ to whom the whole mass of their designs, as well what remained in chaos as what was formed, was more entirely communicated, and more consulted with.

[The preliminaries of the passing of the so-called Self-denying Ordinance, 1644, which removed Essex and Manchester from their command.] That violent party, which had at first cozened the rest into the war, and afterwards obstructed all the approaches towards peace, found now that they had finished as much of their work, as the tools which they had wrought with could be applied to; and what remained to be done, must be despatched by new workmen. They had been long unsatisfied with the earl of Essex, and he was as much with them; both being more solicitous to suppress the other, than to destroy the king. They bore the loss and dishonour he had sustained in Cornwall very well; and would have been glad, that both he and his army had been quite cut off, instead of being dissolved; for most of his officers and soldiers were corrupted in their affections towards them, and desired nothing but peace: so that they resolved never more to trust or employ any of them. But that which troubled them more, was, that their beloved earl of Manchester, upon whom they depended as a fast friend, by whom they might insensibly have divested the earl of Essex of all convenient authority in the army, appeared now as unapplicable to their purposes as the other; and there was a breach fallen out between him and Oliver Cromwell, which was irreconcilable, and which had brought some counsels upon the stage, before they were ripe.

Cromwell accused the earl of Manchester 'of having betrayed the parliament out of cowardice; for that he might, at the king's last being at Newbury, when he drew off his cannon, very easily have defeated his whole army, if he would have permitted it to have been engaged: that he went to him, and shewed him evidently how it might be done; and desired him that he would give him leave, with his own brigade of horse, to charge the king's army in their retreat; and the earl, with the rest of his army, might look on, and do as he should think fit: but that the earl had, notwithstanding all importunity used by him and other officers, positively and obstinately refused to permit him; giving no other reason, but that, he said, if they did engage, and overthrow the king's army, the king would always have another army to keep up the war; but if that army which he commanded should be overthrown, before the other under the earl of Essex should be reinforced, there would be an end of their pretences; and they should be all rebels and traitors, and executed and forfeited by the law.'

This pronunciation what the law would do against them was very heavily taken by the parliament, as if the earl believed the law to be against them, after so many declarations made by them, 'that the law was on their side, and that the King's arms were taken up against the law'. The earl confessed 'he had used words to that effect, that they should be treated as traitors, if their army was defeated, when he did not approve the advice that was given by the lieutenant general; which would have exposed the army to greater hazard, than he thought seasonable in that conjuncture, in the middle of the winter, to expose it to'. He then recriminated Cromwell, 'that at another time, Cromwell discoursing freely with him of the state of the kingdom, and proposing somewhat to be done', the earl had answered, 'that the parliament would never approve it': to which Cromwell presently replied, 'My lord, if you will stick firm to honest men, you shall find yourself in the head of an army, that shall give the law to king and parliament: which discourse, he said, made great impression in him; for he knew the lieutenant general to be a man of very deep designs; and therefore he was the more careful to preserve an army, which he yet thought was very faithful to the parliament.'

This discourse startled those who had always an aversion to Cromwell, and had observed the fierceness of his nature, and the language he commonly used when there was any mention of peace; so that they desired that this matter might be thoroughly examined, and brought to judgment. But the other side put all obstructions in the way, and rather chose to lose the advantage they had against the earl of Manchester, than to have the other matter examined; which would unavoidably have made some discoveries which they were not yet ready to produce. However the animosities increased, and the parties appeared barefaced against each other; which increased the distractions, and divided the city as well as the parliament; and new opinions started up in religion, which made more sub-divisions; and new terms and distinctions were brought into discourse; and fanatics were now first brought into appellation: which kind of confusions exceedingly disposed men of any sober understanding to wish for peace; though none knew how to bring the mention of it into the parliament.

The earl of Manchester, of the whole cabal, was, in a thousand respects, most unfit for the company he kept. He was of a gentle and a generous nature; civilly bred; had reverence and affection for the person of the king, upon whom he had attended in Spain; loved his country with too unskilful a tenderness; and was of so excellent a temper and disposition, that the barbarous times, and the rough parts he was forced to act in them, did not wipe out, or much deface, those marks: insomuch as he was never guilty of any rudeness towards those he was obliged to oppress, but performed always as good offices towards his old friends, and all other persons, as the iniquity of the time, and the nature of the employment he was in, would permit him to do; which kind of humanity could be imputed to very few.

And he was at last dismissed, and removed from any trust, for no other reason, but because he was not wicked enough. He married first into the family of the duke of Buckingham, and, by his favour and interest, was called to the house of peers in the life of his father; and made baron of Kimbolton, though he was commonly treated and known by the name of the lord Mandevile; and was as much addicted to the service of the court as he ought to be. But the death of his lady, and the murder of that great favourite, his second marriage with the daughter of the earl of Warwick, and the very narrow and restrained maintenance, which he received from his father, and which would in no degree defray the expenses of the court, forced him too soon to retire to a country life, and totally to abandon both the court and London; whither he came very seldom in many years. And in this retirement, the discountenance which his father underwent at court, the conversation of that family into which he was married, the bewitching popularity, which flowed upon him with a wonderful torrent, with the want of those guards which a good education should have supplied him with, by the clear notion of the foundation of the ecclesiastical, as well as the civil government, made great impression upon his understanding, (for his nature was never corrupted, but remained still in its integrity,) and made him believe that the court was inclined to hurt, and even to destroy the country; and from particular instances to make general and dangerous conclusions. They who had been always enemies to the church prevailed with him to lessen his reverence for it, and having not been well instructed to defend it, he yielded too easily to those who confidently assaulted it; and thought it had great errors, which were necessary to be reformed; and that all means are lawful to compass that which is necessary. Whereas the true logic is, that the thing desired is not necessary, if the ways are unlawful, which are proposed to bring it to pass. No man was courted with more application, by persons of all conditions and qualities; and his person was not less acceptable to those of steady and uncorrupted principles, than to those of depraved inclinations. And in the end, even his piety administered some excuse to him; for his father's infirmities and transgressions had so far exposed him to the inquisition of justice, that he found it necessary to procure the assistance and protection of those who were strong enough to violate justice itself; and so he adhered to those who were best able to defend his father's honour, and thereby to secure his own fortune; and concurred with them in their most violent designs, and gave reputation to them. And the court as unskilfully took an occasion too soon to make him desperate, by accusing him of high treason, when (though he might be guilty enough) he was, without doubt, in his intentions, at least, as innocent as any of the leading men.

And it is some evidence, that God Almighty saw his heart was not so malicious as the rest, that he preserved him to the end of the confusion; when he appeared as glad of the king's restoration, and had heartily wished it long before, and very few, who had a hand in the contrivance of the rebellion, gave so manifest tokens of repentance as he did; and having, for many years, undergone the jealousy and hatred of Cromwell, as one who abominated the murder of the king, and all the barbarous proceedings against the lives of men in cold blood; the king upon his return received him into grace and favour, which he never forfeited by any undutiful behaviour.

[After the Restoration.] That he [King Charles II] might give a lively instance of his grace to those who had been of the party which had been faulty, according to his declaration from Breda, he made of his own free inclination and choice the earl of Manchester (who was looked upon as one of the principal heads of the presbyterian party) lord chamberlain of his house; who, continuing still to perform all good offices to his old friends, complied very punctually with all the obligations and duties which his place required, never failed being at chapel, and at all the king's devotions with all imaginable decency; and, by his extraordinary civilities and behaviour towards all men, did not only appear the fittest person the king could have chosen for that office in that time, but rendered himself so acceptable to all degrees of men, that none, but such who were implacable towards all who had ever disserved the king, were sorry to see him so promoted. And it must be confessed, that as he had expressed much penitence for what he had done amiss and was mortally hated and persecuted by Cromwell, even for his life, and had done many acts of merit towards the king; so he was of all men, who had ever borne arms against the king, both in the gentleness and justice of his nature, in the sweetness and evenness of his conversation, and in his real principles for monarchy, the most worthy to be received into the trust and confidence in which he was placed.

27. *The Earl of Warwick and the Navy*

Robert Rich, born 1587; M.P. 1610; earl 1619; Lord High Admiral for the Parliament, December 1643 till 1645 and again May 1648 to 1649; died 1658

THE earl of Warwick was of the king's council too, but was not wondered at for leaving the king, whom he had never served; nor did he look upon himself as obliged by that honour, which, he knew, was conferred upon him in the crowd of those whom his majesty had no esteem of, or ever purposed to trust; so his business was to join with those to whom he owed his promotion. He was a man of a pleasant and companionable wit and conversation; of an universal jollity; and such a license in his words, and in his actions, that a man of less virtue could not be found out: so that a man might reasonably have believed, that a man so qualified would not have been able to have contributed much to the overthrow of a nation and kingdom. But, with all these faults, he had great authority and credit, with that people, who, in the beginning of the troubles, did all the mischief; and by opening his doors, and making his house the rendezvous of all the silenced ministers, in the time when there was authority to silence them, and spending a good part of his estate, of which he was very prodigal, upon them, and by being present with them at their devotions, and making himself merry with them, and at them, which they dispensed with, he became the head of that party; and got the style of a godly man. When the king revoked the earl of Northumberland's commission of admiral, he presently accepted the office from the parliament; and never quitted their service; and when Cromwell disbanded that parliament, he betook himself to the protection of the protector; married his heir to his daughter; and lived in so entire a confidence and friendship with him, that, when he died, he had the honour to be exceedingly lamented by him; and left his estate, which before was subject to a vast debt, more improved and repaired, than any man who trafficked in that desperate commodity of rebellion.

[In June 1642] the king thought it time to execute a resolution he had long intended, and which many men wondered he neglected so long; which was, as much as in him lay, to take the admiralty into his own hands. He had long too much cause to be unsatisfied and displeased with the earl of Northumberland; whom he thought he had obliged above any man whatsoever. His delivering the fleet into the hands and command of the earl of Warwick, after his majesty had expressly refused it to the parliament, he resolved never to forgive; however, he thought it not then seasonable to resent it, because he had nothing to object against him, but his compliance with the command of the parliament, which would have made and owned it as their own quarrel; and must have obliged him ⟨that earl⟩ to put his whole interest into their hands, and to have run their fortune; to which he was naturally too much inclined: and then his majesty foresaw, that there would have been no fleet at all set out that year, by their having the command of all the money, which was to be applied to that service. Whereas, by his majesty's concealing his resentment, there was a good fleet made ready, and set out; and many gentlemen settled in the command of ships, of whose affection and fidelity his majesty was assured, that no superior office could corrupt it; but that they would, at all times, repair to his service, whenever he required it. And, indeed, his majesty had an opinion of the devotion of the whole body of the common seamen to his service, because he had, bountifully, so much mended their condition, and increased their pay, that he thought they would have thrown the earl of Warwick overboard, when he should command them; and so the respiting the doing of it would be of little importance. But now, that a ship of his own, in the execution of his commands, should be chased by his own fleet as an enemy, made such a noise in all places, even to his reproach and dishonour, that he could no longer defer the doing what he had so long thought of. He resolved, therefore, to revoke the earl of Northumberland's commission of the office of high admiral of England, and to send the revocation to him under the great seal of England: then, to send sir John Pennington, who was then at York, on board the fleet, and to take the charge of it: and letters were prepared, and signed by the king, to every one of the captains; whereby they were required 'to observe the orders of sir John Pennington'. And all this was carried with all possible secrecy, that none, but those few who were trusted, knew or suspected of any such alteration.

[But by a mishap the scheme could not be carried out as planned. Warwick was alarmed and took prisoner those captains who were royalists.] And thus his majesty was without one ship of his own, in his three kingdoms, at his devotion. As this loss of the whole navy was of unspeakable ill consequence to the king's affairs, and made his condition much less considered by his allies, and neighbour princes; who saw the sovereignty of the seas now in other hands, who were more imperious upon the apprehension of any discourtesies, than regular and lawful monarchs used to be, I cannot but observe some unhappy circumstances and accidents in this important business of the navy which looked like the hand of Providence to take that strength of which his majesty was most confident, out of his hands.

The truth is, the king was so confident upon the general affections of the seamen, who were a tribe of people more particularly countenanced and obliged by him than other men, his majesty having increased their allowance, in provision and money, above the old establishment of the navy, that he did believe no activity of ill officers could have corrupted them; but that, when the parliament had set out and victualled the fleet, it would, upon any occasion, declare itself at his devotion. On the other side, they had been taught to believe, that all the king's bounty and grace towards them had flowed from the mediation of those officers, who were now engaged against the king; and that, the parliament having seized the customs, and all other revenues of the king, they had no other hope of pay or subsistence, but by absolutely devoting themselves to their service; so that a greater or more general defection of any one order or men was never known, than that, at this time, of the seamen; though many gentlemen, and some few of the common sort, to their lasting honour and reputation, either addressed themselves to the active service of their sovereign, or suffered imprisonment, and the loss of all they had, for refusing to serve against him.

[In summer 1648] The prince's remove from Paris on such a sudden, proceeded from an accident in England that was very extraordinary, and looked like a call from Heaven. The parliament had prepared, according to custom, a good fleet of ten or a dozen ships for the summer guard, and appointed Rainsborough to be admiral thereof; who had been bred at sea, and was the son of an eminent commander at sea, lately dead; but he himself, from the time of the new model, had been an officer of foot in the army, and was a colonel of special note and account, and of Cromwell's chief confidents; which offended the earl of Warwick much, and disposed him to concurrence with his brother [the earl of Holland]. And captain Batten was as much unsatisfied, who had acted so great a part in the first alienating the fleet and the affections of the seamen from the king, and had ever been their vice-admiral afterwards, and the person upon whom they principally relied at sea. Rainsborough, as long as he remained in the navy, had been under his command, and both the earl and he well know that this man was now made admiral of the fleet, because they, being presbyterians, should have no credit or influence upon it; which made them solicitous enough that the seamen should not be well pleased with the alteration; and they looked upon Rainsborough as a man that had forsaken them, and preferred the land before the sea service. The seamen are a nation by themselves, a humorous and fantastic people; fierce, and rude in whatsoever they resolve or are inclined to, unsteady and inconstant in pursuing it, and jealous of those to-morrow by whom they are governed to-day. These men, observing the general discontent of the people, and that however the parliament was obeyed by the power of the army, both army and parliament were grown very odious to them, and hearing so much discourse of an army from Scotland ready to enter into the kingdom, they concluded that the king would be restored; and then remembering that the revolt of the fleet was the preamble to the loss of his majesty's authority everywhere else, and the cause of all his misfortunes, imagined it would be a glorious thing to them, if they could lead the way to his majesty's restoration by their declaring for him. This was an agitation among the common seamen, without communicating it to any officer of the quality of master of a ship. This inclination was much improved in them by a general disposition in Kent to an insurrection for the king, and by some gentlemen's coming on board the ships, according to the custom of that country; who fomented the good disposition in the seamen by all the ways they could. [However, nothing came of this agitation at the time; and the story that Warwick was privy to Holland's engagement for the king has to be rejected. On the contrary, when in May 1648 nine ships revolted to the king, Warwick reconstituted the parliamentary navy. He lost his office in February 1649 because of his friendship to Cromwell.]

28. *The Earl of Essex*

Robert Devereux, born 1591; restored in blood and honour 1604; P.C. 1641; parliamentary general 1642; died September 1646

[Having mentioned the earl of Holland and the king's decision to remove both earls from their positions at court, Clarendon continues] Less was to be objected against the earl of Essex, who, as he had been, all his life, without obligations from the court, and believed he had undergone oppression there, so he was, in all respects, the same man he had always professed himself to be, when the king put him into that office; and in receiving of which, many men believed, that he rather gratified the king, than that his majesty had obliged him in conferring it; and it had been, no doubt, the chief reason of putting the staff [of Chamberlain of the King's Household] in his hand because in that conjuncture no other man, who would in any degree have appeared worthy of it, had the courage to receive it. However having taken the charge upon him, he ought, no doubt, to have taken all his master's concernments more to heart, than he had done; and he can never be excused for staying in Whitehall, when the king was with that outrage driven from thence, and for choosing to behold the triumph of the members' return to Westminster, rather than to attend his majesty's person in so great perplexity to Hampton-court; which had been his duty to have done, and for failing wherein no other excuse can be made, but that, after he had taken so full a resolution to have waited upon his majesty thither, that he had dressed himself in his travelling habit, he was diverted from it by the earl of Holland, who ought to have accompanied him in the service, and by his averment, 'that if he went, he should be assassinated'; which was never thought of.

Notwithstanding all this, the persons trusted by his majesty, and remaining at London, had no sooner notice of it, (which his majesty sent to them, that he might be advised the best way of doing it,) but they did all they could to dissuade the pursuing it. They did not think it a good conjuncture to make those two desperate; and they knew that they were not of the temper and inclinations of those, who had too much credit with them, nor did desire to drive things to the utmost extremities, which could never better their conditions; and that they did both rather desire to find any expedients, by which they might make a safe and honourable retreat, than to advance in the way they were engaged. But the argument they chiefly insisted on to the king, was, 'that, being deprived of their offices, they would be able to do more mischief, and ready to embark themselves with the most desperate persons, in the most desperate attempts'; which fell out accordingly. And there is great reason to believe, that if that resolution the king had taken had not been too obstinately pursued at that time, many of the mischiefs, which afterwards fell out, would have been prevented;

and, without doubt, if the staff had remained still in the hands of the earl of Essex, by which he was charged with the defence and security of the king's person, he would never have been prevailed with to have taken upon him the command of that army, which was afterwards raised against the king, and with which so many battles were fought. And there can be as little doubt in any man, who knew well the nature and temper of that time, that it had been utterly impossible, for the two houses of parliament to have raised an army then, if the earl of Essex had not consented to be general of that army.

The earl of Essex hath been enough mentioned before; his nature and his understanding have been described; his former disobligations from the court, and then his introduction into it, and afterwards his being displaced from the office he held in it, have been set forth; and there will be occasion, hereafter, to renew the discourse of him; and therefore it shall suffice, in this place, to say, that a weak judgment, and a little vanity, and as much of pride, will hurry a man into as unwarrantable and as violent attempts, as the greatest, and most unlimited, and insatiable ambition will do. He had no ambition of title, or office, or preferment, but only to be kindly looked upon, and kindly spoken to, and quietly to enjoy his own fortune: and, without doubt, no man in his nature more abhorred rebellion than he did, nor could he have been led into it by any open or transparent temptation, but by a thousand disguises and cozenages. His pride supplied his want of ambition, and he was angry to see any other man more respected than himself, because he thought he deserved it more, and did better requite it. For he was, in his friendships, just and constant; and would not have practised foully against those he took to be enemies. No man had credit enough with him to corrupt him in point of loyalty to the king, whilst he thought himself wise enough to know what treason was. But the new doctrine, and distinction of allegiance, and of the king's power in and out of parliament, and the new notions of ordinances, were too hard for him, and did really intoxicate his understanding, and made him quit his own, to follow theirs, who, he thought, wished as well, and judged better than himself. His vanity disposed him to be his excellency; and his weakness, to believe that he should be the general in the houses, as well as in the field; and be able to govern their counsels, and restrain their passions, as well as to fight their battles; and that, by this means, he should become the preserver, and not the destroyer, of the king and kingdom. And with this ill-grounded confidence, he launched out into that sea, where he met with nothing but rocks and shelves, and from whence he could never discover any safe port to harbour in. [He had been much flattered by the leaders of the opposition and in the end] by these artifices and applications to his vanity, and magnifying the general reputation and credit he had with the people they possessed themselves of the earl of Essex; who, though he was no good speaker in public, yet, having sat long in parliament, and so well acquainted with the order of it in active times, he was a better speaker there than any where else, and being always heard with attention and respect, had much authority in the debates.

29. *The Lord Say*

William Fiennes, born 1582; Viscount Say and Sele 1624; P.C. and Master of the Court of Wards 1641; P.C. and Lord Privy Seal 1660; died 1662

T H E lord viscount Say [was] a man of a close and reserved nature, of a mean and a narrow fortune, of great parts, and of the highest ambition, but whose ambition would not be satisfied with offices and preferment, without some condescensions and alterations in ecclesiastical matters. He had for many years been the oracle of those who were called puritans in the worst sense, and steered all their counsels and designs. He was a notorious enemy to the church, and to most of the eminent churchmen, with some of whom he had particular contests. He had always opposed and contradicted all acts of state, and all taxes and impositions, which were not exactly legal, and so had as eminently and as obstinately refused the payment of

ship-money as Mr. Hambden had done; though the latter,
by the choice of the king's council, had brought his cause
to be first heard and argued, with which judgment that
was intended to conclude the whole right in that matter,
and to overrule all other cases. The lord Say would not
acquiesce, but pressed to have his own case argued, and
was so solicitous in person with all the judges, both
privately at their chambers, and publicly in the court at
Westminster, that he was very grievous to them. His commitment at York the year before, because he refused to
take an oath, or rather subscribe a protestation, against
holding intelligence with the Scots, when the king first
marched against them, had given him much credit. In a
word, he had very great authority with all the discontented
party throughout the kingdom, and a good reputation
with many who were not ⟨discontented,⟩ who believed
him to be a wise man and of a very useful temper, in an age
of license, and one who would still adhere to the law. . . .

The last of those counsellors which were made after the
faction prevailed in parliament, who were all made to
advance an accommodation, and who adhered to the
parliament, was the lord Say; a man, who had the deepest
hand in the original contrivance of all the calamities
which befell this unhappy kingdom, though he had not
the least thought of dissolving the monarchy, and less of
levelling the ranks and distinctions of men. For no man
valued himself more upon his title, or had more ambition
to make it greater, and to raise his fortune, which was but
moderate for his title. He was of a proud, morose, and sullen
nature; conversed much with books, having been bred a
scholar, and (though nobly born) a fellow of New College
in Oxford; to which he claimed a right, by the alliance he
pretended to have from William of Wickham, the founder;
which he made good by such an unreasonable pedigree,
through so many hundred years, half the time whereof
extinguishes all relation of kindred. However upon that
pretence, that college hath been seldom without one of
that lord's family. His parts were not quick, but so much
above those of his own rank, that he had always great
credit and authority in parliament; and the more, for

taking all opportunities to oppose the court; and he had, with his milk, sucked in an implacable malice against the government of the church. When the duke of Buckingham proposed to himself, after his return with the prince from Spain, to make himself popular, by breaking that match, and to be gracious with the parliament, as for a short time he was, he resolved to embrace the friendship of the lord Say; who was as solicitous to climb by that ladder. But the duke quickly found him of too imperious and pedantical a spirit, and to affect too dangerous mutations; and so cast him off; and from that time he gave over any pursuit in court, and lived narrowly and sordidly in the country; having conversation with very few, but such who had great malignity against the church and state, and fomented their inclinations, and gave them instructions how to behave themselves with caution, and to do their business with most security; and was in truth the pilot, that steered all those vessels which were freighted with sedition to destroy the government.

He found always some way to make professions of duty to the king, and made several undertakings to do great services, which he could not, or would not, make good; and made haste to possess himself of any preferment he could compass, whilst his friends were content to attend a more proper conjuncture. So he got the mastership of the wards shortly after the beginning of the parliament, and was as solicitous to be treasurer after the death of the earl of Bedford; and, if he could have satisfied his rancour in any degree against the church, he would have been ready to have carried the prerogative as high as ever it was. When he thought there was mischief enough done, he would have stopped the current, and have diverted farther fury; but he then found he had only authority and credit to do hurt; none to heal the wounds he had given; and fell into as much contempt with those whom he had led, as he was with those whom he had undone.

30. *The Lord Savile*

*Thomas Savile, born 1590?; second baron 1630; first
Earl of Sussex 1644; P.C. and Lord President of
Council of the North 1641; died 1658?*

[In 1644] The lord Savile was likewise of the council,
being first controller, and then treasurer of the household,
in recompense of his discovery of all the treasons and conspiracies, after they had taken effect, and could not be
punished. He was a man of an ambitious and restless
nature; of parts and wit enough; but, in his disposition,
and inclination, so false, that he could never be believed,
or depended upon. His particular malice to the earl of
Strafford, which he had sucked in with his milk, (there
having always been an immortal feud between the families; and the earl had shrewdly overborne his father,)
had engaged him with all persons who were willing, and
like to be able, to do him mischief. And so, having opportunity, when the king was at the Berks, and made the
first unhappy pacification [the treaty of Berwick, 1639],
to enter into conversation, and acquaintance, with those
who were then employed as commissioners from the Scots,
there was a secret intelligence entered into between them
from that time; and he was a principal instrument to
engage that nation to march into England with an army,
which they did the next year after. To which purpose, he
sent them a letter, signed with the names of several of the
English nobility, inviting them to enter the kingdom, and
making great promises of assistance; which names were
forged by himself, without the privity of those who were
named. And when all this mischief was brought to pass,
and he found his credit in the parliament not so great as
other men's, he insinuated himself into credit with somebody, who brought him to the king or queen, to whom he
confessed all he had done to bring in the Scots, and who
had conspired with him, and all the secrets he knew, with
a thousand protestations 'to repair all by future loyalty
and service'; for which he was promised a white staff,
which the king had then resolved to take from sir Henry

Vane, who held it with the secretary's office; which he
had accordingly; though all his discovery was of no other
use, than that the king knew many had been false, whom
he could not punish; and some, whom he could not
suspect. When the king came to York, where this lord's
fortune and interest lay, his reputation was so low, that
the gentlemen of interest, who wished well to the king's
service, would not communicate with him; and, after the
king's remove from thence, the earl of Newcastle found
cause to have such a jealousy of him, that he thought it
necessary to imprison him; and afterwards sent him to
Oxford; where he so well purged himself, that he was
again restored to his office. But in the end he behaved
himself so ill, that the king put him again out of his place,
and committed him to prison, and never after admitted
him to his presence; nor would any man of quality ever
after keep any correspondence with him.

31. *The Opposition disputes with the King the Control of the
Militia, appeals to the Nation by means of the Grand Remonstrance, December 1641 and puts the Country by Ordinance into
'a Posture of Defence' in January 1642.*

[From 10 August to 25 November 1641 the king had
been absent from London.] About the time the news came
of the king's being to begin his journey from Scotland upon
a day appointed; and that he had settled all things in
that kingdom to the general satisfaction; the committee
for preparing the remonstrance offered their report to the
house; which caused the draught they offered to be read.
It contained a very bitter representation of all the illegal
things which had been done, from the first hour of the
king's coming to the crown, to that minute; with all those
sharp reflections which could be made, upon the king
himself, the queen, and council; and published all the unreasonable jealousies of the present government, of the
introducing popery; and all other particulars, which might
disturb the minds of the people; which were enough discomposed.

The house seemed generally to dislike it; many saying

'that it was very unnecessary, and unseasonable: unnecessary, all those grievances being already fully redressed;
and the liberty and property of the subject being as
well secured for the future, as could possibly be done:
and then that it was very unseasonable, after the king
had gratified them, with granting everything which they
had desired of him; and after so long absence, in the
settling the disorders in another kingdom, which he had
happily composed; to be now welcomed home with such
a volume of reproaches, for what others had done amiss,
and which he himself had reformed'. Notwithstanding all
which, all the other party appeared passionately concerned that it might not be rejected; and enlarged themselves with as high expressions against the government, as
at first; with many insinuations, 'that we were in danger
of being deprived of all the good acts which we had gained,
if great care and vigilance was not used, to disappoint
some counsels which were still entertained'; making doubtful glances and reflections upon the rebellion in Ireland,
(with which they perceived many good men were easily
amused,) and in the end prevailed, 'that a day should be
appointed, when the house should be resolved into a grand
committee, and the remonstrance to be then retaken into
consideration': and in the mean time they employed all
their credit and interest with particular men, to persuade
them, 'that the passing that remonstrance was most necessary, for the preservation and maintenance of all those
good laws which they had already made'; giving several
reasons to several persons, according to their natures and
inclinations; assuring many, 'that they intended it only
for the mortification of the court, and manifestation that
that malignant party, which appeared to be growing up
in the house, could not prevail'; and then 'that it should
remain still in the clerk's hands, and never be published'.

And by these, and the like arts, they promised themselves, that they should easily carry it: so that the day it
was to be resumed, they entertained the house all the
morning with other debates, and towards noon called for
the remonstrance; and it being urged by some, 'that it
was too late to enter upon it, with much difficulty they

consented, that it should be entered upon the next morning
at nine of the clock; and every clause should be debated,
the speaker in the chair'; for they would not have the
house resolved into a committee, which they believed
would spend too much time. Oliver Cromwell (who, at
that time, was little taken notice of) asked the lord Falkland, 'Why he would have it put off, for that day would
quickly have determined it?' He answered, 'There would
not have been time enough, for sure it would take some
debate'. The other replied, 'A very sorry one': they supposing, by the computation they had made, that very few
would oppose it.

But he quickly found he was mistaken: for the next
morning, the debate being entered upon about nine of
the clock in the morning, it continued all that day; and
candles being called for when it grew dark, (neither side
being very desirous to adjourn it till the next day; though
it was evident, very many withdrew themselves out of
pure faintness and disability to attend the conclusion,)
the debate continued, till after it was twelve of the clock,
with much passion; and the house being then divided,
upon the passing or not passing it, it was carried for the
affirmative, by nine voices, and no more: and as soon as
it was declared, Mr. Hambden moved, 'that there might
be an order entered for the present printing it'; which
produced a sharper debate than the former. It appeared
then, that they did not intend to send it up to the house of
peers for their concurrence; but that it was upon the
matter an appeal to the people; and to infuse jealousies
into their minds. It had never been the custom to publish
any debates, or determinations of the house, which were
not regularly first transmitted to the house of peers; nor
was it thought, in truth, that the house had authority to
give warrant for the printing of any thing; all which was
offered by Mr. Hyde, with some warmth, as soon as the
motion was made for the printing it; and he said, 'he did
believe the printing it in that manner was not lawful;
and he feared it would produce mischievous effects; and
therefore desired the leave of the house, that if the question should be put, and carried in the affirmative, that he

might have liberty to enter his protestation'; which he no sooner said, than Jeffery Palmer (a man of great reputation, and much esteemed in the house) stood up, and made the same motion for himself, 'that he might likewise protest'. When immediately together many afterwards, without distinction, and in some disorder, cried out, 'They did protest': so that there was after scarce any quiet and regular debate. But the house by degrees being quieted, they all consented, about two of the clock in the morning, to adjourn till two of the clock the next afternoon. And as they went out of the house, the lord Falkland asked Oliver Cromwell, 'Whether there had been a debate?' to which he answered, 'that he would take his word another time'; and whispered him in the ear, with some asseveration, 'that if the remonstrance had been rejected, he would have sold all he had the next morning, and never have seen England more; and he knew there were many other honest men of the same resolution'. So near was the poor kingdom at that time to its deliverance.

And however they got this victory, they did not in a long time recover the spirits they lost, and the agony they sustained, whilst it was in suspense; and they discerned well enough, that the house had not, at that time, half its members; though they had provided, that not a man of their party was absent; and that they had even then carried it by the hour of the night, which drove away a greater number of old and infirm opposers, than would have made those of the negative superior in number: so that they had little hope, in a fuller house, to prevail in any of their unjust designs, except they found some other expedient, by hopes or fears, to work upon the affections of the several members.

In order to which, they spent most part of the next day in their private consultations, how to chastise some of those who most offended them the day before; and resolved in the first place, not to suffer that precedent to be introduced into the house, 'that men should protest against the sense of the house': which, it is true, had not been used in the house of commons.

I know not how those men have already answered it to

their own consciences; or how they will answer it to Him who can discern their consciences; who, having assumed their country's trust, and, it may be, with great earnestness, laboured to procure that trust, by their supine laziness, negligence, and absence, were the first inlets to these inundations; and so contributed to those licenses which have overwhelmed us. For, by this means, a handful of men, much inferior in the beginning, in number and interest, came to give laws to the major part; and to shew that three diligent persons are a greater number in arithmetic, as well as a more significant number in logic, than ten unconcerned, they, by plurality of voices, in the end, converted or reduced the whole body to their opinions. It is true, men of activity and faction, in any design, have many advantages, that a composed and settled council, though industrious enough, usually have not; and some, that gallant men cannot give themselves leave to entertain: for, besides their thorough considering and forming their counsels before they begin to execute them, they contract a habit of ill nature and uningenuity necessary to their affairs, and the temper of those upon whom they are to work, that liberal-minded men would not persuade themselves to entertain, even for the prevention of all the mischief the others intend. And whosoever observed the ill arts, ⟨by which⟩ these men used to prevail upon the people in general; their absurd, ridiculous lying, to win the affections, and corrupt the understandings, of the weak; and the bold scandals, to confirm the wilful; the boundless promises they presented to the ambitious; and their gross, abject flatteries, and applications, to the vulgar-spirited, would hardly give himself leave to use those weapons, for the preservation of the three kingdoms.

The king besides had at that time a greater disadvantage (besides the concurrence of ill and extraordinary accidents) than himself, or any of his progenitors, had ever had before; having no servant in the house of commons of interest, ability, and reputation, of faithfulness and affection to his service. . . . So that, whilst these men, and their consorts, with the greatest deliberation, consulted, and disposed themselves to compass confusion; they, who out of the most abstracted sense of loyalty to the king, and duty to their country, severed from any relations to the king, or hopes from the court, preserved their own innocence, and endeavoured to uphold the good old frame of government, received neither countenance nor conduct from those who were naturally to have taken care of that province. And sure the raging and fanatic distempers of the house of commons (to which all other distempers are to be imputed) must most properly be attributed to the want of good ministers of the crown in that assembly, who being unawed by any guilt of their own, could have watched other men's; and informed, encouraged, and governed those, who stood well inclined to the public peace.

To which purpose, if that stratagem (though none of the best) of winning men by places, had been practised, as soon as the resolution was taken at York to call a parliament, (in which, it was apparent, dangerous attempts would be made; and that the court could not be able to resist those attempts,) and if Mr. Pym, Mr. Hambden, and Mr. Hollis, had been then preferred with Mr. Saint-John, before they were desperately embarked in their desperate designs, and had innocence enough about them, to trust the king, and be trusted by him; having yet contracted no personal animosities against him; it is very possible, that they might either have been made instruments to have done good service; or at least been restrained from endeavouring to subvert the royal building, for supporting whereof they were placed as principal pillars.

But the rule the king gave himself, (very reasonable at another time,) that they should first do service, and compass this or that thing for him before they should receive favour, was then very unseasonable: since, besides that they could not in truth do him that service without the qualification, it could not be expected they would desert that side, by the power of which they were sure to make themselves considerable, without an unquestionable mark of interest in the other, by which they were to keep up their power and reputation: and so, whilst the king expected they should manifest their inclinations to his service, by their temper and moderation in those proceedings that most offended him; and they endeavoured, by doing all the hurt they could, to make evident the power they had to do him good; he grew so far disobliged and provoked, that he could not in honour gratify them; and they so obnoxious and guilty, that they could not think themselves secure in his favour: and thence, according to the policy and method of injustice, combined to oppress that power they had injured; and to raise a security for themselves, by disenabling the king to question their transgressions.

It will be wondered at hereafter, that in a judging and discerning state, where men had, or seemed to have, their faculties of reason and understanding at the height; in a kingdom then unapt, and generally uninclined to war, (how wantonly soever it hath since seemed to throw away its peace,) those men who had the skill and cunning, out of froward and peevish humours, and indispositions, to compound fears and jealousies, and to animate and inflame those fears and jealousies into the most prodigious and the boldest rebellion, that any age or country ever brought forth; who very well saw and felt, that the king had not only, to a degree, wound himself out of that ladyrinth, in which, four months before, they had involved him, with their privileges, fears, and jealousies; but had even so well informed the people, that they began to question both their logic and their law, and to suspect and censure the improvement and gradation of their fears, and the extent and latitude of their privileges; and that they were not only denied by the king, what they required, but that the king's reasons of his denial made very many conclude the unreasonableness of their demands: I say, it may seem strange, that these men could entertain the hope and confidence to obtrude such a declaration and vote upon the people, 'that the king did intend to make war against the parliament'; when they were so far from apprehending, that he would be able to get an army to disturb them, that they were most assured, he would not be able to get bread to sustain himself three months, without submitting all his counsels to their conduct and control; and that the offering to impose it did not awaken the people to an indignation, which might have confounded them: for, besides their presumption in endeavouring to search what the scripture itself told them was unsearchable, the heart of the king; the very law of the land, whose defence they pretended, makes no conclusion of the intention of the meanest subject, in a matter of the highest and tenderest consideration, even treason itself against the life of the king, without some overt, unlawful act, from whence, and other circumstances, the ill intention may be reasonably made appear; and therefore, to declare that the king intended to make war against his parliament, when he had neither ship, harbour, arms, nor money, and knew not how to get either, and when he offered to grant any thing to them, which they could pretend a justifiable reason for asking, was an undertaking of that nature, that even the almightiness of a parliament might have despaired to succeed in.

But, notwithstanding all this, they very well knew what they did, and understood what infinite advantage that vote would (as it did) bring to them; and that a natural way would never bring them to their unnatural end. The power and reputation of parliament, they believed, would implicitly prevail over many; and amaze and terrify others from disputing or censuring what they did, and upon what grounds they did it. The difficulty was, to procure the judgment of parliament; and to incline those different constitutions, and different affections, to such a concurrence as the judgment might not be discredited, by the number of the dissenters; not wounded, or prejudged, by the reasons and arguments given against it: and then, their judgments of the cure being to be grounded upon the nature and information of the disease, it was necessary to confine and contract their fancies and opinions within some bounds and limits: the mystery of rebellion challenging the same encouragement with other sciences, to grow by; that there may be certain postulata, some principles and foundations, upon which the main building may subsist. So, in the case of the militia, an imminent danger

must be first supposed, by which the kingdom is in an
apparent danger, and then the king's refusal to apply any
remedy against that danger, before the two houses would
pretend to the power of disposing that militia; it being too
ridiculous to have pretended the natural and ordinary
jurisdiction over it: but, in case of danger, and danger so
imminent, that the usual recourse would not serve the
turn, and for the saving of a kingdom, which must otherwise be lost, many good men thought it was reasonable to
apply a very extraordinary prevention, without imagining
such a supposition might possibly engage them in any
action, contrary to their own inclinations; and, without
doubt, very many, who frankly voted that imminent
necessity, were induced to it, as an argument, that the
king should be therefore importuned to consent to the
settlement; which would not have appeared so necessary
a request, if the occasion had not been important; never
suspecting, that it would have proved an argument to
them, to adventure the doing it without the king's consent.
And it is not here unseasonable, (how merry soever it may
seem to be,) as an instance of the incogitancy and inad-
vertency of those kind of votes and transactions, to remember, that the first resolution of the power of the militia
being grounded upon a supposition of an imminent necessity, the ordinance first sent up from the commons to the
lords, for the execution of the militia, expressed an eminent necessity; whereupon, some lords, who understood
the difference of the words, and that an *eminent* necessity
might be supplied by the ordinary provision, which, possibly, an *imminent* necessity might not safely attend, desired
a conference with the commons for the amendment;
which, I remember, was at last, with great difficulty, consented to: many (who, I presume, are not yet grown
up to conceive the difference) supposing it an unnecessary contention for a word, and so yielding to them, for
saving of time, rather than of the great moment of the
thing.

They, who contrived this scene, never doubted that,
after a resolution what was to be done upon a supposi-
tious necessity, they should easily, when they found it con-

venient, make that necessity real. It was no hard matter to make the fearful, apprehensive of dangers; and the jealous, of designs; and they wanted not evidence of all kinds; ⟨of⟩ letters from abroad, and discoveries at home, to make those apprehensions formidable enough; and then, though, before the resolution, there was a great latitude in law and reason, what was lawfully to be done, they had now forejudged themselves, and resolved of the proper remedy, except they would argue against the evidence; which usually would have been to discountenance or undervalue some person of notable reputation, or his correspondence; and always to have opposed that that was of such an allay, as, in truth, did operate upon the major part. So, in the case upon which we now discourse, if they had, in the most advantageous article of their fury, professed the raising an army against the king, there was yet that reverence to majesty, and that spirit of subjection and allegiance in most men, that they would have looked upon it with opposition and horror: but defensive arms were more plausible divinity, and if the king should commit such an outrage, as to levy war against his parliament, to destroy the religion, laws, and liberty of the kingdom, good men were persuaded, that such a resistance might be made, as might preserve the whole; and he that would have argued against this thesis, besides the impertinency of arguing against a supposition, that was not like to be real, and in which the corrupt consideration of safety seemed to bribe most men, could never escape the censure of promoting tyranny and lawless dominion. Then to incline men to concur in the declaration 'of the king's intention to make war against the parliament', they were persuaded it might have a good, could have no ill, effect: the remedies, that were to be applied upon an actual levying of war, were not justifiable upon the intention; and the declaring this intention, and the dangers it carried with it to the king himself, and to all those who should assist him, would be a probable means of reforming such intention, and preventing the execution: inconvenience it could produce none, (for the disquieting or displeasing the king was not thought inconvenient,) if there were no progress in the supposed intention; if there were, it were fit the whole kingdom should stand upon its guard, and not be surprised to its confusion.

By these false and fallacious mediums, the clearness of men's understandings were dazzled; and, upon the matter, all their opinions, and judgments for the future, captivated and preengaged by their own votes and determinations. For, how easy a matter was it to make it appear to that man, who consented that the king intended to make war against the parliament, that when he should do it, he had broken his oath, and dissolved his government; and, that whosoever should assist him were traitors; I say, how easy was it to persuade that man, that he was obliged to defend the parliament; to endeavour to uphold that government; and to resist those traitors? and, whosoever considers that the nature of men, especially of men in authority, is inclined rather to commit two errors, than to retract one, will not marvel, that from this root of unadvisedness, so many and tall branches of mischief have proceeded. And therefore it were to be wished, that those, who have the honour to be trusted in public consultations, were endued with so much natural logic, to discern the consequences of every public act and conclusion; and with so much conscience and courage, to watch the first impressions upon ⟨their⟩ understanding and compliance: and, neither out of the impertinency of the thing, which men are too apt to conclude out of impatiency of despatch; or out of stratagem to make men odious, (as in this parliament many forbore to oppose unreasonable resolutions, out of an opinion, that they would make the contrivers odious,) or upon any other (though seeming never so politic) considerations, consent to any propositions, by which truth or justice are invaded. And I am confident, with very good warrant, that many men have, from their souls, abhorred every article of this rebellion; and heartily deprecated the miseries and desolation we have suffered by it, who have themselves, with great alacrity and some industry, contributed to, if not contrived, those very votes and conclusions, from whence the evils they abhor have most naturally and regularly flowed, and been deduced;

and which they could not reasonably, upon their own concessions, contradict and oppose.

But to conclude, a man shall not unprofitably spend his contemplation, that, upon this occasion, considers the method of God's justice, (a method terribly remarkable in many passages, and upon many persons, which we shall be compelled to remember in this discourse,) that the same principles, and the same application of those principles, should be used to the wresting all sovereign power from the crown, which the crown had a little before made use of for the extending its authority and power beyond its bounds, to the prejudice of the just rights of the subject. A supposed necessity was then thought ground enough to create a power, and a bare averment of that necessity, to beget a practice to impose what tax they thought convenient upon the subject, by writs of ship-money never before known; and a supposed necessity now, and a bare averment of that necessity, is as confidently, and more fatally, concluded a good ground to exclude the crown from the use of any power, by an ordinance never before heard of; and the same maxim of *salus populi suprema lex*, which had been used to the infringing the liberties of the one, made use of for the destroying the rights of the other: only that of the psalmist is yet inverted; for many of those, who were the principal makers of the first pit, are so far from falling into it, that they have been the chiefest diggers of the second ditch, in which so many have been confounded.

It is not easily believed, how these gross infusions generally prevailed. [Clarendon speaks here of Somersetshire in 1642.] For though the gentlemen of ancient families and estates in that country were, for the most part, well affected to the king, and easily discerned by what faction the parliament was governed; yet there were a people of an inferior degree, who, by good husbandry, clothing, and other thriving arts, had gotten very great fortunes; and, by degrees, getting themselves into the gentlemen's estates, were angry that they found not themselves in the same esteem and reputation with those whose estates they had; and therefore, with more industry than the other, studied all ways to make themselves considerable. These, from the beginning, were fast friends to the parliament; and many of them were now intrusted by them as deputy lieutenants in their new ordinance of the militia, and having found when the people were ripe, gathered them together, with a purpose on a sudden, before there should be any suspicion, to surround and surprise the marquis [of Hertford] at Wells. For they had always this advantage of the king's party and his counsels, that their resolutions were no sooner published, than they were ready to be executed, there being an absolute implicit obedience in the inferior sort to those who were to command them; and their private agents, with admirable industry and secrecy, preparing all persons and things ready against a call. Whereas all the king's counsels were with great formality deliberated, before concluded; and then, with equal formality, and precise caution of the law, executed; there being no other way to weigh down the prejudice that was contracted against the court, but by the most barefaced publishing all conclusions, and fitting them to that apparent justice and reason, that might prevail over the most ordinary understandings.

32. *Charles I attempts in person to arrest five Members of the House of Commons, 4 January 1642, but is resolutely opposed by the City of London: 'sink of all the ill humour of the kingdom'*

[Advised by lord Digby only the king answered the imprisonment of the twelve bishops by his impeachment of Pym, Hampden, Hollis, Haslerig, Strode, and Lord Kimbolton.] The next day in the afternoon, the king, attended only by his own guard, and some few gentlemen, who put themselves into their company in the way, came to the house of commons; and commanding all his attendants to wait at the door, and to give offence to no man; himself, with his nephew, the prince elector, went into the house, to the great amazement of all: and the speaker leaving the chair, the king went into it; and told the house, 'he was sorry for that occasion of coming to them; that yesterday he had sent his sergeant at arms to apprehend some, that, by his command, were accused of high treason; whereunto he expected obedience, but instead thereof he had received a message. He declared to them, that no king of England had been ever, or should be, more careful to maintain their privileges, than he would be; but that in cases of treason no man had privilege; and therefore he came to see if any of those persons, whom he had accused, were there; for he was resolved to have them, wheresoever he should find them: and looking then about, and asking the speaker whether they were in the house, and he making no answer, he said, he perceived the *birds were all flown*, but expected they should be sent to him, as soon as they returned thither; and assured them in the word of a king, that he never intended any force, but would proceed against them in a fair and legal way;' and so returned to Whitehall.

The next morning, the king, being informed of much that had passed that night, according to the advice he had received, sent to the lord mayor to call a common council immediately; and about ten of the clock, himself, attended only by three or four lords, went to the guildhall; and in the room, where the people were assembled, told them, 'he was very sorry to hear of the apprehensions they had entertained of danger; that he was come to them, to shew how much he relied upon their affections for his security and guard, having brought no other with him; that he had accused certain men of high treason, against whom he would proceed in a legal way; and therefore he presumed they would not shelter them in the city.' And using many other very gracious expressions of his value of them and telling one of the sheriffs, (who was of the two thought less inclined to his service,) 'that he would dine with him', he departed without that applause and cheerfulness, which he might have expected from the extraordinary grace he vouchsafed to them; and in his passage through the city, the rude people flocking together, and crying out, 'Privilege of parliament, privilege of parliament'; some of them pressing very near his own coach, and amongst the rest one calling out with a very loud voice, 'To your tents, O Israel.' However the king, though much mortified, continued his resolution, taking little notice of the distempers;

and, having dined at the sheriff's, returned in the afternoon to Whitehall; and published, the next day, a proclamation for the apprehension of all those, whom he accused of high treason, forbidding any person to harbour them; the articles of their charge being likewise printed and dispersed.

When the house of commons next met, none of the accused members appearing, they had friends enough, who were well enough instructed to aggravate the late proceedings, and to put the house into a thousand jealousies and apprehensions, and every slight circumstance carried weight enough in it to disturb their minds. They took very little notice of the accusing the members; but the king's coming to the house, which had been never known before, and declaring, 'that he would take them wherever he found them, was an evidence, that he meant himself to have brought a force into the house, to apprehend them, if they had been there'; was looked upon as the highest breach of privilege that could possibly be imagined. They who spake most passionately, and probably meant as maliciously, behaved themselves with modesty, and seemed only concerned in what concerned them all; and concluded, after many lamentations, 'that they did not think themselves safe in that house, till the minds of men were better composed; that the city was full of apprehensions, and was very zealous for their security; and therefore wished that they might adjourn the parliament to meet in some place in the city.' But that was found not practicable; since it was not in their own power to do it, without the consent of the peers, and the concurrence of the king; who were both like rather to choose a place more distant from the city. And, with more reason, in the end they concluded, 'that the house should adjourn itself for two or three days, and name a committee, which should sit both morning and afternoon in the city'; and all who came, to have voices: and Merchant-Tailors' hall was appointed for the place of their meeting; they who served for London undertaking, 'that it should be ready against the next morning': no man opposing or contradicting any thing that was said; they, who formerly used to appear for all the rights and authority which belonged to the king, not knowing what to say, and between grief and anger that the violent party had, by these late unskilful actions of the court, gotten great advantage, and recovered new spirits: and the three persons before named [Hyde, Falkland, Colepepper], without whose privity the king had promised that he would enter upon no new counsel, were so much displeased and dejected, that they were inclined never more to take upon them the care of any thing to be transacted in the house: finding already, that they could not avoid being looked upon as the authors of those counsels, to which they were so absolute strangers, and which they so perfectly detested.

And in truth, they had then withdrawn themselves from appearing often in the house, but upon the abstracted consideration of their duty and conscience, and of the present ill condition the king was in; who likewise felt within himself the trouble and agony which usually attends generous and magnanimous minds, upon their having committed errors, which expose them to censure and to damage. In fine, the house of commons adjourned for some days, to consult with their friends in the city; and the house of lords held so good correspondence with them, that they likewise adjourned to the same days they knew, by some intelligence, they intended to meet again. But the lords made no committee to sit in the city.

When the committee met the next morning at Merchant-Tailors' Hall, where all who came were to have voices, and whither all did come at first out of curiosity to observe what method they meant to proceed in, rather than expectation that they should be able to do any good there; they found a guard ready to attend them, of substantial citizens in arms, and a committee from the common council, to bid them welcome into the city; and to assure them, 'that the city would take care, that they and all their members should be secured from violence; and to that purpose had appointed that guard to attend them, which should be always relieved twice a day, if they resolved to sit morning and afternoon'; and acquainted them further, 'that the common council, in contemplation that they might stand in want of any thing, had likewise appointed a committee of so many aldermen, and such a number of the common council, which should always meet at a place named, at those hours, which that committee should appoint to meet at; to the end that, if any thing were to be required of the city, they might still know their pleasure, and take care that it should be obeyed'. And thus they had provided for such a mutual communication and confederacy, that they might be sure always to be of one mind, and the one to help the other in the prosecution of those designs and expedients, which they should find necessary to their common end: the committee of the city consisting of the most eminent persons, aldermen and others, for their disaffection to the government of church and state.

At their first sitting, the committee began with the stating the manner of the king's coming to the house, and all he did there; the several members mentioning all that they would take upon them to remember of his majesty's doing or speaking, both as he came to the house, and after he was there; some of them being walking in Westminster-hall when the king walked through, and so came to the house with him, or near him; others reporting what they heard some of the gentlemen, who attended his majesty, say, as they passed by; every idle word having its commentary; and the persons, whoever were named, being appointed to attend; they having power given to them to send for all persons, and to examine them touching that affair. Nor had any man the courage to refuse to obey their summons; so that all those of the king's servants, who were sent for, appeared punctually at the hour that was assigned them; and were examined upon all questions, which any one of the committee would propose to them, whereof many were very impertinent, and of little respect to the king.

It was very well known where the accused persons were, all together in one house in Coleman Street, near the place where the committee sat; and whither persons trusted passed to and fro to communicate and receive directions; but it was not seasonable time for them yet to appear in public, and to come and sit with the committee, or to own the believing that they thought themselves safe from the violence and the assaults of the court; the power whereof they exceedingly contemned, whilst they seemed to apprehend it: nor was it yet time to model in what manner their friends in the city and the country should appear concerned for them; in preparing whereof no time was lost.

[Because the City sheltered the accused members Clarendon thinks] Neither will it be here unseasonable, to spend a little time in considering how the affections and tempers of so rich and opulent a city, which could naturally expect to prosper only by peace and agreement, were wrought upon and transported to that degree, as to be the only instrument of its own and the kingdom's destruction.

The city of London, as the metropolis of England, by the situation the most capable of trade, and by the most usual residence of the court, and the fixed station of the courts of justice for the public administration of justice throughout the kingdom, the chief seat of trade, was, by the successive countenance and favour of princes, strengthened with great charters and immunities, and was a corporation governed within itself; the mayor, recorder, aldermen, sheriffs, chosen by themselves; several companies incorporated within the great corporation; which, besides notable privileges, enjoyed lands and perquisites to a very great revenue. By the incredible increase of trade, which the distractions of other countries, and the peace of this, brought, and by the great license of resort thither, it was, since the access of the crown to the king, in riches, in people, in buildings, marvellously increased, insomuch as the suburbs were almost equal to the city; a reformation of which had been often in contemplation, never pursued, wise men foreseeing that such a fulness could not be there, without an emptiness in other places; and whilst so many persons of honour and estates were so delighted with the city, the government of the country must be neglected, besides the excess, and ill husbandry, that would be introduced thereby. But such foresight was interpreted a morosity, and too great an oppression upon the common liberty; and so, little was applied to prevent so growing a disease.

As it had these and many other advantages and helps to be rich, so it was looked upon too much of late time as a common stock not easy to be exhausted, and as a body not to be grieved by ordinary acts of injustice; and therefore, it was not only a resort, in all cases of necessity, for the sudden borrowing great sums of money, in which they were commonly too good merchants for the crown, but it was thought reasonable, upon any specious pretences, to void the security, that was at any time given for money so borrowed.

So after many questionings of their charter, which were ever removed by considerable sums of money, a grant made by the king in the beginning of his reign, (in consideration of great sums of money,) of good quantities of land in Ireland, and the city of Londonderry there, was avoided by a suit in the star-chamber; all the lands, after a vast expense in building and planting, resumed into the king's hands, and a fine of fifty thousand pounds imposed upon the city. Which sentence being pronounced after a long and public hearing, during which time they were often invited to a composition, both in respect of the substance, and the circumstances of proceeding, made a general impression in the minds of the citizens of all conditions, much to the disadvantage of the court; and though the king afterwards remitted to them the benefit of that sentence, they imputed that to the power of the parliament, and rather remembered how it had been taken from them, than by whom it was restored: so that, at the beginning of the parliament, the city was as ill affected to the court as the country was; and therefore chose such burgesses to sit there, as had either eminently opposed it, or accidentally been oppressed by it.

The chief government and superintendency of the city is in the mayor and aldermen; which, in that little kingdom, resembles the house of peers; and as subordinate the common council is the representative body thereof, like the house of commons, to order and agree to all taxes, rates, and such particulars belonging to the civil policy. The common council are chosen every year, so many for every parish, of the wisest and most substantial citizens, by the vestry and common convention of the people of that parish; and as the wealthiest and best reputed men were always chosen, so, though the election was once a year, it was scarce ever known, that any man once chosen was afterwards rejected or left out, except upon discovery of an enormous crime, or decaying in fortune to a bankrupt; otherwise, till he was called to be alderman, or died, he continued, and was every year returned of the common council.

After the beginning of this parliament, when they found by their experience in the case of the earl of Strafford, of what consequence the city might be to them, and afterwards found, by the courage of the present lord mayor, sir Richard Gourney, who cannot be too often nor too honourably mentioned, that it might be kept from being disposed by them; and that the men of wealth and ability, who at first had concurred with them, began now to discern that they meant to lead them further than they had a mind to go; they directed their confidents, that at the election of the common councilmen by the concurrence and number of the meaner people, all such who were moderate men, and lovers of the present government, should be rejected; and in their places men of the most active and pragmatical heads, of how mean fortunes soever, should be elected: and by this means all that body consisted of upstart, factious, indigent companions, who were ready to receive all advertisements and directions from those who steered at Westminster, and as forward to encroach upon their superiors, the mayor and aldermen, as the other was upon the house of peers. And so this firebrand of privilege inflamed the city at that time.

The truth is, it cannot be expressed how great a change there appeared to be in the countenance and minds of all sorts of people, in town and country, upon these late proceedings of the king. They, who had before even lost their spirits, having lost their credit and reputation, except amongst the meanest people, who could never have been made use of by them, when the greater should forsake them; and so despairing of ever being able to compass their designs of malice, or ambition, (some of them were

resuming their old resolutions of leaving the kingdom,)
now again recovered greater courage than ever, and
quickly found that their credit and reputation was as great
as ever it had been; the court being reduced to a lower
condition, and to more disesteem and neglect, than ever
it had undergone. All that they had formerly said of plots
and conspiracies against the parliament, which had before
been laughed at, was now thought true and real; and
all their fears and jealousies looked upon as the effects
of their great wisdom and foresight. All that had been
whispered of Ireland was now talked aloud and printed;
as all other seditious pamphlets and libels were. The shops
of the city generally shut up, as if an enemy were at their
gates ready to enter, and to plunder them; and the people
in all places at a gaze, as if they looked only for directions,
and were then disposed to any undertaking.

On the other side, they who had, with the greatest
courage and alacrity, opposed all their seditious prac-
tices, between grief and anger were confounded with the
consideration of what had been done, and what was like
to follow. They were far from thinking that the accused
members had received much wrong; yet they thought it an
unseasonable time to call them to account for it. That if
any thing had been done of that kind, there should have
been a better choice of the persons, there being many of
the house, of more mischievous inclinations, and designs
against the king's person and the government, and were
more exposed to the public prejudice, than the lord
Kimbolton was; who was a civil and well natured man,
and had rather kept ill company, than drank deep of that
infection and poison, that had wrought upon many others.
Then sir Arthur Haslerig and Mr. Strode were persons
of too low an account and esteem; and though their viru-
lence and malice was as conspicuous and transcendent as
any men's, yet their reputation and interest to do any
mischief, otherwise than in concurring in it, was so small,
that they gained credit and authority by being joined
with the rest, who had indeed a great influence. However,
if there was a resolution to proceed against those men, it
would have been much better to have caused them to have

been all severally arrested, and sent to the Tower, or to other prisons, which might have been very easily done before suspected, than to send in that manner to the houses with that formality, which would be liable to so many exceptions. At least, they ought so far to have imparted it to members in both houses, who might have been trusted, that in the instant of the accusation, when both houses were in that consternation, (as in a great consternation they were,) somewhat might have been pressed confidently towards the king's satisfaction; which would have produced some opposition and contradiction, which would have prevented that universal concurrence and dejection of spirit, which seized upon and possessed both houses.

But, above all, the anger and indignation was very great and general, that to all the other oversights and presumptions ⟨was added⟩ the exposing the dignity, and majesty, and safety of the king, in his coming in person, in that manner, to the house of commons; and in going the next day, as he did, to the guildhall, and to the lord mayor's, which drew such reproaches upon him to his face. All which was justly imputed to the lord Digby, who had before fewer true friends than he deserved, and had now almost the whole nation his enemies, being the most universally odious of any man in it.

When the house of commons had passed such votes from the committee at Merchant-Tailors' hall, as they thought necessary, and once more adjourned thither, the committee asked the advice of the house, whether the accused members might be present with them, (who had in truth directed and governed all their proceedings from the time they sat there:) which was not only approved, but those members required to attend the house the next day it was to sit, and so to continue the service of the house, which was then adjourned for three or four days, that the city might appear in such a posture, as should be thought convenient.

The noise was so great of the preparations made in the city to bring the accused members in triumph to the parliament, and that the whole militia would accompany them, whilst the seamen and mariners made an appearance in barges, and other vessels, upon the Thames to Westminster, ⟨that⟩ the king thought it convenient to remove again from Whitehall; and so on the tenth of January, which was the eve to the great festival, his majesty, the queen, and the royal children, went from Whitehall to Hampton-court, attended by some few of their own household servants, and thirty or forty of those officers, who had attended at Whitehall for security against the tumults.

Before his going, he sent to the earls of Essex and Holland to attend him in his journey; who were both by their places, the one being his chamberlain of his household, the other the prime gentleman of his bedchamber, obliged to that duty. The earl of Essex resolved to go; and to that purpose was making himself ready, when the earl of Holland came to him, and privately dissuaded him; assuring him, that if they two went, they should be both murdered at Hampton-court: whereupon they left the king to his small retinue and in a most disconsolate, perplexed condition, in more need of comfort and counsel, than they had ever known him; and, instead of attending their master in that exigent, they went together into the city, where the committee sat, where they were not the less welcome for being known to have been invited to have waited upon their majesties. They who wished the king best, were not sorry that he then withdrew from Whitehall; for the insolence, with which all that people were transported, and the animosity, which was infused into the hearts of the people in general against the court, and even against the person of the king, cannot be expressed.

Whilst the committee sat in London, the common council likewise met, ⟨as hath been said,⟩ to the end they might be ready to comply in any particulars should be desired from the city; and so the committee having resolved, 'that the actions of the citizens of London, or of any other person whatsoever for the defence of the parliament, or the privileges thereof, or the preservation of the members thereof, were according to their duty, and to their late protestation, and the laws of this kingdom': and

if any person should arrest or trouble any of them for so
doing, he was declared 'to be a public enemy of the commonwealth': and in the next place having resolved, 'that
that vote should be made known to the common council
of the city of London', the accused members about two
of the clock in the afternoon on the eleventh of January,
being the next day after the king went to Hampton-court,
came from their lodgings in the city to Westminster,
guarded by the sheriffs, and trained-bands of London and
Westminster, and attended by a conflux of many thousands of people besides, making a great clamour against
bishops and popish lords, and of the privileges of parliament; some of them, as they passed by Whitehall, asking,
with much contempt, 'what was become of the king and
his cavaliers? and whither he was gone?'

From London-bridge to Westminster, the Thames was
guarded with above one hundred lighters and long-boats,
laden with nablettes and murderers, and dressed up with
waist-clothes and streamers, as ready for fight. And that
the trained-bands of London might be under the command of a person fit to lead them, they granted a commission to captain Skippon, who was captain of the
artillery-garden, to be major-general of the militia of the
city of London; an office never before heard of, nor
imagined that they had authority to constitute such an
officer. The man had served very long in Holland, and
from a common soldier had raised himself to the degree
of a captain, and to the reputation of a good officer: he
was a man of order and sobriety, and untainted with any
of those vices, which the officers of that army were exercised in; and had newly given over that service upon
some exceptions he had to it; and, coming to London,
was by some friends preferred to that command in the
artillery-garden, which was to teach the citizens the
posture of their arms. He was altogether illiterate, and
having been bred always in Holland, he brought disaffection enough with him from thence against the church
of England, and so was much caressed and trusted by that
party.

This man marched that day in the head of their army

to the parliament-house; where the accused members were no sooner entered, than they magnified 'the great kindness and affection they had found in the city, and their zeal to the parliament; and if their expressions of it, upon this extraordinary occasion, had been somewhat unusual, that the house was engaged in honour to protect and defend them from receiving any damage'. Whereupon the sheriffs of London were called into the house of commons, and thanked by the speaker for their extraordinary care, and love expressed to the parliament; and told, 'that they should have an ordinance of parliament for their indemnity, declaring that all their actions of respect and kindness, which they had shewed to the lords and commons in London, and their attending them to and at Westminster, was legal and justifiable'. The masters and officers of ships were likewise called in, and most heartily thanked for their kindness; and sergeant-major-general Skippon appointed every day to attend at Westminster, with such a guard as he thought sufficient for the guard of the two houses. There was one circumstance not to be forgotten in the march of the city that day, when the show by water was little inferior to the other by land, that the pikemen had fastened to the tops of their pikes, and the rest in their hats, or their bosoms, printed papers of the protestation which had been taken, and enjoined by the house of commons the year before for the defence of the privilege of parliament; and many of them had the printed votes of the king's breaking their privileges in his coming to the house, and demanding their members.

[This declaration, passed by the Commons only, ended thus:] 'That the publishing the articles of high treason against the persons accused, was a high breach of the privilege of parliament, a great scandal to his majesty and his government, a seditious act, manifestly tending to the subversion of the peace of the kingdom, and an injury and dishonour to the members; that the privileges of parliament, and liberties of the subject, so violated and broken, could not be fully and sufficiently vindicated, unless the king would be graciously pleased to discover the names of those persons, who advised him to do the particular acts before mentioned, that they might receive condign punishment.'

This strange declaration, so contrary to the known rules and judgments of law, and to the known practice and proceedings of parliament, was no sooner framed and agreed upon in the committee, than it was printed, and published throughout the city and kingdom, before it was confirmed by, or reported to the house; which is against the law, and an express statute in that case provided, that no act done at any committee should be divulged before the same be reported to the house.

[The City had already in 1640 interfered effectively in the struggle between the king and parliament.] The two armies were necessarily to be provided for, lest the counties where their quarters were should come to be oppressed by free quarter; which would not only raise a very inconvenient noise, but introduce a necessity of disbanding the armies, which they were in no degree ready for: and money not being to be raised soon enough in the formal way, by act of parliament, which would require some time in the passage; besides, that the manner and way of raising it had not been enough considered; and the collecting it would require much time, even after an act of parliament should be passed; therefore for the present supply they thought fit to make use of their credit with the city; to whom a formal embassy of lords and commons was sent; which were carefully chosen of such persons as carried the business of the house before them, that the performing the service might be as well imputed to their particular reputation and interest, as to the affection of the city: and these men in their orations to the citizens undertook 'that their money should be repaid with interest by the care of the parliament'. And this was the first introduction of the public faith; which grew afterwards to be applied to all monstrous purposes.

And this expedient succeeded twice or thrice for such sums as they thought fit to require; which were only enough to carry on their affairs, and keep them in motion; not proportionable to discharge the debt due to the armies, but to enable them to pay their quarters: it being fit to keep a considerable debt still owing, lest they should appear too ready to be disbanded.

And they had likewise another design in this commerce with the city; for always upon the loan of money they recommended some such thing to the parliament, as might advance the designs of the party; as 'the proceeding against delinquents'; or 'some reformation in the church:' which the managers knew well what use to make of upon any emergency. When they had set this traffick on foot in the city, and so brought their friends there into more reputation and activity; at their election of common-council men, (which is every year before Christmas; and in which new men had rarely used to be chosen, except in case of death, but the old still continued,) all the grave and substantial citizens were left out; and such chosen as were most eminent for opposing the government, and most disaffected to the church, though of never so mean estates: which made a present visible alteration in the temper of the city, (the common-council having so great a share in the management of affairs there,) and even in the government itself.

[Not even the best of Lord Mayors could alter the attitude of the city though] Alderman Gourney, who was lord mayor of London, was a man of courage and discretion, very well affected to the king, and to the government in church and state, and perfectly abhorred the proceedings of the parliament; gave not that obedience to the orders they expected; did all he could to discountenance and suppress the riotous assemblies in the city and especially the insolencies committed in churches; and expressly refused to call common-halls, and sometimes common-councils, when the house of commons desired it, which was the only way they had to scatter their fire about the city, and the refractoriness of this lord mayor discouraged them much by making it evident, that it was only the rabble and inferior sort of the city which was in truth devoted to them.

33. *Denzil Hollis*

Born 1599; M.P. 1624; P.C. and baron 1661; ambassador at Paris 1663–6; died 1680

DENZIL HOLLIS, the younger son and younger brother of the earls of Clare, was as much valued and esteemed by the whole party, as any man; as he deserved to be, being a man of more accomplished parts than any of them, and of great reputation by the part he acted against the court and the duke of Buckingham, in the parliament of the fourth year of the king, (the last parliament that had been before the short one in April,) and his long imprisonment, and sharp prosecution afterwards, upon that account; of which he retained the memory with acrimony enough. But he would in no degree intermeddle in the counsel or prosecution of the earl of Strafford, (which he could not prevent,) who had married his sister, by whom all his children were, which made him a stranger to all those consultations, though it did not otherwise interrupt the friendship he had with the most violent of those prosecutors. In all other contrivances he was in the most secret counsels with those who most governed, and respected by them with very submiss applications as a man of authority. [But later during the war he owned frankly] his animosity and indignation against all the independent party, and was no otherwise affected to the presbyterians than as they constituted a party upon which he depended to oppose the other. [Hence he was amongst the eleven members of Parliament impeached by the army in January 1648. But he survived that trouble and came later to terms with Charles II. He was one of the four peers who protested against Clarendon's banishment in December 1667.]

34. *John Pym*

Born 1584; M.P. 1614; died December 1643

ABOUT this time the councils at Westminster lost a principal supporter, by the death of John Pym; who died with great torment and agony of a disease unusual, and therefore the more spoke of, *morbus pediculosus*, as was reported; which rendered him an object very loathsome to those who had been most delighted with him. No man had more to answer for the miseries of the kingdom, or had his hand, or head, deeper in their contrivance. And yet, I believe, they grew much higher even in his life, than he designed. He was a man of private quality, and condition of life; his education in the office of the exchequer, where he had been a clerk; and his parts rather acquired by industry, than supplied by nature, or adorned by art. He had been well known in former parliaments; and was one of those few, who had sat in many; the long intermission of parliaments having worn out most of those who had been acquainted with the rules and orders observed in those conventions. And this gave him some reputation and reverence amongst those who were but now introduced.

He had been most taken notice of, for being concerned and passionate in the jealousies of religion, and much troubled with the countenance which had been given to those opinions that had been imputed to Arminius; and this gave him great authority and interest with those who were not pleased with the government of the church, or the growing power of the clergy: yet himself industriously took care to be believed, and he professed to be very entire to the doctrine and discipline of the church of England. In the short parliament before this, he spoke much, and appeared to be the most leading man; for besides the exact knowledge of the forms, and orders of that council, which few men had, he had a very comely and grave way of expressing himself, with great volubility of words, natural and proper; and understood the temper and affections of the kingdom as any man; and had observed the errors and mistakes in government; and knew well how to make them appear greater than they were. After the unhappy dissolution of that parliament, he continued for the most part about London, in conversation and great repute amongst those lords who were most strangers to the court, and were believed most averse to it; in whom he improved

all imaginable jealousies and discontents towards the
state; and as soon as this parliament was resolved to be
summoned, he was as diligent to procure such persons to
be elected as he knew to be most inclined to the way he
meant to take.

At the first opening of this parliament, he appeared
passionate and prepared against the earl of Strafford;
and though in private designing he was much governed
by Mr. Hambden, and Mr. Saint-John, yet he seemed to
all men to have the greatest influence upon the house of
commons of any man; and, in truth, I think he was at
that time, and for some months after, the most popular
man, and the most able to do hurt, that hath lived in any
time. Upon the first design of softening and obliging the
powerful persons in both houses, when it was resolved to
make the earl of Bedford lord high treasurer of England,
the king likewise intended to make Mr. Pym chancellor
of the exchequer; for which he received his majesty's
promise, and made a return of a suitable profession of his
service and devotion; and thereupon, the other being
no secret, somewhat declined from that sharpness in the
house, which was more popular than any man's, and made
some overtures to provide for the glory and splendour of
the crown; in which he had so ill success, that his interest
and reputation there visibly abated; and he found that he
was much better able to do hurt than good; which wrought
very much upon him to melancholy, and complaint of
the violence and discomposure of the people's affections
and inclinations. In the end, whether upon the death of
the earl of Bedford he despaired of that preferment, or
whether he was guilty of any thing, which, upon his conversion to the court, he thought might be discovered to
his damage, or for pure want of courage, he suffered himself to be carried by those who would not follow him, and
so continued in the head of those who made the most
desperate propositions.

In the prosecution of the earl of Strafford, his carriage
and language was such that expressed much personal
animosity; and he was accused of having practised some
arts in it not worthy a good man; as an Irishman of very

mean and low condition afterwards acknowledged, that
being brought to him, as an evidence of one part of
the charge against the lord lieutenant, in a particular of
which a person of so vile quality would not be reasonably
thought a competent informer; Mr. Pym gave him money
to buy him a satin suit and cloak; in which equipage he
appeared at the trial, and gave his evidence; which, if
true, may make many other things, which were confidently reported afterwards of him, to be believed; as that
he received a great sum of money from the French ambassador, to hinder the transportation of those regiments
of Ireland into Flanders, upon the disbanding that army
there; which had been prepared by the earl of Strafford
for the business of Scotland; in which if his majesty's
directions and commands had not been diverted and contradicted by the houses, many do believe the rebellion in
Ireland had not happened.

Certain it is, that his power of doing shrewd turns
was extraordinary, and no less in doing good offices for
particular persons; and that he did preserve many from
censure, who were under the severe displeasure of the
houses, and looked upon as eminent delinquents; and the
quality of many of them made it believed that he had sold
that protection for valuable considerations. From the time
of his being accused of high treason by the king, with
the lord Kimbolton, and the other members, he never
entertained thoughts of moderation, but always opposed
all overtures of peace and accommodation, and when the
earl of Essex was disposed, the last summer, by those lords
to an inclination towards a treaty, as is before remembered, Mr. Pym's power and dexterity wholly changed
him, and wrought him to that temper, which he afterwards swerved not from. He was wonderfully solicitous
for the Scots coming in to their assistance, though his
indisposition of body was so great, that it might well have
made another impression upon his mind. During his sickness, he was a very sad spectacle; but none being admitted
to him who had not concurred with him, it is not known
what his last thoughts and considerations were. He died
towards the end of December, before the Scots entered;

and was buried with wonderful pomp and magnificence, in that place where the bones of our English kings and princes are committed to their rest.

35. *The Posture of Affairs when the King set up his Standard, 1642*

According to the proclamation, upon the twentyfifth day of August, the standard was erected, about six of the clock in the evening of a very stormy and tempestuous day. The king himself, with a small train, rode to the top of the castle-hill, Varney the knight-marshal, who was standard-bearer, carrying the standard, which was then erected in that place, with little other ceremony than the sound of drums and trumpets: melancholy men observed many ill presages about that time. There was not one regiment of foot yet levied and brought thither; so that the trained bands, which the sheriff had drawn together, was all the strength the king had for his person, and the guard of the standard. There appeared no conflux of men in obedience to the proclamation; the arms and ammunition were not yet come from York, and a general sadness covered the whole town, and the king himself appeared more melancholic than he used to be. The standard itself was blown down, the same night it had been set up, by a very strong and unruly wind, and could not be fixed again in a day or two, till the tempest was allayed. This was the melancholy state of the king's affairs, when the standard was set up.

Mr. Hyde was wont often to relate a passage in that melancholic time, when the standard was set up at Nottingham, with which he was much affected. Sir Edmund Varney, knight-marshal, who was mentioned before as standard-bearer, with whom he had great familiarity, who was a man of great courage, and generally beloved, came one day to him, and told him, 'he was very glad to see him, in so universal a damp, under which the spirits of most men were oppressed, retain still his natural vivacity and cheerfulness; that he knew that the condition of the king, and the power of the parliament, was not better known to any man than to him; and therefore he hoped that he was able to administer some comfort to his friends, that might raise their spirits, as well as it supported his own'. He answered, 'that he was, in truth, beholden to his constitution, which did not incline him to despair; otherwise, that he had no pleasant prospect before him, but thought as ill of affairs as most men did; that the other was as far from being melancholic as he, and was known to be a man of great courage, (as indeed he was of a very cheerful and a generous nature, and confessedly valiant,) and that they could not do the king better service, than by making it their business to raise the dejected minds of men, and root out those apprehensions which disturbed them, of fear and despair, which could do no good, and did really much mischief'.

He replied smiling, 'I will willingly join with you the best I can, but I shall act it very scurvily. My condition,' said he, 'is much worse than yours, and different, I believe, from any other man's; and will very well justify the melancholic that, I confess to you, possesses me. You have satisfaction in your conscience that you are in the right; that the king ought not to grant what is required of him; and so you do your duty and your business together: but for my part I do not like the quarrel, and do heartily wish that the king would yield and consent to what they desire; so that my conscience is only concerned in honour and in gratitude to follow my master. I have eaten his bread, and served him near thirty years, and will not do so base a thing as to forsake him; and choose rather to lose my life (which I am sure I shall do) to preserve and defend those things which are against my conscience to preserve and defend: for I will deal freely with you, I have no reverence for the bishops, for whom this quarrel ⟨subsists⟩.' It was not a time to dispute; and his affection to the church had never been suspected. He was as good as his word; and was killed, in the battle of Edge-hill, within two months after this discourse. And if those who had the same and greater obligations, had observed the same rules of gratitude and generosity, whatever their

other affections had been, that battle had never been
fought, nor any of that mischief been brought to pass that
succeeded it.

When the king came to Derby, he received clear information from the well affected party in Shrewsbury, that
the town was at his devotion; and that the very rumour of
his majesty's purpose of coming thither had driven away
all those who were most inclined to sedition. And therefore, as well in regard of the strong and pleasant situation
of it, (one side being defended by the Severn, the other
having a secure passage into Wales, the confines of Mont-
gomeryshire extending very near the town,) as for the
correspondence with Worcester, of which city he hoped
well, and that, by his being at Shrewsbury, he should be
as well able to secure Chester, as by carrying his whole
train so far north; besides that the other might give some
apprehension of his going into Ireland, which had been
formerly mentioned, his majesty resolved for that town;
and, after one day's stay at Derby, by easy marches he
went thither, drawing his whole small forces to a rendezvous by Wellington, a day's march short of Shrewsbury;
and that being the first time that they were together, his
majesty then caused his military orders for the discipline
and government of the army to be read at the head of each
regiment; and then, which is not fit ever to be forgotten,
putting himself in the middle, where he might be best
heard, not much unlike the emperor Trajan, who, when
he made Sura great marshal of the empire, gave him a
sword, saying, 'Receive this sword of me; and if I command as I ought, employ it in my defence; if I do otherwise, draw it against me, and take my life from me', his
majesty made this speech to his soldiers:

'Gentlemen, you have heard those orders read: it is
your part, in your several places, to observe them exactly.
The time cannot be long before we come to action, therefore you have the more reason to be careful: and I must
tell you, I shall be very severe in the punishing of those, of
what condition soever, who transgress these instructions.
I cannot suspect your courage and resolution; your conscience and your loyalty hath brought you hither, to fight

for your religion, your king, and the laws of the land. You shall meet with no enemies but traitors, most of them Brownists, anabaptists, and atheists; such who desire to destroy both church and state, and who have already condemned you to ruin for being loyal to us. That you may see what use I mean to make of your valour, if it please God to bless it with success, I have thought fit to publish my resolution to you in protestation; which when you have heard me make, you will believe you cannot fight in a better quarrel; in which I promise to live and die with you.'

It will be, and was then, wondered at, that since the parliament had a full and well formed army, before the king had one full regiment, and the earl of Essex was himself come to Northampton, some days before his majesty went from Nottingham, his lordship neither disquieted the king whilst he stayed there, nor gave him any disturbance in his march to Shrewsbury; which if he had done, he might either have taken him prisoner, or so dispersed his small power, that it would never have been possible for him to have gotten an army together. But as the earl had not yet received his instructions, so they, upon whom he depended, avoided that expedition out of mere pride, and contempt of the king's forces; and upon a presumption, that it would not be possible for him to raise such a power, as would be able to look their army in the face; but that, when he had in vain tried all other ways, and those, who not only followed him upon their own charges, but supported those who were not able to bear their own, (for his army was maintained and paid by the nobility and gentry, who served likewise in their own persons,) were grown weary and unable longer to bear that burden, his majesty would be forced to put himself into their arms for protection and subsistence; and such a victory without blood had crowned all their designs. And if their army, which they pretended to raise only for their defence, and for the safety of the king's person, had been able to prevent the king's raising any; or if the king, in that melancholic conjuncture at Nottingham, had returned to Whitehall, he had justified all their proceedings, and could never after have refused to yield to whatsoever they proposed.

And it is most certain, that the common soldiers of the army were generally persuaded, that they should never be brought to fight; but that the king was in truth little better than imprisoned by evil counsellors, malignants, delinquents, and cavaliers, (the terms applied to his whole party,) and would gladly come to his parliament, if he could break from that company; which he would undoubtedly do, if their army came once to such a distance, that his majesty might make an escape to them. And in this kind of discourse they were so sottish, that they were persuaded, that those persons, of whose piety, honour, and integrity, they had received heretofore the greatest testimony, were now turned papists; and that the small army, and forces the king had, consisted of no other than papists. Insomuch as truly those of the king's party, who promised themselves any support, but from the comfort of their own consciences, or relied upon any other means than from God Almighty, could hardly have made their expectations appear reasonable; for they were in truth possessed of the whole kingdom.

I must not forget, though it cannot be remembered without much horror, that this strange wildfire among the people was not so much and so furiously kindled by the breath of the parliament, as of the clergy, who both administered fuel, and blowed the coals in the houses too. These men having creeped into, and at last driven all learned and orthodox men from, the pulpits, had, as is before remembered, from the beginning of this parliament, under the notion of reformation and extirpating of popery, infused seditious inclinations into the hearts of men against the present government of the church, with many libellous invectives against the state too. But since the raising of an army, and rejecting the king's last overture of a treaty, they contained themselves within no bounds; and as freely and without control inveighed against the person of the king, as they had before against the worst malignant; profanely and blasphemously applying whatsoever had been spoken and declared by God himself, or the prophets, against the most wicked and impious kings, to incense and stir up the people against their most gracious sovereign.

There are monuments enough in the seditious sermons at that time printed, and in the memories of men, of others not printed, of such wresting and perverting of scripture to the odious purposes of the preacher, that pious men will not look over without trembling.

And indeed no good Christian can, without horror, think of those ministers of the church, who, by their function being messengers of peace, were the only trumpets of war, and incendiaries towards rebellion. How much more Christian was that Athenian nun in Plutarch, and how shall she rise up in judgment against those men, who, when Alcibiades was condemned by the public justice of the state, and a decree made that all the religious priests and women would ban and curse him, stoutly refused to perform that office; answering, 'that she was professed religious, to *pray* and to *bless*, not to *curse* and to *ban*'. And if the person and the place can improve and aggravate the offence, (as without doubt it doth, both before God and man,) methinks the preaching treason and rebellion out of the pulpits should be worse than the advancing it in the market, as much as poisoning a man at the communion would be worse than murdering him at a tavern. And it may be, in that catalogue of sins, which the zeal of some men hath thought to be the sin against the Holy Ghost, there may not any one be more reasonably thought to be such, than a minister of Christ's turning rebel against his prince, (which is a most notorious apostasy against his order,) and his preaching rebellion to the people, as the doctrine of Christ; which, adding blasphemy and pertinacy to his apostasy, hath all the marks by which good men are taught to avoid that sin against the Holy Ghost.

[Clarendon returns to the same point when he considers the interference of the Scots in the affairs of England in 1644. They had then asserted in a Declaration that they only did so from a sense of duty and from 'the assurance they had of the assistance of God by whose providence the trust and safety of those kingdoms was put into their hands at this time'. Clarendon rather ingeniously used the very same argument in his rebuttal of their claim. For, says he,] we the rather extracted these short clauses of those two declarations, that posterity may observe the divine hand of Almighty God upon the people of these miserable kingdoms; that after they had broken loose from that excellent form and practice of religion, which their ancestors and themselves had observed and enjoyed, with a greater measure of happiness, than almost any nation lived under, so long a time; and after they had cancelled and thrown off those admirable and incomparable laws of government, which was compounded of so much exact reason, that all possible mischiefs were foreseen, and provided against; they should be now captivated by a profane and presumptuous entitling themselves to God's favour, and using his holy name in that manner, that all sober Christians stand scandalized, and amazed at; and ⟨should⟩ be deluded by such a kind of reasoning and debate, as could only impose upon men unnurtured, and unacquainted with any knowledge or science.

36. *The Duke of Newcastle*

William Cavendish, born 1592; Viscount Mansfield 1620; Earl of Newcastle 1628; marquis 1643; duke 1665; died 1676. Governor of the Prince of Wales 1638–41

[Clarendon's account of the battle of Marston Moor, 1644, has been called by Sir Charles Firth; 'extremely untrustworthy'. But he was correct in thinking that it might not have been so depressing to the royal cause, had not both Prince Rupert and the (then) Marquis of Newcastle left the scene of events so precipitately.] All that can be said for the marquis is, that he was so utterly tired with a condition and employment so contrary to his humour, nature, and education, that he did not at all consider the means, or the way, that would let him out of it, and free him for ever from having more to do with it. And it was a greater wonder, that he sustained the vexation and fatigue of it so long, than that he broke from it with so little circumspection. He was a very fine gentleman, active, and full of courage, and most accomplished in those qualities of horsemanship, dancing, and fencing, which accompany a good breeding; in which his delight was. Besides that he was amorous in poetry and music, to which he indulged the greatest part of his time; and nothing could have tempted him out of those paths of pleasure, which he enjoyed in a full and ample fortune, but honour and ambition to serve the king when he saw him in distress, and abandoned by most of those who were in the highest degree obliged to him, and by him. He loved monarchy, as it was the foundation and support of his own greatness; and the church, as it was well constituted for the splendour and security of the crown; and religion, as it cherished and maintained that order and obedience that was necessary to both; without any other passion for the particular opinions which were grown up in it, and distinguished it into parties, than as he detested whatsoever was like to disturb the public peace.

He had a particular reverence for the person of the king, and the more extraordinary devotion for that of the prince, as he had had the honour to be trusted with his education as his governor; for which office, as he excelled in some, so he wanted other qualifications. Though he had retired from his great trust, and from the court, to decline the insupportable envy which the powerful faction had contracted against him, yet the king was no sooner necessitated to possess himself of some place of strength, and to raise some force for his defence, but the earl of Newcastle (he was made marquis afterwards) obeyed his first call; and, with great expedition and dexterity, seized upon that town; when till then there was not one port town in England that avowed their obedience to the king: and he then presently raised such regiments of horse and foot, as were necessary for the present state of affairs; all which was done purely by his own interest, and the concurrence of his numerous allies in those northern parts; who with all alacrity obeyed his commands, without any charge to the king; which he was not able to supply.

And after the battle of Edge-hill, when the rebels grew so strong in Yorkshire, by the influence their garrison of Hull had upon both the East and West Riding there, that it behoved the king presently to make a general, who might unite all those northern counties in his service, he could not choose any man so fit for it, as the earl of Newcastle, who was not only possessed of a present force, and of that important town, but had a greater reputation and interest in Yorkshire itself, than, at that present, any other man had: the earl of Cumberland being at that time, though of entire affection to the king, much decayed in the vigour of his body and his mind, and unfit for that activity which the season required. And it cannot be denied, that the earl of Newcastle, by his quick march with his troops, as soon as he had received his commission to be general, and in the depth of winter, redeemed, or rescued the city of York from the rebels, when they looked upon it as their own, and had it even within their grasp: and as soon as he was master of it, he raised men apace, and drew an army together, with which he fought many battles, in which he had always (this last only excepted) success and victory.

He liked the pomp and absolute authority of a general well, and preserved the dignity of it to the full; and for the discharge of the outward state, and circumstances of it, in acts of courtesy, affability, bounty, and generosity, he abounded; which, in the infancy of a war, became him, and made him, for some time, very acceptable to men of all conditions. But the substantial part, and fatigue of a general, he did not in any degree understand, (being utterly unacquainted with war,) nor could submit to; but referred all matters of that nature to the discretion of his lieutenant general King; who, no doubt, was an officer of great experience and ability, yet, being a Scotchman, was in that conjuncture upon more disadvantage than he would have been, if the general himself had been more intent upon his command. In all actions of the field he was still present, and never absent in any battle; in all which he gave instances of an invincible courage and fearlessness in danger; in which the exposing of himself notoriously did sometimes change the fortune of the day, when his troops begun to give ground. Such articles of action were no sooner over, than he retired to his delightful company, music, or his softer pleasures, to all which he was so indulgent, and to his ease, that he would not be interrupted upon what occasion soever; insomuch as he sometimes denied admission to the chiefest officers of the army, even to general King himself, for two days together; from whence many inconveniences fell out.

From the beginning, he was without any reverence or regard for the privy-council, with few of whom he had any acquaintance; but was of the other soldiers' mind, that all the business ought to be done by councils of war, and was always angry when there were any overtures of a treaty; and therefore, especially after the queen had landed in Yorkshire, and stayed so long there, he considered any orders he received from Oxford, though from the king himself, more negligently than he ought to have done; and when he thought himself sure of Hull, and was sure that he should be then master entirely of all the north, he had no mind to march nearer the king, (as he had then orders to march into the associated counties, when, upon the taking of Bristol, his majesty had a purpose to have marched towards London on the other side,) out of apprehension that he should be eclipsed by the court, and his authority overshadowed by the superiority of prince Rupert; from whom he desired to be at distance: yet when he found himself in distress, and necessitated to draw his army within the walls of York, and saw no way to be relieved but by Prince Rupert, who had then done great feats of arms in the relief of Newark, and afterwards in his expedition into Lancashire, where he was at that time, he writ to the king to Oxford, either upon the knowledge that the absoluteness and illimitedness of his commission was generally much spoken of, or out of the conscience of some discourse of his own to that purpose; which might have been reported; 'that he hoped his majesty did believe, that he would never make the least scruple to obey the grandchild of king James': and assuredly, if the prince had cultivated the good inclinations the marquis had towards him, with any civil and gracious condescensions, he would have found him full of duty and regard to his service and interest.

But the strange manner of the prince's coming, and undeliberated throwing himself, and all the king's hopes, into that sudden and unnecessary engagement, by which all the force the marquis had raised, and with so many difficulties preserved, was in a moment cast away and destroyed, so transported him with passion and despair, that he could not compose himself to think of beginning the work again, and involving himself in the same undelightful condition of life, from which he might now be free. He hoped his past meritorious actions might outweigh his present abandoning the thought of future action; and so, without further consideration, as hath been said, he transported himself out of the kingdom, and took with him general King.

37. *The Relief of Basing House, 11 September 1644, and the Death of Colonel Gage*

Henry Gage, 1597–1645; knighted November 1644

[Colonel Gage,] having the English regiment in Flanders, had got leave there to make offer of his service to the king, and to that purpose was newly come from thence to Oxford; and was indeed a man of extraordinary parts, both as a soldier and a wise man; of whom there will be hereafter more occasion to enlarge.

He was in truth a very extraordinary man, of a large and very graceful person, of an honourable extraction, his grandfather having been knight of the garter; besides his great experience and abilities as a soldier, which were very eminent, he had very great parts of breeding, being a very good scholar in the polite parts of learning, a great master in the Spanish and Italian tongues, besides the French and the Dutch, which he spoke in great perfection; having scarce been in England in twenty years before.

He was likewise very conversant in courts; having for many years been much esteemed in that of the archduke and duchess, Albert and Isabella, at Brussels; which was a great and very regular court at that time; so that he deserved to be looked upon as a wise and accomplished person. Of this gentleman, the lords of the council had a singular esteem, and consulted frequently with him, whilst they looked to be besieged; and thought Oxford to be the more secure for his being it in; which rendered him so ungrateful to the governor, sir Arthur [Aston], that he crossed him in any thing he proposed, and hated him perfectly; as they were of natures, and manners, as different as men can be.

The garrison of Basing-house, the seat of the marquis of Winchester, in which himself was and commanded, had been now straitly besieged, for the space of above three months, by a conjunction of the parliament troops of Hampshire and Sussex. The lady marchioness, his wife, was then in Oxford; and solicited very diligently the timely preservation of her husband; which made every body desire to gratify her, being a lady of great honour and alliance, as sister to the earl of Essex, and to the lady marchioness of Hertford; who was likewise in the town, and engaged her husband to take this business to heart: and all the Roman catholics, who were numerous in the town, looked upon themselves as concerned to contribute all they could to the good work, and so offered to list themselves and their servants in the service.

The council, both upon public and private motives, was very heartily disposed to effect it; and had several conferences together, and with the officers; in all which the governor too reasonably opposed the design, 'as full of more difficulties, and liable to greater damages, than any soldier who understood command, would expose himself and the king's service to'; and protested, 'that he would not suffer any of the small garrison that was under his charge to be hazarded in the attempt'. It was very true, Basing was near forty miles from Oxford, and, in the way between them, the enemy had a strong garrison of horse and foot at Abingdon, and as strong at Reading, whose

horse every day visited all the highways near, besides a
body of horse and dragoons quartered at Newbury; so
that it appeared to most men hardly possible to send a
party to Basing, and impossible for that party to return to
Oxford, if they should be able to get to Basing: yet new
importunities from the marquis, with a positive declaration, 'that he could not defend it above ten days, and must
then submit to the worst conditions the rebels were like to
grant to his person, and to his religion'; and new instances
from his lady prevailed with the lords to enter upon a new
consultation; in which the governor persisted in his old
resolution, as seeing no cause to change it.

In this debate colonel Gage declared, 'that though he
thought the service full of hazard, especially for the return;
yet if the lords would, by listing their own servants, persuade the gentlemen in the town to do the like, and engage
their own persons, whereby a good troop or two of horse
might be raised, (upon which the principal dependence
must be,) he would willingly, if there were nobody else
thought fitter for it, undertake the conduct of them himself; and hoped he should give a good account of it':
which being offered with great cheerfulness by a person,
of whose prudence, as well as courage, they had a full
confidence, they all resolved to do the utmost that was in
their power to make it effectual.

[Gage was promised help from various small royalist
detachments stationed in the neighbourhood.] After some
hours of refreshment in the morning, and sending this
express to Winchester, the troops marched through by-
lanes to Aldermaston, a village out of any great road;
where they intended to take more rest that night. They
had marched, from the time they left Oxford, with orange-
tawny scarfs and ribbons, that they might be taken for the
parliament soldiers; and hoped, by that artifice to have
passed undiscovered even to the approach upon the be-
siegers. But the party of horse which was sent before to
Aldermaston, found there some of the parliament horse,
and, forgetting their orange-tawny scarfs, fell upon them;
and killed some, and took six or seven prisoners; whereby
the secret was discovered, and notice quickly sent to

Basing of the approaching danger; which accident made their stay shorter at that village than was intended, and than the weariness of the soldiers required. About eleven of the clock, they begun their march again; which they continued all that night; the horsemen often alighting, that the foot might ride, and others taking many of them behind them; however they could not but be extremely weary and surbated.

Between four and five of the clock on Wednesday morning, it having been Monday night that they left Oxford, they arrived within a mile of Basing; where an officer, sent from Sir William Ogle, came to them to let them know, 'that he durst not send his troops so far, in regard many of the enemy's horse lay between Winchester and Basing'. This broke all the colonel's measures; and, since there was no receding, made him change the whole method of his proceedings; and, instead of dividing his forces, and falling on in several places, as he meant to have done if the Winchester forces had complied with their obligation, or if his march had been undiscovered, he resolved now to fall on jointly with all his body in one place; in order to which, he commanded the men to be ranged into battalions; and rid to every squadron, giving them such words as were proper to the occasion; which no man could more pertinently deliver, or with a better grace: he commanded every man to tie a white tape ribbon, or handkerchief, above the elbow of their right arm; and gave them the word *St. George*; which was the sign and the word that he had sent before to the marquis, lest in his sallies their men, for want of distinction, might fall foul of each other.

Thus they marched towards the house, colonel Web leading the right wing, and lieutenant colonel Bunkly the left of the horse; and Gage himself the foot. They had not marched far, when at the upper end of a large campaign field, upon a little rising of an hill, they discerned a body of five cornets of horse very full, standing in very good order to receive them. But before any impression could be made upon them, the colonel must pass between two hedges lined very thick with musketeers; from whom the horse very courageously bore a smart volley, and then charged the enemy's horse so gallantly, that, after a shorter resistance than was expected from the known courage of Norton, though many of his men fell, they gave ground; and at last plainly run to a safe place, beyond which they could not be pursued. The foot disputed the business much better, and being beaten from hedge to hedge, retired into their quarters and works; which they did not abandon in less than two hours; and then a free entrance into the house was gained on that side, where the colonel only stayed to salute the marquis, and to put in the ammunition he had brought with him; which was only twelve barrels of powder, and twelve hundred weight of match; and immediately marched with his horse and foot to Basingstoke, a good market-town two miles from the house; leaving one hundred foot to be led, by some officers of the garrison, to the town of Basing, a village but a mile distant. In Basingstoke they found store of wheat, malt, oats, salt, bacon, cheese, and butter; as much of which was all that day sent to the house, as they could find carts or horses to transport, together with fourteen barrels of powder, and some muskets, and forty or fifty head of cattle, with above one hundred sheep: whilst the other party, that went to Basing town, beat the enemy that was quartered there, after having killed forty or fifty of them; some fled into the church, where they were quickly taken prisoners; and, among them, two captains, Jarvise and Jephson, the two eldest sons of two of the greatest rebels of that county, and both heirs to good fortunes, who were carried prisoners to Basing-house; the rest, who besieged that side, being fled into a strong fort which they had raised in the park. The colonel spent that and the next day in sending all manner of provisions into the house; and then, reasonably computing that the garrison was well provided for two months, he thought of his retreat to Oxford: which it was time to do: for besides that Norton had drawn all his men together, who had been dismayed, with all the troops which lay quartered within any distance, and appeared within sight of the house more numerous and gay than before, as if he meant to be

revenged before they parted; he was likewise well informed by the persons he had employed, that the enemy
from Abingdon had lodged themselves at Aldermaston,
and those from Reading and Newbury, in two other villages upon the river Kennet; over which he was to pass.

Hereupon that he might take away the apprehension
that he meant suddenly to depart, he sent out orders,
which he was sure would come into the enemy's hands, to
two or three villages next the house, 'that they should, by
the next day noon, send such proportions of corn into
Basing-house, as were mentioned in the warrants; upon
pain, if they failed by the time, to have a thousand horse
and dragoons sent to fire the towns'. This being done, and
all his men drawn together about eleven of the clock at
night, Thursday the second night after he came thither,
the marquis giving him two or three guides who knew the
country exactly, he marched from Basing without sound
of drum or trumpet, and passed the Kennet, undiscovered, by a ford near a bridge which the enemy had
broke down; and thereby thought they had secured that
passage; the horse taking the foot *en croupe*; and then,
marching by-ways, in the morning they likewise passed
over the Thames, at a ford little more than a mile from
Reading; and so escaped the enemy, and got before night
to Wallingford; where he securely rested, and refreshed
his men that night; and the next day arrived safe at
Oxford; having lost only two captains, and two or three
other gentlemen, and common men; in all to the number
of eleven; and forty or fifty wounded, but not dangerously.
What number the enemy lost could not be known; but it
was believed they lost many, besides above one hundred
prisoners that were taken; and it was confessed, by enemies
as well as friends, that it was as soldierly an action as had
been performed in the war on either side; and redounded
very much to the reputation of the commander.

[But the royalist camp was riddled with dissensions of
all sorts. These broke out speedily after the king had returned into winter quarters to Oxford, November 1644.]
The king was exceedingly pleased to find how much
the fortifications there had been advanced by the care

and diligence of the lords; and was very gracious in his acknowledgment of it to them. And the governor, sir Arthur Aston, having, some months before, in the managing his horse in the fields, caused him to fall, had in the fall broken his leg, and, shortly after, been compelled to cut it off; so that, if he recovered at all, which was very doubtful, he could not be fit for any active service; his majesty resolved to confer that government upon another. Of which resolution, with all the circumstances of grace and favour, and sending him a warrant for one thousand pounds a year pension for his life, he gave him notice; and then, to the most general satisfaction of all men, he conferred that government upon colonel Gage, whom he had before knighted. Sir Arthur Aston was so much displeased with his successor, that he besought the king to confer that charge upon any other person; and when he found that his majesty would not change his purpose, he sent to some lords to come to him, who he thought were most zealous in religion, and desired them to tell the king from him, 'that, though he was himself a Roman Catholic, he had been very careful to give no scandal to his majesty's protestant subjects; and could not but inform him, that Gage was the most Jesuited papist alive; that he had a Jesuit who lived with him; and that he was present at all the sermons among the catholics; which he believed would be very much to his majesty's disservice'. So much his passion and animosity overruled his conscience.

The king liked the choice he had made; and only advised the new governor, by one of his friends, 'to have so much discretion in his carriage, that there might be no notice taken of the exercise of his religion': to which animadversion he answered, 'that he never had dissembled his religion, nor ever would; but that he had been so wary in the exercise of it, that he knew there could be no witness produced, who had ever seen him at mass in Oxford, though he heard mass every day; and that he had never been but once at a sermon, which was at the lodging of sir Arthur's daughter, to which he had been invited with great importunity and believed now that it was to entrap him'. But the poor gentleman enjoyed the office very little time; for within a month, or thereabout, making an attempt to break down Culham-bridge, near Abingdon, where he intended to erect a royal fort, that should have kept that garrison from that side of the county, he was shot through the heart with a musket bullet. Prince Rupert was present at the action, having approved, and been much pleased with the design, which was never pursued after his death; and in truth the king sustained a wonderful loss in his death; he being a man of great wisdom and temper, and among the very few soldiers, who made himself to be universally loved and esteemed.

38. *The Lord Capel*

Arthur Capel, born 1610; Lord Capel 1641; executed 1649

[At his trial.] The lord Capel appeared undaunted, and utterly refused to submit to their jurisdiction; 'that in the condition and capacity of a soldier and a prisoner of war', he said, 'the lawyers and gownmen had nothing to do with him, and therefore he would not answer to any thing they had said against him'; (Prideaux having treated him with great rudeness and insolence;) but insisted upon 'the law of nations, which exempted all prisoners, though submitting to mercy, from death, if it was not inflicted within so many days: which were long since expired'. He urged 'the declaration which Fairfax the general had made to him, and the rest of the prisoners, after the death of sir Charles Lucas and sir George Lisle; that no other of their lives should be in danger, which he had witnesses ready to prove, if they might be admitted'; and concluded, 'that, if he had committed any offence worthy of death, he might be tried by his peers: which was his right by the laws of the land; the benefit whereof he required'. Ireton, who was present, and sat as one of his judges, denied that the general had made any such promise, and if he had, that the parliament's authority could not be restrained thereby; 'and put him in mind of his carriage at that time, and how much he neglected then the general's civility. The other insisted still on the promise; and urged, that the general might be sent for and examined'; which they knew not how to deny; but, in regard of his indisposition of health, they said they could not expect he should come in person, but they would send to him for his testimony in writing, whilst they proceeded against sir John Owen who was the other prisoner.

The lord Capel, shortly after he was brought prisoner to the Tower from Windsor Castle, had by a wonderful adventure, having a cord and all things necessary conveyed to him, let himself down out of the window of his chamber in the night, over the wall of the Tower; and had been directed through what part of the ditch he might be best able to wade. Whether he found the right place, or whether there was no safer place, he found the water and the mud so deep, that, if he had not been by the head taller than other men, he must have perished, since the water came up to his chin. The way was so long to the other side, and the fatigue of drawing himself out of so much mud so intolerable, that his spirits were near spent, and he was once ready to call out for help, as thinking it better to be carried back again to the prison, than to be found in such a place, from whence he could not extricate himself, and where he was ready to expire. But it pleased God, that he got at last to the other side; where his friends expected him, and carried him to a chamber in the Temple; where he remained two or three nights secure from any discovery, notwithstanding the diligence that could not but be used to recover a man they designed to use no better. After two or three days, a friend whom he trusted much, and who deserved to be trusted, conceiving that he might be more secure in a place to which there was less resort, and where there were so many harboured who were every day sought after, had provided a lodging for him in a private house in Lambeth Marsh; and calling upon him in an evening, when it was dark, to go thither, they chose rather to take any boat they found ready at the Temple stairs, than to trust one of that people with the secret; and it was so late that there was only one boat left there. In that the lord Capel (as well disguised as he thought necessary) and his friend put themselves, and bid the waterman to row them to Lambeth. Whether, in their passage thither, the other gentleman called him *my lord*, as was confidently reported, or whether the waterman had any jealousy by observing what he thought was a disguise, when they were landed, the wicked waterman, undiscerned, followed them, till he saw into what house they went; and then went to an officer, and demanded, 'what he would give him to bring him to the place where the lord Capel lay?' And the officer promising to give him ten pounds, he led him presently to the house, where that excellent person was seized upon, and the next day carried to the Tower.

When the petition, that his wife had delivered, was read, many gentlemen spoke on his behalf; and mentioned the great virtues that were in him; and 'that he had never deceived them, or pretended to be of their party; but always resolutely declared himself for the king': and Cromwell, who had known him very well, spoke so much good of him, and professed to have so much kindness and respect for him, that all men thought he was now safe, when he concluded, 'that his affection to the public so much weighed down his private friendship, that he could not but tell them that the question was now, whether they would preserve the most bitter and the most implacable enemy they had: that he knew the lord Capel very well, and knew that he would be the last man in England that would forsake the royal interest; that he had great courage, industry, and generosity; that he had many friends who would always adhere to him; and that as long as he lived, what condition soever he was in, he would be a thorn in their sides; and therefore for the good of the commonwealth, he should give his vote against the petition'. Ireton's hatred was immortal; he spake of him and against him, as of a man of whom he was heartily afraid.

The lord Capel was then called; who walked through Westminster-hall, saluting such of his friends and acquaintance as he saw there, with a very serene countenance, accompanied with his friend Dr. Morley; who had been with him from the time of his sentence; but, at the foot of the scaffold, his lordship took his leave of him; and embracing him, thanked him; and said, he should go no farther, having some apprehension that he might receive some affront by the soldiers after his death; the chaplains who attended the two other lords being men of the time, and the doctor being well known to be most contrary.

As soon as his lordship had ascended the scaffold, he looked very vigorously about, and asked, 'whether the other lords had spoken to the people with their hats on?' and being told, that 'they were bare'; he gave his hat to his servant, and then with a clear and a strong voice he said, 'that he was brought thither to die for doing that which he could not repent of; that he had been born and bred under the government of a king, whom he was bound in conscience to obey; under laws, to which he had been always obedient; and in the bosom of a church, which he thought the best in the world: that he had never violated his faith to either of those, and was now condemned to die against all the laws of the land; to which sentence he did submit'. He enlarged himself in commending 'the great virtue and piety of the king, whom they had put to death; who was so just and merciful a prince;' and prayed to God, 'to forgive the nation that innocent blood'. Then he recommended to them the present king; 'who', he told them, 'was their true and their lawful sovereign; and was worthy to be so: so that he had the honour to have been some years near his person, and therefore he could not but know him well'; and assured them, 'that he was a prince of great understanding, of an excellent nature, of great courage, an entire lover of justice, and of exemplary piety; that he was not to be shaken in his religion; and had all those princely virtues, which could make a nation happy': and therefore advised them 'to submit to his government, as the only means to preserve themselves, their posterity, and the protestant religion'. And having, with great vehemence, recommended it to them, after some prayers very devoutly pronounced upon his knees, he submitted himself, with an unparalleled Christian courage, to the fatal stroke, which deprived the nation of the noblest champion it had.

He was a man in whom the malice of his enemies could discover very few faults, and whom his friends could not wish better accomplished; whom Cromwell's own character well described; and who indeed would never have been contented to have lived under that government. His memory all men loved and reverenced, though few followed his example. He had always lived in a state of great plenty and general estimation, having a very noble fortune of his own by descent, and a fair addition to it by his marriage with an excellent wife, a lady of very worthy extraction, of great virtue and beauty, by whom he had a numerous issue of both sexes, in which he took great joy and comfort: so that no man was more happy in all his domestic affairs; and he was so much the more happy, in that he thought himself most blessed in them.

And yet the king's honour was no sooner violated, and his just power invaded, than he threw all those blessings behind him; and having no other obligations to the crown, than those which his own honour and conscience suggested to him, he frankly engaged his person and his fortune from the beginning of the troubles, as many others did, in all actions and enterprises of the greatest hazard and danger; and continued to the end, without ever making one false step, as few others did, though he had once, by the iniquity of a faction, that then prevailed, an indignity put upon him that might have excused him for some remission of his former warmth. But it made no other impression upon him, than to be quiet and contented, whilst they would let him alone, and, with the same cheerfulness, to obey the first summons when he was called out; which was quickly after. In a word, he was a man, that whoever shall, after him, deserve best of the English nation, he can never think himself undervalued, when he shall hear, that his courage, virtue, and fidelity, is laid in the balance with, and compared to, that of the lord Capel.

39. *The Lord Hopton*

Born 1598; baron 1643; died at Bruges 1652

THE persons with whom he [King Charles I] only consulted in his martial affairs, and how to carry on the war, were, (besides prince Rupert who was at this time, 1644, absent) the general [Patrick Ruthven, Earl of Forth in Scotland] who was made earl of Brentford; the lord Wilmot who was general of the horse; the lord Hopton who usually commanded an army apart, and was not often with the king's army, but now present; sir Jacob Astley who was major-general of the army; the lord Digby who was secretary of state; and Sir John Colepepper, master of the rolls; for none of the privy council, those two only excepted, were called to those consultations; though some of them were still advised with, for the better execution, or prosecution, of what was then and there resolved.

The lord Hopton was a man superior to any temptation, and abhorred enough the license, and the levities, with which he saw too many corrupted. He had a good understanding, a clear courage, an industry not to be tired, and a generosity that was not to be exhausted; a virtue that none of the rest had: but, in the debates concerning the war, was longer in resolving, and more apt to change his mind after he had resolved, than is agreeable to the office of a commander in chief; which rendered him rather fit for the second, than for the supreme command in an army.

There was only one man in the council of whom nobody spoke ill, or laid anything to his charge; and that was the lord Hopton. But there was then [1648] such a combination, by the countenance of prince Rupert, with all the other lords of the court, and the attorney general, upon former grudges, to undervalue him, that they had drawn the prince [of Wales] himself to have a less esteem of him than his singular virtue, and fidelity, and his unquestionable courage, and industry (all of which his enemies could not deny that he excelled in) did deserve.

40. *Lord George Goring and Henry Wilmot,*
Earl of Rochester

Goring, born 1608; died 1657

*Wilmot, born 1612?; M.P., baron 1643; Viscount of
Athlone 1644; Earl of Rochester 1652; died 1658*

[In 1641 the suspicion that some officers of the army,
led by Goring, plotted to over-awe Parliament by force,
had hastened the fate of Strafford. Clarendon reminds his
readers of this while recounting the events immediately
before the outbreak of war.] We have remembered before,
in the last year, the discourse of the bringing up the army
to London, to awe the parliament, and the unspeakable
dishonour and damage the king sustained by that discourse, how groundless soever it was; all which was imputed to colonel Goring, who, by that means, grew into
great reputation with the parliament, as a man so irre-
coverably lost at court, that he would join with them in
the most desperate designs; yet he carried himself with so
great dexterity, that, within few months, he wrought upon
the king and queen to believe, that he was so much repented that fault, that he would redeem it by any service;
and to trust him to that degree, that the queen once
resolved, when the tumults drove their majesties first from
London, for her security, to put herself into Portsmouth,
which was under his government; whilst his majesty
betook himself to the northern parts; which design was no
sooner over, (if not before,) than he again intimated so
much of it to the lord Kimbolton, and that party, that they
took all the trust he had from court; to proceed from the
confidence their majesties had of his father's interest in
him; whose affection and zeal to their service was ever
most indubitable: but assured themselves he was their
own, even against his own father. So that he carried the
matter so, that at the same time, he received 3000l. from
the queen, (which she raised by the sale of her plate and
some jewels,) to fortify, and victual, and reinforce his

garrison, against the time it should be necessary to declare for the king; and a good supply from the parliament for the payment of the garrison, that it might be kept the better devoted to them, and to their service. All which he performed with that admirable dissimulation, and rare confidence, that, when the house of commons was informed by a member, whose zeal and affection to them was as much valued as any man's, 'that all his correspondence in the county ⟨was⟩ with the most malignant persons; that of those, many frequently resorted to, and continued with him in the garrison; that he was fortifying, and raising batteries towards the land; and that in his discourses, especially in the seasons of his good fellowship, he used to utter threats against the parliament, and sharp censures of their proceedings'; and upon such informations (the author whereof was well known to them, and of great reputation; and lived so near Portsmouth, that he could not be mistaken in the matter of fact) the house sent for him, most thinking he would refuse to come; colonel Goring came, upon the summons, with that undauntedness, that all clouds of distrust immediately vanished, insomuch as no man presumed to whisper the least jealousy of him; which he observing, he came to the house of commons, of which he was a member, and, having sat a day or two patiently, as if he expected some charge, in the end he stood up, with a countenance full of modesty, and yet not without a mixture of anger, (as he could help himself with all the insinuations of doubt, or fear, or shame, or simplicity in his face, that might gain belief, to a greater degree than I ever saw any man; and could seem the most confounded when he was best resolved, and to want words, and the habit of speaking, when they flowed from no man with greater power,) and told them, 'that he had been sent for by them, upon some information given against him, and that, though he believed, the charge being so ridiculous, they might have received, by their own particular inquiry, satisfaction; yet the discourses that had been used, and his being sent for in that manner, had begat some prejudice to him in this reputation; which if he could not preserve, he should be less able to do them service; and therefore desired, that he might have leave (though very unskilful, and unfit to speak, in so wise and judicious an assembly) to present to them the state and condition of that place under his command; and then he doubted not but to give them full satisfaction in those particulars, which possibly had made some impression in them to his disadvantage: that he was far from taking it ill from those, who had given any information against him; for, what he had done, and must do, might give some umbrage to well affected persons, who knew not the grounds and reasons, that induced him so to do; but that if any such person would at any time, resort to him, he would clearly inform them of whatever motives he had; and would be glad of their advice and assistance for the better doing thereof'. Then he took notice of every particular that had been publicly said against him, or privately whispered, and gave such plausible answers to the whole, intermingling sharp taunts, and scorns, to what had been said of him, with pretty application of himself, and flattery to the men that spake it: concluding, 'that they well knew in what esteem he stood with others: so that if, by his ill carriage, he should forfeit the good opinion of that house, upon which he only depended, and to whose service he entirely devoted himself, he were madder than his friends took him to be, and must be as unpitied in any misery, that could befall him, as his enemies would be glad to see him.' With which, as innocently and unaffectedly uttered, as can be imagined, he got so general an applause from the whole house, that, not without some little apology for troubling him, 'they desired him again to repair to his government, and to finish those works, which were necessary for the safety of the place'; and gratified him with consenting to all the propositions he made in behalf of his garrison, and paid him a good sum of money for their arrears; with which, and being privately assured (which was indeed resolved on) that he should be lieutenant-general of their horse in their new army, when it should be formed, he departed again to Portsmouth; in the mean time assuring his majesty, by those who were trusted between them, 'that he would be speedily in a posture to make any such declaration for his service, as he should be required'; which he was forced to do sooner than he was provided for, though not sooner than he had reason to expect.

When the levies for the parliament army were in good forwardness, and he had received his commission for lieutenant-general of the horse, he wrote to the lord Kimbolton, who was his most bosom friend, and a man very powerful, 'that he might not be called to give his attendance upon the army, till it was ready to march; because there were so many things to be done, and perfected, for the safety of that important place, that he was desirous to be present himself at the work as long as was possible. In the mean time, he had given directions to his agent in London, to prepare all things for his equipage; so that he would be ready to appear, at any rendezvous, upon a day's warning.' Though the earl of Essex did much desire his company and assistance in the council of war, and preparing the articles, and forming the discipline for the army, he having been more lately versed in the order and rule of marches, and the provisions necessary or convenient thereunto, than any man then in their service, and of greater command than any man but the general; yet the lord Kimbolton prevailed, that he might not be sent for till things were riper for action. And, when that lord did afterwards write to him, 'that it was time he should come away', he sent such new and reasonable excuses, that they were not unsatisfied with his delay; till he had multiplied those excuses so long, that they begun to suspect; and they no sooner inclined to suspicion, but they met with abundant arguments to cherish it. His behaviour and course of life was very notorious to all the neighbours, nor was he at all reserved in his mirth, and public discourses, to conceal his opinion of the parliament, and their proceedings. So that, at last, the lord Kimbolton writ plainly to him, 'that he could no longer excuse his absence from the army, where he was much wanted; and that, if he did not come to London by such a short day, as he named, he found his integrity would be doubted; and that many things were laid to his charge, of which he doubted not his innocence; and therefore conjured him, immediately, to be at Westminster'. It being now to be no longer deferred, or put off, he writ a jolly letter to that lord, 'that, the truth was, his council advised him, that the parliament did many things which were illegal; and that he might incur much danger by obeying all their orders; that he had received the command of that garrison from the king; and that he durst not be absent from it, without his leave': and concluded with some good counsel to the lord.

[From that time onwards Goring was an eager adherent of the royal cause but did not get on with Prince Rupert, who 'was rough and passionate and loved not debate; liked what was proposed as he liked the persons who proposed it'.] Goring, who was now general of the horse, was no more gracious to prince Rupert, than Wilmot had been; and had all the other's faults, and wanted his regularity, and preserving his respect with the officers. Wilmot loved debauchery, but shut it out from his business; never neglected that, and rarely miscarried in it. Goring had a much better understanding, and a sharper wit, (except in the very exercise of debauchery, and then the other was inspired,) a much keener courage, and presentness of mind in danger: Wilmot discerned it farther off, and because he could not behave himself so well in it, commonly prevented, or warily declined it; and never drank when he was within distance of an enemy: Goring was not able to resist the temptation, when he was in the middle of them, nor would decline it, to obtain a victory; and, in one of those fits, he had suffered the horse to escape out of Cornwall; and the most signal misfortunes of his life in war had their rise from that uncontrollable license. Neither of them valued their promises, professions, or friendships, according to any rules of honour or integrity; but Wilmot violated them the less willingly, and never but for some great benefit or convenience to himself; Goring, without scruple, out of humour, or for wit's sake; and loved no man so well, but that he would cozen him, and then expose him to public mirth for having been cozened: therefore he had always fewer friends than the other, but more company; for no man had a wit that pleased the company better. The ambition of both was unlimited, and so equally incapable of being contented; and both unrestrained, by any respect to good-nature or justice, from pursuing the satisfaction thereof: yet Wilmot had more scruples from religion to startle him, and would not have attained his end by any gross or foul act of wickedness: Goring could have passed through those pleasantly, and would, without hesitation, have broken any trust, or done any act of treachery, to have satisfied an ordinary passion or appetite; and, in truth, wanted nothing but industry (for he had wit, and courage, and understanding, and ambition, uncontrolled by any fear of God or man) to have been as eminent and successful in the highest attempt in wickedness of any man in the age he lived in, or before. Of all his qualifications, dissimulation was his masterpiece; in which he so much excelled, that men were not ordinarily ashamed, or out of countenance, with being deceived but twice by him.

[Goring had been reconciled with the prince and in spring 1645 sent to the west. But by his behaviour there he incurred suspicion, though Clarendon does not doubt his loyalty, strange though his conduct appeared. For] it was very evident, he was resolved never to be in the same army with Prince Rupert under his command; and all his loose and scandalous speeches they imputed to an innate license he had always given himself; and his gross and unfortunate oversights, to the laziness and unactivity of his nature; which could better pursue, and make advantages upon good successes, than struggle and contend with difficulties and straits. And they who had been nearest the observation found a great difference between the presentness of his mind and vivacity in a sudden attempt, though never so full of danger, and an enterprise that required more deliberation, and must be attended with patience, and a steady circumspection; as if his mind could not be long bent. And therefore he had been observed to give over a game, sooner than gamesters that have been thought to have less fire. Many other passages must be attributed to his perfect hatred of all the persons of the council, after he found they would not comply with his desires, and to his particular ambition; and both those passions of ambition and revenge might transport his nature beyond any limits. But what he meant by his discourse at parting to the officers, for the keeping the horse for the service of some foreign prince, was never understood, except he did really believe, that he should shortly return with a body of foot; and so, that they should not be forward to engage with the enemy, or else to keep such a dependence upon him from the officers, that they should always hope for employment under him.

41. *Henry Wilmot and Patrick Ruthven, 'the General'*

Ruthven, born 1573?; baron 1639; Earl of Forth 1642; Earl of Brentford 1644; died 1651. General of all the king's forces after the death of the Earl of Lindsey in 1642 till superseded by Prince Rupert, November 1644

THE general, though he had been, without doubt, a very good officer, and had great experience, and was still a man of unquestionable courage and integrity; yet he was now much decayed in his parts, and, with the long continued custom of immoderate drinking, dozed in his understanding, which had been never quick and vigorous; he having been always illiterate to the greatest degree that can be imagined. He was now become very deaf, yet often pretended not to have heard what he did not then contradict, and thought fit afterwards to disclaim. He was a man of few words, and of great compliance, and usually delivered that as his opinion, which he foresaw would be grateful to the king.

Wilmot was a man of a haughty and ambitious nature, of a pleasant wit, and an ill understanding, as never considering above one thing at once; but he considered that one thing so impatiently, that he would not admit any thing else to be worth any consideration. He had, from the beginning of the war, been very averse to any advice of the privy-council, and thought fit that the king's affairs (which depended upon the success of the war) should entirely be governed and conducted by the soldiers and men of war, and that no other counsellors should have any credit with his majesty. Whilst prince Rupert was present, his exceeding great prejudice, or rather personal animosity against him, made any thing that Wilmot said or proposed, enough slighted and contradicted: and the king himself, upon some former account and observation, was far from any indulgence to his person, or esteem of his parts. But now, by the prince's absence, and his being the second man in the army, and the contempt he had of the old general, who was there the only officer above him, he grew marvellously elated, and looked upon himself as one whose advice ought to be followed, and submitted to in all things. He had, by his excessive good fellowship, (in every part whereof he excelled, and was grateful to all the company,) made himself so popular with all the officers of the army, especially of the horse, that he had, in truth, a very great interest; which he desired might appear to the king, that he might have the more interest in him. He was positive in all his advices in council, and bore contradiction very impatiently; and because he was most contradicted by the two privy-counsellors, the secretary, and the master of the rolls, who, he saw, had the greatest influence upon the king, he used all the artifices he could to render them unacceptable and suspected to the officers of the army, by telling them what they had said in council; which he thought would render them the more ungrateful; and, in the times of jollity, persuaded the old general to believe that they invaded his prerogative, and meddled more in the business of the war, than they ought to do; and thereby made him the less disposed to concur with them in advice, how rational and seasonable soever it was; which often put the king to the trouble of converting him.

42. *The Earl of Lindsey*

Robert Bertie, born 1582; admiral and general 1628;
earl 1626; P.C., K.G. 1630; died at battle of Edgehill
1642

THE earl of Lindsey was a man of very noble extraction,
and inherited a great fortune from his ancestors; which
though he did not manage with so great care, as if he
desired much to improve it, yet he left it in a very fair
condition to his family which more intended the increase
of it. He was a man of great honour, and spent his youth
and the vigour of his age in military actions and commands
abroad; and albeit he indulged to himself great liberties
of life, yet he still preserved a very good reputation with
all men, and a very great interest in his county, as appeared by the supplies he and his son brought to the king's
army; the several companies of his own regiment of foot
being commanded by the principal knights and gentlemen of Lincolnshire, who engaged themselves in the service principally out of their personal affection to him. He
was of a very generous nature, and punctual in what he
undertook, and in exacting what was due to him; which
made him bear that restriction so heavily, which was put
upon him by the commission granted to prince Rupert,
and by the king's preferring the prince's opinion, in all
matters relating to the war, before his. Nor did he conceal
his resentment: the day before the battle, he said to some
friends, with whom he had used freedom, 'that he did not
look upon himself as general; and therefore he was resolved, when the day of battle should come, that he would
be in the head of his regiment as a private colonel, where
he would die'. He was carried out of the field to the next
village; and if he could then have procured surgeons, it
was thought his wound would not have proved mortal.
And it was imputed to the earl of Essex's too well remembering former grudges, that he never sent any surgeon to
him, nor performed any other offices of respect towards
him; but it is most certain that the disorder the earl of

Essex himself was in at that time, by the running away of the horse, and the confusion he saw the army in, and the plundering the carriages, in the town where the surgeons were to attend, was the cause of all the omissions of that kind. And as soon as they were composed by the coming on of the night, about midnight, he sent sir William Balfour, and some other officers, to see him, and to offer him all offices, and meant himself to have visited him. They found him upon a little straw in a poor house, where they had laid him in his blood, which had run from him in great abundance, no surgeon having been yet with him; only he had great vivacity in his looks; and told them, 'he was sorry to see so many gentlemen, some whereof were his old friends, engaged in so foul a rebellion': and principally directed his discourse to sir William Balfour, whom he put in mind of 'the great obligations he had to the king; how much his majesty had disobliged the whole English nation by putting him into the command of the Tower [December 1641]; and that it was the most odious ingratitude in him to make him that return'. He wished them to tell my lord Essex, 'that he ought to cast himself at the king's feet to beg his pardon; which if he did not speedily do, his memory would be odious to the nation'; and continued this kind of discourse with so much vehemence, that the officers by degrees withdrew themselves; and prevented the visit the earl of Essex intended him, who only sent the best surgeons to him; who in the very opening of his wounds died before the morning, only upon the loss of blood. He had very many friends, and very few enemies; and died generally lamented.

43. *The Presbyterians and the Army and the King's Removal to and from Holmby House, 1647*

[The talks between the king and the Scots at Newcastle (1646) had proved unsuccessful as Charles was not prepared to accede to all their demands concerning the future church establishment. Hence the Scots decided to give him up to Parliament, a decision which, unfortunately for their

reputation, coincided with the last payment of the arrears
due to the Scottish army by Parliament. As many others, so
Clarendon too construed the coincidence into a sale and
hence continues] And upon this infamous contract that
excellent prince was, in the end of January, wickedly given
up, by his Scottish subjects, to those of his English who
were entrusted by the parliament to receive him; which
had appointed a committee of lords and commons, to go to
the place agreed upon with a party of horse and foot of the
army, which were subject to the orders of that committee,
and the committee itself to go to Newcastle to receive
that town as well as the king; where, and to whom, his
majesty was delivered.

They received him with the same formality of respect as
he had been treated with by the Scots, and with the same
strictness restrained all resort of those to his majesty, who
were of doubtful affections to them and their cause. Servants were particularly appointed, and named by the
parliament, to attend upon his person and service, in all
relations; amongst which, in the first place, they preferred
those who had faithfully adhered to them against their
master; and, where such were wanting, they found others
who had manifested their affection to them. And, in this
distribution, the presbyterian party in the houses did what
they pleased, and were thought to govern all. The independents craftily letting them enjoy that confidence of
their power and interest, till they had dismissed their
friends, the Scots, out of the kingdom; and permitting
them to put their friends about the person of the king, and
to choose such a guard as they could confide in, to attend
his majesty.

Of the committee employed to govern and direct all,
major general Brown was one, who had a great name and
interest in the city, and with all the presbyterian party, and
had done great service to the parliament in the war under
the earl of Essex, and was a diligent and stout commander.
In this manner, and with this attendance, his majesty was
brought to his own house at Holmby in Northampton-
shire; a place he had taken much delight in: and there he
was to stay till the parliament and the army (for the army

now took upon them to have a share, and to give their opinion in the settlement that should be made) should determine what should be farther done.

From the time that the king was brought to Holmby, and whilst he stayed there, he was afflicted with the same pressures concerning the church, which had disquieted him at Newcastle; the parliament not remitting any of their insolencies in their demands: all which was imputed to the presbyterians, who were thought to exercise the whole power, and begun to give orders for the lessening their great charge by disbanding some troops of their army, and sending others for Ireland; which they made no doubt speedily to reduce; and declared, 'that they would then disband all armies, that the kingdom might be governed by the known laws.'

This temper in the houses raised another spirit in the army; which did neither like the presbyterian government that they saw ready to be settled in the church, nor that the parliament should so absolutely dispose of them, by whom they had gotten power to do all they had done; and Cromwell, who had the sole influence upon the army, underhand, made them petition the houses against any thing that was done contrary to his opinion. He himself, and his officers, took upon them to preach and pray publicly to their troops, and admitted no chaplains in the army, but such as bitterly inveighed against the presbyterian government, as more tyrannical than episcopacy; and the common soldiers, as well as the officers, did not only pray and preach among themselves, but went up into the pulpits in all churches, and preached to the people; who quickly became inspired with the same spirit; women as well as men taking upon them to pray and preach; which made as great a noise and confusion in all opinions concerning religion, as there was in the civil government of the state; no man being suffered to be called in question for delivering any opinion in religion, by speaking or writing, how profane, heretical or blasphemous soever it was; 'which', they said, 'was to restrain the Spirit'.

Liberty of conscience was now the common argument and quarrel, whilst the presbyterian party proceeded with equal bitterness against the several sects as enemies to all godliness, as they had done, and still continued to do, against the prelatical party; and finding themselves superior in the two houses, little doubted, by their authority and power there, to be able to reform the army, and to new model it again; which they would, no doubt, have attempted, if it had not pleased God at that time to have taken away the earl of Essex some months before this; who died without being sensible of sickness, in a time when he might have been able to have undone much of the mischief he had formerly wrought; to which he had great inclinations; and had indignation enough for the indignities himself had received from the ungrateful parliament, and wonderful apprehension and detestation of the ruin he saw like to befall the king and the kingdom. And it is very probable, considering the present temper of the city at that time, and of the two houses, he might, if he had lived, have given some check to the rage and fury that then prevailed. But God would not suffer a man, who, out of the pride and vanity of his nature, rather than the wickedness of his heart, had been made an instrument of so much mischief, to have any share in so glorious a work: though his constitution and temper might very well entitle him to the lethargic indisposition of which he died, yet it was loudly said by many of his friends, 'that he was poisoned'.

Sure it is that Cromwell and his party (for he was now declared head of the army, though Fairfax continued general in name) were wonderfully exalted with his death; he being the only person whose credit and interest they feared without any esteem of his person.

And now, that they might more substantially enter into dispute and competition with the parliament, and go a share with them in settling the kingdom, (as they called it,) the army erected a kind of parliament among themselves. They had, from the time of the defeat of the king's army, and when they had no more enemy to contend with in the field, and after they had purged their army of all those inconvenient officers, of whose entire submission, and obedience to all their dictates, they had not confidence, set aside their self-denying ordinance, and got their principal officers of the army, and others of their friends, whose principles they well knew, to be elected members of the house of commons into their places who were dead, or who had been expelled by them for adhering to the king. By this means, Fairfax himself, Ireton, Harrison, and many other of the independents, officers and gentlemen, of the several counties, who were transported with new fancies in religion, and were called by a new name *fanatics*, sat in the house of commons; notwithstanding all which, the presbyterians still carried it.

So that about this time, that they might be upon a nearer level with the parliament, the army made choice of a number of such officers as they liked; which they called the general's council of officers; who were to resemble the house of peers; and the common soldiers made choice of three or four of each regiment, most corporals or sergeants, and none above the degree of an ensign, who were called agitators, and were to be as a house of commons to the council of officers. These two representatives met severally, and considered of all the acts and orders made by the parliaments towards settling the kingdom, and towards reforming, dividing, or disbanding of the army: and upon mutual messages and conferences between each other, they resolved in the first place, and declared, 'that they would not be divided or disbanded, before their full arrears were paid, and before full provision was made for liberty of conscience; which, they said, was the ground of the quarrel, and for which so many of their friends' lives had been lost, and so much of their own blood had been spilt; and hitherto there was so little security provided in that point, that there was a greater persecution now against religious and godly men, than ever had been in the king's government, when the bishops were their judges'.

They said, 'they did not look upon themselves as a band of janizaries, hired and entertained only to fight their battles; but that they had voluntarily taken up arms for the liberty and defence of the nation of which they were a part; and before they laid down those arms, they would see all those ends well provided for, that the people might not hereafter undergo those grievances which they had formerly suffered. They complained that some members of the army had been sent for by the parliament, and committed to prison, which was against their privilege; since all soldiers ought to be tried by a council of war, and not by any other judicatory; and therefore they desired redress in these, and many other particulars of as ingrateful a nature; and that such as were imprisoned and in custody, might be forthwith set at liberty; without which they could not think themselves justly dealt with'. And with this declaration and address, they sent three or four of their own members to the house of commons; who delivered it at the bar with wonderful confidence [March 1647].

The soldiers published a vindication, as they called it, of their proceedings and resolutions, and directed it to their general; in which they complained of a design to disband and new model the army; 'which, they said, was a plot contrived by some men who had lately tasted of sovereignty; and, being lifted up above the ordinary sphere of servants, endeavoured to become masters, and were degenerated into tyrants'. They therefore declared, 'that they would neither be employed for the service of Ireland, nor suffer themselves to be disbanded, till their desires were granted, and the rights and liberties of the subjects should be vindicated and maintained'. This apology, or vindication, being signed by many inferior officers, the parliament declared them to be enemies to the state: and caused some of them, who talked loudest, to be imprisoned. Upon which a new address was made to their general; wherein they complained 'how disdainfully they were used by the parliament, for whom they had ventured their lives, and lost their blood: that the privileges, which were due to them as soldiers and as subjects, were taken from them; and when they complained of the injuries they received, they were abused, beaten, and dragged into gaols'.

Hereupon, the general was prevailed with to write a letter to a member of parliament, who shewed it to the house; in which he took notice of several petitions, which were prepared in the city of London, and some other counties of the kingdom, against the army; and 'that it was looked upon as very strange, that the officers of the army might not be permitted to petition, when so many petitions were received against them; and that he much doubted that the army might draw to a rendezvous, and think of some other way for their own vindication'.

This manner of proceeding by the soldiers, but especially the general seeming to be of their mind, troubled the parliament; yet they resolved not to suffer their counsels to be censured, or their actions controlled, by those who were retained by them, and who lived upon their pay. And therefore, after many high expressions against the presumption of several officers and soldiers, they declared, 'that whosoever should refuse, being commanded, to engage himself in the service of Ireland, should be disbanded'. The army was resolved not to be subdued in their first so declared resolution, and fell into a direct and high mutiny, and called for the arrears of pay due to them; which they knew where and how to levy for themselves; nor could they be in any degree appeased, till the declaration that the parliament had made against them was rased out of the journal book of both houses, and a month's pay sent to them; nor were they satisfied with all this, but talked very loud, 'that they knew how to make themselves as considerable as the parliament, and where to have their services better valued and rewarded'; which so frighted those at Westminster, that they appointed a committee of lords and commons, whereof some were very acceptable to the army, to go to them, and to treat with a committee chosen of the officers of the army, upon the best expedients that might be applied to the composing these distempers. Now the army thought itself upon a level with the parliament, when they had a committee of the one authorized to treat with a committee of the other; which likewise raised the spirits of Fairfax, who had never thought of opposing or disobeying the parliament; and disposed him to more concurrence with the impetuous humour of the army, when he saw it was so much complied with and submitted to by all men.

Cromwell, hitherto, carried himself with that rare

dissimulation, (in which sure he was a very great master,) that he seemed exceedingly incensed against this insolence of the soldiers; was still in the house of commons when any such addresses were made; and inveighed bitterly against the presumption, and had been the cause of the commitment, of some of the officers. He proposed, 'that the general might be sent down to the army; who', he said, 'would conjure down this mutinous spirit quickly'; and he was so easily believed, that he himself was sent once or twice to compose the army; where after he had stayed two or three days, he would again return to the house, and complain heavily, 'of the great license that was got into the army; that, for his own part, by the artifice of his enemies, and of those who desired that the nation should be again imbrued in blood, he was rendered so odious unto them, that they had a purpose to kill him, if, upon some discovery made to him, he had not escaped out of their hands'. And in these, and the like discourses, when he spake of the nation's being to be involved in new troubles, he would weep bitterly, and appear the most afflicted man in the world with the sense of the calamities which were like to ensue. But, as many of the wiser sort had long discovered his wicked intentions, so his hypocrisy could not longer be concealed. The most active officers and agitators were known to be his own creatures, and such who neither did, not would do, any thing but by his direction. So that it was resolved by the principal persons of the house of commons, that when he came the next day into the house, which he seldom omitted to do, they would send him to the Tower; presuming, that if they had once severed his person from the army, they should easily reduce it to its former temper and obedience. For they had not the least jealousy of the general Fairfax, whom they knew to be a perfect presbyterian in his judgment; and that Cromwell had the ascendant over him purely by his dissimulation, and pretence of conscience and sincerity. There is no doubt Fairfax did not then, nor long after, believe, that the other had those wicked designs in his heart against the king, or the least imagination of disobeying the parliament.

This purpose of seizing upon the person of Cromwell

could not be carried so secretly, but that he had notice
of it; and the very next morning after he had so much
lamented his desperate misfortune in having lost all reputation, and credit, and authority in the army, and that
his life would be in danger if he were with it, when the
house expected every minute his presence, they were informed that he was met out of the town by break of day,
with one servant only, on the way to the army; where he
had appointed a rendezvous of some regiments of the
horse, and from whence he writ a letter to the house of
commons, 'that having the night before received a letter
from some officers of his own regiment, that the jealousy
the troops had conceived of him, and of his want of kindness towards them, was much abated, so that they believed, if he would be quickly present with them, they
would all in a short time by his advice be reclaimed, upon
this he had made all the haste he could; and did find that
the soldiers had been abused by misinformation; and that
he hoped to discover the fountain from whence it sprung;
and in the mean time desired that the general, and the
other officers in the house, and such as remained about the
town, might be presently sent to their quarters; and that
he believed it would be very necessary in order to the
suppression of the late distempers, and for the prevention
of the like for the time to come, that there might be a
general rendezvous of the army; of which the general
would best consider, when he came down; which he
wished might be hastened'. It was now to no purpose to
discover what they had formerly intended, or that they
had any jealousy of a person who was out of their reach;
and so they expected a better conjuncture; and in a few
days after, the general and the other officers left the town,
and went to their quarters.

The same morning that Cromwell left London, cornet
Joyce, who was one of the agitators in the army, a tailor, a
fellow who had two or three years before served in a very
inferior employment in Mr. Hollis's house, came with a
squadron of fifty horse to Holmby, where the king was,
about the break of day; and, without any interruption by
the guard of horse or foot which waited there, came with

two or three more, and knocked at the king's chamber
door, and said 'he must presently speak with the king'.
His majesty, surprised with the manner of it, rose out of his
bed; and, half dressed, caused the door to be opened,
which he knew otherwise would be quickly broken open;
they who waited in the chamber being persons of whom
he had little knowledge, and less confidence. As soon as the
door was opened, Joyce, and two or three more, came into
the chamber, with their hats off, and pistols in their hands.
Joyce told the king, 'that he must go with him'. His
majesty asked, 'whither?' he answered, 'to the army'. The
king asked him, 'where the army was?' he said, 'they
would carry him to the place where it was'. His majesty
asked, 'by what authority they came?' Joyce answered,
'by this'; and shewed him his pistol; and desired his
majesty, 'that he would cause himself to be dressed, because it was necessary they should make haste'. None of
the other soldiers spoke a word; and Joyce, saving the
bluntness and positiveness of the few words he spoke, behaved himself not rudely. The king said, 'he could not
stir before he spoke with the committee to whom he had
been delivered, and who were trusted by the parliament';
and so appointed one of those who waited upon him, to
call them. The committee had been as much surprised
with the noise as the king had been, and quickly came to
his chamber, and asked Joyce, 'whether he had any orders
from the parliament?' he said, *No*. 'From the general?'
No. 'What authority he came by?' to which he made no
other answer, than he had made to the king, and held up
his pistol. They said, 'they would write to the parliament
to know their pleasure'; Joyce said, 'they might do so, but
the king must presently go with him'. Colonel Brown had
sent for some of the troops who were appointed for the
king's guard, but they came not; he spoke then with the
officer who commanded those who were at that time upon
the guard, and found that they would make no resistance:
so that after the king had made all the delays he conveniently could, without giving them cause to believe that
he was resolved not to have gone, which had been to no
purpose, and after he had broken his fast, he went into

his coach, attended by the few servants who were put about him, and went whither cornet Joyce would conduct him; there being no part of the army known to be within twenty miles of Holmby at that time; and that which administered most cause of apprehension, was, that those officers who were of the guard, declared, 'that the squadron which was commanded by Joyce consisted not of soldiers of any one regiment, but were men of several troops, and several regiments, drawn together under him, who was not the proper officer'; so that the king did in truth believe, that their purpose was to carry him to some place where they might more conveniently murder him. The committee quickly gave notice to the parliament of what had passed, with all the circumstances; and it was received with all imaginable consternation; nor could any body imagine what the purpose and resolution was.

From that time both Cromwell and Ireton appeared in the council of officers, which they had never before done; and their expostulations with the parliament begun to be more brisk and contumacious than they had been. The king found himself at Newmarket attended by greater troops and superior officers; so that he was presently freed from any subjection to Mr. Joyce; which was no small satisfaction to him; and they who were about him appeared men of better breeding than the former, and paid his majesty all the respect imaginable, and seemed to desire to please him in all things. All restraint was taken off from persons resorting to him, and he saw every day the faces of many who were grateful to him; and he no sooner desired that some of his chaplains might have leave to attend upon him for his devotion, but it was yielded to, and they who were named by him (who were Dr. Sheldon, Dr. Morley, Dr. Sanderson, and Dr. Hammond) were presently sent, and gave their attendance, and performed their function at the ordinary hours, in their accustomed formalities; all persons, who had a mind to it, being suffered to be present, to his majesty's infinite satisfaction; who begun to believe that the army was not so much his enemy as it was reported to be; and though Fairfax, nor Cromwell, had not yet waited upon him, the

army had sent an address to him full of protestation of
duty, and besought him 'that he would be content, for
some time, to reside among them, until the affairs of the
kingdom were put into such a posture as he might find
all things to his own content and security; which they infinitely desired to see as soon as might be; and to that
purpose made daily instances to the parliament'. In the
mean time his majesty sat still, or removed to such places
as were most convenient for the march of the army; being
in all places as well provided for and accommodated, as
he had used to be in any progress; the best gentlemen of
the several counties through which he passed, daily resorted to him without distinction; he was attended by some
of his old trusty servants in the places nearest his person;
and that which gave him most encouragement to believe
that they meant well, was, that in the army's address to the
parliament, they desired 'that care might be taken for
settling the king's rights, according to the several professions they had made in their declarations; and that the
royal party might be treated with more candour and less
rigour'; and many good officers who had served his
majesty faithfully, were civilly received by the officers of
the army, and lived quietly in their quarters; which they
could not do any where else; which raised a great reputation to the army, throughout the kingdom, and as much
reproach upon the parliament.

The parliament at this time had recovered its spirits,
when they saw the army did not march towards them, and
not only remained at St. Alban's, but was drawn back to a
farther distance; which persuaded them, that their general
was displeased with the former advance: and so they proceeded with all passion and vigour against those principal
officers, who, they knew, contrived all these proceedings.
They published declarations to the kingdom, 'that they
desired to bring the king in honour to his parliament;
which was their business from the beginning, and that he
was detained prisoner against his will in the army; and
that they had great reason to apprehend the safety of his
person'. The army, on the other hand, declared 'that his
majesty was neither prisoner, nor detained against his will;

and appealed to his majesty himself, and to all his friends, who had liberty to repair to him, whether he had not more liberty, and was not treated with more respect, since he came into the army than he had been at Holmby, or during the time he remained in those places, and with that retinue that the parliament had appointed?' The city seemed very unanimously devoted to the parliament, and incensed against the army; and seemed resolute, not only with their trained bands and auxiliary regiments to assist and defend the parliament, but appointed some of the old officers who had served under the earl of Essex, and had been disbanded under the new model, as Waller, Massey, and others, to list new forces; towards which there was not like to be want of men out of their old forces, and such of the king's as would be glad of the employment. There was nothing they did really fear so much, as that the army would make a firm conjunction with the king, and unite with his party, of which there was so much show; and many unskilful men, who wished it, bragged too much; and therefore the parliament sent a committee to his majesty, with an address of another style than they had lately used, with many professions of duty; and declaring, 'that if he was not, in all respects, treated as he ought to be, and as he desired, it was not their fault, who desired he might be at full liberty, and do what he would'; hoping that the king would have been induced to desire to come to London, and to make complaint of the army's having taken him from Holmby; by which they believed the king's party would be disabused, and withdraw their hopes of any good from the army; and then, they thought, they should be hard enough for them.

The king was in great doubt how to carry himself; he thought himself so barbarously used by the presbyterians, and had so ill an opinion of all the principal persons who governed them, that he had no mind to put himself into their hands. On the other side, he was far from being satisfied with the army's good intentions towards him; and though many of his friends were suffered to resort to him, they found that their being long about him, would not be acceptable; and though the officers and soldiers appeared, for the most part, civil to him, they were all at least as vigilant, as the former guards had been; so that he could not, without great difficulty, have got from them if he had desired it. Fairfax had been with him, and kissed his hand, and made such professions as he could well utter; which was with no advantage in the delivery; his authority was of no use, because he resigned himself entirely to Cromwell; who had been, and Ireton likewise, with the king, without either of them offering to kiss his hand; otherwise, they behaved themselves with good manners towards him. His majesty used all the address he could towards them to draw some promise from them; but they were so reserved, and stood so much upon their guard, and used so few words, that nothing could be concluded from what they said: they excused themselves 'for not seeing his majesty often, upon the great jealousies the parliament had of them, towards whom they professed all fidelity'. The persons who resorted to his majesty, and brought advices from others who durst not yet offer to come themselves, brought several opinions to him; some thinking the army would deal sincerely with his majesty, others expecting no better from them than they afterwards performed: so that the king wisely concluded that he would neither reject the parliament addresses by any neglect, nor disoblige the army by appearing to have jealousy of them, or a desire to be out of their hands; which he could hardly have done, if he had known a better place to have resorted to. So he desired both parties 'to hasten their consultations, that the kingdom might enjoy peace and happiness: in which he should not be without a share; and he would pray to God to bring this to pass as soon as was possible'.

[With regard to the repeated negotiations between the king and the Presbyterians, either of England or of Scotland, it is well to bear in mind what Clarendon held to be the king's real conviction—a verdict borne out by historians generally. Clarendon makes the remark re the king's first journey into Scotland, 1633, for his coronation.] The king was always the most punctual observer of all decency in his devotion, and the strictest promoter of the ceremonies of the church, as believing in his soul the church of England to be instituted the nearest to the practice of the apostles, and the best for the propagation and advancement of Christian religion, of any church in the world: and on the other side, though no man was more averse from the Romish church than he was, nor better understood the motives of their separation from us, and animosity against us, he had the highest dislike and prejudice to that part of his own subjects, who were against the government established, and did always look upon them as a very dangerous and seditious people; who would, under pretence of conscience, which kept them from submitting to the spiritual jurisdiction, take the first opportunity they could find, or make, to disturb and withdraw themselves from their temporal subjection; and therefore he had, with the utmost vigilance, caused that temper and disposition to be watched and provided against in England; and if it were then in truth there, it lurked with wonderful secrecy. In Scotland indeed it covered the whole nation, so that though there were bishops in name, the whole jurisdiction, and they themselves were, upon the matter, subject to an assembly, which was purely presbyterian; no form of religion in practice, no liturgy, nor the least appearance of any beauty of holiness: the clergy, for the most part, corrupted in their principles; at least, (for it cannot be denied but that their universities, especially in Aberdeen, flourished under many excellent scholars and very learned men,) none countenanced by the great men, or favoured by the people, but such.

44. *Henry Ireton*

Born 1611; married Bridget Cromwell 1646; Cromwell's deputy in Ireland from May 1650 till his death November 1651

IN Ireland, if that people had not been prepared and ripe for destruction there had happened an alteration which might have given some respite to it, and disposed the nation to have united themselves under their new deputy, whom they had themselves desired, under all the solemn obligations of obedience. Shortly after the departure of the marquis of Ormond, Cromwell's deputy, Ireton, who had married his daughter, died in Limerick of the plague; which was gotten into his army, that was so much weakened by it, and there were so great factions and divisions among the officers after his sudden death, that great advantages might have been gotten by it. His authority was so absolute, that he was entirely submitted to in all the civil, as well as martial affairs. But his death was thought so little possible, that no provision had been made for that contingency. So that no man had authority to take the command upon him, till Cromwell's pleasure was farther known; who put the charge of the army under Ludlow, a man of a very different temper from the other; but appointed the civil government to run in another channel, so that there remained jealousy and discontent enough still between the council and the officers to have shaken a government that was yet no better established.

Ireton, of whom we have had too much occasion to speak formerly, was of a melancholic, reserved, dark nature, who communicated his thoughts to very few; so that, for the most part, he resolved alone, but was never diverted from any resolution he had taken; and he was thought often by his obstinacy to prevail over Cromwell himself, and to extort his concurrence contrary to his own inclinations. But that proceeded only from his dissembling less; for he was never reserved in the owning and communicating his worst and most barbarous purposes; which the other always concealed and disavowed. Hitherto their concurrence had been very natural, since they had the same ends and designs. It was generally conceived by those who had the opportunity to know them both very well, that Ireton was a man so radically averse from monarchy, and so fixed to a republic government, that, if he had lived, he would either, by his counsel and credit, have prevented those tyrannical excesses in Cromwell, or publicly opposed and declared against them, and carried the greatest part of the army with him; and that Cromwell, who best knew his nature and his temper, had therefore carried him into Ireland, and left him there, that he might be without his counsels or importunities, when he should find it necessary to put off his mask, and to act that part which he foresaw it would be requisite to do. Others thought, his parts lay more towards civil affairs; and were fitter for the modelling that government, which his heart was set upon, (being a scholar, conversant in the law, and in all that learning which had expressed the greatest animosity and malice against the regal government,) than for the conduct of an army to support it; his personal courage being never reckoned among his other abilities.

What influence soever his life might have had upon the future transactions, certain it is, his death had none upon the state of Ireland to the king's advantage.

45. *Thomas Harrison*
Born 1606; executed 1660

[To stand his trial in January 1649] The king was now sent for from Hurst castle, and when he came out of the boat which transported him from thence he was received by colonel Harrison with a strong party of horse; by whom he was to be conducted to Windsor castle. Harrison was the son of a butcher near Nantwich in Cheshire, and had been bred up in the place of a clerk under a lawyer of good account in those parts; which kind of education introduces men into the language and practice of business, and, if it be not resisted by the great ingenuity of the person, imbues young men with more pride than any other kind of breeding; and disposes them to be pragmatical and insolent, though they have the skill to conceal it from their masters, except they find them (as they are too often) inclined to cherish it. When the rebellion first began, this man quitted his master, (who had relation to the king's service, and discharged his duty faithfully,) and put himself into the parliament army; where, having first obtained the office of a cornet, he got up, by diligence and sobriety, to the state of a captain, without any signal notice taken of him till the new model of the army; when Cromwell, who, possibly, had knowledge of him before, found him of a spirit and disposition fit for his service, much given to prayer and to preaching, and, otherwise, of an understanding capable to be trusted in any business; to which his clerkship contributed very much: and then he was preferred very fast; so that, by the time the king was brought to the army, he had been a colonel of horse, and looked upon as inferior to few, after Cromwell and Ireton, in the council of officers and in the government of the agitators; and there were few men with whom Cromwell more communicated, or upon whom he more depended for the conduct of any thing committed to him. He received the king with outward respect, kept himself bare; but attended him with great strictness; and was not to be approached by any address; answering questions in short and few words, and, when importuned, with rudeness. He manifested an apprehension that the king had some thought of making an escape, and did all things in order to prevent it.

46. *Dr. George Morley, Bishop of Winchester*

*Born 1597; various preferments; Bishop of Worcester
1660 and of Winchester 1662; died 1684*

DOCTOR MORLEY, of whom more must likewise be said in its place, was a gentleman of very eminent parts in all polite learning; of great wit, and readiness, and subtilty in disputation; and of remarkable temper and prudence in conversation, which rendered him most grateful in all the best company. He was then chaplain in the house, and to the family, of the lord and lady Carnarvon, which needed a wise and a wary director [because of its Roman Catholic affiliations.] From some academic contests he had been engaged in, during his living in Christ Church in Oxford, where he was always of the first eminency, he had by the natural faction and animosity of those disputes, fallen under the reproach of holding some opinions, which were not then grateful to those churchmen who had the greatest power in ecclesiastical promotions; and some sharp answers and replies he used to make in acci-

dental discourses, and which in truth were made for
mirth and pleasantness sake, (as he was of the highest
facetiousness,) were reported, and spread abroad to his
prejudice: as being once asked by a grave country gentleman, (who was desirous to be instructed what their
tenets and opinions were,) 'what the Arminians held', he
pleasantly answered, that *they held all the best bishoprics and
deaneries in England*; which was quickly reported abroad,
as Dr. Morley's definition of the Arminian tenets.

Such and the like harmless and jocular sayings, upon
many accidental occasions, had wrought upon the archbishop of Canterbury, Laud, (who lived to change his
mind, and to have a just esteem of him,) to entertain some
prejudice towards him; and the respect which was paid
him by many eminent persons, as John Hampden, Arthur
Goodwin, and others, who were not thought friends to the
prosperity the church was in, made others apprehend that
he was not enough zealous for it. But that disaffection and
virulency (which few men had then owned and discovered)
no sooner appeared, in those and other men, but Dr.
Morley made haste as publicly to oppose them, both in
private and in public; which had the more effect to the
benefit of the church, by his being a person above all possible reproach, and known and valued by more persons of
honour than most of the clergy were, and being not only
without the envy of any preferment, but under the advantage of a discountenanced person. And as he was afterwards the late king's chaplain, and much regarded by him,
and as long about him as any of his chaplains were permitted to attend him; so presently after his murder he
left the kingdom, and remained in banishment till his
majesty's (king Charles the Second's) happy return.

47. *Presbyterians and Independents, Levellers and Cromwell*

[Having got hold of the king and installed him at Hampton Court the army proceeded against the Presbyterians
in Parliament and in the City of London, courting the
king while matters seemed still to lie in the balance. [But

when the army had thus subdued all opposition, and the parliament and they seemed all of a piece, and the refractory humours of the city seemed to be suppressed, and totally tamed, the army seemed less regardful of the king than they had been; the chief officers came rarely to Hampton Court, nor had they the same countenances towards Ashburnham and Berkley, as they used to have; they were not at leisure to speak with them, and when they did, asked captious questions, and gave answers themselves of no significance. The agitators, and council of officers, sent some propositions to the king, as ruinous to the church, and destructive to the regal power, as had been yet made by the parliament; and, in some respects, much worse, and more dishonourable; and said, 'if his majesty would consent thereunto, they would apply themselves to the parliament, and do the best they could to persuade them to be of the same opinion'. But his majesty rejected them with more than usual indignation, not without some reproaches upon the officers, for having deluded him, and having prevailed in all their own designs, by making the world believe that they intended his majesty's restoration and settlement, upon better conditions than the parliament was willing to admit. By this manner of resentment, the army took itself to be disobliged, and used another language in their discourse of the king than they had for some months used to do; and such officers who had formerly served the king, and had been civilly treated and sheltered in the quarters of the army, were now driven from thence. And they who had been kind to them, withdrew themselves from their acquaintance; and the sequestrations of all the estates of the cavaliers, which had been intermitted, were revived with as much rigour as ever had been before practised, and the declared delinquents racked to as high compositions; which, if they refused to make, their whole estates were taken from them, and their persons exposed to affronts, and insecurity; but this was imputed to the prevalence of the presbyterian humour in the parliament against the judgment of the army: and it is very true, that though the parliament was so far subdued, that it no more found fault with what the army did, nor complained that it meddled in determining what settlement should be made in the government; yet, in all their own acts and proceedings, they prosecuted a presbyterian settlement as earnestly as they could. The covenant was pressed in all places, and the anabaptists and other sects, which begun to abound, were punished, restrained, and discountenanced; which the army liked not, as a violation of the liberty of tender consciences; which, they pretended, was as much the original of the quarrel, as any other grievance whatsoever.

These kinds of proceedings in all places, blasted all the king's hopes, and deprived him of all the rest and quiet he had for some time enjoyed; nor could he devise any remedy. He was weary of depending upon the army, but neither knew how to get from them, nor whither else to resort for help. . . . There was at this time a new faction grown up in the army, which were either by their own denomination, or with their own consent, called levellers; who spoke insolently and confidently against the king and parliament, and the great officers of the army, and professed as great malice against all the lords, as against the king; and declared: 'that all degrees of men should be levelled and an equality should be established, both in titles and estates throughout the kingdoms'. Whether the raising this spirit was a piece of Cromwell's ordinary witchcraft, in order to some of his designs, or whether it grew amongst those tares which had been sowed in that confusion, certain it is, it gave him real trouble at last [and it also had some influence on the king's decision to renew negotiations with the Presbyterians and to escape from Hampton Court, 11 November 1647. He was, however, taken and imprisoned more strictly at Carisbrooke Castle.]

And now the parliament maintained no farther contests with the army, but tamely submitted to whatsoever they proposed; the presbyterians in both houses, and in the city, being in a terrible agony, that some close correspondences they had held with the king during his abode at Hampton Court, would be discovered; and therefore would give no farther occasion of jealousy by any contradictions, leaving it to their clergy to keep the fire burning in the hearts of the people by their pulpit-inflammations; and they stoutly discharged their trust.

But Cromwell had more cause to fear a fire in his own quarters, and that he had raised a spirit in the army which would not easily be quieted again. The agitators, who were first formed by him to oppose the parliament, and to resist the destructive doom of their disbanding, and likewise to prevent any inconvenience, or mischief, that might result from the drowsy, dull presbyterian humour of Fairfax; who wished nothing that Cromwell did, and yet contributed to bring it all to pass: these agitators had hitherto transcribed faithfully all the copies he had given them, and offered such advices to the parliament, and insisted upon such expostulations and demands, as were necessary, whilst there was either any purpose to treat with the king, or any reason to flatter his party. But now the king was gone from the army, and in such a place as the army could have no recourse to him, and that the parliament was become of so soft a temper, that the party of the army that was in it could make all necessary impression upon them, he desired to restrain the agitators ⟨from⟩ that liberty which they had so long enjoyed, and to keep them within stricter rules of obedience to their superiors, and to hinder their future meetings, and consultations concerning the settling the government of the kingdom; which, he thought, ought now to be solely left to the parliament; whose authority, for the present, he thought best to uphold, and by it to establish all that was to be done. But the agitators would not be so dismissed from state affairs, of which they had so pleasant a relish; nor be at the mercy of the parliament, which they had so much provoked; and therefore, when they were admitted no more to consultations with their officers, they continued their meetings without them; and thought there was as great need to reform their officers, as any part of the church or state. They entered into new associations, and made many propositions to their officers, and to the parliament, to introduce an equality into all conditions, and a parity among all men; from whence they had the appellation of *levellers*; which appeared a great party. They did not only meet against the express command of their officers, but drew very considerable parties of the army to rendezvous, without the order or privity of their superiors; and there persuaded them to enter into such engagements, as would in a short time have dissolved the government of the army, and absolved them from a dependence upon their general officers. The suppression of this license put Cromwell to the expense of all his cunning, dexterity, and courage; so that after he had cajoled parliament, as if the preservation of their authority had been all he cared for and took to heart, and sent some false brothers to comply in the counsels of the conspirators, by that means having notice of their rendezvous, he was unexpectedly found with an ordinary guard at those meetings; and, with a marvellous vivacity, having asked some questions of those whom he observed most active, and receiving insolent answers, he knocked two or three of them in the head with his own hand, and then charged the rest with his troop; and took such a number of them as he thought fit; whereof he presently caused some to be hanged, and sent others to London for a more formal trial. By two or three such encounters, for the obstinacy continued long, he totally subdued that spirit in the army, though it continued and increased very much in the kingdom; and if it had not been encountered at that time with that rough and brisk temper of Cromwell, it would presently have produced all imaginable confusion in the parliament, army, and kingdom.

It was a wonderful difference, throughout their whole proceedings, between the heads of those who were thought to sway the presbyterian counsels, and those who governed the independents, though they were equally masters of dissimulation, and had equally malice and wickedness in their intentions, though not of the same kind, and were equally unrestrained by any scruples or motions of conscience, the independents always doing that, which, how ill and unjustifiable soever, contributed still to the end they aimed at, and to the conclusion they meant to bring to pass; whereas the presbyterians, for the most part, did always somewhat that reasonably must destroy their own end, and cross that which they first and principally designed; and there were two reasons that might naturally produce this ill success to the latter, at least hindered the even progress and current which favoured the other. First, their councils were most distracted and divided, being made up of many men, whose humours and natures must be observed, and complied with, and whose concurrence was necessary to the carrying on the same designs, though their inclinations did not concur in them; whereas the other party was entirely led and governed by two or three, to whom they resigned, implicitly, the conduct of their interest; who advanced, when they saw it reasonable, and stood still, or retired, or even declined the way they best liked, when they saw any inconvenient jealousy awakened by the progress they had made.

In the second place, the presbyterians, by whom I mean the Scots, formed all their counsels by the inclinations and affections of the people; and first considered how they might corrupt and seduce, and dispose them to second their purposes; and how far they might depend upon their concurrence and assistance, before they resolved to make any attempt; and this made them in such a degree submit to their senseless and wretched clergy; whose infectious breath corrupted and governed the people, and whose authority was prevalent upon their own wives, and in their domestic affairs; and yet they never communicated to them more than the outside of their designs: whereas, on the other side, Cromwell, and the few others with whom he consulted, first considered what was absolutely necessary to their main and determined end; and then, whether it were right or wrong, to make all other means subservient to it; to cozen and deceive men, as long as they could induce them to contribute to what they desired, upon motives how foreign soever; and when they would keep company with them no longer, or farther serve their purposes, to compel them by force to submit to what they should not be able to oppose; and so the one resolved, only to do what they believed the people would like and approve; and the other, that the people should like and approve what they had resolved. And this difference in the measures they took, was the true cause of so different success in all they undertook. Machiavel, in this, was in the right, though he got an ill name by it with those who take what he says from the report of other men, or do not enough consider themselves what he says, and his method in speaking: (he was as great an enemy to tyranny and injustice in any government, as any man then was, or now is; and says,) 'that a man were better be a dog than be subject to those passions and appetites, which possess all unjust, and ambitious, and tyrannical persons'; but he confesses, 'that they who are so transported, and have entertained such wicked designs as are void of all conscience, must not think to prosecute them by the rules of conscience, which was laid aside, or subdued, before they entered upon them; they must make no scruple of doing all those impious things which are necessary to compass and support the impiety to which they have devoted themselves'; and therefore he commends Caesar Borgia for 'not being startled with breach of faith, perjuries, and murders, for the removal of those men who he was sure would cross and enervate the whole enterprise he had resolved, and addicted himself to; and blames those usurpers, who had made themselves tyrants, for hoping to support a government by justice, which they had assumed unjustly, and which having wickedly attempted, they manifestly lost by not being wicked enough'. The common old adage, 'that he who hath drawn his sword against his prince, ought to throw away the scabbard, never to think of sheathing it again', hath never been received in a neighbour climate; but hath been looked upon in the frolic humour of that nation [France], as a gaiety that manifests a noble spirit, and may conduce to many advantages, and hath been controlled by some wonderful successes in this age, in those parts, which used not to be so favourable to such attempts: yet without doubt the rule will still hold good; and they who enter upon unwarrantable enterprises, must pursue many unwarrantable ways to preserve themselves from the penalty of the first guilt.

Cromwell, though the greatest dissembler living, always made his hypocrisy of singular use and benefit to him; and never did any thing, how ungracious or imprudent soever it seemed to be, but what was necessary to the design; even his roughness and unpolishedness, which, in the beginning of the parliament, he affected to the smoothness and complacency, which his cousin, and bosom friend, Mr Hambden, practised towards all men, was necessary; and his first public declaration, in the beginning of the war, to his troop when it was first mustered, 'that he would not deceive or cozen them by the perplexed and involved expressions in his commission, to fight for king and parliament'; and therefore told them, 'that if the king chanced to be in the body of the enemy that he was to charge, he would as soon discharge his pistol upon him, as any other private person; and if their conscience would not permit them to do the like, he advised them not to list themselves in his troop, or under his command'; which was generally looked upon as imprudent and malicious, and might, by the professions the parliament then made, have proved dangerous to him; yet served his turn, and severed from others, and united among themselves, all the furious and incensed men against the government, whether ecclesiastical or civil, to look upon him as a man for their turn, upon whom they might depend, as one who would go through his work that he undertook. And his strict and unsociable humour in not keeping company with the other officers of the army in their jollities and excesses, to which most of the superior officers under the earl of Essex were inclined, and by which he often made himself ridiculous or contemptible, drew all those of the like sour or reserved natures to his society and conversation, and gave him opportunity to form their understandings, inclinations, and resolutions, to his own model. By this he grew to have a wonderful interest in the common soldiers, out of which, as his authority increased, he made all his officers, well instructed how to live in the same manner with their soldiers, that they might be able to apply them to their own purposes: whilst he looked upon the presbyterian humour as the best incentive to rebellion, no man more a presbyterian; he sung all psalms with them to their tunes, and loved the longest sermons as much as they; but when he discovered that they would prescribe some limits and bounds to their rebellion, that it was not well breathed, and would expire as soon as some few particulars were granted to them in religion, which he cared not for; and then that the government must run still in the same channel; it concerned him to make it believed 'that the state had been more delinquent than the church, and that the people suffered more by the civil than by the ecclesiastical power; and therefore that the change of one would give them little ease, if there were not as great an alteration in the other, and if the whole government in both were not reformed and altered'; which though it made him generally odious ⟨at first⟩, and irreconciled many of his old friends to him; yet it made those who remained more cordial and firm: he could better compute his own strength, and upon whom he might depend. This discovery made him contrive the ⟨new⟩ model of the army; which was the most unpopular act, and disobliged all those who first contrived the rebellion, and who were the very soul of it; and yet, if he had not brought that to pass, and changed a general, who, though not very sharpsighted, would never be governed, nor applied to any thing he did not like, for another who had no eyes, and so would be willing to be led, all his designs must have come to nothing, and he remained a private colonel of horse, not considerable enough to be in any figure upon an advantageous composition.

[Nevertheless Cromwell and his adherents had still to face opposition, especially] from that part of their own army which had contributed most to the grandeur and empire of which they were possessed, the levellers. That people had been countenanced by Cromwell to enter into cabals and confederacies to corrupt and dissolve the discipline of the army, and by his artifices had been applied to bring all his crooked designs to pass. By them he broke the strict union between the parliament and the Scots, and then took the king out of the hands of the parliament, and kept him in the army, with so many fair professions of intending better to his majesty, and his party, than the other did; by them the presbyterians had been affronted and trodden under foot, and the city of London exposed to disgrace and infamy; by them he had broken the treaty of the Isle of Wight; driven out of the parliament, by force of arms, all those who desired peace, and at last executed his barbarous malice upon the sacred person of the king: and when he had applied them to all those uses, for which he thought them to be most fit, he hoped and endeavoured to have reduced them again, by a severe hand, into that order and obedience from whence he had seduced them, and which was now as necessary to his future purpose of government. But they had tasted too much of the pleasure of having their part and share in it, to be willing to be stripped, and deprived of it; and made an unskilful computation of what they should be able to do for the future, by the great things they had done before in those changes and revolutions which are mentioned; not considering, that the superior officers of the army were now united with the parliament, and concurred entirely in the same designs. And therefore when they renewed their former expostulations and demands from the parliament, they were cashiered, and imprisoned, and some of them put to death. Yet after Cromwell, who had persecuted them with great fury, was gone for Ireland, they recovered their courage, and resolved to obtain those concessions by force, which were refused to be granted upon their request: and so they mutinied in several parts, upon presumption that those of the army, who would not join with them in public, would yet never be prevailed with to oppose, and reduce them by force. But this confidence deceived them; for the parliament no sooner commanded their general Fairfax to suppress them, than he drew troops together, and fell upon them at Banbury, and in other places; and by killing some upon the place, and executing others to terrify the rest, he totally suppressed that faction; and the orders of those at Westminster met with no more opposition.

48. *Charles I: Trial and Character*

[After the failure of the second civil war, a committee
of the House of Commons prepared a charge against
Charles 'that the king had been the cause of all the blood
that had been spilt; and therefore, that it was fit that such
a man of blood should be brought to justice, that he might
undergo the penalty that was due to his tyranny and
murders'. But as the House of Lords refused to concur
with them the Commons had to] make a new form to
warrant their proceedings: and a new form they did erect,
never before heard of. They constituted and erected a
court that should be called '*the high court of justice,* to consist
of so many judges, who should have authority to try the
king, whether he were guilty of what he was accused of,
or no; and, in order thereunto, to examine such witnesses
as should be produced': the number of the judges to be
eight and forty, whereof the major part might proceed.

They could not have found such a number yet amongst
themselves, after so many barbarities and impieties, upon
whom they might depend in this last tragical act. And
therefore they laid this for a ground; that if they should
make only their own members to be judges in this case,
they might appear in the eyes of the people to be too much
parties, as having from the beginning maintained a war,
though defensive, as they pretended, against the king, and
so not so fit to be the only judges who were in the fault: on
the other hand, if they should name none of themselves,
it might be interpreted that they looked upon it as too
dangerous a province to engage themselves in, and therefore they had put it off to others; which would discourage
others from undertaking it. Wherefore they resolved, that
the judges should be nominated promiscuously, as well
of members of the house, as of such other of their good and
godly men in the kingdom, as they should think fit to
nominate. Whosoever would not be one himself when
named as there were yet many amongst them, who, out of
conscience, or of fear, utterly protested against it, should
take upon him to name another man; which sure he could

not but think was equally unlawful: so that few took upon them to nominate others who would reject the province themselves.

All the chief officers of the army were named and divers accepted the office; and such aldermen and citizens of London, as had been most violent against peace, and some few country gentlemen, whose zeal had been taken notice of for the cause, and who were like to take such a preferment as a testimony of the parliament's confidence in them, and would thereupon embrace it. When such a number of men were nominated as were thought in all respects to be equal to the work, they were to make choice of a speaker, or prolocutor, who should be called lord president of that high court, who must manage and govern all the proceedings there, ask the witnesses all proper questions, and answer what the prisoner should propose. And to that office one Bradshaw was chosen, a lawyer of Gray's inn, not much known in Westminster-hall, though of good practice in his chamber, and much employed by the factious and discontented persons. He was a gentleman of an ancient family in Cheshire and Lancashire, but of a fortune of his own making. He was not without parts, and of great insolence and ambition. When he was first nominated, he seemed much surprised, and very resolute to refuse it; which he did in such a manner, and so much enlarging upon his own want of abilities to undergo so important a charge, that it was very evident he had expected to be put to that apology. And when he was pressed with more importunity than could have been used by chance, he required 'time to consider of it'; and said, 'he would then give his final answer'; which he did the next day; and with great humility accepted the office, which he administered with all the pride, impudence, and superciliousness imaginable. He was presently invested in great state, and many officers and a guard assigned for the security of his person, and the dean's house at Westminster given to him for ever for his residence and habitation, and a good sum of money, about five thousand pounds, was appointed to be presently paid to him, to put himself in such an equipage and way of living, as the dignity of the office which he held would require. And now, the lord president of the high court of justice seemed to be the greatest magistrate in England. And though it was not thought seasonable to make any such declaration, yet some of those whose opinions grew quickly into ordinances, upon several occasions, declared, 'that they believed that office was not to be looked upon as necessary *pro hac vice* only, but for continuance; and that he who executed it deserved to have an ample and a liberal estate conferred upon him for ever': which sudden mutation and exaltation of fortune, could not but make a great impression upon a vulgar spirit, accustomed to no excesses, and acquainted only with a very moderate fortune. All this being done, they made choice of some lawyers (eminent for nothing but their obscurity, and that they were men scarce known) to perform the offices of attorney general, and solicitor general for the state, to prosecute the prisoner at his trial, and to manage the evidence against him. Other officers, of all kinds, were appointed to attend, and perform the several offices of their new court; which was ordered to be erected in Westminster-hall, for which such architects were appointed as were thought fit to give direction therein.

From the time of the king's being come to St. James's, . . . his majesty was treated with more rudeness and barbarity than he had ever been before. No man was suffered to see or speak to him, but the soldiers who were his guard, some of whom sat up always in his bedchamber, and drank, and took tobacco, as if they had been upon the court of guard; nor was he suffered to go into any other room, either to say his prayers, or to receive the ordinary benefits of nature, but was obliged to do both in their presence and before them: and yet they were so jealous of these their janizaries, that they might be wrought upon by the influence of this innocent prince, or by the remorse of their own conscience upon the exercise of so much barbarity, that they caused the guards to be still changed; and the same men were never suffered twice to perform the same monstrous duty.

When he was first brought to Westminster-hall, which

was upon the twentieth of January, before their high court
of justice, he looked upon them, and sat down, without
any manifestation of trouble, never stirring his hat; all
the impudent judges sitting covered, and fixing their eyes
upon him, without the least show of respect. The odious
libel, which they called a charge and impeachment, was
then read by the clerk; which contained, 'that he had been
admitted king of England, and trusted with a limited
power to govern according to law; and, by his oath and
office, was obliged to use the power committed to him
for the good and benefit of the people: but that he had,
out of a wicked design to erect himself an illimited and
tyrannical power, and to overthrow the rights and liberties
of the people, traitorously levied war against the present
parliament, and the people therein represented'. And then
it mentioned his first appearance at York with a guard,
then his being at Beverly, then his setting up his standard
at Nottingham, the day of the month and the year in
which the battle had been at Edge-hill, and all the other
several battles which had been fought in his presence;
'in which', it said, 'he had caused and procured many
thousands of the freeborn people of the nation to be slain:
that after all his forces had been defeated, and himself
become a prisoner, he had, in that very year, caused many
insurrections, to be made in England, and given a commission to the prince his son to raise a new war against the
parliament; whereby many who were in their service, and
trusted by them, had revolted, broken their trust, and
betook themselves to the service of the prince against the
parliament and the people: that he had been the author
and contriver of the unnatural, cruel, and bloody wars;
and was therein guilty of all the treasons, murders, rapines,
burnings, and spoils, desolations, damage, and mischief
to the nation, which had been committed in the said war,
or been occasioned thereby; and that he was therefore
impeached for the said treasons and crimes, on the behalf
of the people of England, as a tyrant, traitor, and murderer, and a public implacable enemy to the commonwealth of England'. And it was prayed, 'that he might be
put to answer to all the particulars, to the end that such

an examination, trial, and judgment, might be had thereupon, as should be agreeable to justice'.

Which being read, their president Bradshaw, after he had insolently reprehended the king 'for not having stirred his hat, or shewed more respect to that high tribunal', told him, 'that the parliament of England had appointed that court to try him for the several treasons, and misdemeanours, which he had committed against the kingdom during the evil administration of his government; and that, upon the examination thereof, justice might be done'. And, after a great sauciness and impudence of talk, he asked the king, 'what answer he had to make to that impeachment'.

The king, without any alteration in his countenance by all that insolent provocation, told them, 'he would first know of them, by what authority they presumed by force to bring him before them, and who gave them power to judge of his actions, for which he was accountable to none but God; though they had always been such as he need not be ashamed to own them before all the world'. He told them, 'that he was their king, they his subjects; who owed him duty and obedience: that no parliament had authority to call him before them; but that they were not the parliament, nor had any authority from the parliament to sit in that manner: that of all the persons who sat there, and took upon them to judge him, except those persons who being officers of the army he could not but know whilst he was forced to be amongst them, there were only two faces which he had ever seen before, or whose names were known to him'. And, after urging, 'their duty, that was due to him, and his superiority over them', by such lively reasons, and arguments, as were not capable of any answer, he concluded, 'that he would not so much betray himself, and his royal dignity, as to answer any thing they objected against him, which were to acknowledge their authority; though he believed that every one of themselves, as well as the spectators, did, in their own consciences, absolve him from all the material things which were objected against him'.

Bradshaw advised him, in a very arrogant manner, 'not

to deceive himself with an opinion that any thing he had said would do him any good: that the parliament knew their own authority, and would not suffer it to be called in question or debated': therefore wished him, 'to think better of it, against he should be next brought thither, and that he would answer directly to his charge; otherwise, he could not be so ignorant, as not to know what judgment the law pronounced against those who stood mute, and obstinately refused to plead'. So the guard carried his majesty back to St. James's; where they treated him as before.

There was an accident happened that first day, which may be fit to be remembered. When all those who were commissioners had taken their places, and the king was brought in, the first ceremony was, to read their commission; which was the ordinance of parliament for the trial; and then the judges were all called, every man answering to his name as he was called, and the president being first called and making answer, the next who was called being the general, lord Fairfax, and no answer being made, the officer called him the second time, when there was a voice heard that said, 'he had more wit than to be there'; which put the court into some disorder, and somebody asking, who it was, there was no answer but a little murmuring. But, presently, when the impeachment was read, and that expression used, of 'all the good people of England', the same voice in a louder tone answered, 'No, nor the hundredth part of them': upon which, one of the officers bid the soldiers give fire into that box whence those presumptuous words were uttered. But it was quickly discerned that it was the general's wife, the lady Fairfax, who had uttered both those sharp sayings; who was presently persuaded or forced to leave the place, to prevent any new disorder. She was of a very noble extraction, one of the daughters and heirs of Horace Lord Vere of Tilbury; who, having been bred in Holland, had not that reverence for the church of England, as she ought to have had, and so had unhappily concurred in her husband's entering into rebellion, never imagining what misery it would bring upon the kingdom; and now abhorred the work in hand as much as any body could do, and did all she could to hinder her husband from acting any part in it. Nor did he ever sit in that bloody court, though out of the stupidity of his soul he was throughout overwitted by Cromwell, and made a property to bring that to pass which could very hardly have been otherwise effected.

As there was in many persons present at that woeful spectacle a real duty and compassion for the king, so there was in others so barbarous and brutal a behaviour towards him, that they called him tyrant and murderer; and one spit in his face; which his majesty, without expressing any trouble, wiped off with his handkerchief.

The several unheard of insolences which this excellent prince was forced to submit to, at the other times he was brought before that odious judicatory, his majestic behaviour under so much insolence, and resolute insisting upon his own dignity, and defending it by manifest authorities in the law, as well as by the clearest deductions from reason, the pronouncing that horrible sentence upon the most innocent person in the world, the execution of that sentence by the most execrable murder that was ever committed since that of our blessed Saviour, and the circumstances thereof; the application and interposition that was used by some noble persons to prevent that woeful murder, and the hypocrisy with which that interposition was eluded, the saint-like behaviour of that blessed martyr, and his Christian courage and patience at his death, are all particulars so well known, and have been so much enlarged upon in a treatise peculiarly writ to that purpose, that the farther mentioning it in this place would but afflict and grieve the reader, and make the relation itself odious as well as needless; and therefore no more shall be said here of that lamentable tragedy, so much to the dishonour of the nation, and the religion professed by it.

But it will not be unnecessary to add a short character of his person, that posterity may know the inestimable loss, which the nation then underwent, in being deprived of a prince, whose example would have had a greater influence upon the manners and piety of the nation, than the most strict laws can have. To speak first of his private qualifications as a man, before the mention of his princely and royal virtues; he was, if ever any, the most worthy of the title of an honest man; so great a lover of justice, that no temptation could dispose him to a wrongful action, except it was so disguised to him that he believed it to be just. He had a tenderness and compassion of nature, which restrained him from ever doing a hard-hearted thing: and therefore he was so apt to grant pardon to malefactors, that the judges of the land represented to him the damage and insecurity to the public, that flowed from such his indulgence. And then he restrained himself from pardoning either murders or highway robberies, and quickly discerned the fruits of his severity by a wonderful reformation of those enormities. He was very punctual and regular in his devotions; he was never known to enter upon his recreations or sports, though never so early in the morning, before he had been at public prayers; so that on hunting days his chaplains were bound to a very early attendance. He was likewise very strict in observing the hours of his private cabinet devotions; and was so severe an exactor of gravity and reverence in all mention of religion, that he could never endure any light or profane word, with what sharpness of wit soever it was covered: and though he was well pleased and delighted with reading verses made upon any occasion, no man durst bring before him any thing that was profane or unclean. That kind of wit had never any countenance then. He was so great an example of conjugal affection, that they who did not imitate him in that particular did not brag of their liberty: and he did not only permit, but direct his bishops to prosecute those scandalous vices, in the ecclesiastical courts, against persons of eminence and near relation to his service.

His kingly virtues had some mixture and allay, that hindered them from shining in full lustre, and from producing those fruits they should have been attended with. He was not in his nature very bountiful, though he gave very much. This appeared more after the duke of Buckingham's death, after which those showers fell very rarely; and he paused too long in giving, which made those, to whom he gave, less sensible of the benefit. He kept state to the full, which made his court very orderly; no man presuming to be seen in a place where he had no pretence to be. He saw and observed men long, before he received them about his person; and did not love strangers; nor very confident men. He was a patient hearer of causes; which he frequently accustomed himself to at the council board; and judged very well, and was dexterous in the mediating part: so that he often put an end to causes by persuasion, which the stubbornness of men's humours made dilatory in courts of justice.

He was very fearless in his person, but not very enterprising. He had an excellent understanding, but was not confident enough of it; which made him oftentimes change his own opinion for a worse, and follow the advice of men that did not judge so well as himself. This made him more irresolute than the conjecture of his affairs would admit: if he had been of a rougher and more imperious nature he would have found more respect and duty. And his not applying some severe cures to approaching evils proceeded from the lenity of his nature, and the tenderness of his conscience, which, in all cases of blood, made him choose the softer way, and not hearken to severe counsels, how reasonably soever urged. This only restrained him from pursuing his advantage in the first Scottish expedition, when, humanly speaking, he might have reduced that nation to the most slavish obedience that could have been wished. But no man can say he had then many who advised him to it, but the contrary, by a wonderful indisposition all his council had to fighting, or any other fatigue. He was always an immoderate lover of the Scottish nation, having not only been born there, but educated by that people, and besieged by them always, having few English about him till he was king; and the major number of his servants being still of that nation, who he thought could never fail him. And among these, no man had such an ascendant over him, by the humblest insinuations, as duke Hamilton had.

As he excelled in all other virtues, so in temperance he was so strict, that he abhorred all debauchery to that degree, that, at a great festival solemnity, where he once was, when very many of the nobility of the English and Scots were entertained, being told by one who withdrew from thence, what vast draughts of wine they drank, and 'that there was one earl, who had drank most of the rest down, and was not himself moved or altered', the king said, 'that he deserved to be hanged'; and that earl coming shortly after into the room where his majesty was, in some gayety, to shew how unhurt he was from the battle, the king sent one to bid him withdraw from his majesty's presence; nor did he in some days after appear before him.

So many miraculous circumstances contributed to his ruin, that men might well think that heaven and earth and the stars designed it. Though he was, from the first declension of his power, so much betrayed by his own servants, that there were very few who remained faithful to him, yet that treachery proceeded not from any treasonable purpose to do him any harm, but from particular and personal animosities against other men. And, afterwards, the terror all men were under of the parliament, and the guilt they were conscious of themselves, made them watch all opportunities to make themselves gracious to those who could do them good; and so they became spies upon their master, and from one piece of knavery were hardened and confirmed to undertake another; till at last they had no hope of preservation but by the destruction of their master. And after all this, when a man might reasonably believe that less than a universal defection of three nations could not have reduced a great king to so ugly a fate, it is most certain, that, in that very hour when he was thus wickedly murdered in the sight of the sun, he had as great a share in the hearts and affections of his subjects in general, was as much beloved, esteemed, and longed for by the people in general of the three nations, as any of his predecessors had ever been. To conclude, he was the worthiest gentleman, the best master, the best friend, the best husband, the best father, and the best

Christian, that the age in which he lived produced. And if he were not the best king, if he were without some parts and qualities which have made some kings great and happy, no other prince was ever unhappy who was possessed of half his virtues and endowments, and so much without any kind of vice.

49. *The Reactions of other States to the Events in Great Britain*

THERE is not a sadder consideration (and I pray God the almighty justice be not angry with, and weary of the government of kings and princes, for it is a strange declension monarchy is fallen to, in the opinion of the common people within these late years) than this passion and injustice, in Christian princes, that they are not so solicitous that the laws be executed, justice administered, and order preserved within their own kingdoms, as they are that all three may be disturbed and confounded amongst their neighbours. And therefore there is no sooner a spark of dissension, a discomposure in affections, a jealousy in understandings, discerned to be in or to be easy to be infused into a neighbour province, or kingdom, to the hazarding of the peace thereof, but they, though in league and amity, with their utmost art and industry, make it their business to kindle that spark into a flame, and to contract and ripen all unsettled humours, and jealous apprehensions, into a peremptory discontent, and all discontent to sedition, and all sedition to open and professed rebellion. And they have never so ample satisfaction in their own greatness, or so great a sense and value of God's blessing upon them, as when they have been instruments of drawing some notorious calamity upon their neighbours. As if the religion of princes were nothing but policy, enough to make all other kingdoms but their own miserable: and that, because God hath reserved them to be tried only within his own jurisdiction, and before his own tribunal, that he means to try them too by other laws and rules, than he hath published to the world for his servants to walk by. Whereas they ought to consider, that God hath placed them over his people as examples, and to give countenance to his laws by their own strict observation of them; and that as their subjects are to be defended and protected by them, so themselves are to be assisted and supported by one another; the function of kings being a classis by itself: and as a contempt and breach of every law is, in the policy of states, an offence against the person of the king, because there is a kind of violence offered to his person in the transgression of that rule without which he cannot govern; so the rebellion of subjects against their prince ought to be looked upon, by all other kings, as an assault of their own sovereignty, and a design against monarchy itself; and consequently to be suppressed, and extirpated, in what other kingdom soever it is, with the same concernment as if it were in their own bowels.

[After the execution of King Charles I] It will require, at least it may not be unfit, to rest and make a pause in this place, to take a view, and behold with what countenance the kings and princes of Christendom had their eyes fixed upon this woeful bloody spectacle; how they looked upon that issue of blood, at which their own seemed to be so prodigally poured out; with what consternation their hearts laboured to see the impious hands of the lowest and basest subjects bathing in the bowels and reeking blood of their sovereign; a brother king, the anointed of the Lord, dismembered as a malefactor; what combination and union was entered into, to take vengeance upon those monsters, and to vindicate the royal blood thus wickedly spilt. Alas! there was not a murmur amongst any of them at it; but, as if they had been all called upon in the language of the prophet Isaiah, *Go, ye swift messengers, to a nation scattered and peeled, to a people terrible from the beginning hitherto, to a nation meted out, and trodden down, whose lands the rivers have spoiled*, they made haste and sent over, that they might get shares in the spoils of a murdered monarch.

Cardinal Mazarin, who, in the infancy of the French king, managed that sceptre, had long adored the conduct of Cromwell, and sought his friendship by a lower and viler application than was suitable to the purple of a cardinal, sent now to be admitted as a merchant to traffic in the purchase of the rich goods and jewels of the rifled crown, of which he purchased the rich beds, hangings, and carpets, which furnished his palace at Paris. The king of Spain had, from the beginning of the rebellion, kept don Alonzo de Cardinas, who had been his ambassador to the king, residing still at London; and he had, upon several occasions, many audiences from the parliament, and several treaties on foot; and as soon as this dismal murder was over, that ambassador, who had always a great malignity towards the king, bought as many pictures, and other precious goods appertaining to the crown, as, being sent in ships to the Corunna in Spain, were carried from thence to Madrid, upon eighteen mules. Christina, queen of Sweden, purchased the choice of all the medals, and jewels, and some pictures of a great price, and received Cromwell's ambassador with great joy and pomp, and made an alliance with them. The archduke Leopold, who was governor of Flanders, disbursed a great sum of money for many of the best pictures, which adorned the several palaces of the king; which were all brought to him to Brussels, and from thence carried by him into Germany. In this manner did the neighbour princes join to assist Cromwell with very great sums of money, whereby he was enabled to prosecute and finish his wicked victory over what yet remained unconquered, and to extinguish monarchy in this renowned kingdom; whilst they enriched and adorned themselves with the ruins and spoils of the surviving heir, without applying any part thereof to his relief, in the greatest necessities which ever king was subject to. And that which is stranger than all this, and more wonderful, (since most men, by recovering their fortunes, use to recover most of what they were before robbed of, many who joined in the robbery pretending that they took care to preserve it for the true owner,) not one of all these princes, ever restored any of their unlawful purchases to the king, after his blessed restoration.

[Clarendon continues with a description of life in exile, starting the new book with one of his habitual references to scripture texts.]

2 Chron. xxviii. 10. *And now ye purpose to keep under the children of Judah and Jerusalem for bondmen and bondwomen unto you: but are there not with you, even with you, sins against the Lord your God?*

Isaiah xvii. 12. *Woe to the multitude of many people, which make a noise like the noise of the seas; and to the rushing of nations, that make a rushing like the rushing of mighty waters.—*xxix. 10. *For the Lord hath poured out upon you the spirit of deep sleep, and hath closed your eyes: the prophets and your rulers, the seers hath he covered.*

Whilst these tragedies were acting in England, and ordinances formed, as hath been said, to make it penal in the highest degree for any man to assume the title of king, or to acknowledge any man to be so, the king himself remained in a very disconsolate condition at the Hague. Though he had known the desperate state his father was long in, yet the barbarous stroke so surprised him, that he was in all the confusion imaginable, and all about him were almost bereft of their understanding. The truth is, it can hardly be conceived, with what a consternation this terrible news was received by all the common people of that country. There was a woman at the Hague, of the middling rank, who, being with child, with the horror of the mention of it, fell into travail, and in it died. There could not be more evidence of a general detestation than there was, amongst all men of what quality soever. Within two or three days, which they gave to the king's recollection, the States presented themselves in a body to his majesty, to condole with him for the murder of his father, in terms of great sorrow and condolence, save that there was not bitterness enough against the rebels and murderers. The States of Holland, apart, performed the same civility towards his majesty; and the body of the clergy, in a very good Latin oration, delivered by the chief preacher of the Hague, lamented the misfortune, in terms of as much asperity, and detestation of the actors, as unworthy the name of Christians, as could be expressed.

The desperateness of the king's condition could not excuse his sinking under the burden of his grief: but those who were about him besought him to resume so much courage as was necessary for his present state. He thereupon caused those of his father's council who had attended him to be sworn of his privy council, adding only Mr. Long his secretary: who, before, was not of the council. All which was done before he heard from the queen his mother; who, notwithstanding the great agony she was in, which without doubt was as great a passion of sorrow as she was able to sustain, wrote to the king, 'that he could not do better, than to repair into France as soon as was possible, and, in the meantime, desired him not to swear any persons to be of his council, till she could speak with him'. Whether it was, that she did not think those persons to be enough at her devotion; or that she would have them receive that honour upon her recommendation.

The king himself had no mind to go into France, where he thought he had not been treated with excess of courtesy; and he resolved to perform all filial respect towards the queen his mother, without such a condescension and resignation of himself, as she expected; and, to avoid all eclaircissements upon that subject, he heartily desired that any other course might be found more counsellable than that he should go into France. He himself lived with and upon the prince of Orange; who supplied him with all things necessary for his own person, for his mourning, and the like: but towards any other support for himself and his family, his majesty had not enough to maintain them one day: and there were very few of them who could maintain themselves in the most private way: and it was visible enough, that they should not be long able to reside in the Hague.

50. *The Embassy to Spain, 1650–1*

[After the death of Charles I the exiled court hesitated as to what best to do next: the new king intended to attempt Ireland but received also invitations from the Presbyterians of Scotland and from the earl of Montrose. The

Chancellor did not think much of either plan and therefore listened willingly when lord Cottington begged his
company on an embassy to Madrid.] The chancellor was
weary of the company he was in, and the business, which,
having no prospect but towards despair, was yet rendered
more grievous by the continual contentions and animosities between persons. He knew he was not in the queen's
favour at all, and should find no respect in that court.
However, he was very scrupulous, that the king might not
suspect that he was weary of his attendance, or that any
body else might believe that he withdrew himself from
waiting longer upon so desperate a fortune. In the end,
he told the lord Cottington, 'that he would only be passive
in the point, and refer it entirely to him, if he thought fit
to dispose the king to like it by all the arguments he could
use; and if the king approved it so much as to take notice of
it to the chancellor, and commend it as a thing he thought
for his service, he would submit to his command, and very
cheerfully accompany him through the employment';
with which Cottington was very well pleased, taking upon
him what concerned the king.

The lord Cottington's heart was much set upon this
employment, and he knew well, that if it took air before
the king was well prepared and resolved, it would be
much opposed as to the chancellor's part; because many
who did not love him, yet thought his presence about the
king to be of some use, therefore would do all they could
to divert his going: and therefore he managed it so warily
with the king, and presented the whole scheme to him so
dexterously, that his majesty was much pleased with it,
and approved it, and spake of it to the chancellor as a
business he liked, and promised himself much good from
it, and therefore persuaded him to undertake it cheerfully.
Whereupon the chancellor desired him to think well of it,
for he was confident many would dissuade his majesty
from employing him that way; therefore he only besought
him, that when he was so far resolved upon it as to publish
it, he would not be afterwards prevailed with to change
his purpose; which the king said he would not do; and
shortly after declared his resolution publicly to send the

lord Cottington and the chancellor of the exchequer his
ambassadors extraordinary into Spain, and commanded
them to prepare their own commission and instructions,
and to begin their journey as soon as was possible. This
was no sooner known, than all kinds of people, who agreed
in nothing else, murmured and complained of this
counsel, and the more, because it had never been mentioned or debated in council. Only the Scots were very
glad of it, (Mountrose excepted,) believing that when the
chancellor was gone, their beloved covenant would not
be so irreverently mentioned, and that the king would be
wrought upon to withdraw all countenance and favour
from the marquis of Mountrose: and the marquis himself
looked upon it as a deserting him, and complying with the
other party; and from that time, though they lived with
civility towards each other, he withdrew very much of his
confidence, which he had formerly reposed in him. They
who loved him were sorry for him and themselves; they
thought he deserted a path he had long trod, and was well
acquainted with, and was henceforward to move *extra
sphaeram activitatis*, in an office he had not been acquainted
with; and then they should want his credit to support and
confirm them in the king's favour and grace. And there
were many who were very sorry when they heard it, out
of particular duty to the king, who being young, they
thought might be without that counsel and advertisements
which they knew well he would still administer to him.

[Indeed Clarendon never refrained from speaking out.]
In the distress which the king suffered during his abode
in France, the chancellor of the exchequer's part was the
most uneasy and grievous. For though all who were angry
with him were as angry with the marquis of Ormond, who
lived in great friendship with him, and was in the same
trust with the king in all his counsels which were reserved
from others; yet the marquis's quality, and the great
services he had performed, and the great sufferings he
underwent for the crown, made him above all their
exceptions: and they believed his aversion from all their
devices to make marriages, and to traffic in religion, proceeded most from the credit the other had with him. And

the queen's displeasure grew so notorious against the chancellor, that after he found that she would not speak to him, nor take any notice of him when she saw him, he forbore at last coming in her presence; and for many months did not see her face, though he had the honour to lodge in the same house, the palace royal, where both their majesties kept their courts: which encouraged all who desired to ingratiate themselves with her majesty, to express a great prejudice to the chancellor, at least to withdraw from his conversation: and the queen was not reserved in declaring, that she did exceedingly desire to remove him from the king; which nothing kept him from desiring also, in so uncomfortable a condition, but the conscience of his duty, and the confidence his majesty had in his fidelity.

[Thus his farewell audience was stormy.] The queen, with a louder voice, and more emotion than she was accustomed to, told him, 'that she had been contented to see him, and to give him leave to kiss her hand, to comply with the king's desire, who had importuned her to it; otherwise, that he lived in that manner towards her, that he had no reason to expect to be welcome to her: that she need not assign any particular miscarriage of his, since his disrespect towards her was notorious to all men; and that all men took notice, that he never came where she was, though he lodged under her roof', (for the house was hers,) 'and that she thought she had not seen him in six months before; which she looked upon as so high an affront, that only her respect towards the king prevailed with her to endure it'.

When her majesty made a pause, the chancellor said, 'that her majesty had only mentioned his punishment, and nothing of his fault: that how great soever his infirmities were in defect of understanding, or in good manners, he had yet never been in bedlam; which he had deserved to be, if he had affected to publish to the world that he was in the queen's disfavour, by avoiding to be seen by her: that he had no kind of apprehension that they who thought worst of him, would ever believe him to be such a fool, as to provoke the wife of his dead master, the greatness of whose affections to her was well known to him, and the mother of the king, who subsisted by her favour, and all this in France, where himself was a banished person, and she at home, where she might oblige or disoblige him at her pleasure. So that he was well assured, that nobody would think him guilty of so much folly and madness, as not to use all the endeavours he possibly could to obtain her grace and protection: that it was very true, he had been long without the presumption of being in her majesty's presence, after he had undergone many sharp instances of her displeasure, and after he had observed some alteration and aversion in her majesty's looks and countenance, upon his coming into the room where she was, and during the time he stayed there; which others likewise observed so much, that they withdrew from holding any conversation with him in those places, out of fear to offend her majesty: that he had often desired, by several persons, to know the cause of her majesty's displeasure, and that he might be admitted to clear himself from any unworthy suggestions which had been made of him to her majesty; but could never obtain that honour; and therefore he had conceived, that he was obliged, in good manners, to remove so unacceptable an object from the eyes of her majesty, by not coming into her presence; which all who knew him, could not but know to be the greatest mortification that could be inflicted upon him; and therefore he most humbly besought her majesty at this audience, which might be the last he should receive of her, she would dismiss him with the knowledge of what he had done amiss, that he might be able to make his innocence and integrity appear: which he knew had been blasted by the malice of some persons; and thereby misunderstood and misinterpreted by her majesty'. But all this prevailed not with her majesty; who, after she had, with her former passion, objected his credit with the king, and his endeavours to lessen that credit which she ought to have, concluded, 'that she should be glad to see reason to change her opinion'; and so, carelessly, extended her hand towards him: which he kissing, her majesty departed to her chamber.

[But despite these disagreements Henrietta Maria was also on occasion able to appreciate Hyde's services to the monarchy.] During the time of their short stay at Paris, the queen used the chancellor very graciously; but still, expressed trouble that he was sent on that embassy, which she said, would be fruitless, as to any advantage the king would receive from it; and, she said, she must confess, that though she was not confident of his affection and kindness towards her, yet she believed that he did wish that the king's carriage towards her should be always fair and respectful; and that she did desire that he might be always about his majesty's person; not only because she thought he understood the business of England better than any body else, but because she knew that he loved the king, and would always give him good counsel towards his living virtuously; and that she thought he had more credit with him than any other, who would deal plainly and honestly with him.

There was a passage at that time, of which he used to speak often, and looked upon as a great honour to him. The queen one day, amongst some of her ladies in whom she had most confidence, expressed some sharpness towards a lord of the king's council, whom she named not; who, she said, always gave her the fairest words, and promised her every thing she desired, and had persuaded her to affect somewhat that she had before no mind to; and yet she was well assured, that when the same was proposed to the king on her behalf, he was the only man who dissuaded the king from granting it. Some of the ladies seemed to have the curiosity to know who it was; which the queen would not tell: one of them, who was known to have a friendship for him, said, she hoped it was not the chancellor; to which her majesty replied with some quickness, that she might be sure it was not he, who was so far from making promises, or giving fair words, and flattering her, that she did verily believe that 'if he thought her to be a whore, he would tell her of it'; which when that lady told him, he was not displeased with the testimony.

[The embassy proved a failure but there were redeeming moments.] The next day, and so for two or three days together, both the ambassadors had a box prepared for them, to see the *toros*; which is a spectacle very wonderful, different from what they had seen at Burgos, where the bulls were much tamer, and where they were not charged by men on horseback, and little harm done.

Here the place was very noble, being the market-place, a very large square, built with handsome brick houses, which had all balconies, which were adorned with tapestry and very beautiful ladies. Scaffolds were built round to the first story, the lower rooms being shops, and for ordinary use; and in the division of those scaffolds, all the magistrates and officers of the town knew their places. The pavement of the place was all covered with gravel, (which in summer time was upon these occasions watered by carts charged with hogsheads of water.) As soon as the king comes, some officers clear the whole ground from the common people, so that there is no man seen upon the plain but two or three *alguazils*, magistrates with their small white wands. Then one of the four gates which leads into the streets is opened, at which the toreadors enter, all persons of quality richly clad, and upon the best horses of Spain, every one attended by eight or ten or more lackeys, all clinquant with gold and silver lace, who carry the spears, which their masters are to use against the bulls; and with this entry many of the common people break in, for which sometimes they pay very dear. The persons on horseback have all cloaks folded upon their left shoulder, the least disorder of which, much more the letting it fall, is a very great disgrace; and in that grave order they march to the place where the king sits, and after they have made their reverences, they place themselves at a good distance from one another, and expect the bull. The bulls are brought in the night before from the mountains by the people used to that work, who drive them into the town when nobody is in the streets, into a pen made for them, which hath a door, which opens into that large space; the key whereof is sent to the king, which the king, when he sees every thing ready, throws to an *alguazil*, who carries it to the officer that keeps the door, and he causes it to be opened, when a single bull is ready to come out. When the bull enters, the common people, who sit over the door or near to it, strike him, or throw short darts with sharp points of steel, to provoke him to rage. He commonly runs with all his fury against the first man he sees on horseback, who watches him so carefully, and avoids him so dexterously, that when the spectators believe him to be even between the horns of the bull, he avoids by the quick turn of his horse, and with his lance strikes the bull upon a vein that runs through his pole, with which in a moment he falls down dead. But this fatal stroke can never be struck, but when the bull comes so near upon the turn of the horse, that his horn even touches the rider's leg, and so is at such a distance that he can shorten his lance, and use the full strength of his arm in the blow. And they who are the most skilful in the exercise do frequently kill the beast with such an exact stroke, insomuch as in a day two or three fall in that manner: but if they miss the vein, it only gives a wound that the more enrages him. Sometimes the bull runs with so much fierceness (for if he escapes the first man, he runs upon the rest as they are in his way,) that he gores the horse with his horns, that his guts come out, and he falls before the rider can get from his back. Sometimes by the strength of his neck, he raises horse and man from the ground, and throws both down, and then the greatest danger is another gore upon the ground. In any of these disgraces, or any other by which the rider comes to be dismounted, he is obliged in honour to take his revenge upon the bull by his sword, and upon his head, towards which the standers by assist him by running after the bull and hocking him, by which he falls upon his hinder legs; but before that execution can be done, a good bull hath his revenge upon many poor fellows. Sometimes he is so unruly that nobody dares to attack him, and then the king calls for his mastiffs, whereof two are let out at a time, and if they cannot master him, but are themselves killed, as frequently they are, the king then, as a last refuge, calls for the English mastiffs, of which they seldom turn above one at a time; and he rarely misses of taking the bull and holding him by the nose till the men run in; and after they have hocked him, they quickly kill him. In one of those days there were no fewer than sixteen horses, as good as any in Spain, the worst of which would that very morning have yielded three hundred pistoles, killed, and four or five men, besides many more of both hurt: and some men remain perpetually maimed: for after the horsemen have done as much as they can, they withdraw themselves, and then some accustomed nimble fellows, to whom money is thrown when they perform their feats with skill, stand to receive the bull, whereof the worst are reserved till the last: and it is a wonderful thing to see with what steadiness these fellows will stand a full career of the bull, and by a little quick motion upon one foot avoid him, and lay a hand upon his horn, as if he guided him from him; but then the next standers by, who have not the same activity, commonly pay for it, and there is no day without much mischief. It is a very barbarous exercise and triumph, in which so many men's lives are lost, and always ventured; but so rooted in the affections of that nation, that it is not in the king's power, they say, to suppress it, though, if he disliked it enough, he might forbear to be present at it. There are three festival days in the year, whereof midsummer is one, on which the people hold it to be their right to be treated with these spectacles, not only in great cities, where they are never disappointed, but in very ordinary towns, where there are places provided for it. Besides those ordinary annual days, upon any extraordinary accident of joy, as at this time for the arrival of the queen, upon the birth of the king's children, or any signal victory, these triumphs are repeated, which no ecclesiastical censures or authority can suppress or discountenance. For Pope Pius the Fifth, in the time of Philip the Second, and very probably with his approbation, if not upon his desire, published a bull against the *toros* in Spain, which is still in force, in which he declared, that nobody should be capable of Christian burial who lost his life at those spectacles, and that every clergyman who should be present at them stood excommunicated *ipso facto*; and yet there is always one of the largest galleries assigned to the office of the inquisition and the chief of the clergy, which is always filled; besides that many religious men in their habits get other places; only the Jesuits, out of their submission to the supreme authority of the pope, are never present there, but on those days do always appoint some such solemn exercise to be performed, that obliges their whole body to be together.

51. *Sir John Colepepper or Culpepper*

Born ?; baron 1643; P.C. and Chancellor of the Exchequer 1642; Master of the Rolls 1643; surrenders chancellorship to Hyde, February 1643; died 1660

[In 1641] The house of commons being at this time without any member, who, having relation to the king's service, would express any zeal for it, and could take upon him to say to others, whom he would trust, what the king desired, or to whom they who wished well could resort for advice and direction; so that whilst there was a strong conjunction and combination to disturb the government by depraving it, whatever was said or done to support it, was as if it were done by chance, and by the private dictates of the reason of private men; the king resolved to call the lord Falkland, and sir John Colepepper, who was knight of the shire for Kent, to his council; and to make the former secretary of state in the place of Vane, that had been kept vacant; and the latter chancellor of the exchequer, which office the lord Cottington had resigned, that Mr. Pym might be put into that office, when the lord Bedford should have been treasurer, as is mentioned before. They were both of great authority in the house; neither of them any relation to the court; and therefore what they said made the more impression; and they were frequent speakers. The lord Falkland was wonderfully beloved, by all who knew him, as a man of excellent parts, of a wit so sharp, and a nature so sincere, that nothing could be more lovely. The other was generally esteemed as a good speaker, being a man of an universal understanding, a quick comprehension, a wonderful memory, who commonly spake at the end of the debate; when he would recollect all that had been said of weight on all sides with great exactness, and express his own sense with much clearness, and such an application to the house, that no man more gathered a general concurrence to his opinion than he; which was the more notable, because his person, and manner of speaking, were ungracious enough; so that he prevailed only by the strength of his reason, which was enforced with confidence enough. His infirmities were known only to his nearest friends, or those who were admitted into his most intimate conversation.

Sir John Colepepper had spent some years of his youth in foreign parts, and especially in armies; where he had seen good service, and very well observed it; and might have made a very good officer if he had intended it. He was of a rough nature, a hot head, and of great courage; which had engaged him in many quarrels and duels; wherein he still behaved himself very signally. He had in a very good season, and after a small waste of his fortune, retired from that course of life, and married, and betook himself to a country life; and studied the business of the country, and the concernments of it, in which he was very well versed; and being a man of sharpness of parts, and volubility of language, he was frequently made choice of to appear at the council-board, in those matters which related to the country: in the managing whereof, his abilities were well taken notice of. His estate was very moderate, and his usual expense exceeded it not; not being delighted with delicacies of any nature, or indeed ever acquainted with them. He had infirmities which sometimes made a noise; but his parts and abilities made him very acceptable to his neighbours, and to those who were most considerable in their estates, and most popular; so that with very little opposition, he had been chosen to be knight of that great county Kent, for the parliament; where he quickly made himself to be taken notice of. He was proud and ambitious, and very much disposed to improve his fortune; which he knew well how to do, by industry and thrift, without stooping to any corrupt ways, to which he was not inclined.

He did not love the persons of many of those who were

the violent managers, and less their designs; and therefore he no sooner knew that he was well spoken of at court, but he exposed himself to the invitation, and heartily embraced that interest: and when he came thither, he might very well be thought a man of no very good breeding; having never sacrificed to the muses, or conversed in any polite company. He was warm and positive in debates, and of present fancy to object and find fault with what was proposed; and indeed would take any argument in pieces, and expose it excellently to a full view; and leave nothing to chance, or accident, without making it foreseen; but after that, knew not so well what to judge and determine; and was so irresolute, and had a fancy so perpetually working, that, after a conclusion made, he would the next day, in the execution of it, and sometimes after, raise new doubts, and make new objections; which always occasioned trouble, and sometimes produced inconvenience.

In matters of religion he was, in his judgment, very indifferent; but more inclined to what was established, to avoid the accidents which commonly attend a change, without any motives from his conscience; which yet he kept to himself; and was well content to have it believed that the activity proceeded from thence. He had, with all this uncourtliness (for sure no man less appeared a courtier) and ungracefulness in his mien and motion, a wonderful insinuation and address into the acceptation and confidence of the king and queen; and flattery being a weed not so natural to the air and soil of the country where he had wholly lived, he was believed to speak with all plainness and sincerity; when no man more complied with those infirmities they both had, and by that compliance prevailed often over them.

He had a very tragical way in expressing himself, to raise the fears and apprehensions of those who were naturally apprehensive of dangers; and by this means he prevailed marvellously with the queen in those matters to which she was most averse; by representing things as dismally to her as he could well do; and on the other hand, to the king (who was naturally very sanguine) he was full of compliance; cherished all his hopes and imaginations, and raised and improved those hopes very frequently by expedients very unagreeable to the end proposed. He was then (as was said before) very positive in his conclusions; as if he did not propose a thing that might come to pass, but what infallibly must be so: which was a temper the king could not contend with; and did so much suspect himself, (which was his greatest infirmity, and the chief ground of all his sufferings,) that he did believe a man, of whom he thought very well, did know everything that he confidently insisted upon. But his greatest advantage was, (besides his diligence in speaking as often as he could with the king and queen, and always with the queen upon any important counsel,) that he had an entire confidence and friendship with Mr. John Ashburnham, whom the king loved, and trusted very much; and who always imprinted that advice in the king's mind, which the other had infused; and being a member of the house, was always ready to report the service he did his majesty there, as advantageously as the business would bear.

[While Hyde's preferment to the Chancellorship of the Exchequer was under discussion in 1643, the Master of the Rolls died. This place the king had promised to] sir John Colepepper, who would by no means release him. This was no sooner declared, than the lord Falkland (who was much more solicitous to have Mr. Hyde of the council, than he was himself for the honour) took an opportunity to tell the king, that he had now a good opportunity to prefer Mr. Hyde, by making him chancellor of the exchequer in the place of sir John Colepepper; which the king said he had resolved to do, and bid him take no notice of it, until he had told him so himself: and shortly after sent for him, and said, 'that he had now found an office for him, which he hoped he would not refuse: that the chancellorship of the exchequer was void by the promotion of Colepepper, and that he resolved to confer it upon him;' with many gracious expressions of the satisfaction he had in his service. The other answered, 'that though it was an office much above his merit, yet he did not despair of enabling himself by industry to execute it, which he would do with all fidelity'.

As soon as this was known, no man was so much troubled at it as sir John Colepepper, who had in truth an intention to have kept both places, until he should get into the quiet possession of the rolls. And though he professed much friendship to the other, he had no mind he should be upon the same level with him; and believed he would have too much credit in the council. And so delayed, after his patent for the rolls was passed, to surrender that of the chancellorship of the exchequer, until the lord Falkland and the lord Digby expostulated very warmly with him upon it, and until the king took notice of it; and then, seeming very much troubled that any body should doubt the integrity of his friendship to Mr. Hyde, to whom he made all the professions imaginable, he surrendered his office of chancellor of the exchequer: and the next day Mr. Hyde was sworn of the privy-council, and knighted, and had his patents sealed for that office. And the king, after he rose from the council, and after many expressions of the content he took himself in the obligation he had laid upon him, with much grace, that was not natural in him upon such occasions, told him, that 'he was very fortunate, because he verily believed nobody was angry at his preferment; for besides that the earl of Dorset and others, who he knew loved him, had expressed much satisfaction in the king's purpose', he said, 'the lord Maltrevers, and the lord Dunsmore, who he did not think had any acquaintance with him, seemed very much pleased with him; and therefore he thought nobody would envy him; which was a rare felicity'. But his majesty was therein mistaken; for he had great enviers, of many who thought he had run too fast; especially of those of his own profession, who looked upon themselves as his superiors in all respects, and did not think that his age, (which was not then above thirty-three,) or his other parts, did entitle him to such a preference before them. And the news of it at Westminster exceedingly offended those who governed in the parliament; to see the man whom they most hated, and whom they had voted to be incapable of pardon, to be now preferred to an office the chief of them looked for. Besides, there was another unusual circumstance accompanied his preferment, that it was without the interposition or privity of the queen, which was not like to make it the more easy and advantageous; and it was not the more unwelcome to him from that circumstance.

[After the Restoration Colepepper became a member of the Privy Council.] The lord Colepepper was a man of great parts, a very sharp and present wit, and an universal understanding; so that few men filled a place in council with more sufficiency, or expressed themselves upon any subject that occurred with more weight and vigour. He had been trusted by the late king (who had a singular opinion of his courage and other abilities) to wait upon the prince when he left his father, and continued still afterwards with him, or in his service, and in a good correspondence with the chancellor.

52. *The Fate of the Earl of Montrose*

James Graham, born 1612; fifth earl; marquis 1644; executed 21 May 1650

THE earl of Mountrose, a young man of a great spirit and of the most ancient nobility, had been one of the most principal and active covenanters in the beginning of the troubles; but soon after, upon his observation of the unwarrantable prosecution of it, he gave over that party, and his command in that army; and at the king's being in Scotland, after the pacification, 1641, had made full tender of his service to his majesty; and was so much in the jealousy and detestation of the violent party, whereof the earl of Argyle was the head, that there was no cause or room left to doubt his sincerity to the king.

In this state stood the affair in the end of the year 1649: but because of the unfortunate tragedy of that noble person succeeded so soon after, without the intervention of any notable circumstances to interrupt it, we will rather continue the relation of it in this place, than defer it to be resumed in the proper season; which quickly

ensued, in the beginning of the next year. The marquis of
Argyle was vigilant enough, to observe the motion of an
enemy that was so formidable to him; and had present
information of his arrival in the Highlands, and of the
small forces which he had brought with him. The parliament was then sitting at Edinburgh, their messenger being
returned to them from Jersey, with an account, 'that the
king would treat with their commissioners at Breda'; for
whom they were preparing their instructions.

The alarm of Mountrose's being landed startled them
all, and gave them no leisure to think of any thing else
than of sending forces to hinder the recourse of others to
join with him.

So that he had none left, but a company of good officers,
and five or six hundred foreigners, Dutch and Germans,
who had been acquainted with their officers. With these,
he betook himself to a place of some advantage by the
inequality of the ground, and the bushes and small shrubs
which filled it: and there they made a defence for some
time with notable courage.

But the enemy being so much superior in number, the
common soldiers, being all foreigners, after about a hundred of them were killed upon the place, threw down
their arms; and the marquis, seeing all lost, threw away
his ribbon and George, (for he was a knight of the garter,)
and found means to change his clothes with a fellow of the
country, and so after having gone on foot two or three
miles, he got into a house of a gentleman, where he remained concealed about two days: most of the other
officers were shortly after taken prisoners, all the country
desiring to merit from Argyle by betraying all those into
his hands which they believed to be his enemies. And thus,
whether by the owner of the house, or any other way, the
marquis himself became their prisoner. The strangers
who were taken, were set at liberty, and transported themselves into their own countries; and the castle, in which
there was a little garrison, presently rendered itself; so
that there was no more fear of an enemy in those parts.

The marquis of Mountrose, and the rest of the prisoners,
were the next day, or soon after, delivered to David

Lesley; who was come up with his forces, and had now nothing left to do but to carry them in triumph to Edinburgh; whither notice was quickly sent of their great victory; which was received there with wonderful joy and acclamation. David Lesley treated the marquis with great insolence, and for some days carried him in the same clothes, and habit, in which he was taken; but at last permitted him to buy better. His behaviour was, in the whole time, such as became a great man; his countenance serene and cheerful, as one that was superior to all those reproaches, which they had prepared the people to pour out upon him in all the places through which he was to pass.

When he came to one of the gates of Edinburgh, he was met by some of the magistrates, to whom he was delivered, and by them presently put into a new cart, purposely made, in which there was a high chair, or bench, upon which he sat, that the people might have a full view of him, being bound with a cord drawn over his breast and shoulders, and fastened through holes made in the cart. When he was in this posture, the hangman took off his hat, and rode himself before the cart in his livery, and with his bonnet on; the other officers, who were taken prisoners with him, walking two and two before the cart; the streets and windows being full of people to behold the triumph over a person whose name had made them tremble some few years before, and into whose hands the magistrates of that place had, upon their knees, delivered the keys of that city. In this manner he was carried to the common gaol, where he was received and treated as a common malefactor.

That he might not enjoy any ease or quiet during the short remainder of his life, their ministers came presently to insult over him with all the reproaches imaginable; pronounced his damnation; and assured him, 'that the judgment he was the next day to undergo, was but an easy prologue to that which he was to undergo afterwards'. After many such barbarities, they offered to intercede for him to the kirk upon his repentance, and to pray with him; but he too well understood the form of their common prayer, in those cases, to be only the most virulent and insolent imprecations against the persons of those they prayed against, ('Lord, vouchsafe yet to touch the obdurate heart of this proud incorrigible sinner, this wicked, perjured, traitorous, and profane person, who refuses to hearken to the voice of thy kirk', and the like charitable expressions,) and therefore he desired them 'to spare their pains, and to leave him to his devotions'. He told them, 'that they were a miserable, deluded, and deluding people; and would shortly bring that poor nation under the most insupportable servitude ever people had submitted to'. He told them, 'he was prouder to have his head set upon the place it was appointed to be, than he could have been to have his picture hang in the king's bedchamber: that he was so far from being troubled that his four limbs were to be hanged in four cities of the kingdom, that he heartily wished that he had flesh enough to be sent to every city in Christendom, as a testimony of the cause for which he suffered'.

The next day, they executed every part and circumstance of that barbarous sentence, with all the inhumanity imaginable; and he bore it with all the courage and magnanimity, and the greatest piety, that a good Christian could manifest. He magnified the virtue, courage, and religion of the last king, exceedingly commended the justice, and goodness, and understanding of the present king; and prayed, 'that they might not betray him as they had done his father.' When he had ended all he meant to say, and was expecting to expire, they had yet one scene more to act of their tyranny. The hangman brought the book that had been published of his truly heroic actions, whilst he had commanded in that kingdom, which book was tied in a small cord that was put about his neck. The marquis smiled at this new instance of their malice, and thanked them for it; and said, 'he was pleased that it should be there; and was prouder of wearing it, than ever he had been of the garter'; and so renewing some devout ejaculations, he patiently endured the last act of the executioner.

Thus died the gallant marquis of Mountrose, after he had given as great a testimony of loyalty and courage, as a subject can do, and performed as wonderful actions in several battles, upon as great inequality of numbers, and as great disadvantages in respect of arms, and other preparations for war, as have been performed in this age. He was a gentleman of a very ancient extraction, many of whose ancestors had exercised the highest charges under the king of that kingdom, and had been allied to the crown itself. He was of very good parts, which were improved by a good education: he had always a great emulation, or rather a great contempt of the marquis of Argyle, (as he was too apt to contemn those he did not love,) who wanted nothing but honesty and courage to be a very extraordinary man, having all other good talents in a very great degree. Mountrose was in his nature fearless of danger, and never declined any enterprise for the difficulty of going through with it, but exceedingly affected those which seemed desperate to other men, and did believe somewhat to be in himself which other men were not acquainted with, which made him live more easily towards those who were, or were willing to be, inferior to him, (towards whom he exercised wonderful civility and generosity,) than with his superior or equals. He was naturally jealous, and suspected those who did not concur with him in the way, not to mean so well as he. He was not without vanity, but his virtues were much superior, and he well deserved to have his memory preserved, and celebrated amongst the most illustrious persons of the age in which he lived.

The king received an account and information of all these particulars, before he embarked from Holland, without any other apology for the affront and indignity to himself, than that they assured him, 'that the proceeding against the late marquis of Mountrose had been for his service'. They who were most displeased with Argyle and his faction, were not sorry for this inhuman and monstrous prosecution; which at the same time must render him the more odious, and had rid them of an enemy that they thought would have been more dangerous to them; and they persuaded the king, who was enough afflicted with the news, and all the circumstances of it, 'that he might sooner take revenge upon that people by a temporary complying with them, and going to them, than staying away, and absenting himself, which would invest them in an absolute dominion in that kingdom, and give them power to corrupt or destroy all those who yet remained faithful to him, and were ready to spend their lives in his service': and so his majesty pursued his former resolution and embarked for Scotland.

53. *The End of the Commonwealth, 20 April 1653, and Praise-God Barebone's Parliament, 4 July to 12 December 1653*

IF God had not reserved the deliverance and restoration of the king to himself, and resolved to accomplish it when there appeared least hope of it, and least worldly means to bring it to pass; there happened at this time another very great alteration in England, that, together with the continuance of the war with Holland, and affronts every day offered to France, might very reasonably have administered great hopes to the king of a speedy change of government. From the time of the defeat at Worcester, [3 September 1651] and the reduction of Scotland and Ireland to perfect obedience, Cromwell did not find the parliament so supple to observe his orders, as he expected they would have been. The presbyterian party, which he had discountenanced all he could, and made his army of the independent party, were bold in contradicting him in the house, and crossing all his designs in the city, and exceedingly inveighed against the license that was practised in religion, by the several factions of independents, anabaptists, quakers, and the several species of these; who contemned all magistrates, and the laws established. All these, how contradictory soever to one another, Cromwell cherished and protected, that he might not be overrun by the presbyterians; of whom the time was not yet come that he could make use: yet he seemed to shew much respect to some principal preachers of that party, and consulted much with them, how the distempers in religion might be composed.

Though he had been forward enough to enter upon the war of Holland, that so there might be no proposition made for the disbanding any part of his army, which otherwise could not be prevented, yet he found the expense of it was so great, that the nation could never bear that addition of burden to the other of land forces; which how apparent soever, he saw the parliament so fierce for the carrying on that war, that they would not hearken to any reasonable condition of peace; which the Dutch appeared most solicitous to make upon any conditions. But that which troubled him most, was the jealousy that his own party of independents had contracted against him: that party, that had advanced him to the height he was at, and made him superior to all opposition, even his beloved Vane, thought his power and authority to be too great for a commonwealth, and that he and his army had not dependence enough upon, or submission to, the parliament. So that he found those who had exalted him, now most solicitous to bring him lower; and he knew well enough what any diminution of his power and authority must quickly be attended with. He observed, that those his old friends very frankly united themselves with his and their old enemies, the presbyterians, for the prosecution of the war with Holland, and obstructing all the overtures towards peace; which must, in a short time, exhaust the stock, and consequently disturb any settlement in the kingdom.

In this perplexity he resorts to his old remedy, his army: and again erects another council of officers, who, under the style first, of petitions, and then of remonstrances, interposed in whatsoever had any relation to the army; used great importunity for 'the arrears of their pay; that they might not be compelled to take free quarter upon their fellow subjects, who already paid so great contributions and taxes; which they were well assured, if well managed, would abundantly defray all the charges of the war, and of the government'. The sharp answers the parliament gave to their addresses, and the reprehensions for their presumption in meddling with matters above them, gave the army new matter to reply to; and put them in mind of some former professions they had made, 'that they would be glad to be eased of the burden of their employment; and that there might be successive parliaments to undergo the same trouble they had done'. They therefore desired them, 'that they would remember how many years they had sat; and though they had done great things, yet it was a great injury to the rest of the nation, to be utterly excluded from bearing any part in the service of their country, by their engrossing the whole power into their hands; and thereupon besought them, that they would settle a council for the administration of the government during the interval, and then dissolve themselves, and summon a new parliament; which', they told them, 'would be the most popular action they could perform'.

These addresses in the name of the army, being confidently delivered by some officers of it, and as confidently seconded by others who were members of the house, it was thought necessary, that they should receive a solemn debate, to the end that when the parliament had declared its resolution and determination, all persons might be obliged to acquiesce therein, and so there would be an end put to all addresses of that kind.

There were many members of the house, who, either from the justice and reason of the request, or seasonably to comply with the sense of the army, to which they foresaw they should be at last compelled to submit, seemed to think it necessary, for abating the great envy, which was confessedly against the parliament throughout the kingdom, that they should be dissolved, to the end the people might make a new election of such persons as they thought fit to trust with their liberty and property, and whatsoever was dearest to them. But Mr. Martyn told them, 'that he thought they might find the best advice from the scripture, what they were to do in this particular: that when Moses was found upon the river, and brought to Pharaoh's daughter, she took care that the mother might be found out, to whose care he might be committed to be nursed; which succeeded very happily'. He said, 'their commonwealth was yet an infant, of a weak growth, and a very tender constitution; and therefore his opinion was, that nobody could be so fit to nurse it, as the mother who brought it forth; and that they should not think of putting it under any other hands, until it had obtained more years and vigour'. To which he added 'that they had another infant too under their hands, the war with Holland, which had thrived wonderfully under their conduct; but he much doubted that it would be quickly strangled, if it were taken out of their care who had hitherto governed it'.

These reasons prevailed so far, that, whatsoever was said to the contrary, it was determined, that the parliament would not yet think of dissolving, nor would take it well, that any persons should take the presumption any more to make overtures to them of that nature, which was not fit for private and particular persons to meddle with: and, to put a seasonable stop to any farther presumption of that kind, they appointed a committee speedily to prepare an act of parliament by which it should be declared to be high treason, for any man 'to propose or contrive the dissolution of this parliament, or to change the present government settled and established'.

This bill being prepared by the committee, they resolved to pass it with all possible expedition. So Cromwell clearly discerned, that by this means they would never be persuaded to part with that authority and power, which was so profitable, and so pleasant to them: yet the army declared they were not satisfied with the determination, and continued their applications to the same purpose, or to others as unagreeable to the sense of the house; and did all they could to infuse the same spirit into all the parts of the kingdom, to make the parliament odious, as it was already very abundantly; and Cromwell was well pleased that the parliament should express as much prejudice against the army.

All things being thus prepared, Cromwell thought this a good season to expose these enemies of peace to the indignation of the nation; which, he well knew, was generally weary of the war, and hoped, if that were at an end, that they should be eased of the greatest part of their contributions, and other impositions: thereupon, having adjusted all things with the chief officers of the army, who were at his devotion, in the month of April, that was in the year 1653, he came into the house of parliament in a morning when it was sitting, attended with the officers, who were likewise members of the house, and told them, 'that he came thither to put an end to their power and authority; which they had managed so ill, that the nation could be no otherwise preserved than by their dissolution; which he advised them, without farther debate, quietly to submit unto'.

Thereupon another officer, with some files of musketeers, entered into the house, and stayed there till all the members walked out; Cromwell reproaching many of the members by name, as they went out of the house, with their vices and corruptions; and amongst the rest, sir Harry Vane with his breach of faith and corruption; and having given the mace to an officer to be safely kept, he caused the doors to be locked up; and so dissolved that assembly, which had sat almost thirteen years, and under whose name he had wrought so much mischief, and reduced three kingdoms to his own entire obedience and subjection, without any example or precedent in the Christian world that could raise his ambition to such a presumptuous undertaking, and without any rational dependence upon the friendship of one man, who had any other interest to advance his designs, but what he had given him by preferring him in the war.

The method he pursued afterwards, for the composing a government, by first putting it into a most ridiculous confusion, and by divesting himself of all pretences to authority, and putting what he had no title to keep into the hands of men so well chosen that they should shortly after delegate the power legally to him for the preservation of the nation, was not less admirable; and puts me in mind of what Seneca said of Pompey, 'that he had brought the people of Rome to that pass, by magnifying their power and authority, *ut salvus esse non possit nisi beneficio servitutis*'. And if Cromwell had not now made himself a tyrant, all bonds being broken, and the universal guilt diverting all inclinations to return to the king's obedience, they must have perished together in such a confusion, as would rather have exposed them as a prey to foreigners, than dispose them to the only reasonable way for their preservation; there being no man that durst mention the king, or the old form of government.

It was upon the twenty-fourth ⟨twentieth⟩ of April that the parliament had been dissolved; and though Cromwell found that the people were satisfied in it, and the declaration published thereupon, yet he knew it would be necessary to provide some other visible power to settle the government, than the council of officers; all whom he was not sure he should be able long entirely to govern, many of them having clear other notions of a republic than he was willing England should be brought to. A parliament was still a name of more veneration than any other assembly of men was like to be, and the contempt the last was fallen into was like to teach the next to behave itself with more discretion. However the ice was broken for dissolving them, when they should do otherwise; yet he was not so well satisfied in the general temper, as to trust the election of them to the humour and inclination to the people.

He resolved therefore to choose them himself, that he might with the more justice unmake them when he should think fit; and with the advice of his council of officers, for he made yet no other council of state, he made choice of a number of men, consisting of above one hundred and forty persons, who should meet as a parliament to settle the government of the nation. It can hardly be believed that so wild a notion should fall into any man's imagination, that such a people should be fit to contribute towards any settlement, or that from their actions any thing could result, that might advance his particular design. Yet, upon the view and consideration of the persons made choice of, many did conclude, 'that he had made his own scheme entirely to himself; and though he communicated it with no man, concluded it the most natural way to ripen and produce the effects it did afterwards, to the end he proposed to himself'.

There were amongst them some few of the quality and

degree of gentlemen, and who had estates, and such a proportion of credit and reputation, as could consist with the guilt they had contracted. But much the major part of them consisted of inferior persons, of no quality or name, artificers of the meanest trades, known only by their gifts in praying and preaching; which was now practised by all degrees of men, but scholars, throughout the kingdom. In which number, that there may be a better judgment made of the rest, it will not be amiss to name one, from whom that parliament itself was afterwards denominated, who was Praise-God (that was his Christian name) Bare-bone, a leatherseller in Fleet-street, from whom (he being an eminent speaker in it) it was afterwards called Praise-God Barebone's parliament. In a word, they were a pack of weak senseless fellows, fit only to bring the name and reputation of parliaments lower than it was yet.

When they had tired and perplexed themselves so long in such debates [concerning legal and ecclesiastical matters], as soon as they were met in the morning upon the twelfth of December, and before many of them were come who were like to dissent from the motion, one of them stood up and declared, 'that he did believe, they were not equal to the burden that was laid upon them, and therefore that they might dissolve themselves, and deliver back their authority into their hands from whom they had received it'; which being presently consented to, their speaker, with those who were of that mind, went to Whitehall, and redelivered to Cromwell the instrument they had received from him, acknowledged their own impotency, and besought him to take care of the commonwealth.

By this frank donation he and his council of officers were once more possessed of the supreme sovereign power of the nation. And in few days after, his council were too modest to share with him in this royal authority, but declared, 'that the government of the commonwealth should reside in a single person; that that person should be Oliver Cromwell, captain general of all the forces in England, Scotland, and Ireland, and that his title should be lord protector of the commonwealth of England, Scotland, and Ireland, and of the dominions and territories thereunto belonging; and that he should have a council of one and twenty persons to be assistant to him in the government'. [Thus the Protectorate was inaugurated and soon after the nation submitted.]

Though the protector had nothing now to do but at home, Holland having accepted peace upon his own terms, Portugal bought it at a full price, and upon an humble submission, Denmark being contented with such an alliance as he was pleased to make with them, and France and Spain contending, by their ambassadors, which should render themselves most acceptable to him; Scotland lying under a heavy yoke by the severe government of Monk, who after the peace with the Dutch was sent back to govern that province, which was reduced under the government of the English laws, and their kirk, and kirkmen, entirely subdued to the obedience of the state without reference to assemblies, or synods; Ireland being confessedly subdued, and no opposition made to the protector's commands; so that commissions were sent to divide all the lands which had belonged to the Irish, or to those English who had adhered to the king, amongst those adventurers who had supplied money for the war, and the soldiers and officers; who were in great arrears for their pay, and who received liberal assignations in lands; one whole province being reserved for a demesne for the protector; and all these divisions made under the government of his younger son, Harry Cromwell, whom he sent thither as his lieutenant of that kingdom; who lived in the full grandeur of the office: notwithstanding all this, England proved not yet so towardly as he expected. Vane, and the most considerable men of the independent party, from the time he had turned them out of the parliament, and so dissolved it, retired quietly to their houses in the country; poisoned the affections of their neighbours towards the government; and lost nothing of their credit with the people; yet carried themselves so warily, that they did nothing to disturb the peace of the nation, or to give Cromwell any advantage against them upon which to call them in question.

There were another less wary, because a more desperate party, which were the levellers; many whereof had been the most active agitators in the army, who had executed his orders and designs in incensing the army against the parliament, and had been at that time his sole confidents and bed-fellows; who, from the time that he assumed the title of protector, which to them was as odious as that of king, professed a mortal hatred to his person; and he well knew both these people had too much credit in his army, and with some principal officers of it. Of these men he stood in more fear than of all the king's party; of which he had in truth very little apprehension, though he coloured many of the preparations he made against the other, as if providing against the dangers threatened from them.

54. *Blake's Victory at Santa Cruz, April 1657, and Death, August 1657*

Robert Blake, 1599–1657; general-at-sea 1649

[Having mentioned Cromwell's 'domestic triumphs' Clarendon continues] But that which made a noise indeed, and crowned his successes, was the victory his fleet, under the command of Blake, had obtained over the Spaniard; which, in truth, with all its circumstances, was very wonderful, and will never be forgotten in Spain, and the Canaries. That fleet had rode out all the winter storms before Cales and the coast of Portugal, after they had sent home those former ships which they had taken of the West Indian fleet, and understood by the prisoners, that the other fleet from Peru, which is always much richer than that of Mexico, was undoubtedly at sea, and would be on the coast by the beginning of the spring, if they received not advertisement of the presence of the English fleet; in which case they were most like to stay at the Canaries. The admiral concluded, that, notwithstanding all they had done, or could do to block up Cales, one way or other they would not be without that advertisement; and therefore resolved to sail with the whole fleet to the length of the Canaries, that, if it were possible, they might meet with the galleons before they came thither; and if they should be first got in thither, they would then consider what was to be done.

With this resolution the fleet stood for the Canaries, and about the middle of April came thither; and found that the galleons were got thither before them, and had placed themselves, as they thought, in safety. The smaller ships being ten in number, lay in a semicircle, moored along the shore; and the six great galleons, (the fleet consisting of sixteen good ships,) which could not come so near the shore, lay with their broadsides towards the offing. Besides this good posture in which all the ships lay, they were covered with a strong castle well furnished with guns; and there were six or seven small forts, raised in the most advantageous places of the bay, everyone of them furnished with six good pieces of cannon; so that they were without the least apprehension of their want of security, or imagination that any men would be so desperate, as to assault them upon such apparent disadvantage.

When the English fleet came to the mouth of the bay of Santa Cruz, and the general saw in what posture the Spaniard lay, he thought it impossible to bring off any of the galleons; however, he resolved to burn them, (which was by many thought to be equally impossible,) and sent captain Stayner with a squadron of the best ships to fall upon the galleons; which he did very resolutely; whilst other frigates entertained the forts and lesser breastworks, with continual broadsides to hinder their firing. Then the general coming up with the whole fleet, after full four hours' fight, they drove the Spaniards from their ships, and possessed them; yet found that their work was not done; and that it was not only impossible to carry away the ships, which they had taken, but that the wind that had brought them into the bay, and enabled them to conquer the enemy, would not serve to carry them out again; so that they lay exposed to all the cannon from the shore; which thundered upon them. However, they resolved to do what was in their power; and so, discharging their broadsides upon the forts and land, where they did great execution, they set fire to every ship, galleons, and others, and burned every one of them; which they had no sooner done, but the wind turned, and carried the whole fleet without loss of one ship out of the bay, and put them safe to sea again.

The whole action was so miraculous, that all men who knew the place, wondered that any sober men, with what courage soever endued, would ever have undertaken it; and they could hardly persuade themselves to believe what they had done; whilst the Spaniards comforted themselves with the belief, that they were devils, and not men, who had destroyed them in such a manner. So much a strong resolution of bold and courageous men can bring to pass, that no resistance and advantage of ground can disappoint them. And it can hardly be imagined, how small loss the English sustained in this unparalleled action; no one ship being left behind, and the killed and wounded not exceeding two hundred men, when the slaughter on board the Spanish ships, and on the shore, was incredible.

The fleet after this, having been long abroad, found it necessary to return home. And this was the last service performed by Blake; who sickened on his return, and in the very entrance of the fleet into the sound of Plymouth, expired. He wanted no pomp of funeral when he was dead, Cromwell causing him to be brought up by land to London in all the state that could be; and then, according to the method of that time, to encourage his officers to be killed, that they might be pompously buried, he was, with all the solemnity possible, and at the charge of the public, interred in Harry the Seventh's chapel, among the monuments of the kings. He was a man of an ordinary extraction; yet had enough left him by his father to give him a good education; which his own inclination disposed him to receive in the university of Oxford; where he took the degree of a master of arts; and was enough versed in books for a man who intended not to be of any profession, having sufficient of his own to maintain him in the plenty he affected, and having then no appearance of ambition to be a greater man than he was. He was of a melancholic and a sullen nature, and spent his time most with good fellows, who liked his moroseness, and a freedom he used in inveighing against the license of the time, and the power of the court. They who knew him inwardly, discovered that he had an antimonarchical spirit, when few men thought the government in any danger. When the troubles begun, he quickly declared himself against the king; and having some command in Bristol, when it was first taken by prince Rupert and the marquis of Hertford, being trusted with the command of a little fort upon the line, he refused to give it up, after the governor had signed the articles of surrender, and kept it some hours after the prince was in the town, and killed some of the soldiers; for which the prince resolved to hang him, if some friends had not interposed for him, upon his want of experience in war; and prevailed with him to quit the place by very great importunity, and with much difficulty. He then betook himself wholly to the sea; and quickly made himself signal there. He was the first man that declined the old track, and made it manifest that the science might be attained in less time than was imagined ;and despised those rules which had been long in practice, to keep his ship and his men out of danger; which had been held in former times a point of great ability and circumspection; as if the principal art requisite in the captain of a ship had been to be sure to come home safe again. He was the first man who brought the ships to contemn castles on shore, which had been thought ever very formidable, and were discovered by him to make a noise only, and to fright those who could rarely be hurt by them. He was the first that infused that proportion of courage into the seamen, by making them see by experience, what mighty things they could do, if they were resolved; and taught them to fight in fire as well as upon water: and though he hath been very well imitated and followed, he was the first that drew the copy of naval courage, and bold and resolute achievements.

55. *Cromwell's Death, 3 September 1658*

IT had been observed in England, that, though from the dissolution of the last parliament, all things seemed to succeed, at home and abroad, to the protector's wish, and his power and greatness to be better established than ever it had been, yet he never had the same serenity of mind he had been used to, after he had refused the crown; but was out of countenance, and chagrin, as if he were conscious of not having been true to himself; and much more apprehensive of danger to his person than he had used to be. Insomuch as he was not easy of access, nor so much seen abroad; and seemed to be in some disorder, when his eyes found any stranger in the room; upon whom they were still fixed. When he intended to go to Hampton Court, which was his principal delight and diversion, it was never known, till he was in the coach, which way he would go; and he was still hemmed in by his guards both before and behind; and the coach in which he went was always thronged as full as it could be, with his servants; who were armed; and he seldom returned the same way he went; and rarely lodged two nights together in one chamber, but had many furnished and prepared, to which his own key conveyed him and those he would have with him, when he had a mind to go to bed: which made his fears the more taken notice of, and public, because he had never been accustomed to those precautions.

But that which chiefly broke his peace, was the death of his daughter Claypole; who had been always his greatest joy, and who, in her sickness, which was of a nature the physicians knew not how to deal with, had several conferences with him, which exceedingly perplexed him. Though nobody was near enough to hear the particulars, yet her often mentioning, in the pains she endured, the blood her father had spilt, made people conclude, that she had presented his worst actions to his consideration. And though he never made the least show of remorse for any of those actions. it is very certain, that either what she said, or her death, affected him wonderfully.

Whatever it was, about the middle of August, he was seized on by a common tertian ague, from which, he believed, a little ease and divertisement at Hampton Court would have freed him. But the fits grew stronger, and his spirits much abated: so that he returned again to Whitehall, when his physicians began to think him in danger, though the preachers, who prayed always about him, and told God Almighty what great things he had done for him, and how much more need he had still of his service, declared as from God, that he should recover: and he did not think he should die, till even the time that his spirits failed him. Then he declared to them, 'that he did appoint his son to succeed him, his eldest son Richard'; and so expired upon the third day of September, 1658, a day he thought always very propitious to him, and on which he had twice triumphed for several victories; a day very memorable for the greatest storm of wind that had been ever known, for some hours before and after his death, which overthrew trees, houses, and made great wrecks at sea; and ⟨the tempest⟩ was so universal, that the effects of it were terrible both in France and Flanders, where all people trembled at it; for, besides the wrecks all along the sea-coast, many boats were cast away in the very rivers; and within few days after, the circumstance of his death, that accompanied that storm, was known.

He was one of those men, *quos vituperare ne inimici quidem possunt, nisi ut simul laudent*; for he could never have done half that mischief without great parts of courage, industry, and judgment. He must have had a wonderful understanding in the natures and humours of men, and as great a dexterity in applying them; who, from a private and obscure birth, (though of a good family,) without interest or estate, alliance or friendship, could raise himself to such a height, and compound and knead such opposite and contradictory tempers, humours, and interests into a consistence, that contributed to his designs, and to their own destruction; whilst himself grew insensibly powerful enough to cut off those by whom he had climbed, in the instant that they projected to demolish their own building. What Velleius Paterculus said of Cinna may very justly be said of him, *ausum eum, quae nemo auderet bonus; perfecisse, quae a nullo, nisi fortissimo, perfici possent*. Without doubt, no man with more wickedness ever attempted any thing, or brought to pass what he desired more wickedly, more in the face and contempt of religion, and moral honesty; yet wickedness as great as his could never have accomplished those trophies, without the assistance of a great spirit, an admirable circumspection and sagacity, and a most magnanimous resolution.

When he appeared first in the parliament, he seemed to have a person in no degree gracious, no ornament of discourse, none of those talents which use to reconcile the affections of the stander by: yet as he grew into place and authority, his parts seemed to be raised, as if he had had concealed faculties, till he had occasion to use them; and when he was to act the part of a great man, he did it without any indecency, notwithstanding the want of custom.

After he was confirmed and invested protector by the *humble petition and advice*, he consulted with very few upon any action of importance, nor communicated any enterprise he resolved upon, with more than those who were to have principal parts in the execution of it; nor with them sooner than was absolutely necessary. What he once resolved, in which he was not rash, he would not be dissuaded from, nor endure any contradiction of his power and authority; but extorted obedience from them who were not willing to yield it.

When he had laid some very extraordinary tax upon the city, one Cony, an eminent fanatic, and one, who had heretofore served him very notably, positively refused to pay his part; and loudly dissuaded others from submitting to it, 'as an imposition notoriously against the law, and the property of the subject, which all honest men were bound to defend'. Cromwell sent for him, and cajoled him with the memory of 'the old kindness, and friendship, that had been between them; and that of all men he did not expect this opposition from him, in a matter that was so necessary for the good of the commonwealth'. But it was always his fortune to meet with the most rude and obstinate behaviour from those who had formerly been governed by him; and they commonly put him in mind of some expressions and sayings of his own, in cases of the like nature: so this man remembered him, how great an enemy he had expressed himself to such grievances, and had declared, 'that all who submitted to them, and paid illegal taxes, were more to blame, and greater enemies to their country, than they who had imposed them; and that the tyranny of princes could never be grievous, but by the tameness and stupidity of the people'. When Cromwell saw that he could not convert him, he told him, 'that he had a will as stubborn as his, and he would try which of them two should be master'. Thereupon, with some terms of reproach and contempt, he committed the man to prison; whose courage was nothing abated by it; but as soon as the term came, he brought his habeas corpus in the king's bench, which they then called the upper bench. Maynard, who was of council with the prisoner, demanded his liberty, with great confidence, both upon the illegality of the commitment, and the illegality of the imposition, as being laid without any lawful authority. The judges could not maintain or defend either, and enough declared what their sentence would be; and therefore the protector's attorney required a farther day, to answer what had been urged. Before that day, Maynard was committed to the Tower, for presuming to question or make doubt of his authority; and the judges were sent for, and severely reprehended for suffering that license; when they, with all humility, mentioned the law and magna carta, Cromwell told them, 'their magna f—— should not control his actions; which he knew were for the safety of the commonwealth'. He asked them, 'who made them judges? whether they had any authority to sit there, but what he gave them? and if his authority were at an end, they knew well enough what would become of themselves; and therefore advised them to be more tender of that which could only preserve them'; and so dismissed them with caution, 'that they should not suffer the lawyers to prate what it would not become them to hear'.

Thus he subdued a spirit that had been often troublesome to the most sovereign power, and made Westminster-hall as obedient, and subservient to his commands, as any of the rest of his quarters. In all other matters, which did not concern the life of his jurisdiction, he seemed to have great reverence for the law, rarely interposing between party and party. As he proceeded with this kind of indignation and haughtiness with those who were refractory, and dared to contend with his greatness, so towards all who complied with his good pleasure, and courted his protection, he used a wonderful civility, generosity and bounty.

To reduce three nations, which perfectly hated him, to an entire obedience, to all his dictates; to awe and govern those nations by an army that was indevoted to him, and wished his ruin, was an instance of a very prodigious address. But his greatness at home was but a shadow of the glory he had abroad. It was hard to discover, which feared him most, France, Spain, or the Low Countries, where his friendship was current at the value he put upon it. As they did all sacrifice their honour and their interest to his pleasure, so there is nothing he could have demanded, that either of them would have denied him.

He was not a man of blood, and totally declined Machiavel's method; which prescribes, upon any alteration of government, as a thing absolutely necessary, to cut off all the heads of those, and extirpate their families, who are friends to the old one. It was confidently reported, that, in the council of officers, it was more than once proposed, 'that there might be a general massacre of all the royal party, as the only expedient to secure the government', but that Cromwell would never consent to it; it may be, out of too much contempt of his enemies. In a word, as he had all the wickedness against which damnation is denounced, and for which hell-fire is prepared, so he had some virtues which have caused the memory of some men in all ages to be celebrated; and he will be looked upon by posterity as a brave bad man.

56. *Monk and the Restoration, 1659–60*

George Monk, born 1608; Duke of Albemarle, July
1660; died 1670

GENERAL MONK was a gentleman of a very good extraction, of a very ancient family in Devonshire, always very loyally affected. Being a younger brother, he entered early into the life and condition of a soldier, upon that stage where some of all Europe then acted, between the Spaniard and the Dutch; and had the reputation of a very good foot-officer in the lord Vere's regiment in Holland, at the time when he assigned it to the command of Colonel Goring. When the first troubles begun in Scotland, Monk, and many other officers of the nation, left the Dutch service, and betook themselves to the service of the king. In the beginning of the Irish rebellion, he was sent thither, with the command of the lord Leicester's own regiment of foot, (who was then lieutenant of Ireland,) and continued in that service with singular reputation of courage and conduct. When the war broke out in England between the king and the parliament, he fell under some discountenance, upon a suspicion of an inclination to the parliament; which proceeded from his want of bitterness in his discourses against them, rather than from any inclination towards them; as appeared by his behaviour at Nantwich, where he was taken prisoner, and remained in the Tower till the end of the war. For though his behaviour had been such in Ireland, when the transportation of the regiment from thence, to serve the king in England, was in debate, that it was evident enough he had no mind his regiment should be sent on that expedition, and his answer to the lord of Ormond was so rough and doubtful, (having had no other education but Dutch and Devonshire,) that he thought not fit to trust him, but gave the command of the regiment to Harry Warren, the lieutenant colonel of it, an excellent officer, generally known, and exceedingly beloved where he was known; yet when those regiments were sent to Chester, and there were others at the same time sent to Bristol, and with them Monk was sent prisoner, and from Bristol to the king at Oxford, where he was known to many persons of quality, (and his eldest brother being at the same time most zealous in the king's service in the west, and most useful,) his professions were so sincere, (he being, throughout his whole life, never suspected of dissimulation,) that all men there thought him very worthy of all trust; and the king was willing to send him into the west, where the gentlemen had a great opinion of his ability to command. But he desired that he might serve with his old friends and companions; and so, with the king's leave, made all haste towards Chester; where he arrived the very day before the defeat at Nantwich; and though his lieutenant colonel was very desirous to give up the command again to him, and to receive his orders, he would by no means at that time take it, but chose to serve, as a volunteer, in the first rank, with a pike in his hand; and was the next day, as was said, taken prisoner with the rest, and with most of the other officers sent to Hull, and shortly after from thence to the Tower of London.

He was no sooner there, than the lord Lisle, who had great kindness for him, and good interest in the parliament, with much importunity persuaded him to take a commission in that service, and offered him a command superior to what he had ever had before; which he positively and disdainfully refused to accept, though the straits he suffered in prison were very great, and he thought himself not kindly dealt with, that there was neither care for his exchange, nor money sent for his support. But there was all possible endeavour used for the first, by offering several officers of the same quality for his exchange; which was always refused; there having been an ordinance made, 'that no officer who had been transported out of Ireland should ever be exchanged'; so that most of them remained still in prison with him in the Tower, and the rest in other prisons; who all underwent the same hardships by the extreme necessity of the king's condition, which could not provide money enough for their supply; yet all was done towards it that was possible.

When the war was at an end, and the king a prisoner,

Cromwell prevailed with Monk, for his liberty and money, which he loved heartily, to engage himself again in the war of Ireland. And, from that time, Monk continued very firm to Cromwell; who was liberal and bountiful to him, and took him into his entire confidence; and after he had put the command of Scotland into his hands, he feared nothing from those quarters; nor was there any man in either of the armies, upon whose fidelity to himself Cromwell more depended. And those of his western friends, who thought best of him, thought it to no purpose to make any attempt upon him whilst Cromwell lived. But as soon as he was dead, Monk was generally looked upon as a man more inclined to the king, than any other in great authority, if he might discover it without too much loss or hazard. His elder brother had been entirely devoted to the king's service; and all his relations were of the same faith. He himself had no fumes of religion to turn his head, nor any credit with, or dependence upon any who were swayed by those trances; only he was cursed after a long familiarity to marry a woman of the lowest extraction, the least wit, and less beauty; who, taking no care for any other part of herself, had deposited her soul with some presbyterian ministers, who disposed her to that interest. She was a woman, *nihil muliebre praeter corpus gerens,* so utterly unacquainted with all persons of quality of either sex, that there was no possible approach to him by her.

There remained only within the king's own breast some faint hope (and God knows it was very faint) that Monk's march into England might yet produce some alteration. His majesty had a secret correspondence with some principal officers in his army, who were much trusted by him, and had promised great services; and it was presumed that they would undertake no such perilous engagement without his privity and connivance. Besides, it might be expected from his judgment, that, whatever present conditions the governing party might give him, for the service he had done, he could not but conclude, that they would be always jealous of the power they saw he was possessed of, and that an army that had marched so far barely upon his word, would be as ready to march to any place, or for any purpose, he would conduct them. And it was evident enough that the parliament resolved to new model their army, and to have no man in any such extent of command, as to be able to control their counsels. Then his majesty knew they were jealous of his fidelity, how much soever they courted him at that time; and therefore Monk would think himself obliged to provide for his own safety and security.

But, I say, these were but faint hopes grounded upon such probabilities as despairing men are willing to entertain. The truth is, those officers had honest inclinations; and, as wise men, had concluded, that, from those frequent shuffles, some game at last might fall out, that might prove to the king's advantage, and so were willing to bespeak their own welcome by an early application; which, in regard of the persons trusted by them, they concluded would be attended with no danger. But it never appeared they ever gave the general the least cause to imagine they had any such affection; and if they had, it is likely they had paid dearly for it. And for the second presumption upon his understanding and ratiocination, alas! it was not equal to the enterprise. He could not bear so many and so different contrivances in his head together, as were necessary to that work. And it was the king's great happiness that he never had it in his purpose to serve him, till it fell to be in his power; and indeed till he had nothing else to do. If he had resolved it sooner, he had been destroyed himself; the whole machine being so infinitely above his strength, that it could be only moved by a divine hand; and it is glory enough to his memory, that he was instrumental in bringing those mighty things to pass, which he had neither wisdom to foresee, nor courage to attempt, nor understanding to contrive.

When the king, who had rather an imagination, than an expectation, that the march of general Monk to London with his army might produce some alteration that might be useful to him, heard of his entire submission to the parliament, and of his entering the city, and disarming it, the commitment of the principal citizens, and breaking their gates and portcullises, all the little remainder of his hopes was extinguished, and he had nothing left before his eyes but a perpetual exile, attended with all those discomforts, whereof he had too long experience, and which, he must now expect, would be improved with the worst circumstances of neglect, which use to wait upon that condition. A greater consternation and dejection of mind cannot be imagined than at that time covered the whole court of the king; but God did not suffer him long to be wrapped up in that melancholic cloud. As the general's second march into the city was the very next day after his first, and dispelled the mists and fogs which the other had raised, so the very evening of that day which had brought the news of the first in the morning, brought likewise an account to his majesty of the second, with all the circumstances of bells, and bonfires, and burning of rumps, and such other additions, as might reasonably be true, and which a willing relator would not omit.

[Charles had at last written both to Monk and to Parliament.] The general, upon the perusal of the copies of the several despatches, liked all very well. And it ought to be remembered for his honour, that from this time he behaved himself with great affection towards the king; and though he was offered all the authority that Cromwell had enjoyed, and the title of king, he used all his endeavours to promote and advance the interest of his majesty: yet he as carefully retained the secret, and did not communicate to any person living, (Mr. Morrice only excepted,) that he had received any letter from the king, till the very minute that he presented it to the house of commons.

There happened at the same time a concurrence which much facilitated the great work in hand. For since a great obstruction, that hindered the universal consent to call in the king, was the conscience of the personal injuries, incivilities, reproaches, which all the royal party had sustained, and the apprehension that their animosities were so great, that, notwithstanding all acts of pardon and indemnity granted by the king, all opportunities would be embraced for secret revenge, and that they, who had been kept under and oppressed for near twenty years, would for the future use the power they could not be without upon the king's restoration, with extreme license and insolence; to obviate this too reasonable imagination, some discreet persons of the king's party caused a profession and protestation to be prepared, in which they declared that they looked upon their late sufferings as the effect of God's judgments upon their own particular sins, which had as much contributed to the miseries of the nation, as any other cause had done; and they did therefore protest and call God to witness of such their protestation, that if it should please God to restore the king, they would be so far from remembering any injuries or discourtesies which they had sustained, in order to return the like to any who had disobliged them, that they resolved on nothing more than to live with the same affection and good neighbourhood towards them, as towards each other, and never to make the least reflection upon any thing that was past.

These professions, or to the same purpose, under the title of a declaration of all those that had served the late king, or his present majesty, or adhered to the royal party in such a city or county, which was named, were signed by all the considerable persons therein; and then all printed with their names, and published to the view of the world; which were received with great joy, and did much to allay those jealousies, which obstructed the confidence that was necessary to establish a good understanding between them.

[The Convention Parliament met 25 April 1660.] They begun chiefly with bitter invectives against the memory of Cromwell, as an odious and perjured tyrant, with execrations upon the unchristian murder of the late king. And in these generals they spent the first five days of sitting; no man having the courage, how loyal soever their wishes were, to mention his majesty, till they could make a discovery what mind the general was of; who could only protect such a proposition from being penal to the person that made it, by the former ordinances of the rump parliament.

After the general had well surveyed the temper of the house, upon the first of May he came into the house, and told them, 'one sir John Greenvil, [Greenville] who was a servant of the king's, had brought him a letter from his majesty; which he had in his hand, but would not presume to open it without their direction; and that the same gentleman was at the door, and had a letter to the house'; which was no sooner said, than with a general acclamation he was called for; and being brought to the bar, he said, 'that he was commanded by the king his master, having been lately with him at Breda, to deliver that letter to the house': which he was ready to do; and so, giving it by the sergeant to be delivered to the speaker, he withdrew.

The house immediately called to have both letters read, that to the general, and that to the speaker; which being done, the declaration was as greedily called for, and read. And from this time Charles Stuart was no more heard of: and so universal a joy was never within those walls; and though there were some members there, who were nothing delighted with the temper of the house, nor with the argument of it, and probably had malice enough to make within themselves the most execrable wishes, yet they had not the hardiness to appear less transported than the rest: who, not deferring it one moment, and without one contradicting voice, appointed a committee to prepare an answer to his majesty's letter, expressing the great and joyful sense the house had of his gracious offers, and their humble and hearty thanks for the same, and with professions of their loyalty and duty to his majesty; and that the house would give a speedy answer to his majesty's gracious proposals. They likewise ordered, at the same time, that both his majesty's letters, that to the house, and that to the general, with his majesty's declaration therein enclosed, and the resolution of the house thereupon, should be forthwith printed and published.

This kind of reception was beyond what the best affected, nay, even the king, could expect or hope; and all that followed went in the same pace. The lords, when they saw what spirit the house of commons was possessed of, would not lose their share of thanks, but made haste into their house without excluding any who had been sequestered from sitting there for their delinquency; and then they received likewise the letter from sir John Greenvil which his majesty had directed to them; and they received it with the same duty and acknowledgment. The lord mayor, aldermen, and common council, were likewise transported with the king's goodness towards them, and with the expressions of his royal clemency; and entered into close deliberation, what return they should make to him to manifest their duty and gratitude. And the officers of the army, upon the sight of the letters to their general, and his majesty's declaration, thought themselves highly honoured, in that they were looked upon as good instruments of his majesty's restoration; and made those vows, and published such declarations of their loyalty and duty, as their general caused to be provided for them; which they signed with the loudest alacrity. And the truth is, the general managed the business, which he had now undertaken, with wonderful prudence and dexterity. And, as the nature and humour of his officers was well known to him, so he removed such from their commands whose affections he suspected, and conferred their places upon others, of whom he was most assured. In a word, there was either real joy in the hearts of all men, or at least their countenance appeared such as if they were glad at the heart.

After eight or ten days spent at the Hague in triumphs and festivals, which could not have been more splendid if all the monarchs of Europe had met there, and which were concluded with several rich presents made to his majesty, the king took his leave of the States, with all the professions of amity their civilities deserved; and embarked himself on the Prince; which had been before called the Protector, but had been new christened the day before, as many others had been, in the presence, and by the order, of his royal highness the admiral [James, Duke of York]. Upon the four and twentieth day of May, the fleet set sail; and, in one continued thunder of cannon, arrived at Dover so early on the six and twentieth, that his majesty disembarked; and being received by the general at the brink of the sea, he presently took coach, and came that night to Canterbury; where he stayed the next day, being Sunday; and went to his devotions to the cathedral, which he found very much dilapidated, and out of repair; yet the people seemed glad to hear the Common Prayer again. Thither came very many of the nobility, and other persons of quality, to present themselves to the king; and there his majesty assembled his council; and swore the general of the council, and Mr. Morrice, whom he there knighted, and gave him the signet, and swore him secretary of state. That day his majesty gave the garter to the general, and likewise to the marquis of Hertford, and the earl of Southampton, (who had been elected many years before), and sent it likewise by garter, herald and king at arms, to admiral Mountague, who remained in the Downs.

On Monday he went to Rochester; and the next day, being the nine and twentieth of May, and his birthday, he entered London; all the ways from Dover thither being so full of people, and acclamations, as if the whole kingdom had been gathered. About or above Greenwich the lord mayor and aldermen met him, with all such protestations of joy as can hardly be imagined. And the concourse was so great, that the king rode in a crowd from the bridge to Temple-bar; all the companies of the city standing in order on both sides, and giving loud thanks to God for his majesty's presence. And he no sooner came to Whitehall, but the two houses of parliament solemnly cast themselves at his feet, with all vows of affection and fidelity to the world's end. In a word, the joy was so unexpressible, and so universal, that his majesty said smilingly to some about him, 'he doubted it had been his own fault he had been absent so long; for he saw nobody that did not protest, he had ever wished for his return'.

In this wonderful manner, and with this miraculous expedition, did God put an end in one month (for it was the first of May that the king's letter was delivered to the parliament, and his majesty was at Whitehall upon the twenty-ninth of the same month) to a rebellion that had raged near twenty years, and been carried on with all the horrid circumstances of parricide, murder, and devastation, that fire and the sword, in the hands of the most wicked men in the world, could be ministers of; almost to the desolation of two kingdoms, and the exceeding defacing and deforming the third. Yet did the merciful hand of God in one month bind up all those wounds, and even made the scars as undiscernible, as, in respect of the deepness, was possible; which was a glorious addition to the deliverance; and if there wanted more glorious monuments of this deliverance, posterity would know the time of it, by the death of the two great favourites of the two crowns [France and Spain], cardinal Mazarin and don Lewis de Haro, who both died within three or four months, with the wonder if not the agony of this undreamed of prosperity; and as if they had taken it ill that God Almighty would bring such a work to pass in Europe without their concurrence, and against all their machinations. . . . [Clarendon repeats the story in his] reflections upon the most material passages which happened after the king's restoration to the time of the chancellor's banishment; out of which his children, for whose information they are only collected, may add some important passages to his Life, as the true cause of his misfortunes.

The easy and glorious reception of the king, in the manner that hath been mentioned, without any other conditions than what had been frankly offered by himself in his declaration and letters from Breda; the parliament's casting themselves in a body at his feet, in the minute of his arrival at Whitehall, with all the professions of duty and submission imaginable; and no man having authority there, but they who had either eminently served the late king, or who were since grown up out of their nonage from such fathers, and had thoroughly manifested their fast fidelity to his present majesty; the rest, who had been enough criminal, shewing more animosity towards the severe punishment of those, who having more power in the late times had exceeded them in mischief, than care for their own indemnity: this temper sufficiently evident, and the universal joy of the people, which was equally visible, for the total suppression of all those who had so many years exercised tyranny over them, made most men believe, both abroad and at home, that God had not only restored the king miraculously to his throne, but that he had, as he did in the time of Hezekiah, 'prepared the people, for the thing was done suddenly', (2 Chron. xxix. 36) in such a manner that his authority and greatness would have been more illustrious than it had been in any of his ancestors. And it is most true, and must never be denied, that the people were so admirably disposed and prepared to pay all the subjection, duty, and obedience, that a just and prudent king could expect from them, and had a very sharp aversion and detestation of all those who had formerly misled and corrupted them; so that except the general, who seemed to be possessed entirely of the affection of the army, and whose fidelity was now above any misapprehension, there appeared no man whose power and interest could in any degree shake or endanger the peace and security the king was in; the congratulations for his return being so universal from all the counties of England, as well as from the parliament and city; from all those who had most signally disserved and disclaimed him, as well as from those of his own party, and those who were descended from them: insomuch as the king was wont merrily to say, as hath been mentioned before, 'that it could be nobody's fault but his own that he had stayed so long abroad, when all mankind wished him so heartily at home'. It cannot therefore but be concluded by the standers by, and the spectators of this wonderful change and exclamation of all degrees of men, that there must be some wonderful miscarriages in the state, or some unheard of defect of understanding in those who were trusted by the king in the administration of his affairs; that there could in so short a time be a new revolution in the general affections of the people, that they grew even weary of that happiness they were possessed of and had so much valued, and fell into the same discontents and murmurings which had naturally accompanied them in the worst times. From what fatal causes these miserable effects were produced, is the business of this present disquisition to examine, and in some degree to discover; and therefore must be of such a nature, as must be as tenderly handled, with reference to things and persons, as the discovery of the truth will permit; and cannot be presumed to be intended ever for a public view, or for more than the information of his children of the true source and grounds from whence their father's misfortunes proceeded, in which nothing can be found that can make them ashamed of his memory.

Upon the 29th of May, which was his majesty's birth-day, and now again the day of his restoration and triumph, he entered London, the highway from Rochester to Black-heath being on both sides so full of acclamations of joy, and crowded with such a multitude of people, that it seemed one continued street wonderfully inhabited. Upon Blackheath the army was drawn up, consisting of above fifty thousand men, horse and foot, in excellent order and equipage, where the general presented the chief officers to kiss the king's hands, which grace they seemed to receive with all humility and cheerfulness. Shortly after, the lord mayor of London, the sheriffs, and body of the aldermen, with the whole militia of the city, appeared with great lustre; whom the king received with a most graceful and obliging countenance, and knighted the mayor, and all the aldermen, and sheriffs, and the principal officers of the militia: an honour the city had been without near eigh-teen years, and therefore abundantly welcome to the hus-bands and their wives. With this equipage the king was attended through the city of London, where the streets were railed in on both sides, that the livery of all the com-panies of the city might appear with the more order and decency, till he came to Whitehall; the windows all the way being full of ladies and persons of quality, who were impatient to fill their eyes with a beloved spectacle, of which they had been so long deprived. The king was no sooner at Whitehall but (as hath been said) the speakers and both houses of parliament presented themselves with all possible professions of duty and obedience at his royal feet, and were even ravished with the cheerful reception they had from him. The joy was universal; and whosoever was not pleased at heart, took the more care to appear as if he was; and no voice was heard but of the highest con-gratulation, of extolling the person of the king, admiring his condescensions and affability, raising his praises to heaven, and cursing and detesting the memory of those villains who had so long excluded so meritorious a prince, and thereby withheld that happiness from them, which they should enjoy in the largest measure they could desire or wish. The joy on all sides was with the greatest excess, so that most men thought, and had reason enough to think, that the king was even already that great and glorious prince which the parliament had wantonly and hypocritically promised to raise his father to be.

57. *Admiral Edward Montague*

Born 1625; general-at-sea with Blake and Monk;
Earl of Sandwich 1660; died 1672

[After the dissolution of the Long Parliament, March 1660, the council of state 'did many prudent actions'.] But that which seemed of most importance, was the reformation they made in the navy; which was full of sectaries, and under the government of those who of all men were declared the most republican. The present fleet prepared for the summer service was under the command of vice-admiral Lawson; an excellent seaman, but then a notorious anabaptist; who had filled the fleet with officers and mariners of the same principles. And they well remembered how he had lately besieged the city; and, by the power of his fleet, given that turn which helped to ruin the committee of safety, and restore the rump parliament to the exercise of their jurisdiction; for which he stood high in reputation with all that party. The parliament resolved, though they thought it not fit or safe to remove Lawson, yet so far to eclipse him, that he should not have it so absolutely in his power to control them. In order to this they concluded, that they would call Mountague, who had lain privately in his own house, under a cloud, and jealousy of being inclined too much to the king, and made him and the general (who was not to be left out in any thing) joint admirals of the fleet; whereby Mountague only would go to sea, and have the ships under his command; by which he might take care for good officers, and seamen, for such other ships as they meant to add to the fleet, and would be able to observe, if not reform the rest. Mountague sent privately over to the king for his approbation, before he would accept the charge; which being speedily sent to him, he came to London, and entered into that joint command with the general; and immediately applied himself to put the fleet into so good order, that he might comfortably serve in it. Since there was no man who betook himself to his majesty's service with more generosity than this gentleman, it is fit in this place to enlarge concerning him, and the correspondence which he held with the king.

Mountague was of a noble family, of which some were too much addicted to innovations in religion, and in the beginning of the troubles, appeared against the king; though his father [Sir Sidney], who had been long a servant to the crown, never could be prevailed upon to swerve from his allegiance, and took all the care he could to restrain this his only son within those limits: but being young, and more out of his father's control by being married into a family [Crewe of Stene], which, at that time, also trod awry, he was so far wrought upon by the caresses of Cromwell, that, out of pure affection to him, he was persuaded to take command in the army, when it was new modelled under Fairfax, and when he was little more than twenty years of age. He served in that army in the condition of a colonel to the end of the war, with the reputation of a very stout and sober young man. And from that time Cromwell, to whom he passionately adhered, took him into his nearest confidence, and sent him, first, joined in commission with Blake; and then, in the sole command of several expeditions by sea; in which he was discreet and successful. And though men looked upon him as devoted to Cromwell's interest, in all other respects he behaved himself with civility to all men, and without the least show of acrimony towards any who had served the king; and was so much in love with monarchy, that he was one of those who most desired and advised Cromwell to accept and assume that title, when it was offered to him by his parliament. He was designed by him to command the fleet that was to mediate, as was pretended, in the Sound, between the two kings of Sweden and Denmark; but was, in truth, to hinder the Dutch from assisting the Dane against the Swede; with whom Oliver was engaged in an inseparable alliance. He was upon this expedition, when Richard was scornfully thrown out of the protectorship; and was afterwards joined (for they knew not how to leave him out, whilst he had that command) with Algernon Sidney, and the other plenipotentiaries which the rump parliament sent to reconcile those crowns. As soon as Richard was so cast down, the king thought Mountague's relations and obligations were at an end, and was advised by those who knew him, to invite him to his service.

[Soon after the Convention Parliament decided to send the fleet to fetch Charles II from the United Province.] The king had been very few days at the Hague, when he heard that the English fleet was in sight of Scheveling; and shortly after, an officer from admiral Mountague was sent to the king, to present his duty to him, and to the duke of York, their high admiral, to receive orders. As soon as Mountague came on board the fleet in the Downs, and found those officers more frank in declaring their duty to the king, and resolution to serve him, than he expected, that he might not seem to be sent by the parliament to his majesty, but to be carried by his own affection and duty, without expecting any command from them, the wind coming fair, he set up his sails, and stood for the coast of Holland, leaving only two or three of the lesser ships to receive their orders, and to bring over those persons, who, he knew, were designed to wait upon his majesty; which expedition was never forgiven him by some men, who took all occasions afterwards to revenge themselves upon him.

The duke of York went the next day on board the fleet, to take possession of his command; where he was received by all the officers and seamen, with all possible duty and submission, and with those acclamations which are peculiar to that people, and in which they excel. After he had spent the day there, in receiving information of the state of the fleet, and a catalogue of the names of the several ships, his highness returned with it that night to the king, that his majesty might make alterations, and new christen those ships which too much preserved the memory of the late governors, and of the republic.

58. *The Temper and Spirit of the Nation after 1660*

I T will be convenient here, before we descend to those particulars which had an influence upon the minds of men, to take a clear view of the temper and spirit of that time; of the nature and inclination of the army; of the disposition and interest of the several factions in religion; all which appeared in their several colours, without dissembling their principles, and with equal confidence demanded the liberty of conscience they had enjoyed in and since the time of Cromwell; and the humour and the present purpose and design of the parliament itself, to whose judgment and determination the whole settlement of the kingdom, both in church and state, stood referred by the king's own declaration from Breda, which by God's inspiration had been the sole visible motive to that wonderful change that had ensued. And whosoever takes a prospect of all those several passions and appetites and interests, together with the divided affections, jealousies, and animosities of those who had been always looked upon as the king's party, which, if united, would in that conjuncture have been powerful enough to have balanced all the other; I say, whoever truly and ingenuously considers and reflects upon all this composition of contradictory wishes and expectations, must confess that the king was not yet the master of the kingdom, nor his authority and security such as the general noise and acclamation, the bells and the bonfires, proclaimed it to be; and that there was in no conjuncture more need, that the virtue and wisdom and industry of a prince should be evident, and made manifest in the preservation of his dignity, and in the application of his mind to the government of his affairs; and that all who were eminently trusted by him should be men of unquestionable sincerity, who with industry and dexterity should first endeavour to compose the public disorders, and to provide for the peace and settlement of the kingdom, before they applied themselves to make or improve their own particular fortunes. And there is little question, but if this good method had been pursued, and the resolutions of that kind, which the king had seriously taken beyond the seas, when he first discerned his good fortune coming towards him, had been executed and improved; the hearts and affections of all degrees of men were so prepared by their own natural inclinations and integrity, by what they had seen and what they had suffered, by their observations and experience, by their fears, or by their hopes; that they might have been all kneaded into as firm and constant an obedience and resignation to the king's authority, and to a lasting establishment of monarchic power, in all the just extents which the king could expect, or men of any public or honest affections could wish or submit to.

There was yet added to this slippery and uneasy posture of affairs, another mortification, which made a deeper impression upon the king's spirit than all the rest, and without which the worst of the other would have been in some degree remediable; that was, the constitution and disunion of those who were called and looked upon as his own party, which without doubt in the whole kingdom was numerous enough, and capable of being powerful enough to give the law to all the rest; which had been the ground of many unhappy attempts in the late time; that if any present force could be drawn together, and possessed of any such place in which they might make a stand without being overrun in a moment, the general concurrence of the kingdom would in a short time reduce the army, and make the king superior to all his enemies; which imagination was enough confuted, though not enough extinguished, by the dearbought experience in the woeful enterprise at Worcester. However, it had been now a very justifiable presumption in the king, to believe as well as hope, that he could not be long in England without such an apparency of his own party, that wished all that he himself desired, and such a manifestation of their authority, interest and power, that would prevent, or be sufficient to subdue, any froward disposition that might grow up in the parliament, or more extravagant demands in the army itself. An apparance there was of that people, great enough, who had all the wishes for the king which he entertained for himself. But they were so divided and disunited by private quarrels, factions, and animosities; or so unacquainted with each other; or, which was worse, so jealous of each other; the understandings and faculties of many honest men were so weak and shallow, that they could not be applied to any great trust; and others, who wished and meant well, had a peevishness, frowardness, and opiniatrety, that they would be engaged only in what pleased themselves, nor would join in any thing with such and such men whom they disliked. The severe and tyrannical government of Cromwell and the parliament had so often banished and imprisoned them upon mere jealousies, that they were grown strangers to one another, without any communication between them: and there had been so frequent betrayings and treacheries used, so many discoveries of meetings privately contrived, and of discourses accidentally entered into, and words and expressions rashly and unadvisedly uttered without any design, upon which multitudes were still imprisoned and many put to death; so that the jealousy was so universal, that few men who had never so good affections for the king, durst confer with any freedom together.

But these unhappy and fatal miscarriages, and the sad spectacles which ensued, made not those impressions upon the affections and spirits of the king's friends as they ought to have done; nor rendered the wariness and discretion of those who had dissuaded the enterprise, and who were always imprisoned upon suspicion, how innocent soever, the more valued and esteemed: on the contrary, it increased the reproaches against the knot, as if their lâcheté and want of appearance and engaging had been the sole cause of the misfortune.[1] And after some short fits

---

[1] Concerning the 'Sealed Knot' see *The Letter-Book of John Viscount Mordaunt, 1658–60*, ed. M. Coate, London, 1945.

of dejection and acquiescence, upon the shedding so much
blood of their friends and confederates, and the notorious
discovery of being betrayed by those, who had been
trusted by them, of the army; they began again to resume courage, to meet and enter upon new counsels and
designs, imputing the former want of success to the want
of skill and conduct in the undertakers, not to the all-
seeing vigilance of Cromwell and his instruments, or to
the formed strength of his government, not to be shaken
by weak or ill-seconded conspiracies. Young men were
grown up, who inherited their fathers' malignity, and
were too impatient to revenge their death, or to be even
with their oppressors, and so entered into new combinations as unskilful, and therefore as unfortunate as the
former; and being discovered even before they were
formed, Cromwell had occasion given him to make himself more terrible in new executions, and to exercise
greater tyranny upon the whole party, in imprisonments,
penalties, and sequestrations; making those who heartily
desired to be quiet, and who as much abhorred any rash
and desperate insurrection, to pay their full shares of the
folly of the other, as if all were animated by the same
spirit. And this unjust and unreasonable rigour increased
the reproaches and animosities in the king's friends against
each other: the wiser and more sober part, who had most
experience, and knew how impossible it was to succeed
in such enterprises, and had yet preserved or redeemed
enough of their fortunes to sit still and expect some hopeful
revolution, were unexpressibly offended, and bitterly inveighed against those, who without reason disturbed their
peace and quiet, by provoking the state to fresh persecu-
tions of them who had given them no offence: and the
other stirring and enraged party, with more fierceness
and public disdain, protested against and reviled those
who refused to join with them, as men who had spent all
their stock of allegiance, and meant to acquiesce with
what they had left under the tyranny and in the subjection of Cromwell. And thus they who did really wish
the same things, and equally the overthrow of that government, which hindered the restoration of the king, grew into

more implacable jealousies and virulencies against each other, than against that power that oppressed them both, and 'poured out their blood like water'. And either party conveyed their apologies and accusations to the king: one insisting upon the impertinency of all such attempts; and the other insisting that they were ready for a very solid and well-grounded enterprise, were sure to be possessed of good towns, if, by his majesty's positive command, the rest, who professed such obedience to him, would join with them.

I have thought myself obliged to renew the memory of all these particulars, that the several vicissitudes and stages may be known, by which the jealousies, murmurs, and disaffections in the royal party amongst themselves, and against each other, had mounted to that height which the king found them at when he returned; when in truth very few men of active minds, and upon whom he could depend in any sudden occasion that might probably press him, can be named, who had any confidence in each other. All men were full of bitter reflections upon the actions and behaviour of others, or of excuses and apologies for themselves for what they thought might be charged upon them. The woeful vice of drinking, from the uneasiness of their fortune, or the necessity of frequent meetings together, for which taverns were the most secure places, had spread itself very far in that classis of men, as well as upon other parts of the nation, in all counties; and had exceedingly weakened the parts, and broken the understandings of many, who had formerly competent judgments, and had been in all respects fit for any trust; and had prevented the growth of parts in many young men, who had good affections, but had been from their entering into the world so corrupted with that excess, and other license of the time, that they only made much noise, and, by their extravagant and scandalous debauches, brought many calumnies and disestimation upon that cause which they pretended to advance. They who had suffered much in their fortunes, and by frequent imprisonments and sequestrations and compositions, expected large recompenses and reparations in honours which they could not support, or offices which they could not discharge, or lands and money which the king had not to give; as all dispassioned men knew the conditions which the king was obliged to perform, and that the act of indemnity discharged all those forfeitures which could have been applied to their benefit: and therefore they who had been without comparison the greatest sufferers in their fortunes, and in all respects had merited most, never made any inconvenient suits to the king, but modestly left the memory and consideration of all they had done or undergone, to his majesty's own gracious reflections. They were observed to be most importunate, who had deserved least, and were least capable to perform any notable service; and none had more esteem of themselves, and believed preferment to be more due to them, than a sort of men, who had most loudly begun the king's health in taverns, especially if for any disorders which had accompanied it they had suffered imprisonment, without any other pretence of merit, or running any other hazard.

This unhappy temper and constitution of the royal party, with whom he had always intended to have made a firm conjunction against all accidents and occurrences which might happen at home or from abroad, did wonderfully displease and trouble the king; and, with the other perplexities, which are mentioned before, did so break his mind, and had that operation upon his spirits, that finding he could not propose any such method to himself, by which he might extricate himself out of those many difficulties and labyrinths in which he was involved, nor expedite those important matters which depended upon the goodwill and despatch of the parliament, which would proceed by its own rules, and with its accustomed formalities, he grew more disposed to leave all things to their natural course, and God's providence; and by degrees unbent his mind from the knotty and ungrateful part of his business, grew more remiss in his application to it, and indulged to his youth and appetite that license and satisfaction that it desired, and for which he had opportunity enough, and could not be without ministers abundant for any such negotiations; the time itself, and the young people thereof of either sex having been educated in all the liberty of vice, without reprehension or restraint. All relations were confounded by the several sects in religion, which discountenanced all forms of reverence and respect, as relics and marks of superstition. Children asked not blessing of their parents; nor did they concern themselves in the education of their children; but were well content that they should take any course to maintain themselves, that they might be free from that expense. The young women conversed without any circumspection or modesty, and frequently met at taverns and common eating houses; and they who were stricter and more severe in their comportment, became the wives of the seditious preachers, or of officers of the army. The daughters of noble and illustrious families bestowed themselves upon the divines of the time, or other low and unequal matches. Parents had no manner of authority over their children, nor children any obedience or submission to their parents; but 'everyone did that which was good in his own eyes'. This unnatural antipathy had its first rise from the beginning of the rebellion, when the fathers and sons engaged themselves in the contrary parties, the one choosing to serve the king, and the other the parliament; which division and contradiction of affections was afterwards improved to mutual animosities and direct malice, by the help of the preachers, and the several factions in religion, or by the absence of all religion: so that there were never such examples of impiety between such relations in any age of the world, Christian or heathen, as that wicked time, from the beginning of the rebellion to the king's return; of which the families of Hotham and Vane are sufficient instances; though other more illustrious houses may be named, where the same accursed fruit was too plentifully gathered, and too notorious to the world. The relation between masters and servants had been long since dissolved by the parliament, that their army might be increased by the prentices against their masters' consent, and that they might have intelligence of the secret meetings and transactions in those houses and families which were not devoted to them; from whence issued the foulest treacheries and perfidiousness that were ever practised: and the blood of the master was frequently the price of the servant's villany.

Cromwell had been most strict and severe in the forming the manners of his army, and in chastising all irregularities; insomuch that sure there was never any such body of men so without rapine, swearing, drinking, or any other debauchery, but the wickedness of their hearts: and all persons cherished by him, were of the same leaven, and to common appearance without the practice of any of those vices which were most infamous to the people, and which drew the public hatred upon those who were notoriously guilty of them. But then he was well pleased with the most scandalous lives of those who pretended to be for the king, and wished that all his were such, and took all the pains he could that they might be generally thought to be such; whereas in truth the greatest part of those who were guilty of those disorders were young men, who had never seen the king, and had been born and bred in those corrupt times, 'when there was no king in Israel'. He was equally delighted with the luxury and voluptuousness of the presbyterians, who, in contempt of the thrift, sordidness, and affected ill-breeding of the independents, thought it became them to live more generously, and were not strict in restraining or mortifying the unruly and inordinate appetite of flesh and blood, but indulged it with too much and too open scandal, from which he reaped no small advantage; and wished all those, who were not his friends, should not only be infected, but given over to the practice of the most odious vices and wickedness.

In a word, the nation was corrupted from that integrity, good nature, and generosity, that had been peculiar to it, and for which it had been signal and celebrated throughout the world; in the room whereof the vilest craft and dissembling had succeeded. The tenderness of the bowels, which is the quintessence of justice and compassion, the very mention of good nature was laughed at and looked upon as the mark and character of a fool; and a roughness of manners, or hard-heartedness and cruelty was affected. In the place of generosity, a vile and sordid love of money was entertained as the truest wisdom, and any thing lawful that would contribute towards being rich. There was a total decay, or rather a final expiration of all friendship;

and to dissuade a man from any thing he affected, or to reprove him for any thing he had done amiss, or to advise him to do any thing he had no mind to do, was thought an impertinence unworthy a wise man, and received with reproach and contempt. These dilapidations and ruins of the ancient candour and discipline were not taken enough to heart, and repaired with that early care and severity that they might have been; for they were not then incorrigible; but by the remissness of applying remedies to some, and the unwariness in giving a kind of countenance to others, too much of that poison insinuated itself into minds not well fortified against such infection: so that much of the malignity was transplanted, instead of being extinguished, to the corruption of many wholesome bodies, which, being corrupted, spread the diseases more powerfully and more mischievously.

59. *Clarendon and the Pension Parliament*

[After the first few years Clarendon lost his hold over Parliament. This became first noticeable in 1663 when] the parliament assembled together at the same time in February to which they had been adjourned or prorogued, and continued together till the end of July following. They brought the same affection and duty with them towards the king, which they had formerly; but were much troubled at what they had heard and what they had observed of the divisions in court. They had the same fidelity for the king's service, but not the same alacrity in it: the despatch was much slower in all matters depending, than it had used to be. The truth is; the house of commons was upon the matter not the same: three years sitting, for it was very near so long since they had been first assembled, had consumed very many of their members; and in the places of those who died, great pains were taken to have some of the king's menial servants chosen; so that there was a very great number of men in all stations in the court, as well below stairs as above, who were members of the house of commons. And they were very few of them, who did not think themselves qualified to reform whatsoever was amiss in church or state, and to procure whatsoever supply the king would require.

They, who either out of their own modesty, or in regard of their distant relation to his service, had seldom had access to his presence, never had presumed to speak to him; now by the privilege of parliament every day resorted to him, and had as much conference with him as they desired. They, according to the comprehension they had of affairs, represented their advice to him for the conducting his affairs; according to their several opinions and observations represented those and those men as well affected to his service, and others, much better than they, who did not pay them so much respect, to be ill-affected and to want duty for his majesty. They brought those, who appeared to them to be most zealous for his service, because they professed to be ready to do any thing he pleased to prescribe, to receive his majesty's thanks, and from himself his immediate directions how to behave themselves in the house; when the men were capable of no other instruction, than to follow the example of some discreet man in whatsoever he should vote, and behave themselves accordingly.

To this time, the king had been content to refer the conduct of his affairs in the parliament to the chancellor and the treasurer; who had every day conference with some select persons of the house of commons, who had always served the king, and upon that account had great interest in that assembly, and in regard of the experience they had and their good parts were hearkened to with reverence. And with those they consulted in what method to proceed in disposing the house, sometimes to propose, sometimes to consent to what should be most necessary for the public; and by them to assign parts to other men, whom they found disposed and willing to concur in what was to be desired: and all this without any noise, or bringing many together to design, which ever was and ever will be ingrateful to parliaments, and, however it may succeed for a little time, will in the end be attended with prejudice.

[Three years later the opposition to Clarendon and his

ways was more determined still.] The house of commons seemed much more morose and obstinate than it had formerly appeared to be, and solicitous to grasp as much power and authority as any of their predecessors had done, though no doubt with no ill intention: and it may be this would not have so much appeared, if there had been the same vigour in those who had used to conduct the king's business in that house, as there had used to be. But that spirit was much fallen. The chief men of the court, upon whose example other men looked, were much more humble than they had used to be, and took more pains to ingratiate themselves than to advance the interest of their master: and instead of pressing what was desirable upon the strength of reason and policy, as they had used to do, and by which the major part of the house had usually concurred with them, they now applied themselves with addresses to those, who had always frowardly opposed whatsoever they thought would be grateful to the king; and desired rather to buy their votes and concurrence by promises of reward and preferment, (which is the most dishonourable and unthrifty brokery that can be practised in a parliament, which from this time was much practised, and brought many ill things to pass,) than to prevail upon those weighty and important arguments which would bear the light. Which low artifice raised the insolence of those, which would, as easily as it had been, have been still overruled and suppressed; and was quickly discerned by those others, who, upon the principles of honour and wisdom, had hitherto swayed the house in all matters of public concernment, and who now concluded by those new condescensions that the former sober spirit and resolution was laid aside, and that peevish men would be compounded with; and so resolved to sit still or look on, till the success of this stratagem might be discerned.

[In many debates] the chancellor had the misfortune to lose much credit in the house of commons, not only by a very ⟨strong⟩ and cordial opposition to what they desired, but by taking all occasions, which were offered by the frequent arguments which were urged 'of the opinion and the authority of the house of commons, and that it was

fit and necessary to concur with them', to mention them
with less reverence than they expected. It is very true:
he had always used in such provocations to desire the
lords, 'to be more solicitous in preserving their own unquestionable rights and most important privileges, and
less tender in restraining the excess and new encroach-
ments of the house of commons, which extended their
jurisdiction beyond their limits'. He put them often in
mind 'of the mischiefs which had their original from the
liberties the house of commons assumed, and the compliance the house of peers had descended to, in the late ill
times, and which produced the rebellion; and were carried
so far, till after the multiplied affronts, they had wrested
the whole authority out of the hands of the house of peers,
the commonwealth, and shut up the door of their house
with a padlock, which they had never power to unfasten
till the king's return'. And in those occasions his expressions
were many times so lively, that they offended many of the
lords who were present, and had too much contributed to
those extravagancies, as much as it could do any of the
commons.

The truth is, he did never dissemble from the time of
his return with the king, whom he had likewise prepared
and disposed to the same sentiments whilst his majesty
was abroad, that his opinion was, 'that the late rebellion
could never be extirpated and pulled up by the roots, till
the king's regal and inherent power and prerogative
should be fully avowed and vindicated; and till the usurpations in both houses of parliament since the year 1640
were disclaimed and made odious; and many other excesses, which had been affected by both before that time
under the name of privileges, should be restrained or explained': for all which reformation the kingdom in general
was very well disposed, when it pleased God to restore the
king to it. Nor did the convention, which proclaimed the
king and invited him to return, exercise after his return
any exorbitant power, but what was of necessity upon
former irregularities, and contributed to the present ends
and desires of the king.

And this parliament, that was upon the dissolution of

the former quickly summoned by the king's writ, willingly inclined to that method, as appears by those many excellent acts which vindicated the king's sovereign power over parliaments, and declared the nullity of all acts done by one or both houses without the king's assent; declared and settled the absolute power of the crown over the militia; repealed that act of parliament that had excluded the bishops from being members of the house of peers, and restored them to their session there; and repealed that other infamous act for triennial parliaments, which had clauses in it to have led the people into rebellion; and would willingly have prosecuted the same method, if they had had the same advice and encouragement.

But they had continued to sit too long together, and were invited to meddle and interpose in matters out of their own sphere, to give their advice with reference to peace and war, to hold conferences with the king, and to offer their advices to him, and to receive orders from himself; when his majesty was persuaded by very unskilful men, 'that they were so absolutely at his disposal, that he need never doubt their undertaking any thing that would be ingrateful to him, and that whilst he preserved that entire interest he had in the lower house, (which he might easily do,) he need not care what the other house did or had a mind to do'; and so induced his majesty to undervalue his house of peers as of little power to do him good or harm, and prevailed with him too far to countenance that false doctrine; towards which the house of peers themselves contributed too much, by not inquiring into or considering the public state of the kingdom, or providing remedies for growing evils, or indeed meddling with any thing in the government till they were invited to it by some message or overture from the house of commons: insomuch as they sat not early in the morning, according to the former custom of parliaments, but came not together till ten of the clock; and very often adjourned as soon as they met, because that nothing was brought from the house of commons that administered cause of consultation; and upon that ground often adjourned for one or two days together, whilst the other house sat, and drew the eyes of the kingdom upon them, as the only vigilant people for their good.

The chancellor had always as earnestly opposed the over-captious insisting upon privilege in the lords' house, either when in truth there was not a just ground for it, or when they would extend it further than it would regularly reach; and oftentimes put them in mind 'of many exorbitant acts which stood still mentioned in their journal-books, of their proceedings in the late rebellious times, which might be looked upon as precedents by posterity, and in which the house of commons had really invaded their greatest privileges, and trampled upon their highest jurisdiction; which was worthy of their most strict ⟨proceedings⟩ to vindicate by protestation, and by expunging the memorial thereof out of all their books and records, that there might be no footsteps left to mislead the succeeding ages'; and often desired them 'to preserve a power in themselves to put the house of commons in mind of their exceeding their limits, for which they often gave them occasion, and particularly as often as they sent to quicken them in any debate, which was a very modern presumption, and derogatory from that respect which a house of commons had always paid to the house of lords. And this they could not reasonably or effectually do, till they declined all unjust or unnecessary pretences to privileges which were not their due, and especially to a power of calling private cases of right and justice, which ought to be determined by the law and in courts of justice, to be heard and adjudged before themselves in parliament; of which there were too frequent occasions to oppose and contradict their jurisdiction'.

This free way of discourse offended many of the lords, who thought him not jealous enough of nor zealous for the privilege of the peerage: and they were now very glad that he used so much more freedom against the proceedings of the house of commons, which they were sure would be resented below, more than it had been above. And many of his friends informed him 'how ill it was taken; and how carefully all that he said, and much that he did not say, was transmitted by some of the lords to them, who would not fail in some season to remember and apply it to his highest disadvantage'; and therefore desired him 'to use less fervour in those argumentations'. But he was in that, as in many things of that kind that related to the offending other men, for his own sake uncounsellable: not that he did not know that it exposed him to the censure of some men who lay in wait to do him hurt, but because he neglected those censures, nor valued the persons who promoted them; being confident that he would be liable to no charge that he should be ashamed of, and well knowing that he had, and being well known to have, a higher esteem of parliament, and a greater desire to preserve the just privileges of both houses, than they had who seemed to be angry with him on that behalf; and that the extending ⟨them⟩ beyond their due length would in the end endanger the destruction of parliaments.

But he shortly after found, that this guard was not secure enough to defend him. What he said in parliament was the sense of more who would not speak it, than there were of those who disliked it; and how much soever it offended them, they could not out of it find a crime to accuse him of. But they who were more concerned to remove him from a post, where he too narrowly watched and too often obstructed the liberties they took, resolved to sacrifice all their oaths and obligations, which obliged them to the contrary, to the satisfaction of their envy and their malice: and so whatsoever he said or advised in the most secret council to the king himself with reference to things or persons, they communicated all to those who had most reason to be angry, yet could not own the information. Of all which he had advertisement, and that a storm would be shortly raised to shake him, of which he had little apprehension; never suspecting that it would arise out of that quarter, from whence he soon after discerned it to proceed.

60. *The Marriage of Anne Hyde to the Duke of York*

[In 1660] The first matter of general and public importance, and which resulted not from any debate in parliament, was the discovery of a great affection that the duke
had for the chancellor's daughter, who was a maid of
honour to the king's sister, the princess royal of Orange,
and of a contract of marriage between them: with which
nobody was so surprised and confounded as the chancellor
himself, who being of a nature free from any jealousy, and
very confident of an entire affection and obedience from
all his children, and particularly from that daughter,
whom he had always loved dearly, never had in the least
degree suspected any such thing; though he knew afterwards, that the duke's affection and kindness had been
much spoken of beyond the seas, but without the least suspicion in any body that it could ever tend to marriage.
And therefore it was cherished and promoted in the duke
by those, and only by those, who were declared enemies to
the chancellor, and who hoped from thence, that some
signal disgrace and dishonour would befall the chancellor
and his family; in which they were the more reasonably
confirmed by the manner of the duke's living towards him,
which had never any thing of grace in it, but very much of
disfavour, to which the lord Berkley, and most of his other
servants to please the lord Berkley, had contributed all they
could; and the queen's notorious prejudice to him had
made it part of his duty to her majesty, which had been
a very great discomfort to the chancellor, in his whole
administration beyond the seas. But now, upon this discovery and the consequence thereof, he looked upon himself as a ruined person, and that the king's indignation
ought to fall upon him as the contriver of that indignity
to the crown, which as himself from his soul abhorred, and
would have had the presumption of his daughter to be
punished with the utmost severity, so he believed the
whole kingdom would be inflamed to the punishment of it,
and to prevent the dishonour which might result from it.

And the least calamity that he expected upon himself and family, how innocent soever, was an everlasting banishment out of the kingdom, and to end his days in foreign parts in poverty and misery. All which undoubtedly must have come to pass upon that occasion, if the king had either had that indignation which had been just in him; or if he had withdrawn his grace and favour from him, and left him to be sacrificed by the envy and rage of others; though at this time he was not thought to have many enemies, nor indeed any who were friends to any other honest men. But the king's own knowledge of his innocence, and thereupon his gracious condescension and interposition diverting any rough proceeding, and so a contrary effect to what hath been mentioned having been produced from thence; the chancellor's greatness seemed to be thereby confirmed, his family established above the reach of common envy, and his fortune to be in a growing and prosperous condition not like to be shaken. And since after many years possession of this prosperity, an unexpected gust of displeasure took again its rise from this original, and overwhelmed him with variety and succession of misfortunes; it is very reasonable to relate from before this time all the passages and circumstances, which accompanied or attended that lady's first promotion in the service of the princess royal, in which the extreme averseness in her father and mother from embracing that opportunity, and the unusual grace and importunity from them who conferred the honour, being considered, there may appear to many an extraordinary operation of Providence, in giving the first rise to what afterwards succeeded, though of a nature so transcendent as cannot be thought to have any relation to it.

[After being advised of the duke's owning his marriage to the king] The manner of the chancellor's receiving this advertisement made it evident enough that he was struck with it to the heart, and had never had the least jealousy or apprehension of it. He broke out into a very immoderate passion against the wickedness of his daughter, and said with all imaginable earnestness, 'that as soon as he came home he would turn her out of his house, as a strumpet, to shift for herself, and would never see her again'. They told him, 'that his passion was too violent to administer good counsel to him, that they thought that the duke was married to his daughter, and that there were other measures to be taken than those which the disorder he was in had suggested to him'. Whereupon he fell into new commotions, and said, 'if that were true, he was well prepared to advise what was to be done: that he had much rather his daughter should be the duke's whore than his wife: in the former case nobody could blame him for the resolution he had taken, for he was not obliged to keep a whore for the greatest prince alive; and the indignity to himself he would submit to the good pleasure of God. But if there were any reason to suspect the other, he was ready to give a positive judgment, in which he hoped their lord-ships would concur with him; that the king should im-mediately cause the woman to be sent to the Tower, and to be cast into a dungeon, under so strict a guard, that no person living should be admitted to come to her; and then that an act of parliament should be immediately passed for the cutting off her head, to which he would not only give his consent, but would very willingly be the first man that should propose it': and whoever knew the man, will believe that he said all this very heartily.

In this point of time the king entered the room, and sat down at the table; and perceiving by his countenance the agony the chancellor was in, and his swollen eyes from whence a flood of tears were fallen, he asked the other lords, 'what they had done, and whether they had resolved on any thing'. The earl of Southampton said, 'his majesty must consult with soberer men; that he' (pointing to the chancellor) 'was mad, and had proposed such extravagant things, that he was no more to be consulted with'. Where-upon his majesty, looking upon him with a wonderful benignity, said, 'Chancellor, I knew this business would trouble you, and therefore I appointed your two friends to confer first with you upon it, before I would speak with you myself: but you must now lay aside all passion that disturbs you, and consider that this business will not do itself, that it will quickly take air; and therefore it is fit that I first resolve what to do, before other men uncalled presume to give their counsel: tell me therefore what you would have me do, and I will follow your advice.' Then his majesty enlarged upon the passion of his brother, and the expressions he had often used, 'that he was not capable of having any other wife, and the like'. Upon which the chancellor arose, and with a little composedness said, 'Sir, I hope I need make no apology to you for myself, and of my own in this matter, upon which I look with so much detestation, that though I could have wished that your brother had not thought it fit to have put this disgrace upon me, I had much rather submit and bear it with all humility, than that it should be repaired by making her his wife; the thought whereof I do so much abominate, that I had much rather see her dead, with all the infamy that is due to her presumption.' And then he repeated all that he had before said to the lords, of sending her presently to the Tower, and the rest; and concluded, 'Sir, I do upon all my oaths which I have taken to you to give you faithful counsels, and from all the sincere gratitude I stand obliged to you for so many obligations, renew this counsel to you; and do beseech you to pursue it, as the only expedient that can free you from the evils that this business will otherwise bring upon you.' And observing by the king's countenance, that he was not pleased with his advice, he continued, and said, 'I am the dullest creature alive, if, having been with your majesty so many years, I do not know your infirmities better than other men. You are of too easy and gentle a nature to contend with those rough affronts, which the iniquity and license of the late times is like to put upon you, before it be subdued and reformed. The presumption all kind of men have upon your temper is too notorious to all men, and lamented by all who wish you well: and, trust me, an example of the highest severity in a case that so nearly concerns you, and that relates to the person who is nearest to you, will be so seasonable, that your reign, during the remaining part of your life, will be the easier to you, and all men will take heed how they impudently offend you.'

He had scarce done speaking, when the duke of York came in; whereupon the king spake of some other business, and shortly after went out of the room with his brother, whom (as was shortly known) he informed of all that the chancellor had said, who, as soon as he came to his house, sent his wife to command his daughter to keep her chamber, and not to admit any visits; whereas before she had always been at dinner and supper, and had much company resorting to her: which was all that he thought fit to do upon the first assault, and till he had slept upon it, (which he did very unquietly,) and reflected upon what was like to be the effect of so extravagant a cause. And this was quickly known to the duke, who was exceedingly offended at it, and complained to the king, 'as of an indignity offered to him'. And the next morning the king chid the chancellor for proceeding with so much precipitation, and required him 'to take off that restraint, and to leave her to the liberty she had been accustomed to'. To which he replied, 'that her having not discharged the duty of a daughter ought not to deprive him of the authority of a father; and therefore he must humbly beg his majesty not to interpose his commands against his doing any thing that his own dignity required: that he only expected what his majesty would do upon the advice he had humbly offered to him, and when he saw that, he would himself proceed as he was sure would become him': nor did he take off any of the restraint he had imposed. Yet he discovered after, that even in that time the duke had found ways to come to her, and to stay whole nights with her, by the administration of those who were not suspected by him, and who had the excuse, 'that they knew that they were married'.

This subject was quickly the matter of all men's discourse, and did not produce those murmurs and discontented reflections which were expected. The parliament was sitting, and took not the least notice of it; nor could it be discerned that many were scandalized at it. The chancellor received the same respects from all men which he had been accustomed to: and the duke himself, in the house of peers, frequently sat by him upon the woolsack, that he might the more easily confer with him upon the matters which were debated, and receive his advice how to behave himself; which made all men believe that there had been a good understanding between them. And yet it is very true, that, in all that time, the duke never spake one word to him of that affair. The king spake every day about it, and told the chancellor, 'that he must behave himself wisely, for that the thing was remediless; and that his majesty knew that they were married, which would quickly appear to all men, who knew that nothing could be done upon it'. In this time the chancellor had conferred with his daughter, without any thing of indulgence, and not only discovered that they were unquestionably married, but by whom, and who were present at it, who would be ready to avow it; which pleased him not, though it diverted him from using some of that rigour which he intended. And he saw no other remedy could be applied, but that which he had proposed to the king, who thought of nothing like it.

The greatness and power of the chancellor, by this marriage of his daughter, with all the circumstances which had accompanied and attended it, seemed to all men to have established his fortune, and that of his family; I say, to all men but to himself, who was not in the least degree exalted with it. He knew well upon how slippery ground he stood, and how naturally averse the nation was from approving an exorbitant power in any subject. He saw that the king grew every day more inclined to his pleasures, which involved him in expense, and company that did not desire that he should intend his business, or be conversant with sober men. He knew well that the servants who were about the duke were as much his enemies as ever, and intended their own profit only, by what means soever, without considering his honour; that they formed his household, officers, and equipage, by the model of France, and against all the rules and precedents of England for a brother of the crown; and every day put into his head, 'that if he were not supplied for all those expenses, it was the chancellor's fault, who could effect it if he would'. Nor was he able to prevent those infusions, nor the effects of them, because they were so artificially administered, as if their end was to raise a confidence in him of the chancellor, not to weaken it; though he knew well that their design was to create by degrees in him a jealousy of his power and credit with the king, as if it eclipsed his. But this was only in their own dark purpose, which had been blasted, if they had been apparent; for the duke did not only profess a very great affection for the chancellor, but gave all the demonstration of it that was possible, and desired nothing more, than that it should be manifest to all men, that he had an entire trust from the king in all his affairs, and that he would employ all his interest to support that trust: whilst the chancellor himself declined all the occasions, which were offered for the advancement of his fortune, and desired wholly to be left to the discharge of his office, and that all other officers might diligently look to their own provinces, and be accountable for them; and detested nothing more than that title and appellation, which he saw he should not always be able to avoid, of principal minister or favourite, and which was never cast on him by any designation of the king, (who abhorred to be thought to be governed by any single person,) but by his preferring his pleasures before his business, and so sending all men to the chancellor to receive advice. And hereby the secretaries of state, not finding a present access to him, when the occasions pressed, resorted to the chancellor, with whom his majesty spent most time, to be resolved by him; which method exceedingly grieved him, and to which he endeavoured to apply a remedy, by putting all things in their proper channel, and by prevailing with the king, when he should be a little satiated with the divertisements he affected, to be vacant to so much of his business, as could not be managed and conducted by any body else.

And here it may be seasonable to insert at large some instances, which I promised before, and by which it will be manifest, how far the chancellor was from an immoderate appetite to be rich, and to raise his fortune, which he proposed only to do by the perquisites of his office, which were considerable at the first, and by such bounty of the king as might hereafter, without noise or scandal, be conferred on him in proper seasons and occurrences; and ⟨that he was⟩ as far from affecting such an unlimited power as he was believed afterwards to be possessed of, (and of which no footsteps could ever be discovered in any of his actions, or in any one particular that was the effect of such power,) or that he did desire any other extent of power than was agreeable to the great office he held, and which had been enjoyed by most of those who had been his predecessors in that trust.

61. *The Queen and the Lady*

Catherine of Braganza 1638–1705
Barbara Villiers 1641–1709; married Palmer 1659;
Countess of Castlemaine 1661; Duchess of Cleveland
1669

[After agreement had been reached with regard to her dowry] the queen with all her court and retinue were embarked on board the fleet; and without any ill accidents her majesty arrived safely at Portsmouth: and having rested only three or four days there, to recover the indisposition contracted in so long a voyage at sea, her majesty, together with the king, came to Hampton-court at the time mentioned before, the twenty-ninth of May, the king's birth-day, full two years after his majesty's return and entering London.

However the public joy of the kingdom was very manifest upon this conjunction, yet in a short time there appeared not that serenity in the court that was expected. They who had formerly endeavoured to prevent it, used ever after all the ill arts they could to make it disagreeable, and to alienate the king's affection from the queen to such a degree, that it might never be in her power to prevail with him to their disadvantage; an effect they had reason to expect from any notable interest she might gain in his affections, since she could not be uninformed by the ambassador of the disservice they had formerly endeavoured to do her.

There was a lady of youth and beauty, with whom the king had lived in great and notorious familiarity from the

time of his coming into England, and who, at the time of
the queen's coming, or a little before, had been delivered
of a son whom the king owned. And as that amour had
been generally taken notice of, to the lessening of the good
reputation the king had with the people; so it underwent
the less reproach from the king's being young, vigorous,
and in his full strength; and upon a full presumption,
that when he should be married, he would contain himself within the strict bounds of virtue and conscience. And
that his majesty himself had that firm resolution, there
want not many arguments, as well from the excellent
temper and justice of his own nature, as from the professions he had made with some solemnity to persons who
were believed to have much credit, and who had not
failed to do their duty, in putting him in mind 'of the infinite obligations he had to God Almighty, and that he
expected another kind of return from him, in the purity
of mind and integrity of life': of which his majesty was
piously sensible, albeit there was all possible pains taken
by that company which were admitted to his hours of
pleasure, to divert and corrupt all those impressions and
principles, which his own conscience and reverent esteem
of Providence did suggest to him; turning all discourse
and mention of religion into ridicule, as if it were only an
invention of divines to impose upon men of parts, and to
restrain them from the liberty and use of those faculties
which God and nature had given them, that they might be
subject to their reproofs and determinations; which kind
of license was not grateful to the king, and therefore
warily and accidentally used by those who had pleasant
wit, and in whose company he took too much delight.

The queen had beauty and wit enough to make herself
very agreeable to him; and it is very certain, that at their
first meeting, and for some time after, the king had very
good satisfaction in her, and without doubt made very
good resolutions within himself, and promised himself a
happy and an innocent life in her company, without any
such uxoriousness, as might draw the reputation upon him
of being governed by his wife, of which he had observed
or been too largely informed of some inconvenient effects

in the fortune of some of his nearest friends, and had long protested against such a resignation; though they who knew him well, did not think him so much superior to such a condescension, but that if the queen had had that craft and address and dexterity that some former queens had, she might have prevailed as far by degrees as they had done. But the truth is, though she was of years enough to have had more experience of the world, and of as much wit as could be wished, and of a humour very agreeable at some seasons; yet she had been bred, according to the mode and discipline of her country, in a monastery, where she had only seen the women who attended her, and conversed with the religious who resided there, and without doubt in her inclinations was enough disposed to have been one of that number. And from this restraint she was called out to be a great queen, and to a free conversation in a court that was to be upon the matter new formed, and reduced from the manners of a licentious age to the old rules and limits which had been observed in better times; and to which regular and decent conformity the present disposition of men or women was not enough inclined to submit, nor the king enough disposed to exact.

There was a numerous family of men and women that were sent from Portugal, the most improper to promote that conformity in the queen that was necessary for her condition and future happiness, that could be chosen: the women for the most part old and ugly and proud, incapable of any conversation with persons of quality and a liberal education. And they desired and indeed had conspired so far to possess the queen themselves, that she should neither learn the English language, nor use their habit, nor depart from the manners and fashions of her own country in any particulars; 'which resolution', they told her, 'would be for the dignity of Portugal, and would quickly induce the English ladies to conform to her majesty's practice': and this imagination had made that impression, that the tailor who had been sent into Portugal to make her clothes, could never be admitted to see her or receive any employment. Nor when she came to Portsmouth, and found there several ladies of honour and prime quality to attend her in the places to which they were assigned by the king, did she receive any of them, till the king himself came; nor then with any grace, or the liberty that belonged to their places and offices. She could not be persuaded to be dressed out of the wardrobe that the king had sent to her, but would wear the clothes which she had brought, until she found that the king was displeased, and would be obeyed: whereupon she conformed against the advice of her women, who continued their opiniatrety, without any one of them receding from their own mode, which exposed them the more to reproach.

When the queen came to Hampton-court, she brought with her a formed resolution, that she would never suffer the lady who was so much spoken of to be in her presence: and afterwards to those she would trust she said, 'her mother had enjoined her so to do'. On the other hand, the king thought that he had so well prepared her to give her a civil reception, that within a day or two after her majesty's being there, himself led her into her chamber, and presented her to the queen, who received her with the same grace as she had done the rest; there being many lords and other ladies at the same time there. But whether her majesty in the instant knew who she was, or upon recollection found it afterwards, she was no sooner sat in her chair, but her colour changed, and tears gushed out of her eyes, and her nose bled, and she fainted; so that she was forthwith removed into another room, and all the company retired out of that where she was before. And this falling out so notoriously when so many persons were present, the king looked upon it with wonderful indignation, and as an earnest of defiance for the decision of the supremacy and who should govern, upon which point he was the most jealous and the most resolute of any man; and the answer he received from the queen, which kept up the obstinacy, displeased him more. Now the breach of the conditions grew matter of reproach; the payment of but half the portion was objected to the ambassador, who would have been very glad that the quarrel had been upon no other point. He knew not what to say or do; the king being offended with him for having said so much in Portugal to provoke the queen, and not instructing her enough to make her unconcerned in what had been before her time, and in which she could not reasonably be concerned; and the queen with more indignation reproaching him with the character he had given of the king, of his virtue and good-nature: whilst the poor man, not able to endure the tempest of so much injustice from both, thought it best to satisfy both by dying; and from the extreme affliction of mind which he underwent, he sustained such a fever as brought him to the brink of his grave, till some grace from both their majesties contributed much to the recovery of his spirits.

In the meantime the king forbore her majesty's company, and sought ease and refreshment in that jolly company, to which in the evenings he grew every day more indulgent, and in which there were some who desired rather to inflame than pacify his discontent. And they found an expedient to vindicate his royal jurisdiction, and to make it manifest to the world, that he would not be governed; which could never without much artifice have got entrance into his princely breast, which always entertained the most tender affections; nor was ever any man's nature more remote from thoughts of roughness or hardheartedness. They magnified the temper and constitution of his grandfather [Henry IV of France], who indeed to all other purposes was a glorious example: 'that when he was enamoured, and found a return answerable to his merit, he did not dissemble his passion, nor suffered it to be matter of reproach to the persons whom he loved; but made all others pay them that respect which he thought them worthy of; brought them to the court, and obliged his own wife the queen to treat them with grace and favour; gave them the highest titles of honour, to draw reverence and application to them from all the court and all the kingdom; raised the children he had by them to the reputation, state, and degree of princes of the blood, and conferred fortunes and offices upon them accordingly. That his majesty, who inherited the same passions, was without the gratitude and noble inclination to make returns proportionable to the obligations he received. That he had, by the charms of his person and of his professions, prevailed upon the affections and heart of a young and beautiful lady of a noble extraction, whose father had lost his life in the service of the crown. That she had provoked the jealousy and rage of her husband to that degree, that he had separated himself from her: and now the queen's indignation had made the matter so notorious to the world, that the disconsolate lady had no place of retreat left, but must be made an object of infamy and contempt to all her sex, and to the whole world'.

Those discourses, together with a little book newly printed at Paris, according to the license of that nation, of the amours of Henry IV which was by them presented to him, and too concernedly read by him, made that impression upon his mind, that he resolved to raise the quality and degree of that lady, who was married to a private gentleman of a competent fortune, that had not the ambition to be a better man than he was born. And that he might do so, he made her husband an earl of Ireland, who knew too well the consideration that he paid for it, and abhorred the brand of such a nobility, and did not in a long time assume the title. The lady thus qualified was now made fit for higher preferment: and the king resolved, for the vindication of her honour and innocence, that she should be admitted of the bedchamber of the queen, as the only means to convince the world, that all aspersions upon her had been without ground. The king used all the ways he could, by treating the queen with all caresses, to dispose her to gratify him in this particular, as a matter in which his honour was concerned and engaged; and protested unto her, which at that time he did not intend to observe, 'that he had not had the least familiarity with her since her majesty's arrival, nor would ever after be guilty of it again, but would live always with her majesty in all fidelity for conscience sake.' The queen, who was naturally more transported with choler than her countenance declared her to be, had not the temper to entertain him with those discourses, which the vivacity of her wit could very plentifully have suggested to her; but brake out into a torrent of rage, which increased the former prejudice, confirmed the king in the resolution he had taken, gave ill people more credit to mention her disrespectfully, and more increased his aversion from her company, and which was worse, his delight in those, ⟨who meant⟩ that he should neither love his wife or his business, or any thing but their conversation.

These domestic indispositions and distempers, and the impressions they made of several kinds upon the king's spirit and his humour, exceedingly discomposed the minds of the gravest and most serious men; gave the people generally occasion of speaking loudly, and with a license that the magistrates knew not how to punish, for the publication of the scandal: and the wisest men despaired of finding remedies to apply to the dissoluteness and debauchery of the time, which visibly increased. No man appeared to suffer or likely to suffer more than the chancellor, against whom though no particular person owned a malignity, the congregation of the witty men for the evening conversation were enough united against his interest; and thought his influence upon the king's actions and counsels would be too much augmented, if the queen came to have any power, who had a very good opinion of him: and it is very probable, that even that apprehension increased the combination against her majesty.

The lady had reason to hate him mortally, well knowing that there had been an inviolable friendship between her father and him to his death, which had been notorious to all men; and that he was an implacable enemy to the power and interest she had with the king, and had used all the endeavours he could to destroy it. Yet neither she nor any of the other adventured to speak ill of him to the king, who at that time would not have borne it; except for wit's sake they sometimes reflected upon somewhat he had said, or acted some of his postures and manner of speaking, (the skill in mimicry being the best faculty in wit many of them had;) which license they practised often towards the king himself, and therefore his majesty thought it to be the more free from malice. But by these liberties, which at first only raised laughter, they by degrees got the hardiness to censure both the persons, counsels, and actions of those who were nearest his majesty's trust, with the highest malice and presumption; and too often suspended or totally disappointed some resolutions, which had been taken upon very mature deliberation, and which ought to have been pursued. But (as hath been said before) this presumption had not yet come to this length.

The king imparted the trouble and unquietness of his mind to nobody with equal freedom, as he did to the chancellor: to him he complained of all the queen's perverseness and ill humours, and informed him of all that passed between them, and obliged him to confer and advise the queen, who, he knew, looked upon him as a man devoted to her service, and that he would speak very confidently to her whatsoever he thought; and therefore gave him leave to take notice to her of any thing he had told him. It was too delicate a province for so plain-dealing a man as he was to undertake: and yet he knew not how to refuse it, nor indeed did despair totally of being able to do some good, since the queen was not yet more acquainted with any man than with him, nor spake so much with any man as with him; and he believed, that he might hereby have opportunity to speak sometimes to the king of some particulars with more freedom, than otherwise he could well do, at least more effectually.

He had never heard before of the honour the king had done that lady, nor of the purpose he had to make her of his wife's bedchamber. He spake with great boldness to him upon both; and did not believe that the first was proceeded in beyond revocation, because it had not come to the great seal, and gave him many arguments against it, which he thought of weight. But upon the other point he took more liberty, and spake 'of the hardheartedness and cruelty in laying such a command upon the queen, which flesh and blood could not comply with'.

[Clarendon was sent to the queen to try to persuade her to accede to the king's demands.] The chancellor addressed himself to the queen with as full liberty and plainness as he had presumed to use to his majesty, but could not proceed so far at a time, nor hold so long conferences at once. When he first lamented the misintelligence he observed to be between their majesties, and she perceived the king had told him some particulars, she protested her own innocence, but with so much passion and such a torrent of tears, that there was nothing left for him to do, but to retire, and tell her, 'that he would wait upon her in a fitter season, and when she should be more capable of receiving humble advice from her servants, who wished her well'; and so departed.

The next day he waited upon her again at the hour assigned by her, and found her much better composed than he had left her. She vouchsafed to excuse the passion she had been in, and confessed 'she looked upon him as one of the few friends she had, and from whom she would most willingly at all times receive counsel: but that she hoped he would not wonder or blame her, if having greater misfortunes upon her, and being to struggle with more difficulties, than any woman had ever been put to of her condition, she sometimes gave vent to that passion that was ready to break her heart'. He told her, 'he was desirous indeed to serve her, of which he would not make great or many protestations, since she could not but believe it, except she thought him to be a fool, or mad, since nothing could contribute so much to his happiness, as an eminent sympathy between the king and her in all things: and he could not give her a greater evidence of his devotion, than in always saying that to her which was fit for her to hear, though it did not please her; and he would observe no other rule towards her, though it should render him ungracious to her'.

She seemed well satisfied with what he said, and told him 'he should never be more welcome to her, than when he told her of her faults': to which he replied, 'that it was the province he was accused of usurping with reference to all his friends'. He told her, 'that he doubted she was little beholden to her education, that had given her no better information of the follies and iniquities of mankind, of which he presumed the climate from whence she came could have given more instances, than this cold region would afford'; though at that time it was indeed very hot. He said, 'if her majesty had been fairly dealt with in that particular, she could never have thought herself so miserable, and her condition so insupportable as she seemed to think it to be; the ground of which heavy complaint he could not comprehend'. Whereupon with some blushing and confusion and some tears ⟨she said⟩, 'she did not think that she should have found the king engaged in his affection to another lady'; and then was able to say no more: which gave the chancellor opportunity to say, 'that he knew well, that she had been very little acquainted with or informed of the world; yet he could not believe that she was so utterly ignorant, as to expect that the king her husband, in the full strength and vigour of his ⟨youth⟩, was of so innocent a constitution, as to be reserved for her whom he had never seen, and to have had no acquaintance or familiarity with the sex'; and ⟨asked⟩ 'whether she believed, when it should please God to send a queen to Portugal, she should find that court so full of chaste affections'. Upon which her majesty smiled, and spake pleasantly enough, but as if she thought it did not concern her case, and as if the king's affection had not wandered, but remained fixed.

Upon which the chancellor replied with some warmth, 'that he came to her with a message from the king, which if she received as she ought to do, and as he hoped she would, she would be the happiest queen in the world'.

[Peace appeared in sight but] the fire flamed that night higher than ever: the king reproached the queen with stubbornness and want of duty, and she him with tyranny and want of affection: he used threats and menaces, which he never intended to put in execution, and she talked loudly 'how ill she was treated, and that she would return again to Portugal'. He replied, 'that she should do well first to know whether her mother would receive her: and he would give her a fit opportunity to know that, by sending to their home all her Portuguese servants; and that he would forthwith give order for the discharge of them all, since they behaved themselves so ill, for to them and their counsels he imputed all her perverseness'.

The passion and noise of the night reached too many ears to be a secret the next day; and the whole court was full of that, which ought to have been known to nobody. And the mutual carriage and behaviour between their majesties confirmed all that they had heard or could imagine: they spake not, hardly looked on one another. Every body was glad that they were so far from the town, (for they were still at Hampton-court,) and that there were so few witnesses of all that passed. The queen sat melancholic in her chamber in tears, except when she drove them away by a more violent passion in choleric discourse: and the king sought his divertisements in that company that said and did all things to please him; and there he spent all the nights, and in the morning came to the queen's chamber, for he never slept in any other place. Nobody knew how to interpose, or indeed how to behave themselves, the court being far from one mind; with this difference, that the young and frolic people of either sex talked loudly all that they thought the king would like and be pleased with, whilst the other more grave and serious people did in their souls pity the queen, and thought that she was put to bear more than her strength could sustain.

In all this time the king pursued his point: the lady came to the court, was lodged there, was every day in the queen's presence, and the king in continual conference with her; whilst the queen sat untaken notice of: and if her majesty rose at the indignity and retired into her chamber, it may be one or two attended her; but all the company remained in the room she left, and too often said those things aloud which nobody ought to have whispered. The king (who had in the beginning of this conflict appeared still with a countenance of trouble and sadness, which had been manifest to every body, and no doubt was really afflicted, and sometimes wished that he had not proceeded so far, until he was again new chafed with the reproach of being governed, which he received with the most sensible indignation, and was commonly provoked with it most by those who intended most to govern him) had now vanquished or suppressed all those tendernesses and reluctances, and appeared every day more gay and pleasant, without any clouds in his face, and full of good humour; saving that the close observers thought it more feigned and affected than of a natural growth. However, to the queen it appeared very real, and made her the more sensible, that she alone was left out in all jollities, and not suffered to have any part of those pleasant applications and caresses, which she saw made almost to every body else; an universal mirth in all company but in hers, and in all places but in her chamber; her own servants shewing more respect and more diligence to the person of the lady, than towards their own mistress, who they found could do them less good. The nightly meeting continued with the same or more license; and the discourses which passed there, of what argument soever, were the discourse of the whole court and of the town the day following: whilst the queen had the king's company those few hours which remained of the preceding night, and which were too little for sleep.

All these mortifications were too heavy to be borne: so that at last, when it was least expected or suspected, the queen on a sudden let herself fall first to conversation and then to familiarity, and even in the same instant to a confidence with the lady; was merry with her in public, talked kindly of her, and in private used nobody more friendly. This excess of condescension, without any provocation or invitation, except by multiplication of injuries and neglect, and after all friendships were renewed, and indulgence yielded to new liberty, did the queen less good than her former resoluteness had done. Very many looked upon her with much compassion, commended the greatness of her spirit, detested the barbarity of the affronts she underwent, and censured them as loudly as they durst; not without assuming the liberty sometimes of insinuating to the king himself, 'how much his own honour suffered in the neglect and disrespect of her own servants, who ought at least in public to manifest some duty and reverence towards her majesty; and how much he lost in the general affections of his subjects: and that, besides the displeasure of God Almighty, he could not reasonably hope for children by the queen, which was the great if not the only blessing of which he stood in need, whilst her heart was so full of grief, and whilst she was continually exercised with such insupportable afflictions'. And many, who were not wholly unconversant with the king, nor strangers to his temper and constitution, did believe that he grew weary of the struggle, and even ready to avoid the scandal that was so notorious, by the lady's withdrawing from the verge of the court and being no longer seen there, how firmly soever the friendship might be established. But this sudden downfall and total abandoning her own greatness, this low demeanour and even application to a person she had justly abhorred and worthily contemned, made all men conclude, that it was a hard matter to know her, and consequently to serve her. And the king himself was so far from being reconciled by it, that the esteem, which he could not hitherto but retain in his heart for her, grew now much less. He concluded that all her former aversion expressed in those lively passions, which seemed not capable of dissimulation, was all fiction, and purely acted to the life by a nature crafty, perverse, and inconstant. He congratulated his own ill-natured perseverance, by which he had discovered how he was to behave himself hereafter, and what remedies he was to apply to all future indispositions: nor had he ever after the same value of her wit, judgment, and understanding, which he had formerly; and was well enough pleased to observe, that the reverence others had for all three was somewhat diminished.

[Because of the plague Parliament in 1666 met in Oxford.] When the parliament at Oxford was prorogued it was to a day in April: but the king had reason to believe that they would not so soon be in good humour enough to give more money, which was the principal end of calling them together. And the dregs of the plague still remaining, and venting its malignity in many burials every week, his majesty thought fit to dispense with their attendance at that time by a proclamation: and he caused it at the day to be prorogued to the twentieth of September following. In the mean time the court abounded in all its excesses. There had been some hope during the abode at Oxford, that the queen had been with child; and whilst that hope lasted, the king lived with more constraint and caution, and prepared to make himself worthy of that blessing: and there are many reasons to believe, besides his own natural good inclinations, that if God had vouchsafed to have given him a child, and the queen that blessing to have merited from him, he would have restrained all those inordinate appetites and delights; and that he would seriously have applied himself to his government, and cut off all those extravagant expenses of money and time, which disturbed and corrupted the evenness of his own nature and the sincerity of his intentions, and exposed him to the temptations of those who had all the traps and snares to catch and detain him.

The imagination of the queen's breeding was one cause of her stay there; and her stay there was the longer, because she miscarried when she intended to begin her journey. And though the doctors declared that it was a real miscarriage, ripe enough to make a judgment of the sex; yet some of the women who had more credit with the king assured him, 'that it was only a false conception, and that she had not been at all with child:' insomuch that his majesty, who had been so confident upon a former ⟨occasion⟩, as to declare to the queen his mother, and to others, 'that upon his own knowledge her majesty had miscarried of a son', suffered himself now to be so totally convinced by those ladies and other women, that he did as positively believe that she never had, never could be, with child. And from that time he took little pleasure in her conversation, and more indulged to himself all liberties in the conversation of those, who used all their skill to supply him with divertisements, which might drive all that was serious out of his thoughts, and make him undervalue those whom he had used, and still did most trust and employ, in what he thought most important; though he sometimes thought many things not of importance, which in the consequence were of the highest.

The lady, who had never declined in favour, was now greater in power than ever: she was with child again, and well enough contented that his majesty should entertain an amour with another lady, and made a very strict friendship with her, it may be more diligently out of confidence that he would never prevail with her, which many others believed too. But without doubt the king's passion was stronger towards that other lady, than ever it was to any other woman: and she carried it with that discretion and modesty, that she made no other use of it than for the convenience of her own fortune and subsistence, which was narrow enough; never seemed disposed to interpose in the least degree in business, not to speak ill of any body; which kind of nature and temper the more inflamed the king's affection, who did not in his nature love a busy woman, and had an aversion from speaking with any woman, or hearing them speak, of any business but to that purpose he thought them all made for, however they broke in afterwards upon him to all other purposes.

[The other lady was Frances Stewart, later Duchess of Richmond.]

62. *The Plague and the Fire of London, 1665–6*

[In 1665] There begun now to appear another enemy, much more formidable than the Dutch, and more difficult to be struggled with; which was the plague, that brake out in the winter, and made such an early progress in the spring, that though the weekly numbers did not rise high, and it appeared to be only in the outskirts of the town, and in the most obscure alleys, amongst the poorest people; yet the ancient men, who well remembered in what manner the last great plague (which had been near forty years before) first brake out, and the progress it afterwards made, foretold a terrible summer. And many of them removed their families out of the city to country habitations; when their neighbours laughed at their providence, and thought they might have stayed without danger: but they found shortly that they had done wisely.

In March it spread so much, that the parliament was very willing to part: which was likewise the more necessary, in regard that so many of the members of the house of commons were assigned to so many offices and employments which related to the war, and which required their immediate attendance.

After Christmas the rage and fury of the pestilence began in some degree to be mitigated, but so little, that nobody who had left the town had yet the courage to return thither: nor had they reason; for though it was a considerable abatement from the height it had been at, yet there died still between three and four thousand in the week, and of those, some men of better condition than had fallen before. The general [Albemarle] writ from thence, 'that there still arose new difficulties in providing for the setting out the fleet, and some of such a nature, that he could not easily remove them without communication with his majesty, and receiving his more positive directions; and how to bring that to pass he knew not, for as he could by no means advise his majesty to leave Oxford, so he found many objections against his own being absent from London'. Windsor was thought upon as a place where the king might safely reside, there being then no infection there: but the king had adjourned the term thither, which had possessed the whole town; and he was not without some apprehension, that the plague had got into one house.

In the end, towards the end of February, the king resolved that the queen and duchess and all their families should remain in Oxford; and that his majesty and his brother, with prince Rupert, and such of his council and other servants as were thought necessary or fit, would make a quick journey to Hampton-Court, where the general might be every day, and return again to London at night, and his majesty gave such orders as were requisite for the carrying on his service, and so after two or three days' stay there return again to Oxford; for no man did believe it counsellable, that his majesty should reside longer there, than the despatch of the most important business required: and with this resolution his majesty made his journey to Hampton-Court.

It pleased God, that the next week after his majesty came thither, the number of those who died of the plague in the city decreased one thousand; and there was a strange universal joy there for the king's being so near. The weather was as it could be wished, deep snow and terrible frost, which very probably stopped the spreading of the infection, though it might put an end to those who were already infected, as it did, for in a week or two the number of the dead was very little diminished. The general came and went as was intended: but the business every day increased; and his majesty's remove to a further distance was thought inconvenient, since there appeared no danger in remaining where he was.

And after a fortnight's or three weeks' stay, he resolved, for the quicker despatch of all that was to be done, to go to Whitehall, when there died above fifteen hundred in the week, and when there was not in a day seen a coach in the streets, but those which came in his majesty's train; so much all men were terrified from returning to a place of so much mortality. Yet it can hardly be imagined what numbers flocked thither from all parts upon the fame of the king's being at Whitehall, all men being ashamed of their fears for their own safety, when the king ventured his person. The judges at Windsor adjourned the last return of the term to Westminster-hall, and the town every day filled marvellously; and which was more wonderful, the plague every day decreased. Upon which the king changed his purpose, and, instead of returning to Oxford, sent for the queen and all the family to come to Whitehall: so that before the end of March the streets were as full, the exchange as much crowded, and the people in all places as numerous, as they had ever been seen, few persons missing any of their acquaintance, though by the weekly bills there appeared to have died above one hundred and threescore thousand persons: and many, who could compute very well, concluded that there were in truth double that number who died; and that in one week, when the bill mentioned only six thousand, there had in truth fourteen thousand died. The frequent deaths of the clerks and sextons of parishes hindered the exact account every week; but that which left it without any certainty was the vast number that was buried in the fields, of which no account was kept. Then of the ana-baptists and other sectaries, who abounded in the city, very few left their habitations; and multitudes of them died, whereof no churchwarden or other officer had notice; but they found burials, according to their own fancies, in small gardens or the next fields. The greatest number of those who died consisted of women and children, and the lowest and poorest sort of the people; so that, as I said before, few men missed any of their acquaintance when they returned, not many of wealth or quality or of much conversation being dead; yet some of either sort there were.

The Fire

It was upon the first day of that September, in the dismal year of 1666, (in which many prodigies were expected, and so many really fell out,) that that memorable and terrible fire brake out in London, which begun about midnight, or nearer the morning of Sunday, in a baker's house at the end of Thames-street next the Tower, there being many little narrow alleys and very poor houses about the place where it first appeared; and then finding such store of combustible materials, as that street is always furnished with in timber-houses, the fire prevailed so powerfully, that that whole street and the neighbourhood was in so short a time turned to ashes, that few persons had time to save and preserve any of their goods; but were a heap of people almost as dead with the sudden distraction, as the ruins were which they sustained. The magistrates of the city assembled quickly together, and with the usual remedies of buckets, which they were provided with: but the fire was too ravenous to be extinguished with such quantities of water as those instruments could apply to it, and fastened still upon new materials before it had destroyed the old. And though it raged furiously all that day, to that degree that all men stood amazed as spectators only, no man knowing what remedy to apply, nor the magistrates what orders to give; yet it kept within some compass, burned what was next, and laid hold only on both sides; and the greatest apprehension was of the Tower, and all considerations entered upon how to secure that place.

But in the night the wind changed, and carried the danger from thence, but with so great and irresistible violence, that as it kept the English and Dutch fleets from grappling when they were so near each other, so it scattered the fire from pursuing the line it was in with all its force, and spread it over the city: so that they, who went late to bed at a great distance from any place where the fire prevailed, were awakened before morning with their own houses being in a flame; and whilst endeavour was used to quench that, other houses were discovered to be burning, which were near no place from whence they could imagine the fire could come; all which kindled another fire in the breasts of men, almost as dangerous as that within their houses.

Monday morning produced first a jealousy, and then an universal conclusion, that this fire came not by chance, nor did they care where it began; but the breaking out in several places at so great distance from each other made it evident, that it was by conspiracy and combination. And this determination could not hold long without discovery of the wicked authors, who were concluded to be all the Dutch and all the French in the town, though they had inhabited the same places above twenty years. All of that kind, or, if they were strangers, of what nation soever, were laid hold of; and after all the ill usage that can consist in words, and some blows and kicks, they were thrown into prison. And shortly after, the same conclusion comprehended all the Roman Catholics, the papists, who were in the same predicament of guilt and danger, and quickly found that their only safety consisted in keeping within doors; and yet some of them, and of quality, were taken by force out of their houses, and carried to prison.

When this rage spread as far as the fire, and every hour brought reports of some bloody effects of it, worse than in truth they were, the king distributed many of the privy-council into several quarters of the city, to prevent, by their authorities, those inhumanities which he heard were committed. In the mean time, even they or any other person thought it ⟨not⟩ safe to declare, 'that they believed that the fire came by accident, or that it was not a plot of the Dutch, and the French and papists to burn the city'; which was so generally believed, and in the best

company, that he who said the contrary was suspected for
a conspirator, or at best a favourer of them. It could not
be conceived how a house that was distant a mile from
any part of the fire could suddenly be in a flame, without
some particular malice; and this case fell out every hour.
When a man at the furthest end of Bread-street, had made
a shift to get out of his house his best and most portable
goods, because the fire had approached near them; he no
sooner had secured them, as he thought, in some friend's
house in Holborn, which was believed a safe distance, but
he saw that very house, and none else near it, in a sudden
flame. Nor did there want, in this woeful distemper, the
testimony of witnesses who saw this villany committed,
and apprehended men who they were ready to swear threw
fire-balls into houses, which were presently burning.

The lord Hollis and lord Ashley, who had their quarters
assigned about Newgate-market and the streets adjacent,
had many brought to them in custody for crimes of this
nature; and saw, within a very little distance from the
place where they were, the people gathered together in
great disorder; and as they came nearer saw a man in the
middle of them without a hat or cloak, pulled and hauled
and very ill used, whom they knew to be a servant to the
Portugal ambassador, who was presently brought to them.
And a substantial citizen was ready to take his oath,
'that he saw that man put his hand in his pocket, and
throw into a shop a fireball; upon which he saw the house
immediately on fire: whereupon, being on the other side
of the way, and seeing this, he cried out to the people
to stop that gentleman, and made all the haste he could
himself'; but the people had first seized upon him, and
taken away his sword, which he was ready to draw; and he
not speaking nor understanding English, they had used
him in the manner set down before. The lord Hollis told
him what he was accused of, and 'that he was seen to have
thrown somewhat out of his pocket, which they thought
to be a fireball, into a house which was now on fire':
and the people had diligently searched his pockets to
find more of the same commodities, but found nothing
that they meant to accuse him of. The man standing in

great amazement to hear he was so charged, the lord Hollis asked him, 'what it was that he pulled out of his pocket, and what it was he threw into the house': to which he answered, 'that he did not think that he had put his hand into his pocket; but he remembered very well, that as he walked in the street, he saw a piece of bread upon the ground, which he took up, and laid upon a shelf in the next house'; which is a custom or superstition so natural to the Portuguese, that if the king of Portugal were walking, and saw a piece of bread upon the ground, he would take it up with his own hand, and keep it till he saw a fit place to lay it down.

The house being in view, the lords with many of the people walked to it, and found the piece of bread just within the door upon a board, where he said he laid it; and the house on fire was two doors beyond it, which the man who was on the other side of the way, and saw this man put his hand into the house without staying, and presently after the fire break out, concluded to be the same house; which was very natural in the fright that all men were in: nor did the lords, though they were satisfied, set the poor man at liberty; but, as if there remained ground enough of suspicion, committed him to the constable, to be kept by him in his own house for some hours, when they pretended they would examine him again. Nor were any persons who were seized upon in the same manner, as multitudes were in all the parts of the town, especially if they were strangers or papists, presently discharged, when there was no reasonable ground to suspect; but all sent to prison, where they were in much more security than they could have been in full liberty, after they were once known to have been suspected; and most of them understood their commitment to be upon that ground, and were glad of it.

The fire and the wind continued in the same excess all Monday, Tuesday, and Wednesday, till afternoon, and flung and scattered brands burning into all quarters; the nights more terrible than the days, and the light the same, the light of the fire supplying that of the sun. And indeed whoever was an eyewitness of that terrible prospect, can

never have so lively an image of the last conflagration
till he beholds it; the faces of all people in a wonderful
dejection and discomposure, not knowing where they
could repose themselves for one hour's sleep, and no distance thought secure from the fire, which suddenly started
up before it was suspected; so that people left their houses
and carried away their goods from many places which
received no hurt, and whither they afterwards returned
again; all the fields full of women and children, who had
made a shift to bring thither some goods and conveniences
to rest upon, as safer than any houses, where yet they felt
such intolerable heat and drought, as if they had been
in the middle of the fire. The king and the duke, who rode
from one place to another, and put themselves into great
dangers amongst the burning and falling houses, to give
advice and direction what was to be done, underwent as
much fatigue as the meanest, and had as little sleep or
rest; and the faces of all men appeared ghastly and in the
highest confusion. The country sent in carts to help those
miserable people who had saved any goods: and by this
means, and the help of coaches, all the neighbour villages
were filled with more people than they could contain, and
more goods than they could find room for; so that those
fields became likewise as full as the other about London
and Westminster.

It was observed that where the fire prevailed most, when
it met with brick buildings, if it was not repulsed, it
was so well resisted that it made a much slower progress;
and when it had done its worst, that the timber and all
the combustible matter fell, it fell down to the bottom
within the house, and the walls stood and enclosed the fire,
and it was burned out without making a further progress in
many of those places; and then the vacancy so interrupted
the fury of it, that many times the two or three next
houses stood without much damage. Besides the spreading,
insomuch as all London seemed but one fire in the breadth
of it, it seemed to continue in its full fury a direct line
to the Thames side, all Cheapside from beyond the Exchange, through Fleet-street; insomuch as for that breadth,
taking in both sides as far as the Thames, there was

scarce a house or church standing from the bridge to Dorset-house, which was burned on Tuesday night after Baynard's-castle.

On Wednesday morning, when the king saw that neither the fire decreased nor the wind lessened, he even despaired of preserving Whitehall, but was more afraid of Westminster-abbey. But having observed by his having visited all places, that where there were any vacant places between the houses, by which the progress of the fire was interrupted, it changed its course and went to the other side; he gave order for pulling down many houses about Whitehall, some whereof were newly built and hardly finished, and sent many of his choice goods by water to Hampton-Court; as most of the persons of quality in the Strand, who had the benefit of the river, got barges and other vessels, and sent their furniture for their houses to some houses some miles out of the town. And very many on both sides the Strand, who knew not whither to go, and scarce what they did, fled with their families out of their houses into the streets, that they might not be within when the fire fell upon their houses.

But it pleased God, contrary to all expectation, that on Wednesday [really Tuesday], about four or five of the clock in the afternoon, the wind fell: and as in an instant the fire decreased, having burned all on the Thames side to the new buildings of the Inner Temple next to White-friars, and having consumed them, was stopped by that vacancy from proceeding further into that house; but laid hold on some old buildings which joined to Ram-alley, and swept all those into Fleet-street. And the other side being likewise destroyed to Fetter-lane, it advanced no further; but left the other part of Fleet-street to the Temple-bar, and all the Strand, unhurt, but what damage the owners of the houses had done to themselves by endeavouring to remove; and it ceased in all other parts of the town near the same time: so that the greatest care then was, to keep good guards to watch the fire that was upon the ground, that it might not break out again. And this was the better performed, because they who had yet their houses standing had not the courage to sleep, but watched with much less distraction; though the same distemper still remained in the utmost extent, 'that all this had fallen out by the conspiracy of the French and Dutch with the papists'; and all gaols were filled with those who were every hour apprehended upon that jealousy; or rather upon some evidence that they were guilty of the crime. And the people were so sottish, that they believed that all the French in the town (which no doubt were a very great number) were drawn into a body, to prosecute those by the sword who were preserved from the fire: and the inhabitants of a whole street have ran in a great tumult one way, upon the rumour that the French were marching at the other end of it; so terrified men were with their own apprehensions.

When the night, though far from being a quiet one, had somewhat lessened the consternation, the first care the king took was, that the country might speedily supply markets in all places, that they who had saved themselves from burning might not be in danger of starving; and if there had not been extraordinary care and diligence used, many would have perished that way. The vast destruction of corn, and all other sorts of provisions, in those parts where the fire had prevailed, had not only left all that people destitute of all that was to be eat or drank; but the bakers and brewers, which inhabited the other parts which were unhurt, had forsaken their houses, and carried away all that was portable: insomuch as many days passed, before they were enough in their wits and in their houses to fall to their occupations; and those parts of the town which God had spared and preserved were many hours without anything to eat, as well as they who were in the fields. And yet it can hardly be conceived, how great a supply of all kinds was brought from all places within four and twenty hours. And which was more miraculous, in four days, in all the fields about the town, which had seemed covered with those whose habitations were burned, and with the goods which they had saved, there was scarce a man to be seen: all found shelter in so short a time, either in those parts which remained of the city and in the suburbs, or in the neighbour villages; all kind of people expressing a marvellous charity towards those who appeared to be undone. And very many, with more expedition than can be conceived, set up little sheds of brick and timber upon the ruins of their own houses, where they chose rather to inhabit than in more convenient places, though they knew they could not long reside in those new buildings.

The king was not more troubled at any particular, than at the imagination which possessed the hearts of so many, that all this mischief had fallen out by a real and formed conspiracy; which, albeit he saw no colour to believe, he found very many intelligent men, and even some of his own council, who did really believe it. Whereupon he appointed the privy-council to sit both morning and evening, to examine all evidence of that kind that should be brought before them, and to send for any persons who had been committed to prison upon some evidence that made the greatest noise; and sent for the lord chief justice, who was in the country, to come to the town for the better examination of all suggestions and allegations of that kind, there having been some malicious report scattered about the town, 'that the court had so great a prejudice against any kind of testimony of such a conspiracy, that they discountenanced all witnesses who came before them to testify what they knew'; which was without any colour of truth. Yet many who were produced as if their testimony would remove all doubts, made such senseless relations of what they had been told, without knowing the condition of the persons who told them, or where to find them, that it was a hard matter to forbear smiling at their evidence. Some Frenchmen's houses had been searched, in which had been found many of those shells for squibs and other fireworks, frequently used in nights of joy and triumph; and the men were well known, and had lived many years there by that trade, and had no other: and one of these was the king's servant, and employed by the office of ordnance for making grenades of all kinds, as well for the hand as for mortarpieces. Yet these men were looked upon as in the number of the conspirators, and remained still in prison till their neighbours solicited for their liberty. And it cannot be enough wondered at, that in this general rage of the people no mischief was done to the strangers, that no one of them was assassinated outright, though many were sorely beaten and bruised.

Let the cause be what it would, the effect was very terrible; for above two parts of three of that great city were burned to ashes, and those the most rich and wealthy parts of the city, where the greatest warehouses and the best shops stood. The Royal Exchange, with all the streets about it, Lombard-street, Cheapside, Paternoster-row, St. Paul's church, and almost all the other churches in the city, with the Old Bailey, Ludgate, all Paul's churchyard even to the Thames, and the greatest part of Fleet-street, all which were places the best inhabited, were all burned without one house remaining.

The value or estimate of what that devouring fire consumed, over and above the houses, could never be computed in any degree: for besides that the first night (which in a moment swept away the vast wealth of Thames-street) there was ⟨not⟩ any thing that could be preserved in respect of the suddenness and amazement, (all people being in their beds till the fire was in their houses, and so could save nothing but themselves,) the next day with the violence of the wind increased the distraction; nor did many believe that the fire was near them, or that they had reason to remove their goods, till it was upon them, and rendered it impossible. Then it fell out at a season in the year, the beginning of September, when very many of the substantial citizens and other wealthy men were in the country, whereof many had not left a servant in their houses, thinking themselves upon all ordinary accidents more secure in the goodness and kindness of their neighbours, than they could be in the fidelity of a servant; and whatsoever was in such houses was entirely consumed by the fire, or lost as to the owners. And of this classis of absent men, when the fire came where the lawyers had houses, as they had in many places, especially Sergeants-Inn in Fleet street, with that part of the Inner Temple that was next it and White-friars, there was scarce a man to whom those lodgings appertained who was in

Town: so that whatsoever was there, their money, books, and papers, besides the evidences of many men's estates deposited in their hands, were all burned or lost, to a very great value. But of particular men's losses could never be made any computation.

It was an incredible damage that was and might rationally be computed to be sustained by one small company, the company of stationers, in books, paper, and the other lesser commodities which are vendible in that corporation, which amounted to no less than two hundred thousand pounds: in which prodigious loss there was one circumstance very lamentable. All those who dwelt near Paul's carried their goods, books, paper, and the like, as others of greater trades did their commodities, into the large vaults which were under St. Paul's church, before the fire came thither: which vaults, though all the church above the ground was afterwards burned, with all the houses round about, still stood firm and supported the foundation, and preserved all that was within them; until the impatience of those who had lost their houses, and whatsoever they had else, in the fire, made them very desirous to see what they had ⟨saved⟩, upon which all their hopes were founded to repair the rest.

It was the fourth day after the fire ceased to flame, though it still burned in the ruins, from whence there was still an intolerable heat, when the booksellers especially, and some other tradesmen, who had deposited all they had preserved in the greatest and most spacious vault, came to behold all their wealth, which to that moment was safe: But the doors were no sooner opened, and the air from without fanned the strong heat within, but first the driest and most combustible matters, broke into a flame, which consumed all, of what kind soever, that till then had been unhurt there. Yet they who had committed their goods to some lesser vaults, at a distance from that greater, had better fortune; and having learned from the second ruin of their friends to have more patience, attended till the rain fell, and extinguished the fire in all places, and cooled the air: and then they securely opened the doors, and received all from thence that they had there.

If so vast a damage as two hundred thousand pounds befell that little company of stationers in books and paper and the like, what shall we conceive was lost in cloth, (of which the country clothiers lost all that they had brought up to Blackwell-hall against Michaelmas, which was all burned with that fair structure,) in silks of all kinds, in linen, and those richer manufactures? Not to speak of money, plate, and jewels, whereof some were recovered out of the ruins of those houses which the owners took care to watch, as containing somewhat that was worth the looking for, and in which deluge there were men ready enough to fish.

The lord mayor, though a very honest man, was much blamed for want of sagacity in the first night of the fire, before the wind gave it much advancement: for though he came with great diligence as soon as he had notice of it, and was present with the first, yet having never been used to such spectacles, his consternation was equal to that of other men, nor did he know how to apply his authority to the remedying the present distress; and when men who were less terrified with the object pressed him very earnestly, 'that he would give order for the present pulling down those houses which were nearest, and by which the fire climbed to go further', (the doing whereof at that time might probably have prevented much of the mischief that succeeded,) he thought it not safe counsel, and made no other answer, 'than that he durst not do it without the consent of the owners'. His want of skill was the less wondered at, when it was known afterwards, that some gentlemen of the Inner Temple would not endeavour to preserve the goods which were in the lodgings of absent persons, nor suffer others to do it, 'because', they said, 'it was against the law to break up any man's chamber'.

The so sudden repair of those formidable ruins, and the giving so great beauty to all deformity, (a beauty and a lustre that city had never before been acquainted with,) is little less wonderful than the fire that consumed it.

It was hoped and expected that this prodigious and universal calamity, for the effects of it covered the whole kingdom, would have made impression, and produced some reformation in the license of the court: for as the pains the king had taken night and day during the fire, and the dangers he had exposed himself to, even for the saving the citizens' goods, had been very notorious, and in the mouths of all men, with good wishes and prayers for him; so his majesty had been heard during that time to speak with great piety and devotion of the displeasure that God was provoked to. And no doubt the deep sense of it did raise many good thoughts and purposes in his royal breast. But he was narrowly watched and looked to, that such melancholic ⟨thoughts⟩ might not long possess him, the consequence and effect whereof was like to be more grievous than that of the fire itself; of which that loose company that was too much cherished, even before it was extinguished, discoursed as of an argument for mirth and wit to describe the wildness of the confusion all people were in; which the scripture itself was used with equal liberty, when they could apply it to their profane purposes. And Mr. May presumed to assure the king, 'that this was the greatest blessing that God had ever conferred upon him, his restoration only excepted: for the walls and gates being now burned and thrown down of that rebellious city, which was always an enemy to the crown, his majesty would never suffer them to repair and build them up again, to be a bit in his mouth and a bridle upon his neck; but would keep all open, that his troops might enter upon them whenever he thought necessary for his service, there being no other way to govern that rude multitude but by force'.

This kind of discourse did not please the king, but was highly approved by the company; and for the wit and pleasantness of it was repeated in all companies, infinitely to the king's disservice, and corrupted the affections of the citizens and of the country, who used and assumed the same liberty to publish the profaneness and atheism of the court. And as nothing was done there in private, so it was made more public in pasquils and libels, which were as bold with reflections of the broadest nature upon the king himself, and upon those in whose company he was most delighted, as upon the meanest person.[1]

[1] Clarendon's story should be checked by G. W. Bell: *The Great Fire*, edition of 1951.

63. *The Royal Brothers*

THE king had in his nature so little reverence or esteem for antiquity, and did in truth so much contemn old orders, forms and institutions, that the objections of novelty rather advanced than obstructed any proposition. He was a great lover of new inventions, and thought them the effects of wit and spirit, and fit to control the superstitious observation of the dictates of our ancestors. [The hangers-on of the court found it therefore easy to work on him as they did during the Dutch war.]

The chief design they now began to design, and the worst they could ever design, was to raise a jealousy in the king of his brother, to which his majesty was not in any degree inclined, and had in truth a just affection for him and confidence in him, without thinking better of his natural parts than he thought there was cause for; and yet, which made it the more wondered at, he did very often depart in matters of the highest moment from his own judgment to comply with his brother, who was instructed, by those who too well knew the king's nature, to adhere to any thing he once advised, and to be importunate in any thing he proposed; in which he prevailed the more easily, because he never used it in any thing that concerned himself or his own benefit.

The truth is, it was the unhappy fate and constitution of that family, that they trusted naturally the judgments of those, who were as much inferior to them in understanding as they were in quality, before their own, which was very good; and suffered even their natures, which disposed them to virtue and justice, to be prevailed upon and altered and corrupted by those, who knew how to make use of some one infirmity that they discovered in them; and by complying with that, and cherishing and serving it, they by degrees wrought upon the mass, and sacrificed all the other good inclinations to that single vice. They were too much inclined to like men at first sight, and did not love the conversation of men of many more years than themselves, and thought age not only troublesome but

impertinent. They did not love to deny, and less to strangers than to their friends; not out of bounty or generosity,
which was a flower that did never grow naturally in the
heart of either of the families, that of Stuart or the other of
Bourbon, but out of an unskilfulness and defect in the
countenance: and when they prevailed with themselves to
make some pause rather ⟨than⟩ to deny, importunity removed all resolution, which they knew neither how to shut
out nor to defend themselves against, even when it was
evident enough that they had much rather not consent;
which often made that which would have looked like
bounty lose all its grace and lustre.

If the duke seemed to be more firm and fixed in his
resolutions, it was rather from an obstinacy in his will,
which he defended by aversion from the debate, than by
the constancy of his judgment, which was more subject to
persons than to arguments, and so as changeable at least
as the king's, which was in greatest danger by surprise:
and from this want of steadiness and irresolution (whence-
soever the infirmity proceeded) most of the misfortunes,
which attended either of them or their servants who
served them honestly, had ⟨their⟩ rise and growth; of
which there will be shortly an occasion, and too frequently,
to say much more. In the mean time it cannot be denied,
and was observed and confessed by all, that never any
prince had a more humble and dutiful condescension and
submission to an elder brother, than the duke had towards
the king; his whole demeanour and behaviour was so full
of reverence, that ⟨it⟩ might have given example to be
imitated by those, who ought but did not observe a
greater distance. And the conscience and resentment he
had within himself, for the sally he had made in Flanders
[autumn, 1650], made him after so wary in his actions,
and so abhorring to heed anything that might lessen
his awe for the king, that no man who had most credit
with ⟨him⟩ durst approach towards any thing of that
kind; so that there was never less ground of jealousy than
of him. And (as was said before) the king (who was in his
nature so far from any kind of jealousy, that he was too
much inclined to make interpretations of many words

and actions, which might reasonably harbour other apprehensions) was as incapable of any infusions which might lessen his confidence in his brother, as any noble and virtuous mind could be. And therefore those ill men, who began about this time to sow that cursed seed that grew up to bear a large crop of the worst and rankest jealousy in the succeeding time, did not presume to make any reflection upon the duke himself, but upon his wife, 'upon the state she assumed, and the height of the whole family, that lived in much more plenty', they said, 'than the king's, and were more regarded abroad.'

Such kind of people are never without some particular stories of the persons whom they desire to deprave: and so had many instances, which they used upon all occasions, of some levity or vanity, of some words affected by the duchess, or some outward carriage, true or false, which for the most part concluded in mirth and laughter, and seemed ridiculous; which was the method they used in all their approaches of that kind towards the highest acts of malice, first to make the person, whom they hoped to ruin in the end, less esteemed, by the acting and presentation of his words and gestures and motions; which commonly is attended with laughter. And this is the first breach they make upon any man's reputation; and the frequent custom of this kind of laughter and mirth, which is easily produced without any malice, doth in the end open a space large enough to let ⟨in⟩ calumny and scandal enough to weaken, if not destroy, the best built reputation.

[Clarendon found himself increasingly unable to adapt himself to the atmosphere at court, nor was he any longer able to keep the king's favour.] The truth is, he had a very hard province, and found his credit every day to decay with the king: whilst they who prevailed against him used all the skill and cunning they had to make it believed, 'that his power with his majesty was as great as it had ever been, and that all those things which he most opposed were acted by his advice'. And whilst they procured all those for whom he had kindness, or who professed any respect towards him, to be discountenanced and undervalued, and preferred none but such who were known to have an aversion for him upon somewhat that he had, or they had been told that he had, obstructed their pretences in; they persuaded men, 'that nobody had any credit with the king to dispose of any place but he'.

Those very men would often profess to him, 'that they were so much afflicted at the king's course of life, that they even despaired that he would be able to master those difficulties which would still press him'; and would then tell him some particulars which he himself had said or done, or had been said or done lately in his own presence, and of which he had never heard before; which gave him occasion often to blame them, 'that they, having the opportunity to see and know many things which he had no notice of or could not take any, and foresaw the consequence that did attend them, did yet forbear to use the credit they had with his majesty, in advertising him what they thought and heard all others say'; and he offered 'to go with them to his majesty, and make a lively representation to him of the great decay of his reputation with the people upon his exorbitant excesses, which God could never bless': to all which they were not ashamed to confess, 'that they never had nor durst speak to his majesty to that purpose, or in such a dialect'. Indeed they were the honester men in not doing it, for it had been gross hypocrisy to have found fault with those actions, upon the pursuing whereof they most depended; and the reformation which they would have been glad to have seen, had no relation to those inordinate and unlawful appetites, which were the root from whence all the other mischiefs had their birth. They did not wish that the lady's authority and power should be lessened, much less extinguished; and that which would have been the most universal blessing to the whole kingdom, would have been received by them as the greatest curse that could befall them.

One day the chancellor and the lord Arlington were together alone, and the secretary, according to his custom, was speaking soberly of many great miscarriages by the license of the court, and how much his majesty suffered thereby; when the king suddenly came into the room to them, and after he was sat asked them what they were talking of: to which the chancellor answered, 'that he would tell him honestly and truly, and was not sorry for the opportunity'. And the other looking with a very troubled countenance, he proceeded and said, 'that they were speaking of his majesty, and, as they did frequently, were bewailing the unhappy life he lived, both with respect to himself, who, by the excess of pleasures which he indulged to himself, was indeed without the true delight and relish of any; and in respect to his government, which he totally neglected, and of which the kingdom was so sensible, that it could not be long before he felt the ill effects of it. That the people were well prepared and well inclined to obey; but if they found that he either would not or could not command, their temper would quickly be changed, and he would find less obedience in all places, than was necessary for his affairs: and that it was too evident and visible, that he had already lost very much of the affection and reverence the nation had for him'.

He said, 'that this was the subject they two were discoursing upon when his majesty entered; and that it is the argument, upon which all those of his council with whom he had any conversation did every day enlarge, when they were together, with grief of heart, and even with tears; and that he hoped that some of them did, with that duty that became them, represent to his majesty their own sense, and the sense his good subjects had, of his condition of living, both with reference to God, who had wrought such miracles for him, and expected some proportionable return; and with reference to his people, who were in the highest discontent. He doubted all men did not discharge their duty this way; and some had confessed to him that they durst not do it, lest they might offend him, which he had assured them often that they would not do, having had so often experience himself of his goodness; and that he had rather taken this opportunity to make this representation to him in the presence of another, which he had never used to do': and concluded 'with beseeching his majesty to believe that which he had often said to him, that no prince could be more miserable, nor could have more reason to fear his own ruin, than he who hath no servants who dare contradict him in his opinions, or advise him against his inclinations, how natural soever'.

The king heard all this and more to the same effect with his usual temper, (for he was a patient hearer,) and spake sensibly, as if he thought that much that had been said was with too much reason; when the other, who wished not such an effect from the discourse, instead of seconding any thing that had been said, made use of the warmth the chancellor was in, and of some expressions he had used, to fall into raillery, which was his best faculty; with which he diverted the king from any further serious reflections; and both of them grew very merry with the other, and reproached his overmuch severity, now he grew old, and considered not the infirmities of younger men: which increased the passion he was in, and provoked him to say, 'that it was observed abroad, that it was a faculty very much improved of late in the court, to laugh at those arguments they could not answer, and which would always be requited with the same mirth amongst those who were enemies to it, and therefore it was pity that it should be so much embraced by those who pretended to be friends'; and to use some other, too plain, expressions, which it may be were not warily enough used, and which the good lord forgot not to put the king in mind of, and to descant upon the presumption, in a season that was more ripe for such reflections, which at the present he forebore to do, and for some time after remembered only in merry occasions.

Though the king did not yet, nor in a good time after, appear to dislike the liberty the chancellor presumed to take with him, (who often told him, 'that he knew he made himself grievous to him, and gave his enemies too great advantages against him; but that the conscience of having done his duty, and having never failed to inform his majesty of any thing that was fit for him to know and to believe, was the only support he had to bear the present trouble of his mind, and to prepare him for those distresses which he foresaw he was to undergo': which his majesty heard with great goodness, and condescension, and vouchsafed still to tell him, 'that it was in nobody's

power to divert his kindness from him':) yet he found
every day that some arguments grew less acceptable to
him, and that the constant conversation with men of great
profaneness, whose wit consisted in abusing scripture, and
in repeating and acting what the preachers said in their
sermons, and turning it into ridicule, (a faculty in which
the duke of Buckingham excelled,) did much lessen the
natural esteem and reverence he had for the clergy, as
a rank of men that compounded a religion for their own
advantage, and to serve their own turns. Nor was all he
could say to him of weight enough to make impression to
the contrary.

And then he seemed to think, 'that men were bolder in
the examining his actions and censuring them than they
ought to be': and once he told him, 'that he thought
he was more severe against common infirmities than he
should be; and that his wife was not courteous in returning
visits and civilities to those who paid her respect; and that
he expected that all his friends should be very kind to those
who they knew were much loved by him, and that he
thought so much justice was due to him'.

The chancellor, who had never dissembled with him,
but on the contrary, had always endeavoured to persuade
him to believe, that dissimulation was the most dishonest
and ungentlemanly quality that could be affected, answered him very roundly, 'that he might seem not to
understand his meaning, and so make no reply to the discourse he had made: but that he understood it all, and the
meaning of every word of it; and therefore that it would
not become him to suffer his majesty to depart with an
opinion, that what he had said would produce any alteration in his behaviour towards him, or reformation of his
manners towards any other persons.

That for the first part, the liberty men took to speak of
him and to censure his actions, he was of the opinion that
it was a very great presumption, and a crime very fit to be
punished: for let it be true or false, men had been always
severely chastised for that license, because it tended to
sedition. However, he put his majesty in mind of the example of Philip of Macedon, who, when one of his servants

accused a person of condition to him of having spoken ill of him, and offered to go himself to the magistrate and make proof of it, answered him; that the person he accused was a man of the greatest reputation of wisdom and integrity in the kingdom, and therefore it would be fit in the first place to examine, whether himself, the king, had not done somewhat by which he had deserved to be so spoken of: indeed this way the best men would often receive benefit from their worst enemies. For the matter itself', he said, 'he need make no apology: for that it was notoriously known, that he had constantly given it in charge to all the judges, to make diligent inquiry into misdemeanours and transgressions of that magnitude, and to punish those who were guilty in the most exemplary manner; and that he took not more pains any way, than to preserve in the hearts of the people that veneration for his person that is due to his dignity, and to persuade many who appeared afflicted with the reports they heard, that they heard more than was true; and that the suppressing all reports of that kind was the duty of every good subject, and would contribute more towards the reforming any thing that in truth is amiss, than the propagating the scandal by spreading it in discourses could do. However, that all this, which was his duty, and but his duty, did not make it unfit for him, or any other under his obligations, in fit seasons to make a lively representation to his majesty of what is done, and how secretly soever, that cannot be justified or excused; and of the untruths and scandals which spring from thence to his irreparable dishonour and prejudice.

For the other part, of want of ceremony and respect to those who were loved and esteemed by his majesty, he might likewise avoid enlarging upon that subject, by putting his majesty in mind, that he had the honour to serve him in a province that excused him from making visits, and exempted him from all ceremonies of that kind. But he would not shelter himself under such a general defence, when he perceived that his majesty had in the reprehension a particular intention: and therefore he confessed ingenuously to his majesty, that he did deny himself many liberties, which in themselves might be innocent

enough and agreeable to his person, because they would
not be decent or agreeable to the office he held, which
obliged him, for his majesty's honour, and to preserve him
from the reproach of having put a light person into a grave
place, to have the more care of his own carriage and behaviour. And that, as it would reflect upon his majesty
himself, if his chancellor was known or thought to be of
dissolute and debauched manners, which would make
him as uncapable as unworthy to do him service; so it
would be a blemish and taint upon him to give any countenance, or to pay more than ordinary, cursory, and unavoidable civilities, to persons infamous for any vice, for
which by the laws of God and man they ought to be odious,
and to be exposed to the judgment of the church and state.
And that he would not for his own sake and for his own
dignity, to how low a condition soever he might be reduced, stoop to such a condescension as to have the least
commerce, or to make the application of a visit, to any
such person, for any benefit or advantage that it might
bring to him. He did beseech his majesty not to believe,
that he hath a prerogative to declare vice virtue; or to
qualify any person who lives in a sin and avows it, against
which God himself hath pronounced damnation, for the
company and conversation of innocent and worthy persons.
And that whatever low obedience, which was in truth
gross flattery, some people might pay to what they believed would be grateful to his majesty, they had in their
hearts a perfect detestation of the persons they made address to: and that for his part he was long resolved that
his wife should not be one of those courtiers; and that he
would himself much less like her company, if she put herself into theirs who had not the same innocence.'

The king was not the more pleased for the defence he
made, and did not dissemble his dislike of it, without any
other sharpness, than by telling him 'that he was in the
wrong, and had an understanding different from all other
men who had experience in the world'. And it is most certain, it was an avowed doctrine, and with great address
daily insinuated to the king, 'that princes had many liberties which private persons have not; and that a lady of

honour who dedicates herself only to please a king, and continues faithful to him, ought not to be branded with any name or mark of infamy, but hath been always looked upon by all persons well-bred as worthy of respect': and to this purpose the history of all the amours of his grandfather were carefully presented to him, and with what indignation he suffered any disrespect towards any of his mistresses.

But of all these artifices the chancellor had no apprehension, out of the confidence he had in the integrity of the king's nature; and that though he might be swayed to sacrifice his present affections to his appetite, he could never be prevailed upon to entertain a real suspicion of his very passionate affection and duty to his person. That which gave him most trouble, and many times made him wish himself in any private condition separated from the court, was that unfixedness and irresolution of judgment that was natural to all his family of the male line, which often exposed them all to the importunities of bold, and to the snares of crafty, men.

64. *The Earl of Arlington, Sir William Coventry, and Sir George Downing: Parliamentary and Financial Affairs, 1663–6*

Bennet, born 1618; occupied with Spanish affairs till after the Restoration; Secretary of State October 1662; M.P. 1663; Baron Arlington 1663; Earl of Arlington 1672; died 1685

Coventry, born 1628; M.P. 1661; Commissioner of the Navy with Sir George Carteret 1662; P.C. 1665; left service of the Duke of York, August 1667; died 1686

Downing, born 1623?; Cromwell's Resident at The Hague 1657; stays on as Charles's Resident; baronet 1663; Commissioner of the Army 1667; died 1684

[During 1662–3] But there were two persons now introduced to act upon that stage, who disdained to receive orders, or to have any method prescribed to them; who took upon them to judge of other men's defects, and thought their own abilities beyond exception.

The one was sir Harry Bennet, who had procured himself to be sent agent or envoy into Spain, as soon as the king came from Brussels; being a man very well known to the king, and for his pleasant and agreeable humour acceptable to him: and he remained there at much ease till the king returned to England, having waited upon his majesty at Fuentarabia in the close of the treaty between the two crowns,[1] and there appeared by his dexterity to have gained good credit in the court of Spain, and particularly with don Lewis de Haro; and by that short negociation he renewed and confirmed the former good inclinations of his master to him. He had been obliged always to correspond with the chancellor, by whom his instructions had been drawn, and to receive the king's pleasure by his signification; which he had always done, and professed much respect and submission to him: though whatever orders he received, and how positive soever, in particulars which highly concerned the king's honour and dignity, he observed them so far and no further than his own humour disposed him; and in some cases flatly disobeyed what the king enjoined.

But he was very well received by the king, in whose affections he had a very good place: and shortly after his arrival, though not so soon as he thought his high merit deserved, his majesty conferred the only place then void (and that had been long promised to a noble person, who had behaved himself very well towards his majesty and his blessed father) upon him, which was the office of privy purse; received him into great familiarity, and into the nightly meeting, in which he filled a principal place to all intents and purposes. The king very much desired to have him elected a member in the house of commons, and commanded the chancellor to use his credit to obtain it upon the first opportunity: and in obedience to that command, he did procure him to be chosen about the time

[1] The negotiations of autumn 1659 leading to the Peace of the Pyrenees between Spain and France.

we are now speaking of, when the parliament assembled in February.

The other person was Mr. William Coventry, the youngest son to a very wise father, the lord Coventry, who had been lord keeper of the great seal of England for many years with a universal reputation. This gentleman was young whilst the war continued: yet he had put himself before the end of it into the army, and had the command of a foot company, and shortly after travelled into France; where he remained whilst there was any hope of getting another army for the king, or that either of the other crowns would engage in his quarrel. But when all thoughts of that were desperate, he returned into England; where he remained for many years without the least correspondence with any of his friends beyond the seas, and with so little reputation of caring much for the king's restoration, that some of his own family, who were most zealous for his majesty's service, and had always some signal part in any reasonable design, took care of nothing more, than that nothing they did should come to his knowledge; and gave the same advice to those about the king, with whom they corresponded, to use the same caution. Not that any body suspected his being inclined to the rebels, or to do any act of treachery; but that the pride and censoriousness of his nature made him unconversable, and his despair that any thing could be effectually done made him incompetent to consult the ways of doing it. Nor had he any conversation with any of the king's party, nor they with him, till the king was proclaimed in London; and then he came over with the rest to offer his service to his majesty at the Hague, and had the good fortune to find the duke of York without a secretary. For though he had a Walloon that was, in respect of the languages of which he was master, fit for that function in the army, and had discharged it very well for some years; yet for the province the duke was now to govern, having the office of high admiral of England, he was without any fit person to discharge the office of secretary with any tolerable sufficiency: so that Mr. Coventry no sooner offered his service to the duke, but he was received into that employment, very honourable under such a master, and in itself of the greatest profit next the secretaries of state, if they in that respect be to be preferred.

He had been well known to the king and duke in France, and had a brother whom the king loved well and had promised to take into his bedchamber, as he shortly after did, Harry Coventry, who was beloved by every body, which made them glad of the preferment of the other; whilst they who knew the worst of him, yet knew him able to discharge that office, and so contributed to the duke's receiving him. He was a sullen, ill-natured, proud man, whose ambition had no limits, nor could be contained within any. His parts were very good, if he had not thought them better than any other man's; and he had diligence and industry, which men of good parts are too often without, which made ⟨him⟩ quickly to have at least credit and power enough with the duke; and he was without those vices which were too much in request, and which make men most unfit for business and the trust that cannot be separated from it.

He had sat a member in the house of commons, from the beginning of the parliament, with very much reputation of an able man. He spake pertinently, and was always very acceptable and well heard; and was one of those with whom they, who were trusted by the king in conducting his affairs in the lower house, consulted very frequently; but not so much, nor relied equally upon his advice, as upon some few others who had much more experience, which he thought was of use only to ignorant and dull men, and that men of sagacity could see and determine at a little light, and ought rather to persuade and engage men to do that which they judged fit, than consider what themselves were inclined to do: and so did not think himself to be enough valued and relied upon, and only to be made use of to the celebrating the designs and contrivance of other men, without being signal in the managery, which he aspired to be. Nor did any man envy him the province, if he could indeed have governed it, and that others who had more useful talents would have been ruled by him. However, being a man who naturally loved faction and contradiction, he often made experiments how far he could prevail in the house, by declining the method that was prescribed, and proposing somewhat to the house that was either beside or contrary to it, and which the others would not oppose, believing, in regard of his relation, that he had received newer directions: and then if it succeeded well, (as sometimes it did,) he had argument enough to censure and inveigh against the chancellor, for having taken so ill measures of the temper and affections of the house; for he did not dissemble in his private conversation (though his outward carriage was very fair) that he had no kindness for him, which in gratitude he ought to have had; nor had he any thing to complain of from him, but that he wished well and did all he could to defend and support a very worthy person, who had deserved very well from the king, against whom he manifested a great and causeless animosity, and desired to oppress for his own profit, of which he had an immoderate appetite.

When those two persons, sir Harry Bennet and Mr. Coventry, (between whom there had been as great a league of friendship, as can be between two very proud men equally ill-natured,) came now to sit together in the house of commons; though the former of them knew no more of the constitution and laws of England than he did of China, nor had in truth a care or tenderness for church or state, but believed France was the best pattern in the world[1]; they thought they should have the greatest wrong imaginable, if they did not entirely govern it, and if the king took his measures of what should be done there from any body but themselves. They made friendships with some young men, who spake confidently and often, ⟨and⟩ upon some occasions seemed to have credit in the house. And upon a little conversation with those men, who, being country gentlemen of ordinary condition and mean fortunes, were desirous to have interest in such a person as sir Harry Bennet, who was believed to have great credit with the king; he believed he understood the house, and what was to be done there, as well as any man in England.

---

[1] Regarding these allegations, see V. Barbour: *Henry Bennet, Earl of Arlington*, 1914.

He recommended those men to the king 'as persons of sublime parts, worthy of his majesty's caressing: that he would undertake to fix them to his service; and when they were his own, he might carry what he would in the house of commons'. The men had parts indeed and good affections, and often had resorted to the chancellor, received advice from him, and thought themselves beholden to him; being at that time entirely governed by sir Hugh Pollard, who was himself still advised by the Chancellor (with whom he had a long and fast friendship) how he should direct his friends, having indeed a greater party in the house of commons willing to be disposed of by him, than any man that ever sat there in my time. But now these gentlemen had got a better patron; the new courtier had raised their value, and talked in another dialect to them, of recompenses and rewards, than they had heard formerly. He carried them to the king, and told his majesty in their own hearing, 'what men of parts they were, what services they had done for him, and how much greater they could do': and his majesty received and conferred with them very graciously and dismissed them with promises which made them rich already.

The two friends before mentioned agreed so well between themselves, that whether they spake together or apart to the king, they said always the same things, gave the same information, and took care that both their masters might have the same opinions and judgments. They magnified the affections of the house of commons, 'which were so great and united, that they would do whatsoever his majesty would require. That there were many worthy and able men, of whose wisdom the house was so well persuaded, that they commonly consented to whatsoever they proposed: and that these men complained, that they had no directions given to them which way they might best serve the king; they knew not what he desired, which when they should do, it would quickly appear how much they were at the king's disposal, and all things which now depended long would be hereafter despatched in half the time'.

The king wondered very much, 'that his friends in the

house were no better informed, of which he had never heard any complaint before, and wished them to speak with the chancellor'; for neither of these men were yet arrived at the confidence to insinuate in the least degree any ill-will or prejudice to him, though they were not united in any one thing more than the desire of his ruin, and the resolution to compass it by all the ill arts and devices they could use; but till it should be more seasonable, they dissembled to both their masters to have a high esteem of him, having not yet credit enough with either to do him harm. They said, 'they would very willingly repair to him, and be directed by him: but they desired that his majesty himself would first speak to him (because it would not so well become them) to call those persons, whom they had recommended to him, to meet together with the rest with whom he used to advise; which the persons they named they were sure would be very glad of, having all of them a great esteem of the chancellor, and being well known to him', as indeed they were, and most of them obliged by him.

The king willingly undertook it: and being shortly after attended by the chancellor, his majesty told him all that the other two had said to him, and did not forget to let him know the great good-will they had both professed towards him.

[Clarendon answered and] besought his majesty to consider, 'whether any thing had hitherto, in near three years, fallen out amiss, or short of what he had expected, in the wary administration that had been in that affair'; and did not conceal his own fears, 'that putting it into a more open and wider channel, his majesty's own too public speaking with the members of parliament, and believing what every man who was present told him passed in debates, and who for want of comprehension as well as memory committed many mistakes in their relations, would be attended with some inconveniences not easy to be remedied'. The king was not dissatisfied with the discourse, but seemed to approve it: however he would have sir Harry Bennet, Mr. Clifford, and Churchill, called to the next meeting; and because they were to be introduced into company they had not used to converse with, that it should be at the chancellor's chamber, who should let the rest know the good opinion his majesty had of those who were added to the number.

By this means and with these circumstances this alteration was made in the conduct of the king's service in the parliament; upon which many other alterations followed by degrees, though not at once. Yet presently it appeared, that this introduction of new confidents was not acceptable to those, who thought they had very well discharged their trust. Sir Harry Bennet was utterly unknown to them, a man unversed in any business, who never had nor ever was like to speak in the house, except in his ear who sat next him to the disadvantage of some who had spoken, and was thought by all men to be a Roman catholic, for which they had not any other reason but from his indifference in all things which concerned the church.

When they met first at the chancellor's chamber, as the king had directed, they conferred freely together with little difference of opinion: though it appeared that they, who had used to be together before, did not use the same freedom as formerly in delivering their particular judgments, not having confidence enough in the new comers, who in their private meetings afterwards took more upon them, rather to direct than to advise; so that the other grew unsatisfied in their ⟨conversation⟩. And though the meetings continued at one of the places before mentioned, some always discontinued their attendance; so that by degrees there were less resolutions taken than had been formerly; nor was there so cheerful a concurrence, or so speedy a despatch of the business depending in the house, as had been.

However, there appeared nothing of disunion in the parliament, but the same zeal and concurrence in all things which related to the king. The murmurs and discontents were most in the country, where the people began to talk with more license and less reverence of the court, and of the king himself, and to reproach the parliament for their raising so much money, and increasing of the impositions upon the kingdom, without having done any thing for the redress of any grievance that lay upon the people. The license with reference to religion grew every day greater, the conventicles more frequent and more insolent, which disturbed the country exceedingly; but not so much as the liberty the papists assumed, who behaved themselves with indiscretion, and bragged as if they had a toleration and cared not what the magistrates could do. The parliament had a desire to have provided against those evils with the same rigour: but though there would have been a general consent in any provision that could be made against the fanatics and the conventicles, yet there would not be the like concurrence against the papists; and it was not possible to carry on the one without the other. And therefore the court, that they might be sure to prevent the last, interrupted all that was proposed against the former, which they wished provided against, and chose to have neither out of fear of both; which increased the disorders in the country, and caused more reflections upon the court: so that this session of parliament produced less of moment than any other.

During the interval of the parliament, there was not such a vacation from trouble and anxiety as was expected. The domestic unquietness in the court made every day more noise abroad: infinite scandals and calumnies were scattered amongst the people; and they expressed their discontents upon the great taxes and impositions which they were compelled to pay, and publicly reproached the parliament; when they were in truth vexed and grieved at heart for that which they durst not avow, and did really believe that God was angry with the nation, and resolved to exercise it under greater tribulation than he had so lately freed them from. The general want of money was complained of, and a great decay of trade; so that the native commodities of the kingdom were not transported. Yet both these were but pretences, and resulted from combinations rather than from reason. For it appeared by the customs, that the trade was greater than it had ever been, though some of our native commodities, especially cloth, seemed for some time to be at a stand; which proceeded rather from the present glut, which in the general license the interlopers had irregularly transported in great quantities, by which the prices were brought low, and could only be recovered by a restraint for some time, which the merchant adventurers put upon themselves, and would have put upon the interlopers, who were at last too hard for them, even upon the matter to the suppressing the company, that had stood in great reputation for very many years, and had advanced that manufacture to a great height; and whether it deserved that discountenance, time must decide. How unreasonable the other discourse was of want of money, there needs no other argument, but the great purchases which were every day made of great estates; nor was any considerable parcel of land in any part of England offered to be sold, but there was a purchaser at hand ready to buy it.

However, these pretences, together with the sudden bringing up all the money, that was collected for the king, in specie to London, which proceeded from the bankers' advancing so much present money for the emergent occasions, for which they had those assignments upon the money of the country, did really produce such a sudden fall of the rents throughout the kingdom, as had never been known before: so that men were compelled to abate generally a fourth part of their annual rents at the least, or to take their lands into their own hands, for which they were as ill provided. All this mischief fell upon the nobility and greatest gentry, who were owners of the greatest estates, every body whose estate lay in land undergoing a share in the suffering, which made the discontent general; which they thought the best ⟨way⟩ to remedy would be to raise no more taxes, which they took to be the cause why the rents fell. In the mean time the expenses of the court, and of all who depended upon it, grew still higher, and the king himself less intent upon his business, and more loved his pleasures, to which he prescribed no limits, nor to the expenses which could not but accompany them.

[While others were preferred Clarendon lost an old friend and ally in Secretary Nicholas and was impeached, though unsuccessfully, by the Earl of Bristol, 1663.] His majesty did not in the least degree withdraw his favour from him, heard him as willingly, came as often to him, was as little reserved in any thing; only in one particular he did with some solemnity conjure him never to mention it to him again, in which he did not yet punctually obey him, nor avoid seasonably saying any thing to him which he believed to be his duty, and which his majesty never seemed to take ill. And whenever he spake to him of either of the other two gentlemen, which he frequently did with much kindness, he always added somewhat of both their respects and esteem for him, as a thing that pleased him well; and said once, 'that it concerned them, for whenever he should discern it to be otherwise, he should make them repent it'. Yet notwithstanding all this, from that time counsels were not so secret, and greater liberty taken to talk of the public affairs in the evening conversation, than had been before, when they happened sometimes to be shortly mentioned in the production of some wit or jest; but now they were often taken into debate, and censured with too much liberty with reference to things and persons; and the king himself was less fixed and more irresolute in his counsels; and inconvenient grants came every day to the seal for the benefit of particular persons, against which the king had particularly resolved, and at last by importunity would have passed. Lastly, both these persons were most devoted to the lady, and much depended upon her interest, and consequently were ready to do any thing that would be grateful to her.

There was another mischief contrived about this time, that had a much worse influence upon the public, except we shall call it the same, because it did in truth proceed from it. Though the public state of affairs, in respect of the distempers and discomposures which are mentioned before, and that the expenses exceeded what was assigned to support it, whereby the great debt was little diminished, yielded little delight to those who were most trusted to manage and provide for them, and who had a melancholic and dreadful apprehension of consequences: yet whilst the nation continued in peace, and without any danger from any foreign enemy, that the prospect was so pleasant, especially to those who stood at a distance, that they saw nothing worthy of any man's fear; and there was reasonable hope, that the expenses might every year be reduced within reasonable ⟨bounds⟩. But all that hope vanished, when there appeared an immoderate desire to engage the nation in a war.

Upon the king's first arrival in England, he manifested a very great desire to improve the general traffick and trade of the kingdom, and upon all occasions, conferred with the most active merchants upon it, and offered all that he could contribute to the advancement thereof. He erected a council of trade, which produced little other effect than the opportunity of men's speaking together, which possibly disposed them to think more, and to consult more effectually in private, than they could in such a crowd of commissioners. Some merchants and seamen made a proposition by Mr. William Coventry, and some few others to the duke of York, 'for the erection of a company in which they desired his royal highness to preside', (and from thence it was called the Royal Company,) 'to which his majesty should grant the sole trade of Guinea, which in a short time they presumed would bring great advantage to the public, and much profit to the adventurers, who should begin upon a joint stock, to be managed by a council of such as should be chosen out of the adventurers'. [The Royal Africa Company flourished; soon after the merchants began to agitate for war against the Dutch.]

The merchants in the committee of trade much lamented the obstructions and discouragements, which they had long found in their commerce by sea, and with other nations, and which were not removed even by the blessed return of the king; all which they imputed to the pride and insolence of the Hollanders, 'who', they said, 'observed no laws of commerce, or any conditions which themselves consented to. That by their fraud and practice the English were almost driven out of the East and West Indies, and had their trade in Turkey and in Africa much diminished. In sum, that besides many insufferable indignities offered by them to his majesty and to the crown of England, his subjects had in few years sustained the damage of seven or eight hundred thousand pounds sterling.'

All which with some particular instances being reported from the committee of trade to the house, they had desired an audience from his majesty, and then presented this grievance to him, and desired his majesty, 'that he would give such order in it, as to his wisdom should seem fit, that might produce just and honourable satisfaction'. The king, who continued firm to his former resolution, answered them, 'that he would transmit the address they had presented to him to his resident at the Hague, with order that he should inform the States of it, and require satisfaction, which he hoped the States General would yield unto, rather than they compel him to demand justice in another way'. The answer pleased them well, nor could they wish that the prosecution should be put into a better hand than the resident's, who was a member of the house, and a man who had inflamed them more than the merchants themselves against the Dutch.

That resident was sir George Downing, a man of an obscure birth, and more obscure education, which he had received in part in New England: he had passed through many offices in Cromwell's army, of chaplain, scoutmaster, and other employments, and at last got a very particular credit and confidence with him, and under that countenance married a beautiful lady of a very noble extraction, which was the fate of many bold men in that presumptuous time.[1] And when Cromwell had subdued the Dutch to that temper he wished, and had thereupon made a peace with them, he sent this man to reside as his agent with them, being a man of a proud and insolent spirit, and ⟨who⟩ would add to any imperious command of his somewhat of the bitterness of his own spirit.

And he did so fully execute his charge in all things, especially when he might manifest his animosity against the royal party, that when the king himself had once, during his residence at Brussels, for his divertisement made a journey incognito, with not above four persons, to see Amsterdam, and from thence the towns of North Holland;

[1] Downing was in New England 1638–45, the second graduate of Harvard College; his wife Frances was the daughter of Sir William Howard of Naworth.

Downing coming to have notice of it delivered a memorial to the States of Holland, wherein he enclosed the third article of their treaty, by which they were obliged 'not to suffer any traitor, rebel, or any other person, who was declared an enemy to the commonwealth of England, to reside or stay in their dominions;' and told them, 'that Charles Stuart and the marquis of Ormond had been lately in Amsterdam, and were still in some places adjacent'; and required, 'that they might not be permitted to remain in any part of their dominions'. Whereupon the States of Holland sent presently to the princess royal [Mary Stuart, Princess of Orange], who was then at her country house at Hounslerdike, 'that if her brother were then with her or should come to her, he should forthwith depart out of their province': and not satisfied herewith, they published an order in the Hague to the same purpose, which was sent to Amsterdam and other towns according to their custom.

With this rude punctuality he behaved himself during the life of Cromwell, and whilst his son retained the usurpation; but when he saw him thrown out with that contempt, and that the government was not like to be settled again till there was a resort to the old foundation, he bethought himself how he might have a reserve of the king's favour. And the marquis of Ormond making about that time a journey incognito to the Hague, ⟨to treat of⟩ a marriage for his eldest son with a noble lady whose friends lived there, Downing found opportunity to have a private conference with him, and made offer of his service to the king, if his devotion be concealed, without which it would be useless to his majesty. And for an earnest of his fidelity, he informed him of some particulars which were of moment for the king to know: amongst which one was, 'that a person, who in respect of his very honourable extraction, and the present obligations himself had to the royal family, was not suspected, gave him, as he had long done, constant intelligence of what the king did, and of many particulars which in their nature deserved to be more secret, which he had always sent to Cromwell whilst he was living; but since his death, having a resolution to serve the king, he had never disserved him, and would hereafter give him notice of any thing that it would be necessary ⟨for him⟩ to be informed of with reference to England or to Holland'.

The marquis thought it very fit to accept of such an instrument, and promised him 'to acquaint his majesty with his good affection, who he presumed would receive it graciously, and give him as much encouragement to continue it as his present condition would permit'. To which the other replied, 'that he knew the king's present condition too well to expect any reward from him: but if his majesty would vouchsafe, when he should be restored, to confirm to him the office he then held of a teller in the exchequer, and continue him in this employment he then had in Holland, where he presumed he should be able to do him more service than a stranger could do, he would think himself abundantly rewarded'. Of all which when the marquis advertised the king at his return to Brussels, he had authority to assure him 'of the king's acceptation, and that all that he expected should be made good'.

This was the ground and reason, that when the king came to the Hague the year following to embark for England, he received Downing so graciously, and knighted him, and left him there as his resident; which they who were near the king, and knew nothing of what had passed, wondered at as much as strangers who had observed his former behaviour. And the States themselves, who would not at such a time of public joy do any thing that might be ingrateful to his majesty, could not forbear to lament in private, 'that his majesty would depute a person to have his authority, who had never used any other dialect to persuade them to do any thing he proposed, but threats if they should not do it, and who at several times had disobliged most of their persons by his insolence'. And from the time of his majesty's departure from thence, he never made those representations which men in those ministeries used to do, but put the worst commentaries upon all their actions. And when he sat afterwards as a member of the house, returning still in the interval of parliament to his employment at the Hague, he took all opportunities to inveigh against their usurpations in trade;

and either did or pretended to know many of their mysteries of iniquity, in opening of which he rendered himself acceptable to the house, though he was a voluminous speaker, which naturally they do not like. [Finally war was declared and Parliament voted the extraordinary sum of £2,500,000 'for the carrying on the war', 25 November 1664.]

[The war at sea had not gone well at the beginning and the plague had begun to ravish the country. Parliament had met at Oxford but] Though the parliament at Oxford had preserved that excellent harmony that the king had proposed, and hardly wished any thing in which they had not concurred, insomuch as never parliament so entirely sympathised with his majesty; and ⟨though⟩ it passed more acts for his honour and security than any other had ever done in so short a session: yet it introduced a precedent of a very unhappy nature, the circumstances whereof in the present were unusual and pernicious, and the consequences in the future very mischievous, and therefore not unfit to be set out at large.

The lord Arlington and sir William Coventry, closely united in the same purposes, and especially against the chancellor, had a great desire to find some means to change the course and method of the king's counsels; which they could hardly do whilst the same persons continued still in the same employments. Their malice was most against the chancellor: yet they knew not what suggestions to make to the king against him, having always pretended to his majesty, how falsely soever, to have a great esteem of him. Their project therefore was to remove the treasurer [the Earl of Southampton], who was as weary of his office and of the court as any body could be of him: but his reputation was so great, his wisdom so unquestionable, and his integrity so confessed, that they knew in neither of those points he could be impeached. And the king himself had kindness and reverence towards him, though he had for some years thought him less active, and so less fit for that administration, than every body else knew him to be: and these men had long insinuated unto his ⟨majesty⟩, 'how ill all the business of the exchequer was managed by the continual infirmities of the treasurer, who, between the gout and the stone, had not ease enough to attend the painful function of that office.

There was a man who hath been often named, sir George Downing, who by having been some years in the office of one of the tellers of the exchequer, and being of a restless brain, did understand enough of the nature of the revenue and of the course of the receipt, to make others who understood less of it to think that he knew the bottom of it, and that the expedients, which should be proposed by him towards a reformation, could not but be very pertinent and practicable. And he was not unhurt in the emoluments of his own office, which were lessened by the assignations made to the bankers, upon the receipts themselves, without the money's ever passing through the tellers' office; by which, though they did receive their just fees, they had not what they would have taken, if the money had passed through their own hands. He was a member of parliament, and a very voluminous speaker, who would be thought wiser in trade than any of the merchants, and to understand the mystery of all professions much better than the professors of them. And such a kind of chat is always acceptable in a crowd, (where few understand many subjects,) ⟨who⟩ are always glad to find those put out of countenance who thought they understood it best: and so they were much pleased to hear sir George Downing inveigh against the ignorance of those, who could only smile at his want of knowledge. [Downing proposed a sharper application of the novel principle of appropriation. But his proviso, though it became law in 1665, raised the further question as to who was to control that appropriation, the king or Parliament. This question was only finally settled in the future. At the beginning Charles liked the notion well enough.] And because it was foreseen, that it would be opposed by many of those who were known to be very affectionate of the king's service, they had all authority privately to assure them, that it was offered with the king's approbation.

Against the time that the bill was to be brought in, they prepared the house by many unseasonable bitter invectives against the bankers, called them cheats, blood-suckers, extortioners, and loaded them with all the re-proaches which can be cast upon the worst men in the world, and would have them looked upon as the causes of all the king's necessities, and of the want of monies throughout the kingdom: all which was a plausible argu-ment, as all invectives against particular men are; and all men who had faculties of depraving, and of making ill things appear worse than they are, were easily engaged with them. The bankers did not consist of above the num-ber of five or six men, some whereof were aldermen, and had been lord mayors of London, and all the rest were aldermen, or had fined for aldermen. They were a tribe that had risen and grown up in Cromwell's time, and never heard of before the late troubles, till when the whole trade of money had passed through the hands of the scriveners: they were for the most part goldsmiths, men known to be so rich, and of so good reputation, that all the money of the kingdom would be trusted or deposited in their hands.

From the time of the king's return, when though great and vast sums were granted, yet such vast debts were presently to be paid, the armies by land and sea to be presently discharged, ⟨that⟩ the money that was to be collected in six and six months would not provide for those present unavoidable issues; but there must be two or three hundred thousand pounds gotten together in few days, before they could begin to disband the armies or to pay the seamen off; the deferring whereof every month increased the charge to an incredible proportion: none could supply those occasions but the bankers, which brought the king's ministers first acquainted with them; and they were so well satisfied with their proceedings, that they did always declare, 'that they were so necessary to the king's affairs, that they knew not how to have con-ducted them without that assistance'.

The method of proceeding with them was thus. As soon as an act of parliament was passed, the king sent for those bankers, (for there was never any contract made with them but in his majesty's presence:) and being attended by the ministers of the revenue, and commonly the chancellor and others of the council, the lord treasurer presented a particular information to the king of the most urgent occasions for present money, either for disbanding troops, or discharging ships, or setting out fleets, (all which are to be done together, and not by parcels;) so that it was easily foreseen what ready money must be provided. And this account being made, the bankers were called in, and told, 'that the king had occasion to use such a sum of ready money within such a day; they understood the act of parliament, and so might determine what money they could lend the king, and what manner of security would best satisfy them'. Whereupon one said, 'he would within such a time pay one hundred thousand pounds', another more, and another less, as they found themselves provided; for there was no joint stock amongst them, but every one supplied according to his ability. They were desirous to have eight in the hundred, which was not unreasonable to ask, and the king was 'willing to give': but upon better consideration amongst themselves, they thought fit to decline that demand, as being capable of turning to their disadvantage, and would leave the interest to the king's own bounty, declaring 'that themselves paid six in the hundred for all the money with which they were intrusted', which was known to be true.

Then they demanded such a receipt and assignment to be made to them by the lord treasurer, for the payment of the first money that should be payable upon that act of parliament, or a branch of that act, or tallies upon the farmers of the customs or excise, or such other branches of the revenue as were least charged; having the king's own word and the faith of the treasurer, that they should be exactly complied with; for, let the security be what they could desire, it would still be in the power of the king or of the lord treasurer to divert what was assigned to them to other purposes. Therefore there is nothing surer, than that the confidence in the king's justice, and the unquestionable reputation of the lord treasurer's honour and integrity, was the true foundation of that credit which supplied all his majesty's necessities and occasions; and his majesty always treated those men very graciously, as his very good servants, and all his ministers looked upon them as very honest and valuable men. And in this manner, for many years after his majesty's return, even to the unhappy beginning of the Dutch war, the public expenses were carried on, it may be, with too little difficulty, which possibly increased some expenses; and nobody opened his mouth against the bankers, who every day increased in credit and reputation, and had the money of all men at their disposal.

[But Downing's Bill passed the Commons with some amendments in October 1665. Clarendon's description of its fate in the Lords is inaccurate. He was laid up with gout most of this time. Once there was a debate concerning the proviso in his room in front of the king. It is one of the many examples of his impolitic behaviour to Charles II.]

In this debate, upon the insolent behaviour of Downing in the defence of that which could not be defended, and it may be out of the extremity of the pain which at that time he endured in his bed, the ⟨chancellor⟩ had given some very sharp reprehensions to Downing, for his presumption in undertaking to set such a design on foot that concerned the whole fabric of the exchequer, (in which he was an inferior officer,) and such a branch of the king's revenue, without first communicating it to his superior officers, and receiving their advice; and told him, 'that it was impossible for the king to be well served, whilst fellows of his condition were admitted to speak as much as they had a mind to; and that in the best times such presumptions had been punished with imprisonment by the lords of the council, without the king's taking notice of it': which, with what sharpness soever uttered, (in which he naturally exceeded in such occasions,) in a case of this nature, in which, with reference to any disrespect towards himself, he was not concerned, he thought did not exceed the privilege and dignity of the place he held; and for which there were many precedents in the past times.

At the present there was no notice taken, nor reply made to what he said. But they who knew themselves equally guilty, and believed they were reflected upon, found quickly opportunity to incense the king, and to persuade him to believe, 'that the chancellor's behaviour was a greater affront to him than to Downing: that a servant should undergo such reproaches in the king's own presence, for no other reason but having, with all humility, presented an information to his majesty, which was natural for him to understand in the office in which he served him, and afterwards followed and observed the orders and directions which himself had prescribed; that this must terrify all men from giving the king any light in his affairs, that he may know nothing of his own nearest concernments but what his chief ministers thought fit to impart to him'. All which, and whatsoever else was natural to wit sharpened with malice to suggest upon such an argument, they enforced with warmth, that they desired might be taken for zeal for his ⟨service⟩ and dignity, which was prostituted by those presumptions of the chancellor.

And herewith they so inflamed the king, that he was much offended, and expressed to them such a dislike that pleased them well, and gave them opportunity to add more fuel to the fire and told them, 'that the chancellor should find that he was not pleased'; as indeed he did, by a greater reservedness in his countenance than his majesty used to carry towards him; the reason whereof his innocence kept him from comprehending, till in a short time he vouchsafed plainly to put him in mind of his behaviour at that time, and to express a great resentment of it, and urged all those glosses which had been made to him upon it, and 'what interpretation all men must make of such an action, and be terrified by it from offering any thing, of what importance soever to his service, if it would offend his ministers'; and all this in a choler very unnatural to him, which exceedingly troubled the chancellor, and made him more discern, though he had evidence enough of it before, that he stood upon very slippery ground.

[The dislocation of trade because of the Dutch war and of the fire of London had an adverse effect on financial affairs. The Parliament of 1666 was disinclined to grant any further supplies without an inspection and audit of accounts, a demand which led to further strife between the government and the Commons.] Indeed the king did not till now understand the damage he had sustained by the plague, much less what he must sustain from the fire. Monies could neither be collected nor borrowed where the plague had prevailed, which was over all the city and over a great part of the country; the collectors durst not go to require it or receive it. Yet the fountains remained yet clear, and the waters would run again: but this late conflagration had dried up or so stopped the very fountains, that there was no prospect when they would flow again. The two great branches of the revenue, the customs and excise, which was the great and almost inexhaustible security to borrow money upon, were now bankrupt, and would neither bring in money nor supply credit: all the measures by which computations had been made were so broken, that they could not be brought to meet again. By a medium of the constant receipts it had been depended upon, that what had been borrowed upon that fund would by this time have been fully satisfied with all the interest, whereby the money would have been replaced in the hands to which it was due, which would have been glad to have laid it out again; and the security remained still in vigour to be applied to any other urgent occasions: but now the plague had routed all those receipts, especially in London, where the great conduits of those receipts still ran. The plague and the war had so totally broken and distracted those receipts, that the farmers of either had not received enough to discharge the constant burden of the officers, and were so far from paying any part of the principal that was secured upon it, that it left the interest unpaid to swell the principal. And now this deluge by fire had dissipated the persons, and destroyed the houses, which were liable to the reimbursement of all arrears; and the very stocks were consumed which should carry on and revive the trade. And the third next considerable branch of the revenue, the chimney-money, was determined; and the city must be rebuilt before any body could be required to pay for his chimneys.

65. Sir Edward Nicholas

Born 1593; M.P. 1621–8; Clerk of the Council 1626–
41; knighted, P.C., and Secretary of State 1641–62;
died 1669

SECRETARY NICHOLAS was a very honest and industrious man, and always versed in business; which few of
the others were, or had been. After some time spent in the
university of Oxford, and then in the Middle Temple, he
lived some years in France; and was afterwards secretary
to the lord Zouch, who was a privy-counsellor, and warden
of the cinque ports; and thereby he understood all that
jurisdiction, which is very great, and exclusive to the
admiral. And when that lord, many years after, surrendered that office to the king [1618], to the end that it
might be conferred upon the duke of Buckingham, his
secretary was likewise preferred with the office; and so, in
a short time, became secretary of the admiralty, as well
as of the cinque ports; and was entirely trusted, and
esteemed by that great favourite. After his death, he continued in the same place, whilst the office was in commission, and was then made clerk of the council, from
whence the king called him to be secretary of state, after
secretary Windebank fled the kingdom; upon his majesty's
own observation of his virtue and fidelity, and without
any other recommendation: and he was in truth, throughout his whole life, a person of very good reputation, and
of singular integrity.

[After the Restoration Sir Edward was one of the 'Privy
council'.] Secretary Nicholas was a man of general good
reputation with all men, of unquestionable integrity and
long experience in the service of the crown; whom the late
king trusted as much as any man to his death. He was one
of those who were excepted by the parliament from pardon
or composition, and so was compelled to leave the kingdom
shortly after Oxford was delivered up, when the king was
in the hands of the Scots. The present king continued
him in the office of secretary of state, which he had so long
held under his father. He was a man of great gravity, and

without any ambitious or private designs; and had so fast a
friendship with the chancellor for many years, that he was
very well content, and without any jealousy for his making
many despatches and other transactions, which more
immediately related to his office, and which indeed were
always made with his privity and concurrence.

[When it was proposed to make Sir Henry Bennet
secretary some courtiers] made no scruple to insinuate to
the king, 'that the abilities of neither of his secretaries were
so great but that he might be better served'. Indeed his
majesty, who did not naturally love old men, had not so
much esteem of them as their parts and industry and integrity deserved, and would not have been sorry if either or
both of them had died.

Secretary Nicholas had served the crown very many
years with a very good acceptation, was made secretary of
state by the late king, and loved and trusted by him in his
nearest concernments to his death: nor had any man, who
served him, a more general reputation of virtue and piety
and unquestionable integrity throughout the kingdom.
He was a man to whom the rebels had been always irreconcilable; and from the end of the war lived in banishment
beyond the seas, was with his majesty from the time he left
France (for whilst the king was in France with his mother,
to whom the secretary was not gracious, he remained at a
distance; but from the time that his majesty came into
Germany he was always with him) in the exercise of the
same function he had under his father, and returned into
England with him, with hope to repair his fortune by the
just perquisites of his office, which had been very much
impaired by his long sufferings and banishment. He had
never been in his youth a man of quick and sudden parts,
but full of industry and application, (which it may be is the
better composition,) and always versed in business and all
the forms of despatch. He was now some years above
seventy, yet truly performed his office with punctuality,
and to the satisfaction of all men who repaired to him:
and the king thought it an envious as well as an ill-natured
thing, to discharge such an officer because he lived too
long. [Yet Bennet succeeded in his design in October 1662.]

66. *Sir William Morrice*

Born 1602; knighted, P.C., and Secretary of State
1660; died 1676

THE other secretary was secretary Morrice, whose merit
had been his having transacted all that had been between
the king and the general [Monk, his kinsman] which was
thought to be much more than it was. Yet he had behaved himself very well, and as much disposed the general
as he was capable of being disposed; and his majesty had
preferred him to that office purely to gratify and oblige
the general; and he had behaved himself very honestly
and diligently in the king's service, and had a good
reputation in the house of commons, and did the business
of his office without reproach. He had lived most part of
his time in the country, with the repute of a wise man
and a very good scholar, as indeed he was both in the
Latin and Greek learning; but being without knowledge
in the modern languages, he gave the king often occasion
to laugh at his unskilful pronunciation of many words.
In the Latin despatches, which concern all the northern
parts, he was ready, and treated with those ambassadors
fluently and elegantly; and for all domestic affairs no
man doubted his sufficiency, except in the garb and mode
and humour of the court.

67. *The Earl of Southampton*

Thomas Wriothesley, born 1607; fourth earl 1624;
P.C. 1642; P.C., K.G. 1660; Lord High Treasurer,
September 1660 till death 1667

THE earl of Southampton was indeed a great man in all
respects, and brought very much reputation to the king's
cause. He was of a nature much inclined to melancholy,
and being born a younger brother, and his father and his
elder brother dying upon the point together, whilst he
was but a boy, he was much troubled to be called *my lord*,

and with the noise of attendance; so much he then delighted to be alone. Yet he had a great spirit, and exacted the respect that was due to his quality; he had never had any conversation in the court, nor obligation to it. On the contrary, he had undergone some hardship from it; which made it believed, that he would have been ready to have taken all occasions to have been severe towards it. And therefore, in the beginning of the parliament, no man was more courted by the managers of those designs. He had great dislike of the high courses, which had been taken in the government, and a particular prejudice to the earl of Strafford, for some exorbitant proceedings. But, as soon as he saw the ways of reverence and duty towards the king declined, and the prosecution of the earl of Strafford to exceed the limits of justice, he opposed them vigorously in all their proceedings. He was a man of a great sharpness of judgment, a very quick apprehension, and that readiness of expression upon any sudden debate, that no man delivered himself more advantageously and weightily, and more efficaciously with the hearers; so that no man gave them more trouble in his opposition, or drew so many to a concurrence with him in opinion. He had no relation to, or dependence upon, the court, or purpose to have any; but wholly pursued the public interest. It was long before he could be prevailed with to be a counsellor, and longer before he would be admitted to be of the bedchamber; and received both honours the rather, because, after he had refused to take a protestation, which both houses had ordered to be taken by all their members, they had likewise voted, 'that no man should be capable of any preferment in church or state, who refused to take the same;' and he would shew how much he contemned those votes. He went with the king to York; was most solicitous, as hath been said, for the offer of peace at Nottingham; and was then with him at Edge-hill; and came and stayed with him at Oxford to the end of the war, taking all opportunities to advance all motions towards peace; and, as no man was more punctual in performing his own duty, so no man had more melancholy apprehensions of the issue of the war; which is all shall be said of him in this place, there being frequent occasions to mention him, in the continuance of this discourse, there being always a fast friendship between him and the chancellor of the exchequer, which lasted to his death.

[16 May 1667 the Treasurer died.] There happened at this time an accident that made a fatal breach into the chancellor's fortune with a gap wide enough to let in all that ruin which soon after was poured upon him. The earl of Southampton, the treasurer, with whom he had an entire fast friendship, and who, when they were together, had credit enough with the king and at the board to prevent, at least to defer, any very unreasonable resolution, was now ready to expire with the stone; a disease that had kept him in great pain many months, and for which he had sent to Paris for a surgeon to be cut, but had deferred it too long by the physicians not agreeing what the disease was: so that at last he grew too weak to apply that remedy. They who had with so much industry, and as they thought certainty, prevailed with the king at Oxford to have removed him from that office, had never since intermitted the pursuing the design, and persuaded his majesty, 'that his service had suffered exceedingly by his receding from his purpose'; and did not think their triumph notorious enough, if they suffered him to die in the office: insomuch as when he grew so weak, that it is true he could not sign any orders with his hand, which was four or five days before his death, they had again persuaded the king to send for the staff. But the chancellor again prevailed with him not to do so ungracious an act to a servant who had served him and his father so long and so eminently, to so little purpose as the ravishing an office unseasonably, which must within five or six days fall into his hands, as it did within less time, by his death.

He was a person of extraordinary parts, of faculties very discerning, and a judgment very profound, great eloquence in his delivery, without the least affectation of words, for he always spake best on the sudden. In the beginning of the troubles, he was looked upon amongst those lords who were least inclined to the court, and so most acceptable to the people: he was in truth not obliged by the court, and thought himself oppressed by it, which his great spirit could not bear; and so he had for some years forbore to be much seen there, which was imputed to a habit of melancholy, to which he was naturally inclined, though it appeared more in his countenance than in his conversation, which to those with whom he was acquainted was very cheerful.

The great friendship that had been between their fathers made many believe, that there was a confidence between the earl of Essex and him; which was true to that degree as could be between men of so different natures and understandings. And when they came to the parliament in the year 1640 they appeared both unsatisfied with the prudence and politics of the court, and were not reserved in declaring it, when the great officers were called in question for great transgressions in their several administrations: but in the prosecution there was great difference in their passions and their ends. The earl of Essex was a great lover of justice, and could not have been tempted to consent to the oppression of an innocent man: but in the discerning the several species of guilt, and in the proportioning the degrees of punishment to the degree of guilt, he had no faculties or measure of judging; nor was above the temptation of general prejudice, and it may be of particular disobligations and resentments, which proceeded from the weakness of his judgment, not the malice of his nature. The earl of Southampton was not only an exact observer of justice, but so clearsighted a discerner of all the circumstances which might disguise it, that no false or fraudulent colour could impose upon him; and of so sincere and impartial a judgment, that no prejudice to the person of any man made him less awake to his cause; but believed that there is 'aliquid et in hostem nefas', and that a very ill man might be very unjustly dealt with.

This difference of faculties divided them quickly in the progress of those businesses, in the beginning whereof they were both of one mind. They both thought the crown had committed great excesses in the exercise of its power, which the one thought could not be otherwise prevented, than by being deprived of it: the consequence whereof the

other too well understood, and that the absolute taking
away that power that might do hurt, would likewise take
away some of that which was necessary for the doing good;
and that a monarch cannot be deprived of a fundamental
right, without such a lasting wound to monarchy itself,
that they who have most shelter from it and stand nearest
to it, the nobility, could ⟨not⟩ continue long in their native
strength, if the crown received a maim. Which if the earl
of Essex had comprehended, who set as great a price upon
nobility as any man living did, he could never have been
wrought upon to have contributed to his own undoing;
which the other knew was unavoidable, if the king were
undone. So they were both satisfied that the earl of
Strafford had countenanced some high proceedings, which
could not be supported by any rules of justice, though the
policy of Ireland, and the constant course observed in the
government of Ireland, might have excused and justified
many of the high proceedings with which he was reproached: and they who had now the advantage-ground,
by being thought to be most solicitous for the liberty of
the subject, and most vigilant that the same outrages
might not be transplanted out of the other kingdom into
this, looked upon him as having the strongest influence
upon the counsels of England as well as governor of Ireland. Then he had declared himself so averse and irreconcilable to the sedition and rebellion of the Scots, that the
whole nation had contracted so great an animosity against
him, that less than his life could not secure them from the
fears they had conceived of him: and this fury of theirs
met with a full concurrence from those of the English, who
could not compass their own ends without their help. And
this combination too soon drew the earl of Essex, who had
none of their ends, into their party, to satisfy his pride
and his passion, in removing a man who seemed to have no
regard for him; for the stories, which were then made of
disobligations from the earl of Strafford towards the earl
of Clanrickard, were without any foundation of truth.[1]

The earl of Southampton, who had nothing of obligation,
and somewhat of prejudice to some high acts of power

[1] Richard de Burgh, 4th earl of Clanricarde, died 1635.

which had been exercised by the earl of Strafford, was not unwilling that they should be so far looked into and examined, as might raise more caution and apprehension in men of great authority of the consequence of such excesses. But when he discerned irregular ways entered into to punish those irregularities, and which might be attended with as ill consequences, and that they intended to compound one great crime out of several smaller trespasses, and, to use their own style, to complicate a treason out of misdemeanours, and so to take away his life for what he might be fined and imprisoned; he first dissuaded and then abhorred that exorbitance, and more abhorred it, when he found it passionately and maliciously resolved by a direct combination.

From this time he and the earl of Essex were perfectly divided and separated, and seldom afterwards concurred in the same opinion: but as he worthily and bravely stood in the gap in the defence of that great man's life, so he did afterwards oppose all those invasions, which were every day made by the house of commons upon the rights of the crown, or the privileges of the peers which the lords were willing to sacrifice to the useful humour of the other. And by this means, whilst most of the king's servants listed themselves with the conspirators in promoting all things which were ingrateful to him, this lord, who had no relation to his service, was looked upon as a courtier; and by the strength of his reason gave such a check to their proceedings, that he became little less odious to them than the court itself; and so much the more odious, because as he was superior to their temptations, so his unquestionable integrity was out of their reach, and made him contemn their power as much as their malice.

He had all the detestation imaginable of the civil war, and discerned the dismal effects it would produce, more than most other men, which made him do all he could to prevent it. But when it could not be avoided, he made no scruple how to dispose of himself, but frankly declared for the king, who had a just sense of the service he had done him, and made him then both of his privy-council and gentleman of his bedchamber, without the least application or desire of his, and when most of those who were under both those relations had chosen, as the much stronger, the rebels' side: and his receiving those obligations at that present was known to proceed more from his duty than his ambition. He had all the fidelity that God requires, and all the affection to the person of the king that his duty suggested to him was due, without any reverence for or compliance with his infirmities or weakness; which made him many times uneasy to the king, especially in all consultations towards peace, in which he was always desirous that his majesty should yield more than he was inclined to do.

He was in his nature melancholic, and reserved in his conversation, except towards those with whom he was very well acquainted; with whom he was not only cheerful, but upon occasion light and pleasant. He was naturally lazy, and indulged overmuch ease to himself: yet as no man had a quicker apprehension or solider judgment in business of all kinds, so, when it had a hopeful prospect, no man could keep his mind longer bent, and take more pains in it. In the treaty at Uxbridge [1645], which was a continued fatigue of twenty days, he never slept four hours in a night, who had never used to allow himself less than ten, and at the end of the treaty was much more vigorous than in the beginning; which made the chancellor to tell the king when they returned to Oxford, 'that if he would have the earl of Southampton in good health and good humour, he must give him good store of business to do'.

His person was of a small stature, his courage, as all his other faculties, very great, having no sign of fear or sense of danger; when he was in a place where he ought to be found.

After the murder of the king [Charles I], the earl of Southampton remained in his own house, without the least application to those powers, which had made themselves so terrible, and which seemed to resolve to root out the whole party as well as the royal family; and would not receive a civility from any of them: and when Cromwell was near his house in the country, upon the marriage of his son in those parts, and had a purpose to

have made a visit to him; upon a private notice thereof,
he immediately removed to another house at a greater
distance. He sent frequently some trusty person to the
king [Charles II] with such presents of money, as he
could receive out of the fortune they had left to him, which
was scarce enough to support him in that retirement: and
after the battle of Worcester, when the rebels had set a
price upon the king's head, and denounced the most terrible judgment upon whomsoever, and his posterity, that
should presume to give any shelter or assistance to Charles
Stuart towards his escape; he sent a faithful servant to all
those persons, who in respect of their fidelity and activity
were most like to be trusted upon such an occasion, that
they should advertise the king, 'that he would most willingly receive him into his house, and provide a ship for
his escape'. And his majesty received this advertisement
from him the day before he was ready to embark in a small
vessel prepared for him in Sussex; which his majesty always
remembered as a worthy testimony of his affection and
courage in so general a consternation. And the earl was
used to say, 'that after that miraculous escape, how dismal soever the prospect was, he had still a confidence of his
majesty's restoration'.

His own natural disposition inclined to melancholic;
and his retirement from all conversation, in which he
might have given some vent to his own thoughts, with the
discontinuance of all those bodily exercises and recreations to which he had been accustomed, brought many
diseases upon him, which made his life less pleasant to
him; so that from the time of the king's return, between
the gout and the stone, he underwent great affliction. Yet
upon the happy return of his majesty he seemed to recover
great vigour of mind, and undertook the charge of high
treasurer with much alacrity and industry, as long as he
had any hope to get a revenue settled proportionable to
the expense of the crown, (towards which his interest and
authority and counsel contributed very much,) or to reduce
the expense of the court within the limits of the revenue.
But when he discerned that the last did and would still
make the former impossible, (upon which he made as

frequent and lively representations as he thought himself obliged to do,) and when he saw irregularities and excesses to abound, and to overflow all the banks which should restrain them; he grew more dispirited, and weary of that province, which exposed him to the reproaches which others ought to undergo, and which supplied him not with authority to prevent them. And he had then withdrawn from the burden, which he infinitely desired to be eased of, but out of conscience of his duty to the king, who he knew would suffer in it; and that the people who knew his affections very well, and already opened their mouths wide against the license of the court, would believe it worse and incurable if he quitted the station he was in. This, and this only, prevailed with him still to undergo that burden, even when he knew that they who enjoyed the benefit of it were as weary that he should be disquieted with it.

He was a man of great and exemplary virtue and piety, and very regular in his devotions; yet was not generally believed by the bishops to have an affection keen enough for the government of the church, because he was willing and desirous, that somewhat more might have been done to gratify the presbyterians than they thought just. But the truth is; he had a perfect detestation of all the presbyterian principles, nor had ever had any conversation with their persons, having during all those wicked times strictly observed the devotions prescribed by the church of England; in the performance whereof he had always an orthodox chaplain, ⟨one of those⟩ deprived of their estates by that government, which disposed of the church as well as of the state. But it is very true, that upon the observation of the great power and authority which the presbyterians usurped and were possessed of, even when Cromwell did all he could to divest them of it, and applied all his interest to oppress or suppress them, insomuch as they did often give a check to and divert many of his designs; he did believe that their numbers and their credit had been much greater than in truth it was. And then some persons, who had credit with him by being thought to have an equal aversion ᵻrom them, persuaded him to

believe, that they would be satisfied with very easy concessions, which would bring no prejudice or inconvenience to the church. And this imagination prevailed with
him, and more with others who loved them not, to wish
that there might be some indulgence towards them. But
that which had the strongest influence upon him, and
which made him less apprehensive of the venom of any
other sect, was the extreme jealousy he had of the power
and malignity of the Roman catholics; whose behaviour
from the time of the suppression of the regal power, and
more scandalously at and from the time of the murder of
the king, had very much irreconciled him towards them:
and he did believe, that the king and the duke of York had
a better opinion of their fidelity, and less jealousy of their
affections, than they deserved; and so thought there could
not be too great an union of all other interests to control
the exorbitance of that. And upon this argument, with his
private friends, he was more passionate than in any other.

He had a marvellous zeal and affection for the royal
family; insomuch as the two sons of the duke of York
falling both into distempers, (of which they both shortly
after died,) very few days before his death, he was so marvellously affected with it, that many believed the trouble
of it, or a presage what might befall the kingdom by
it, hastened his death some hours: and in the agony of
death, the very morning he died, he sent to know how they
did; and seemed to receive some relief, when the messenger
returned with the news, that they were both alive and in
some degree mended.

68. *The Marquis of Ormonde*

*James Butler, born 1610; courtesy title Lord Thurles;
twelfth earl 1632; Lord General of Irish army 1641;
P.C. 1651; first duke, Lord High Steward, &c., of
England and Lord Lieutenant of Ireland 1661; died
1688*

[When Clarendon returned from Madrid to Paris, 1651,
he met again the marquis: 'a man so accomplished that
he had either no enemies or such who were ashamed to

profess they were so'.] There had been a great acquaintance between the marquis of Ormond, when he was lord Thurles, in the life of his grandfather, and the chancellor of the exchequer, which was renewed, by a mutual correspondence, when they both came to have shares in the public business, the one in Ireland, and the other in England: so that when they now met at Paris, they met as old friends, and quickly understood each other so well, that there could not be a more entire confidence between men. The marquis consulted with him in his nearest concernments, and the chancellor esteemed and cultivated the friendship with all possible industry and application. The king was abundantly satisfied in the friendship they had for each other, and trusted them both entirely; nor was it in the power of any, though it was often endeavoured by persons of no ordinary account, to break or interrupt that mutual confidence between them, during the whole time the king remained beyond the seas; whereby the king's perplexed affairs were carried on with the less trouble. And the chancellor did always acknowledge, that the benefit of this friendship was so great to him, that, without it, he could not have borne the weight of that part of the king's business which was incumbent on him, nor the envy and reproach that attended the trust.

The marquis of Ormond and the chancellor of the exchequer believed that the king had nothing at this time to do but to be quiet, and that all his activity was to consist in carefully avoiding to do anything that might do him hurt, and to expect some blessed conjuncture from the amity of Christian princes, or some such revolution of affairs in England by their own discontents and divisions amongst themselves, as might make it seasonable for his majesty again to shew himself.

The marquis of Ormond was the person of the greatest quality, estate, and reputation, who had frankly engaged his person and his fortune in the king's service from the first hour of the troubles, and pursued it with that courage and constancy, that when the king was murdered, and he deserted by the Irish, contrary to the articles of the peace which they had made with him [at Kilkenny in January

1649] and when he could make no longer defence, he refused all the conditions which Cromwell offered, who would have given him all his vast estate, if he would have been contented to have lived quietly in some of his own houses, without further concerning himself in the quarrel; and transported himself, without so much as accepting a pass from his authority, in a little weak vessel into France, where he found the king, from whom he never parted till he returned with him into England. And having thus merited as much as a subject can do from a prince, he had much more credit and esteem with the king than any other man: and the lustre the chancellor was in, was no less from the declared friendship the marquis had for him, than from the great trust his majesty reposed in him.

[The Restoration had not settled affairs in Ireland.] And they who took the most dispassioned survey of all that had been done, and of what remained to be done, did conclude that nothing could reasonably produce a settlement there, but the deputing one single person to exercise that government. And the duke of Albemarle himself, who had a great estate in that kingdom, which made him the more long for a settlement, and who had before the king's return and ever since dissuaded the king from thinking of employing the duke of Ormond there, who had himself aversion enough from that command, of which he had sufficient experience; I say, the general had now so totally changed his mind, that he plainly told the king, 'that there was no way to explicate that kingdom out of those intricacies in which it was involved, but by sending over a lord lieutenant thither. That he thought it not fit for his majesty's service, that himself, who had that commission of lord lieutenant, should be absent from his person; and therefore that he was very ready and desirous to give up his commission: and that in his judgment nobody would be able to settle and compose the several factions in that kingdom, but the duke of Ormond, who he believed would be grateful to all sorts of people'.

And therefore he advised his majesty very positively, 'that he would immediately give him the commission, and as soon as should be possible send him away into

Ireland'. And both the king and the general spake with the duke of Ormond, and prevailed with him to accept it, before either of them communicated it to the chancellor, who the king well knew would for many reasons, and out of his great friendship to the duke, dissuade him from undertaking it; which was very true.

The duke, who never took any thing ill he said to him, told him, 'that nobody knew better than he the aversion he had to that command, when it may be he might have undertaken it with more advantage'. He confessed, 'he saw many dangers with reference to himself, which he knew not how to avoid, and many difficulties with reference to the public, which he had little hope to overcome; yet Ireland must not be given over: yet since there seemed to be a general opinion, with which the king concurred, that he could be able to contribute to the composing the distempers, and the settling the government; he would not suspect himself, but believe that he might be able to do somewhat towards it'. And he gave his word to him, that nothing should be defective on his part in point of industry; for he was resolved to take indefatigable pains for a year or two, in which he hoped the settlement would be completed, that he might have ease and recreation for the other part of his life'. And he confessed, 'that he did the more willingly enter upon that province, that he might have the opportunity to settle his own fortune, which, how great soever in extent of lands, did not yet, by reason of the general unsettlement, yield him a quarter of the revenue it ought to do. That for what concerned himself, and the disadvantages he might undergo by his absence, he referred it to Providence and the king's good nature; who', he said, 'knew him better than any of his enemies did; and therefore, he hoped, he would believe himself before them'. However, the truth is, he was the more disposed to that journey, by the dislike he had of the court, and the necessary exercises which men there were to excel in, for which he was superannuated: and if he did not already discern any lessening of the king's grace towards him, he saw enough to make him believe, that the contrary ought not to be depended upon.

69. *The Second Duke of Buckingham*

George Villiers, born 1628; P.C. 1650 and 1662;
died 1687

[At the time of the attack on Clarendon in 1666–7, Buckingham was one of the leaders of the opposition.] The duke ⟨of Buckingham⟩ took more pains than was agreeable to his constitution to get an interest in all such persons, invited them to his table, pretended to have a great esteem of their parts, asked counsel of them, lamented the king's neglecting his business, and committing it to other people who were not fit for it; and then reported all the license and debauchery of the court in the most lively ⟨colours⟩, being himself a frequent eye and earwitness of it. He had a mortal quarrel with the lady, and was at this time so much in the king's displeasure, (as he was very frequently,) that he forbore going to the court, and revenged himself upon it by all the merry tales he could tell of what was done there.

It cannot be imagined, considering the loose life he led (which was a life more by night than by day) in all the liberties that nature could desire or wit invent, how great an interest he had in both houses of parliament; that is, how many in both would follow his advice, and concur in what he proposed. His quality and condescensions, the pleasantness of his humour and conversation, the extravagance and sharpness of his wit, unrestrained by any modesty or religion, drew persons of all affections and inclinations to like his company; and to believe that the levities and the vanities would be wrought off by age, and there would enough of good be left to become a great man, and make him useful to his country, for which he pretended to have a wonderful affection and reverence; and that all his displeasure against the court proceeded from their declared malignity against the liberty of the subject, and their desire that the king should govern by the example of France. He had always held intelligence with the principal persons of the levelling party, and professed to desire that

liberty of conscience might be granted to all; and exercised his wit with most licence against the church, the
law, and the court.

The king had constant intelligence of all his behaviour,
and the liberty he took in his discourses of him for which
he had indignation enough: but of this new stratagem to
make himself great in parliament, and to have a faction
there to disturb his business, his majesty had no apprehension, believing it impossible for the duke to keep his
mind long bent upon any particular design, or to keep and
observe those hours and orders of sleeping and eating, as
men who pretend to business are obliged to; and that it
was more impossible, for him to make and preserve a
friendship with any serious persons, whom he could never
restrain himself from abusing and making ridiculous, as
soon as he was out of their company. Yet, with all these infirmities and vices, he found a respect and concurrence
from all men of different tempers and talents, and had an
incredible opinion with the people.

70. *Clarendon's Fall and Exile, 1667*

[After its last meeting Parliament had been prorogued
to 20 October 1667. Foreign and financial matters made it,
however, appear advisable to some of the king's council-
lors to call it already in summer. Clarendon opposed this,
advocating rather a dissolution. But Charles was afraid
that a new Parliament might not be agreeable to his
wishes and therefore called the old one for 25 June. The
members were, however, too excited about the army then
in England for the purpose of the Dutch war to be willing
to consider the king's business. Hence the king prorogued
them on 29 June to the original date, only informing
them shortly of the peace concluded with the Dutch.]
The public no sooner entered into this repose, than the
storm began to arise that destroyed all the prosperity,
ruined the fortune, and shipwrecked all the hopes, of the
chancellor, who had been the principal instrument in the
providing that repose. The parliament, that had been so

unseasonably called together from their business and recreations, in a season of the year that they most desired to
be vacant, were not pleased to be so soon dismissed: and
very great pains were taken by those, who were thought
to be able to do him the least harm, because they were
known to be his enemies, to persuade the members of
parliament, 'that it was the chancellor only who had
hindered their continuing together, and that he had
advised the king to dissolve them'; which exceedingly
inflamed them.

And sir William Coventry was so far from being reserved
in his malice, that the very day that the parliament was
dismissed, after he had incensed them against the chancellor, in the presence of six or seven of the members, who
were not all of the same mind, he declared, 'that if at their
next meeting, which would be within little more than two
months, they had a mind to remove the chancellor from
the court, they should easily bring it to pass': of all which
he had quickly information, and had several other advertisements from persons of honour, 'that there was a
strong combination entered into against him'; and ⟨they⟩
mentioned some particulars to have been told the king
concerning him, which had exceedingly offended his
majesty. All which particulars, being without any colour
or ground of truth, he believed were inventions (though
not from those who informed him) only to amuse him.

Yet he took an opportunity to acquaint the king with it,
who, with the same openness he had always used, conferred
with him about his present business, but only of the business.
He besought his majesty to let him know, 'whether he had
received any information that he had done or said such and
such things', which he made appear to him to be in themselves so incredible and improbable, that it could hardly be
in his majesty's power to believe ⟨them⟩; to which the king
answered, 'that nobody had told him any such thing'.
To which the other replied, 'that he did really think they
had not, though he knew that they had bragged they had
done so, and thereby incensed his majesty against him;
which they desired should be generally believed'.

The truth is; the chancellor was guilty of that himself

which he had used to accuse the archbishop Laud of, that he was too proud of a good conscience. He knew his own innocence, and had no kind of apprehension of being publicly charged with any crime. He knew well he had many enemies who had credit with the king, and that they did him all the ill offices they could: and he knew that the lady's power and credit increased, and that she desired nothing more than to remove him from his majesty's confidence; in which he never thought her to blame, since she well knew that he employed all the credit he had to remove her from the court. But he thought himself very secure in the king's justice: and though his kindness was much lessened, he was confident his majesty would protect him from being oppressed, since he knew his integrity; and never suspected that he would consent to his ruin. He was in truth weary of the condition he was in, and had in the last year undergone much mortification; and desired nothing more, than to be divested of all other trusts and employments than what concerned the chancery only, in which he could have no rival, and in the administration whereof he had not heard of any complaint: and this he thought might have satisfied all parties; and had sometimes desired the king, 'that he might retire from all other business, than that of the judicatory', for he plainly discerned he was not able to contend with other struggles.

About this time, or in a few days afterwards, a great affliction befell the chancellor in his domestics, which prepared him to bear all the unexpected accidents that suddenly succeeded that more insupportable misfortune. His wife, the mother of all his children, and his companion in all his banishment, and who had made all his former calamities less grievous by her company and courage, having made a journey to Tunbridge for her health, returned from thence without the benefit she expected, yet without being thought by the physicians to be in any danger; and within less than three days died: which was so sudden, unexpected, and irreparable a loss, that he had not courage to support; which nobody wondered at who knew the mutual satisfaction and comfort they had in each other. And he might possibly have sunk under it, if his enemies had not found out a new kind of consolation to him, which his friends could never have thought of.

Within few days after his wife's death, the king vouchsafed to come to his house to condole with him, and used many gracious expressions to him: yet within less than a fortnight the duke (who was seldom a day without doing him the honour to see him) came to him and with very much trouble told him, 'that such a day, that was past, walking with the king in the park, his majesty asked him how the chancellor did: to which his highness had made answer, that he was the ⟨most⟩ disconsolate person he ever ⟨saw⟩; and that he had lamented himself to him not only upon the loss of his wife, but out of apprehension that his majesty had of late withdrawn his countenance from him; to which his majesty replied, that he wondered he should think so, but that he would speak more to him of that subject the next day. And that that morning his majesty had held a long discourse with him, in which he told him, that he had received very particular and certain intelligence, that when the parliament should meet again, they were resolved to impeach the chancellor, who was grown very odious to them, not only for his having opposed them in all those things upon which they had set their hearts, but that they had been informed that he had proposed and advised their dissolution; which had enraged them to that degree, that they had taken a resolution as soon as they came together again to send up an impeachment against him; which would be a great dishonour to his majesty, and obstruct all his affairs, nor should he be able to protect him or divert them: and therefore that it would be necessary for his service, and likewise for the preservation of the chancellor, that he should deliver up the seal to him. All which he desired the duke (who confessed that he had likewise received the same advertisement) to inform him of: and that the chancellor himself should choose the way and the manner of delivering up the seal, whether he would wait upon the king and give it into his own hand, or whether the king should send a secretary or a privy counsellor for it'. When the duke had said all that the king had given him in charge, he declared himself 'to be much unsatisfied with the king's resolution; and though he had received the same advertisement, and believed that there was a real combination and conspiracy against him, yet he knew the chancellor's innocence would not be frighted with it'.

The chancellor was indeed as much surprised with this relation, as he could have been at the sight of a warrant for his execution.

[The king and the duke then came to see Clarendon on 26 August to press him to resign. He concluded his answer thus:] 'That he was so far from fearing the justice of the parliament, that he renounced his majesty's protection or interposition towards his preservation: and that though the earl of Strafford had undergone a sentence he did not deserve, yet he could not acknowledge their cases to be parallel. That though that great person had never committed any offence that could amount to treason, yet he had done many things which he could not justify, and which were transgressions against the law: whereas he was not guilty of any action, whereof he did not desire the law might be the judge. And if his majesty himself should discover all that he had said to him in secret, he feared not any censure that should attend it: if any body could charge him with any crime or offence, he would most willingly undergo the punishment that belonged to it.

But', he said, 'he doubted very much, that the throwing off an old servant, who had served the crown in some trust near thirty years, (who had the honour by the command of his blessed father, who had left good evidence of the esteem he had of his fidelity, to wait upon his majesty when he went out of the kingdom, and by the great blessing of God had the honour to return with him again; which no other counsellor alive could say,) on the sudden, without any suggestion of a crime, nay, with a declaration of innocence, would call his majesty's justice and goodnature into question; and men would not know how securely to serve him, when they should see it was in the power of three or four persons who had never done him any notable service, nor were in the opinion of those who knew them best like to do, to dispose him to so ungracious an act'.

The king seemed very much troubled and irresolute; then repeated 'the great power of the parliament, and the clear information he had of their purposes, which they were resolved to go through with, right or wrong; and that his own condition was such, that he could not dispute with them, but was upon the matter at their mercy'.

The chancellor told him, 'it was not possible for his majesty to have any probable assurance what the parliament would do. And though he knew he had offended some of the house of commons, in opposing their desires in such particulars as his majesty thought were prejudicial to his service; yet he did not doubt but his reputation was much greater in both houses, than either of theirs who were known to be his enemies, and to have this influence upon his majesty, who were all known to be guilty of some transgressions, which they would have been called in question for in parliament, if he had not very industriously, out of the tenderness he had for his majesty's honour and service, prevented it; somewhat whereof was not unknown to his majesty'. He concluded 'with beseeching him, whatever resolution he took in his particular, not to suffer his spirits to fall, nor himself to be dejected with the apprehension of the formidable power of the parliament, which was more or less or nothing, as he pleased to make it: that it was yet in his own power to govern them; but if they found it was in theirs to govern him, nobody knew what the end would be'. And thereupon he made him a short relation of the method that was used in the time of Richard the Second, 'when they terrified the king with the power and the purposes of the parliament, till they brought him to consent to that from which he could not redeem himself, and without which they could have done him no harm'. And in the warmth of this relation he found a seasonable opportunity to mention the lady with some reflections and cautions, which he might more advisedly have declined.

After two hours' discourse, the king rose without saying any thing, but appeared not well pleased with all that had been said; and the duke of York found he was offended with the last part of it. The garden, that used to be private, had now many in it to observe the countenance of the king when he came out of the room: and when the chancellor returned, the lady, the lord Arlington, and Mr. May, looked together out of her open window with great gaiety and triumph, which all people observed.

In this suspension, the common argument was, 'that it was not now the question whether the chancellor was innocent; but whether, when the king had so long resolved to remove him, and had now proceeded so far towards it, he should retract his resolution, and be governed by his brother: it was enough that he was not beloved, and that the court wished him removed'. And Mr. [Henry] Brounker openly declared, that the resolution had been taken above two months before; and that it would not consist with his majesty's honour to be hectored out of it by his brother, who was wrought upon by his wife's crying'. And this kind of argumentation was every moment inculcated by the lady and her party: insomuch as when the duke made his instances with all the importunity he could use, and put his majesty in mind 'of many discourses his majesty had formerly held with him, of the chancellor's honesty, and discretion, conjuring him to love and esteem him accordingly, when his highness had not so good an opinion of him'; and, 'that now he had found by good experience that he deserved that character, his majesty would withdraw his kindness from him, and rather believe others, who he knew were his enemies, than his own judgment': the king gave no other answer, than 'that he had proceeded too far to retire; and that he should be looked upon as a child, if he receded from his purpose'.

And so being reconfirmed, upon the 30th of August in the year 1667 he sent secretary Morrice, who had no mind to the employment, with a warrant under the sign manual, to require and receive the great seal; which the chancellor immediately delivered to him with all the expressions of duty to the king. And as soon as the secretary had delivered it to the king in his closet, Mr. May went into the closet, and fell upon his knees, and kissed his majesty's hand, telling him 'that he was now king, which he had never been before.'

[Clarendon was advised by many to flee and] there could not be a more terrifying or prevalent argument used towards his withdrawing, than that of a prison; the thought and apprehension whereof was more grievous to him than of death itself, which he was confident would quickly be the effect of the other. However, he very resolutely refused to follow their advice; and urged to them, 'the advantage he should give his enemies, and the dishonour he should bring upon himself, by flying, in having his integrity condemned, if he had not the confidence to defend it.' He said, 'he could now appear, wherever he should be required, with an honest countenance, and the courage of an innocent man: but if he should be apprehended in a disguise running away, which he could not but expect by the vigilance of his enemies, (since he could not make any journey by land, being at that time very weak and infirm,) he should be very much out of countenance, and should be exposed to public scorn and contempt. And if he should make his escape into foreign parts, it would not be reasonable to expect or imagine that his enemies, who had so far aliened the king's affection from him, and in spite of his innocence prevailed thus far, would want power to prosecute the advantage they should get by his flight, which would be interpreted as a confession of his guilt; and thereupon they would procure such proceedings in the parliament as might ruin both his fortune and his fame'.

His friends, how unsatisfied soever with his resolution, acquiesced for the present, after having first prevailed with him to write himself to the king; which he did, though without any hope that it would make any impression upon him.

The king's discourse was according to the persons with whom he conferred. To those who were engaged in the violent prosecution he spake with great bitterness of him, repeating many particular passages, in which he had shewed much passion because his majesty did not concur with him in what he advised. To those who he knew were his friends he mentioned him without any bitterness, and with some testimony of his having served him long and usefully, and as if he had pity and compassion for him: yet, 'that he wondered that he did not absent himself, since it could not but be very manifest to him and to all his friends, that it was not in his majesty's power to protect him against the prejudice that was against him in both houses; which', he said, 'could not but be increased by the obstruction his particular concernment gave to all public affairs in this conjuncture; in which', he said, 'he was sure he would prevail at last'. All these advertisements could not prevail over the chancellor, for the reasons mentioned before; though he was very much afflicted at the division between the two houses, the evil consequence whereof he well understood, and could have been well content that the lords would have consented to his imprisonment.

[At last the king became peremptory and] as soon as the chancellor received this advice and command, he resolved with great reluctancy to obey, and to be gone that very night: and having, by the friendship of sir John Wolstenholme, caused the farmers' boat to wait for him at Erith, as soon as it was dark he took coach at his house Saturday night, the 29th of November 1667, with two servants only. And being accompanied with his two sons and two or three other friends on horseback as far as Erith, he found the boat ready; and so embarked about eleven of the clock that night, the wind indifferently good: but before midnight it changed, and carried him back almost as far as he had advanced. And in this perplexity he remained three days and nights before he arrived at Calais, which was not a port chosen by him, all places out of England being indifferent, and France not being in his inclination, because of the reproach and calumny that was cast upon him: but since it was the first that offered itself, and it was not seasonable to affect another, he was very glad to disembark there, and to find himself safe on shore.

All these particulars, of which many may seem too trivial to be remembered, have been thought necessary to be related, it being a principal part of his vindication for going away, and not insisting upon his innocence; which at that time made a greater impression upon many worthy persons to his disadvantage, than any particular that was contained in the charge that had been offered to the house. And therefore though he forebore, when all the promises were broken which had been made to him, and his enemies' malice and insolence increased by his absence, to publish or in the least degree to communicate the true ground and reasons of absenting himself, to avoid any inconvenience that in so captious a season might thereby have befallen the king's service; yet it cannot be thought unreasonable to preserve this memorial of all the circumstances, as well as the substantial reasons, which disposed him to make that flight, for the clear information of those who in a fit season may understand his innocence without any inconvenience to his majesty, of whose goodness and honour and justice it may be hoped, that his majesty himself will give his own testimony, both of this particular of his withdrawing, and a vindication of his innocence from all the other reproaches with which it was aspersed.

INDEX

1·95